ADVANCE PR/
On a Collision Course

"Professor Sakata's pioneering archival work and scholarship anticipated the transnational turn in United States immigration and ethnic
history while also challenging perspectives in Japanese studies. In particular, his broad and deep knowledge of both English and Japanese
language sources informs these original and important essays on early
Japanese migration that will be of interest to a wide range of scholars
across multiple fields and areas of study."

—David K. Yoo, vice provost and professor, UCLA

"At last, *On a Collision Course* provides English-speaking readers with
invaluable access to the scholarship of Yasuo Sakata, arguably one of the
foremost trailblazers in Japanese American studies. Superbly translated,
the volume highlights the contemporary relevance of Sakata's works published in Japan over a quarter of a century ago. While based on impec-
cable empirical research, the selected essays offer an in-depth look at how
the early Japanese immigrant experience unfolded in the intertwined contexts of US-Japan diplomacy and the local race politics of the American
West. Still with ample power to inspire, Sakata's studies represent migration history writing at its best and are a must-read for anyone interested
in transpacific working-class migration and Japanese American history."

—Eiichiro Azuma, associate professor of history and
Asian American studies, University of Pennsylvania

"Yasuo Sakata in *On a Collision Course* lays out the challenges of
researching the Japanese American history: the massive loss of historical archives during the 1906 San Francisco Great Fire and the 1942–5
internment; and the commonplace practice of secondhand citations
and historical distortions in the *Nikkei* communities' publications in
early decades. How could one overcome these problems, if at all? This
is a must-read text for those who seek an answer to this question."

—Yuma Totani, professor of history, University of Hawaii,
and author of *The Tokyo War Crimes Trial*

"This is an exceptionally erudite and timely publication of Yasuo Sakata's historical studies of migration between Japan and the United States during the Meiji era. Sakata's research amounts to essential reading on the place of Issei labor and patterns of mobility caught between the expansionist and exclusionist policies of two rising world powers. Appearing for the first time in English translation, with a preface by Kaoru Ueda and critical introduction by Masako Iino, it provides nuanced, multilayered analyses of the archives on both sides of the Pacific instrumental for restoring this vital transnational history."

—Seth Jacobowitz, assistant professor of East Asian languages and literatures, Yale University, and author of *Writing Technology in Meiji Japan*

"Yasuo Sakata was a pioneer, approaching early Japanese American studies as a field deserving of scholarly attention from both sides of the Pacific. His insistence on the need for bilingual facility and reliance on trustworthy historical documents and archives was only rarely possible, but it will continue to be a beacon and vision for aspiring scholars in the field. This translated volume is most welcome; it is a major contribution."

—Franklin Odo, John J. McCloy Visiting Professor of American Institutions and International Diplomacy, Amherst College

"Revisiting pioneers' works always results in 'new' findings, perspectives, and surprises. This translated collection of essays written by a pioneer scholar of Japanese American history, Yasuo Sakata, shows us the significance of how historians decipher primary sources, master the languages of research, and pay attention to both micro- and macro-perspectives. Scholars who are interested in the US-Japan history, immigration history, and Japanese American studies will benefit from reading his valuable essays for better understanding the development of historical researches on Japanese immigrants and their descendants in the United States."

—Mariko Iijima, associate professor, Sophia University

On a Collision Course

On a Collision Course

The Dawn of Japanese Migration
in the Nineteenth Century

Yasuo Sakata

Edited by Kaoru Ueda
Introduction by Masako Iino

HOOVER INSTITUTION PRESS

STANFORD UNIVERSITY   STANFORD, CALIFORNIA

hoover.org

Hoover Institution Press Publication No. 709

Hoover Institution at Leland Stanford Junior University, Stanford, California 94305-6003

Cover image: *Tanaka Tsurukichi*, from the series "Kyōdō risshi no motoi" (Foundations of Teaching and Achievement) by Inoue Yasuji (1889); Hoover Library & Archives, Japanese woodblock print collection, box no. 2.

First printing 2020
26 25 24 23 22 21 20   7 6 5 4 3 2 1

Manufactured in the United States of America

The paper used in this publication meets the minimum requirements of the American National Standard for Information Sciences—Permanence of Paper for Printed Library Materials, ANSI/NISO Z39.48-1992. ∞

Library of Congress Cataloging-in-Publication Data

Names: Sakata, Yasuo, 1931– author. | Ueda, Kaoru (Kay), editor. | Iino, Masako, 1944– writer of introduction.
Title: On a collision course : the dawn of Japanese migration in the nineteenth century / Yasuo Sakata ; edited by Kaoru Ueda ; introduction by Masako Iino.
Other titles: Hoover Institution Press publication ; 709.
Description: Stanford, California : Hoover Institution Press, 2020. | Series: Hoover Institution Press publication ; No. 709 | Five translated essays, originally published in Japanese between 1991 and 1994. | Includes bibliographical references and index. | Summary: "Essays on Japanese migration to the United States from an international and historical perspective, considering impacts from social and political events on both sides of the Pacific"—Provided by publisher.
Identifiers: LCCN 2020005025 (print) | LCCN 2020005026 (ebook) | ISBN 9780817923556 (paperback) | ISBN 9780817923563 (epub) | ISBN 9780817923570 (mobi) | ISBN 9780817923587 (pdf)
Subjects: LCSH: Foreign workers, Japanese—United States—History—19th century. | Japanese—United States—History—19th century. | Immigrants—United States—History—19th century. | Japan—Emigration and immigration—History—19th century. | United States—Emigration and immigration—History—19th century.
Classification: LCC HD8081.J3 S25 2020 (print) | LCC HD8081.J3 (ebook) | DDC 331.6/25207309034—dc23
LC record available at https://lccn.loc.gov/2020005025
LC ebook record available at https://lccn.loc.gov/2020005026

Contents

Foreword

An archive thrives through its scholarly and educational output. The Hoover Institution Library & Archives, founded a decade before the US National Archives, was established because of Herbert Hoover's strong belief in the significance of primary sources as the basis for empirical inquiry to inform our understanding of history.

The Japanese Diaspora Initiative, generously endowed by an anonymous gift, is closely aligned with our core mission to collect, preserve, describe, make available, and encourage the scholarly and educational uses of primary source materials. The initiative's focus is on the history of overseas Japanese during the Empire of Japan period (1868–1945), but especially in the twentieth century. Supporting the initiative are Hoover's existing and continuously growing archival collections on Japan and Japanese Americans, in physical and digital forms.

The drive behind the establishment of our current core Japan collection was the Stanford Alumni Association of Tokyo. As Yoshio Higashiuchi (Stanford '37), a second-generation Japanese American, recalls, just over a month after the Japanese Instrument of Surrender was signed on the USS *Missouri*, some members of the association gathered amid the ruins of Tokyo, capital of the Empire of the Rising Sun. They recognized the strong need to document the Pacific War and processes leading up to the final rupture of the US-Japan relationship. The Tokyo office of the Hoover Library on War, Revolution and Peace was established in November 1945 after obtaining the permission of the Supreme Commander for the Allied Powers. The Tokyo office collected material in Japan for the Archives until 1952.

Given Hoover's long history of collecting and preserving material on the Empire of Japan, it is a great pleasure to present *On a Collision Course: The Dawn of Japanese Migration in the Nineteenth Century*, translated from Yasuo Sakata's five seminal papers in order to reach an English-speaking readership. Sakata, a pioneer scholar in Japanese migration studies, constantly challenges widely accepted paradigms due to his deeply researched historical evidence, and his work raises the scholarly standard of the discipline. His meticulous research, broad vision, and uncompromising efforts in collecting and compiling Japanese American historical documents have earned him a highly respected place in the field. His emphasis on studying primary source materials on both sides of the Pacific has produced holistic research results.

In his essays Sakata performs a great service for future scholars. He raises awareness of historical bias in the preservation of records in the United States, noting how events and experiences of Japanese and Japanese Americans in America have left gaps in the record and impacted the veracity of what remains. He emphasizes the importance of reading both Japanese and English documents, recognizing how a language as challenging to master as Japanese also stands in the way of scholarly research.

Sakata further takes the reader beyond Japanese migration history to US-Japan diplomatic history and to political and economic currents in Asia. Together, his essays take a *longue durée* approach to historical understanding and place Japanese migration within a broader social and cultural context. Many of the issues Sakata raised with regard to Japanese migration and Japanese American studies are still relevant today, as we study contemporary migration. We hope current and future generations of scholars and students alike are informed by his research and use it to further shape their own work and the discipline of history going forward.

Sakata's contributions to the field don't end here. He generously donated materials he had accumulated over many years of research to the Hoover Institution, including primary sources, for other researchers to study. He also allowed us to host summary transcriptions of handwritten Japanese newspapers published in San Francisco on the Hoji Shinbun Digital Collection, making the headlines searchable online. These resources that Sakata graciously made available to researchers demonstrate his keen interest in preserving sources, providing better access, and improving research opportunities. His work clearly illustrates that we have much to learn from the past.

ERIC WAKIN
Robert H. Malott Director, Hoover Institution Library & Archives
Deputy Director and Research Fellow, Hoover Institution
Stanford University

Preface

The Japanese Diaspora Initiative at the Hoover Institution Library & Archives is delighted to introduce to English-speaking researchers Yasuo Sakata's key Japanese-language articles on Japanese emigration and immigration. Sakata's meticulous and uncompromising research conducted using both Japanese and English materials set a milestone for scholars of Japanese migration studies.

Sakata received a BA in history (1962) and a PhD in East Asian history (1969) from the University of California–Los Angeles. He was instrumental in compiling materials for its Japanese American Research Project and published *A Buried Past: An Annotated Bibliography of the Japanese American Research Project Collection* (1974), compiled with Yuji Ichioka, Nobuya Tsuchida, and Eri Yasuhara; and *Fading Footsteps of the Issei: An Annotated Check List of the Manuscript Holdings of the Japanese American Research Project Collection* (1992). After returning to Japan in 1990, he taught at the Faculty of International Studies, Osaka Gakuin University. He also served as the president of the Japanese Association for Migration Studies.

Sakata's exposure to a wide range of primary sources and his interviews with Issei (first-generation Japanese immigrants to the United States) as a graduate student and a researcher at UCLA, his remarkable energy and passion for conducting research on Japanese emigration and immigration, his uncompromising search for historical evidence, and his ability to read both classical Japanese and English fluently are only some of his exceptional qualities. With these capabilities and keen interest, Sakata brought an international perspective to the academic discipline, opening the door for a broader discourse of Japanese migration studies and placing the subject within the context of transnational history.

Sakata has an avid interest and a strong belief in the value of primary-source documents, both in Japanese and in the local languages of the immigrants' new homes. We at the Hoover Institution Library & Archives at Stanford University share these values. Supported by a generous anonymous gift, the Japanese Diaspora Initiative at Hoover aims to promote the study of the modern Japanese diaspora and its relationship with the history of Japan, focusing mainly on Japanese Americans and other overseas Japanese communities. To this end, we have created the Hoji Shinbun Digital Collection, an open-access online resource of overseas Japanese newspapers published during the Empire of Japan period (1868–1945). Sakata has generously allowed his many years of transcription work of handwritten Japanese newspapers from the late nineteenth and early twentieth centuries to be incorporated into the digital collection to make them searchable. Together with the Sakata papers now housed at our archives, we hope this translated volume of Sakata's seminal works will contribute to bringing an international perspective to the discipline of migration studies and open up a more robust dialogue among scholars across borders.

Sakata and we have selected the five articles in this volume as a contribution to this long-term vision, and we hope they serve at least four purposes: to disseminate the results of Sakata's research to a broader audience; to question some established ideas and historical understandings; to increase awareness among English-speaking scholars of Japanese migration studies on the importance of both English and Japanese primary sources; and to alert scholars of historical and current biases in the availability of resources.

The first article, "A Historical Study of Migration Research and Its Challenges," was translated from "Imin kenkyū no rekishiteki kōsatsu to sono kadai" 移民研究の歴史的考察とその課題, which was originally published in 1991 as part of Sakata's seminal work compiling and reprinting critical materials related to Japanese emigration and immigration, a series titled *Nihon imin shiryōshū dai 1-ki Hokubei-hen dai 18-kan* 日本移民資料集第1期 北米編 第18巻. In this article, Sakata provides an overview of Japanese American studies from a historical perspective and warns against the biases of resources. The 1906 earthquake and subsequent fires most likely destroyed many of the important early documents of the Japanese community in San Francisco, the first entry point for Japanese on the continental United States in the late nineteenth century. Arguably more damaging was World War II's impact on Japanese and Japanese American records in the United States, which includes FBI confiscations; limited preservation capabilities left to the community before and during the forced removal to camps; and postwar bias among Japanese Americans against openly discussing Japanese patriotism in the United States before the war and making related resources available to the public. Sakata also blames missing or false information on the Japanese tradition of not citing sources, as well as on the cultural tendency to not question the veracity of authorities or seniors, which provides a possible basis for the repeated publishing of incorrect historical information without critical review.

The year 1991 was a productive publication year for Sakata. "Unequal Treaties and Japanese Migrant Workers in the United States" was translated from "Fubyōdō jōyaku to Amerika dekasegi" 不平等条約とアメリカ出稼ぎ, an extracted chapter from *Hokubei Nihonjin Kirisutokyō undōshi* 北米日本人キリスト教運動史. Sakata conducted meticulous research based on historical Japanese- and English-language documents, underscoring the nuanced early US-Japan diplomatic relationship, full of idiosyncratic interpretations on both sides, and the haphazard beginnings of Japanese going abroad. His research scope went beyond a traditional emigration study to examine the conditions of Chinese migrant workers sent overseas as an underlying political and economic current for the Japanese government while it made crucial diplomatic decisions and created an immigration-related regulatory framework.

Three chapters, "On a Collision Course: The Migration of Japanese *Dekasegi* Laborers to the United States during the Meiji Era," parts I, II, and III, are translated from articles with the original bilingual titles in English and Japanese. The Japanese titles are *Shōtotsuten e mukau kidō: Meijiki ni okeru Nihonjin no Amerika dekasegi* 衝突点へ向かう軌道: 明治期における日本人のアメリカ出稼ぎ (I, II, III), and the first two were published in 1992 and the last in 1994. What is particularly significant in our view is that Sakata broadened the scope of Japanese migration research by holistically studying the history using resources from both sides of the Pacific, and by demonstrating the importance of early US-Japanese diplomatic relationships, the mass media, and the American view of Asian populations in California as a whole.

The first article in this series highlights the Japanese inability to recognize the fact that Americans at large gave little credit to Japanese who tried to behave in a more "civilized" and westernized manner and instead grouped the Japanese with the Chinese, whom Americans considered unable to assimilate. The second article, "On a Collision Course (II)," attempts to answer why the Japanese government did not grasp the gravity of American concern about immigration and their response. The third article, "On a Collision Course (III)," deals with the worsening and more widely spread fissure between Japan and the United States after the Japanese victory in the first Sino-Japanese war (1894–95). This military success boosted Japanese confidence in their superiority over the Chinese. However, US government officials joined forces with the exclusionists, fueling the populace's anxiety over the increasing arrivals of "cheap" Japanese labor.

Sakata published the series as "incomplete," planning to conduct further research. Unfortunately, his intention of revising his original articles for this publication expressed in our initial conversation did not come to fruition due to his health conditions. Thus, readers should be aware that Sakata may have more historical evidence to revise his earlier findings.

We deliberately retained some Japanese terms in this translated volume not only because it is a widely used practice in the field but also because the early Japanese migration to Hawai'i and North America was conceptually, legally, and diplomatically structured differently from what Americans would commonly define as "immigration." Sakata emphasizes the importance of distinguishing between *dekasegi*, literally meaning "moving out to earn money," the movement of Japanese who came to the United States to work but who planned to return to Japan; and *imin*, Japanese who planned to move to the United States permanently. As Sakata suggests, the most pressing diplomatic agenda for the Japanese government in the early Meiji era (the first forty-four years of the Empire period, 1868–1912) was to amend the so-called unequal treaties signed with Western powers. For this purpose, Japan felt the need to boost its image abroad as a modern westernized nation, deserving of equal treatment with Western countries. Against this backdrop, the early Japanese migration abroad was carefully formulated: migrants were compelled to prearrange the means of their own support and their eventual return to the homeland. Thus, many of the early Japanese *dekasegi* workers were inevitably contract laborers.

Sakata suggests that the traditional methodologies of studying Japanese immigration have conflated three distinct periods: first, the *dekasegi* period, when Japanese crossed the Pacific and sojourned in the United States and Hawai'i intending to return home; second, the transition period, when the Japanese began to shift toward a permanent settlement in new homes; and third, the *imin* period, when they became immigrants or permanent residents. To gain a holistic understanding of Japanese immigration, Sakata urges, it is necessary to study these three periods independently and investigate the internal relationships among them, instead of erroneously citing parts that do not fit into a preconceived singular history as exceptional conditions or reasons.

The birth of the Empire of Japan under the Meiji emperor in 1868 and its transition periods of pre- and post-Meiji Restoration brought sweeping political and social changes to Japan. Two of these changes were the opening of Japanese ports to Western nations and Japan's eventual overseas expansion. We hope this translated volume of Sakata's work will bring this critical chapter of Japanese overseas migration to an international readership and stimulate scholars to reconsider the established understanding of early Japanese American history.

KAORU UEDA
Curator of the Japanese Diaspora Collection
Hoover Institution Library & Archives
Stanford University

Editor's Note on Translation and Acknowledgments

A team of four bilingual Japanese and English speakers translated the five articles in this book. We took both conventional and unconventional approaches to translation. A professional translator, Fukuko Kitano, translated chapters 1 and 4, "A Historical Study of Migration Research and Its Challenges" and "On a Collision Course (II)," and I reviewed the completed text. Recognizing the importance of readability to English speakers, we also took an unconventional approach: I translated the original Japanese into English for the other chapters and discussed the best possible translations with Japanese-language-trained graduate students at Stanford University, Koji Lau-Ozawa and Frank Vito Mondelli. The two individually wrote the final English translations, and I reviewed them. Lau-Ozawa completed chapters 3 and 5, "On a Collision Course (I)" and "On a Collision Course (III)," and Mondelli translated chapter 2, "Unequal Treaties and Japanese Migrant Workers in the United States." After we received reviewers' comments, Kitano revised her translations, and Lau-Ozawa and I edited the other three chapters. Unfortunately, although author Yasuo Sakata wrote adroitly in English, his health did not allow him to review the translations; thus, any misinterpretations are my fault.

After our first translations, four of the translated articles were sent to scholars of Japanese history and Japanese migration studies to read for fidelity to the original text. Comments from these reviewers focused on the consistency of language: the preservation of Sakata's distinctions between terms such as *migration* and *immigration* and his employment of historical terminology. We used the term *migration* to translate *imin* because Sakata demonstrates that the first groups of Japanese traveling abroad to work or study could not have been "immigrants"—they were required to return to Japan by the Japanese government. We used the term *immigration* only when the time period covered by Sakata's *imin* study extended beyond the initial *dekasegi* (temporarily working away from home) stage to permanent settlement. These details are essential to representing the nuances of his work.

With Sakata unavailable for reviewing these translations, we attempted to remain as close as possible to his writing in the original Japanese text and English abstract, and the only major deviations from the original document are to reduce his frequent use of quotation marks and to reduce redundancy across chapters. We incorporated Sakata's English abstract into the translation, where applicable. We also made a stylistic decision to keep the Japanese tradition of writing a family name first, followed by a given name, both in the main text and in the endnotes. For Western names, we followed the Western tradition. The final text presented here reflects these decisions.

This publication would not have been possible without the respect that many scholars of migration study have for Sakata's scholarly work and leadership in the field. Professor Masako Iino graciously accepted Sakata's and my request to write an introduction. With Sakata's long scholarly career and achievements, I am grateful for Iino's brilliant and insightful introduction. I am also deeply indebted to three reviewers: Yuma Totani, professor in the Department of History, the University of Hawai'i at Mānoa; Toyotomi Morimoto, professor of the Graduate School of Human Sciences, Waseda University; and Tomoko Ozawa, professor of the College of Art and Design, Musashino Art University. They helped us shape the translation to be in line with scholarly expectations of Japanese history and migration studies. We also thank the original Japanese publishers, the International Studies Association of Osaka Gakuin University, Nihon Tosho Sentā, and Doshisha University Institute for the Study of Humanities and Social Sciences, for allowing us to publish the English translations.

We are also excited that Sakata selected the Hoover Institution Library & Archives as the permanent home for his private library and archival material. Over the course of the last three years, I visited

Sakata's residence and shipped nearly his entire private library to Hoover. We are fortunate to have been able to complete this acquisition under his direct guidance. He made an invaluable contribution to our organizing the Sakata papers at Hoover by explaining the history of the materials and their importance. Borrowing his word, some of the "gems" in his papers include lists of Japanese passports issued and returned in 1868–1910 and of Japanese residents by occupation in the United States in 1890–1936 compiled by Sakata, and questionnaires filled out by Issei and collected by Zaibei Nihonjin Jiseki Hozonkai 在米日本人事績保存会 (Preservation Committee of Japanese Footsteps in America) in 1939. Sakata believes that the latter is a critical, unstudied resource well worth a doctoral thesis. Details of the Sakata papers are found at the Online Archive of California (oac.cdlib.org, collection number 2018C9).

When I met Professor Sakata nearly three years ago, he was enthusiastically transcribing late nineteenth-century Japanese newspapers and magazines published in San Francisco: *Aikoku*; *Dai Nippon*; *Jiyū*; *Daijūkyūseiki*; *Ensei*; and *Sōkō jiji*. Later he entrusted us with the safekeeping of these transcriptions and allowed us to make the key transcriptions available on the Hoji Shinbun Digital Collection (hojishinbun .hoover.org). This significant contribution allows researchers to search keywords on otherwise unsearchable handwritten newspaper articles. I hope that making the Sakata papers available at the Hoover Institution Library & Archives continues to inspire the current and future generations of scholars of Japanese emigration and immigration studies and help them further the high standards Sakata set for research.

KAORU UEDA
Curator of the Japanese Diaspora Collection
Hoover Institution Library & Archives
Stanford University

Introduction

Masako Iino

Dr. Yasuo Sakata is a leading scholar in immigration/emigration studies, or migration studies, as well as in Japanese American studies in
both Japan and the United States. He has published a great number of
books and essays on themes in these fields. The essays compiled in this
volume are typical of his work and present his great accomplishments.
His contributions started as early as the 1970s, when the situation in
these fields was exactly what he describes: that is, many improvements
were needed. He then brought about great change.

Sakata, who does his research in both Japanese and English, has long
been aware of the situation of researchers in migration studies in Japan
and the United States, as his papers indicate. And he had critical views
on what was needed. Though he saw the development of the field to be
quite slow, he was always in a position to change it. His contribution
to the development of migration studies in both countries is significant.

In 1991 (see chapter 1 of this volume), Sakata described the situation
of immigration studies/Japanese American studies in the United States
as follows:

> Since the 1950s innovative studies have been published that are
> based on detailed research and the examination of documents
> and on new analytical concepts regarding the history of Japanese
> Americans and their communities. Some ethnic studies researchers
> also began engaging in studies of Japanese Americans, recognizing
> that they have played a key role in America's multiethnic society.

And he saw that research on Japanese immigrants and Japanese Americans was well received in academic circles in the United States at the time. There were, however, a few areas of concern. For one, studies using Japanese documents and records were exceptions. If the research relied solely on English-language documents and resources, he argued, American perspectives and opinions would outweigh Japanese perspectives. Sakata maintained that immigration studies should emphasize an international point of view. Thus, he argued that the perspectives of the immigrant and emigrant countries should be examined equally and objectively, even if they had different societies, cultures, or environments. His idea was this: in Japanese American studies, mastering the English and the Japanese languages was crucial to conducting comprehensive research.

Sakata has perfect command of both English and Japanese. With his training in Japanese history, he has also mastered classical Japanese. The documents that researchers rely on in Japanese history, particularly before World War II, are mostly handwritten in classical Japanese. Therefore, researchers in immigration/emigration studies need this training, he insists, and not many researchers, either in the United States or in Japan, have it.

He has also quite critically observed the condition of migration studies and Japanese American studies in Japan (see chapter 1):

> In Japan, even before World War II, researchers, institutions, and local government agencies were studying emigration from their local communities and prefectures, producing highly regarded results. Unfortunately, research on overseas emigration and migration conducted from an international perspective is extremely limited. Japanese researchers have focused on emigrants' former lives in Japan and have shown little interest in their lives in America.

He points out that such academic interest created a bias favoring research focusing on specific regions and issues, making it difficult to grasp the bigger picture.

Actually, in Japan, the field of migration studies was, for a long time, considered to be a part of Japanese history. The focus of research was mainly on the so-called push factors of emigration, with reference to the conditions of areas—the *imin-ken* (literally "emigration prefectures")—that sent out large numbers of emigrants. Naturally the sources that researchers mainly used were part of the local history of Japan, written in Japanese. Research on the emigration policies of the Japanese government was also an important theme of migration studies then.

Even in the 1990s, when Sakata was deeply involved in research on Japanese emigration to the United States, he saw that it was still difficult for Japanese scholars to conduct research from a global perspective despite evaluating works by American experts in immigration studies. For the most part, Japanese scholars of emigration studies had not been able to establish their own research methods.

Sakata speculated that many Japanese scholars who took an interest in American immigration studies or Japanese American studies were primarily experts in general American studies. Thus, their interests were often too broad for Japanese American studies as the field was then constituted in Japan. Moreover, American researchers in Japanese American studies used fundamentally different methodologies, objectives, and approaches than did Japanese researchers, most of whom focused on their own field of emigration studies. The crucial problem, he concluded, was that neither party recognized the differences in their methodologies and did not cooperate with the other to improve and standardize their respective methods.

There were other obstacles to a comprehensive approach, he argued. One was the tendency in Japan to look down on emigrants as "losers." Moreover, the general perception of academics was that immigration studies was not a significant field. Sakata observed that outside the immigrant community itself, there was little enthusiasm to develop immigration studies. Thus, he found, few efforts were made to collect and preserve emigration-related documents left in town halls in the emigrants' prefectures, and it was difficult to find helpful documents or catalogs of articles. It became his mission to improve this situation both in the United States and in Japan.

The situation started to change in Japan in the late 1970s and the 1980s, though very slowly. In the 1970s, a small number of Japanese researchers who were interested in, and doing research on, Japanese emigration to the United States started to discuss which direction they should take. The majority of them were in American studies programs, and they were exploring the experiences of Japanese emigrants and their children. "Immigration studies" was an important part of studies about the United States, which drew immigrants from all over the world. According to the strongly held assimilation theory, all those who came to this promised land would be welcomed and incorporated into American society. Many researchers in Japan were finding that this theory did not hold true for Japanese Americans, as their history showed that they were discriminated against and excluded from the mainstream of American society.

Thus, with the realization that research on migration should not be limited to the field of American studies nor to discussions of push factors, researchers started collaborative efforts in migration studies. The idea was that migration should be viewed from both sides: from the perspective of the country that people left and the country that people entered, exactly as Sakata posited while he was doing research in the United States in the 1970s. Naturally the sources that researchers used were in both Japanese and English. In order to grasp how Japanese Americans saw themselves being treated by the larger society in the United States, researchers looked at Japanese-language newspapers published in Japanese American communities.

At the same time, many Japanese researchers studying Japanese emigrants to the United States and their children, that is, Japanese Americans, realized that their focus should not be limited to how Japanese immigrants were discriminated against. Their realization that they should pay attention to how Japanese Americans contributed to American society or to friendly relations between the two countries led them to apply a comparative approach in their research. They started to see the experiences of Japanese Americans in a larger context, comparing them with those of other ethnic groups in the United States: for example, they compared the history of Japanese Americans with that of Chinese Americans, African Americans, and Hispanic Americans.

The comparative approach was also observed in collaborations between scholars doing research on migration in two or more countries, including the United States, Canada, and Australia. For example,

Japanese migration to Canada was compared with migration to the United States, showing the differences in the ways Japanese immigrants were received by the two countries.

In the 1980s, research on migration was growing in various fields, not only in history, sociology, geography, demography, anthropology, and area studies but also in the fields of literature, legal studies, medicine, psychology, ethnology, philology, gender studies, art, and sports, among others. Also, as Japanese researchers considered those areas where Japanese emigrants moved to, as well as those where people crossed borders as immigrants or refugees, they started to pay attention not only to the Americas but also to Asian and European countries. The sources they used became more various in multiple languages. Their research also became interdisciplinary. Results of these changes were clearly seen in international symposiums and journals containing collected papers on "people on the move."

Another important change that influenced the nature of migration studies occurred in Japan in the 1980s. A large number of Latin Americans of Japanese descent entered Japan to seek employment as temporary workers. They were often called "return migrants," and many of them settled in such areas as Aichi, Tochigi, and Kanagawa; their children went to schools in those areas, creating the phenomenon of "multicultural coexistence." This situation generated more research in the field of migration studies. Researchers in Japanese history who focused on those return migrants naturally had to deal with why their parents and grandparents had left Japan to go to Latin America in the first place.

At this time researchers in Japanese history also declared that they had become aware that migration studies should pay attention to the Japanese whom the Japanese government had sent to Southeast Asia, the South Sea islands, Russia, and Sakhalin. Researchers paid more attention than before to government documents to find out the motives and effects of its migration policies. This trend invited more researchers to collaborate with each other in migration studies.

With such trends as a background, the Japanese Association for Migration Studies was established in 1991, combining several groups of researchers, with Sakata as its president. The establishment of this academic association responded to the need for a place where scholars with various backgrounds could exchange their research results in the international field of immigration/emigration studies. This meant that migration studies in Japan was very much broadened and became interdisciplinary, supported by Sakata's contribution to the field. The association did not focus exclusively on Japanese people who moved beyond Japan's borders, but included research on those who moved from one country to another, for instance, from European countries to the United States, from France to England, or from Mexico to Canada, as well as those who came to work and eventually settled in Japan. Again, the sources that researchers needed to analyze this phenomenon became multilingual. Because of his fluency in both English and Japanese, including classical Japanese, as well as his knowledge of research materials, Sakata himself demonstrated what was needed to proceed in international and global research collaboration.

All the research he published shows his inflexible stand to take materials and documents very seriously and to study them critically before referring to them in publications. Researchers must judge materials before using them to support their own arguments, he maintains. His works show that he takes a serious view of how researchers should find and use materials to reach their conclusions. In chapter 1 of this book, he gives examples of neglected materials and warns that researchers should be aware that some materials may have been misused and that the results of research using these inappropriate materials may be considered plagiarized. His attitude toward research based on reliable materials is always evident in the work he has produced. All researchers in whatever field should learn from his attitude.

Sakata's emphasis on finding and relying on original records leads to his criticism of research that does not show enough serious effort to distinguish original records from forged or secondhand resources. For instance, in his essay "Unequal Treaties and Japanese Migrant Workers in the United States" (chapter 2), which focuses on the overseas *dekasegi* system of the Japanese government and its policies during the early to middle Meiji period, he critically points out that many researchers do not distinguish "immigrants" from "*dekasegi* workers" simply because their research does not rely on original documents. He explains:

The history of Japanese migration to the Americas consists of three periods. First came the *dekasegi* period, when Japanese crossed the Pacific and sojourned in the United States and Hawai'i. Second came the transition period, when the Japanese began to change into immigrants, distinct from *dekasegi* laborers. Third came the *imin* period, when they became immigrants or permanent residents. To gain a holistic understanding of Japanese immigration, it is necessary to study these three periods independently and investigate the internal relationships among them. I suggest that the traditional methodologies of studying Japanese immigration have conflated these three distinct periods, which would erroneously cite parts that do not fit into a preconceived singular history as exceptional conditions or reasons.

Sakata claims that researchers before him did not, or could not, argue that the majority of Japanese laborers were inevitably denied landing from the 1890s, as they were unable to unearth the documents that supported their discourse. Thus he repeatedly addresses the need of efforts on the side of researchers to look for appropriate materials and documents in order to judge and support their argument. Even for scholars with a command of the Japanese language, it is often difficult to fully understand official documents written in classical Japanese, and this might bring about selecting and using the wrong documents. In order to grasp how Japanese intellectual leaders, government officials, and *dekasegi* laborers understood emigration to the United States, what *dekasegi* laborers aspired to do, and how they attempted to deal with immigration issues in the United States, researchers dealing with immigration phenomena should be well acquainted with the original documents, he says.

He goes as far as giving an example of how a US immigration supervisor played a "nonnegligible" role in shifting the exclusionists' target from certain Japanese people (*dekasegi* immigrants) to the Japanese as a whole. This shift was one reason for the deterioration of the US-Japan relationship. Thus, Sakata argues that even official documents should be read critically, taking into account the situation of the time as well as the background of the person who wrote the document or report.

One more instance of Sakata's great contribution to the field of migration studies in Japan is the establishment in 2002 of the Japanese Overseas Migration Museum under the Japan International Cooperation Agency, with the basic theme "Dedicated to Those Japanese Who Have Taken Part in Molding a New Civilization in the Americas." The Japanese government felt the need for a center that helped preserve the records of Japanese migration, mainly to the Americas, and that helped people in the world, as well as in Japan, to understand its importance. The center states its mission as follows: "This museum aims to accurately position in history the paths traced by overseas migrants through exhibits of materials, literature, photographs, etc., as we consider these migrants as pioneers of international cooperation who took part in the planning and formation of new cultures in new lands."

The museum offers exhibits on Japanese migration as well as a variety of resources and learning materials. The museum also supports research projects dealing with migration and migrants, by funding them and organizing workshops and lectures for the general public to participate in learning opportunities. From the time of conception for the idea of establishing a museum that was related to, or concentrated on, Japanese who left Japan for the outer world, Sakata was a major driving force in realizing the dream. When the museum was opened to the public, Sakata became chair of the museum's academic advisory committee, from which he would oversee the direction in which the museum was to develop as well as the direction of migration studies in Japan. Both the essays included in this volume and those not included show not only Sakata's superb scholarship but also his great efforts to nourish the next generation of scholars in the field. He has been a pioneer scholar both in the United States and in Japan, mentoring other scholars by giving them important practical advice. Now, in Japan, the field of migration studies has produced a significant amount of multilingual and diversified research results through global and international collaborations of researchers, just as Sakata wished to see in the 1980s. His contribution to the field is impressive.

CHAPTER I

A Historical Study of Migration Research and Its Challenges

Since around the 1960s, when many in the United States began recognizing the need to reexamine foundational ideas governing human rights, researchers in the social sciences started to review the history of this "immigrant nation" and especially the history and experiences of immigrants and citizens of color. Consequently, thorough analyses and candid criticisms were produced regarding the prejudices and supremacist attitudes held by Americans of European ancestry, who had constituted the majority of American people.[1] That said, Americans of today [when this article was written in 1991] continue to take pride in the American dream, as symbolized by the erection of the Statue of Liberty in 1886. They still support the idealized notion that the United States offers a sanctuary to those abject persons who undergo hardship in another region and warmheartedly welcomes them to start a new life, even if these are empty promises that do not reflect reality.

In this seemingly contradictory America, the land of immigrants, Japanese immigrants and their American descendants, the so-called Japanese Americans (Nikkei), experienced persistent legal harassment and discrimination arising from the racial prejudice of Americans of European ancestry. After the Pacific War broke out, Japanese Americans were forced to "relocate" to incarceration camps pursuant to President Franklin D. Roosevelt's Executive Order 9066. This

This paper was translated from Sakata Yasuo, "Imin kenkyū no rekishiteki kōsatsu to sono kadai," in *Nihon imin shiryōshū dai 1-ki: Hokubei hen dai 18-kan*, ed. Sakata Yasuo (Tokyo: Nihon Tosho Sentā, 1991), 1–81.

executive order neglected the protection of human rights guaranteed in the Constitution, which prohibits discriminatory practices based on ethnicity, and contradicted the ideals of the land of liberty. Consequently, Japanese Americans were forcibly removed to "relocation centers," a phenomenon far from the utopia that the Statue of Liberty symbolized. Since the 1950s innovative studies have been published that are based on detailed research and the examination of documents and on new analytical concepts regarding the history of Japanese Americans and their communities.[2] Some ethnic studies researchers also began engaging in studies of Japanese Americans, recognizing that they have played a key role in America's multiethnic society.[3]

Although recent research on Japanese migrants and Japanese Americans has been well received, one of its shortcomings is that studies using Japanese-language documents and records, such as *The Issei* by Yuji Ichioka and *Planted in Good Soil* by Masakazu Iwata, are exceptions, not the rule.[4] One can expect that American perspectives and opinions will outweigh Japanese perspectives if the research relies solely on English-language documents and resources. From an international perspective, it is ideal to examine the immigrant and emigrant perspectives equally and objectively, even if the homeland and destination countries have completely different ethnicities, societies, cultures, living environments, and customs. For Japanese American studies, the first desirable step is to acquire a sufficient command of both English and Japanese when conducting research. Since it takes years of effort to master both languages, however, this becomes an obstacle in fostering excellent researchers. Moreover, the reproduction and compilation of Japanese documents to aid bilingual and cross-cultural researchers has just begun, and comprehensive descriptions of related documents have not yet been published. These delays have hindered the development of strong cross-cultural scholarship. For these reasons, only a few American researchers are currently interested in the issue of what types of Japanese-language resources are necessary for Japanese American studies, and how they can be used effectively.

Given this, how are Japanese American studies considered in Japan, the ancestral land of Japanese immigrants? In Japan, even before World War II, researchers, institutions, and local government agencies were studying emigration from their local communities and prefectures,

producing highly regarded results.[5] Unfortunately, research on overseas emigration and migration conducted from an international perspective is extremely limited.[6] Japanese researchers have focused on
emigrants' former lives in Japan and have shown little interest in their
lives in America. Current affairs and academic interest tend to influence the direction of migration studies in Japan, creating a bias favoring research focusing on specific Japanese regions and issues, thus
making it difficult to grasp the big picture. One researcher pointed out
that "Japanese prewar emigration studies tended to focus on emigration to Japanese colonies rather than to North and South America or
other Pacific regions."[7]

From the late 1900s till the 1920s, Japan's general public became
increasingly disturbed by the white supremacist attitude of the US
government and its citizens. The rising cries of "yellow peril"—and
Japan's victory in the Russo-Japanese War—led to a serious discussion of a possible war between the United States and Japan. Alien land
laws, which clearly targeted Japanese farmers and farmworkers on the
West Coast, were enacted in California and other states. Furthermore,
due to the Immigration Act of 1924 (commonly referred to as *Hainichi
iminhō* in Japanese), Japanese immigration to America was completely
banned when the US Supreme Court ruled that the Japanese were
"ineligible to be naturalized."[8] Many Japanese writers paid attention
to anti-Japanese incidents and the racial prejudice of white Americans.
In those publications, I observed that the writers projected much anger
at Americans and their government and that the victimized Japanese
immigrants in the United States played a minor role in their accounts.
In the 1930s, as US-Japan tensions worsened, expectations increased
for the second generation of Japanese immigrants (Nisei) to bridge
the gap between two countries. Many writings on "Nisei issues" were
published, but in most cases the discussions were dominated by selfish
views that did not consider the Nisei's positions or views as American
citizens.[9] After World War II, for a while, the general public began to
pay attention to the topic of Japanese Americans' forced removal and
incarceration.

The current situation of migration studies in Japan, unfortunately,
may make it difficult to develop holistic research that can evaluate and
counter the predominating American perspectives. This may be a harsh

criticism, but I think Japanese scholars of migration, except for those in a few specific emigration areas with excellent empirical research results, have not yet been able to grasp the new trends and orientation of studies in the United States and evaluate their results fully, and thus cannot respond from a Japanese researcher's perspective. One reason for this weakness might be that many Japanese scholars who are interested in the history of American immigration or Japanese Americans are specializing in "American studies." Naturally, those scholars have a strong interest in American researchers' methodologies, research results, new English-language research literature and resources, and new analyses in the field of American studies. Moreover, researchers in American studies who specialize in immigration or Nikkei studies have fundamentally different views on methodologies, objectives, approaches, and analyses from those of researchers who conduct emigrant studies in Japan. Though this situation is nothing unusual, it appears that neither party has recognized the differences, demonstrated their problems to one another, or seriously exchanged their views. It is safe to say that we have not yet seen full-scale joint research projects in these fields.

There are other obstacles to a holistic study. One is the tendency in Japan to look down on Japanese emigrants as "losers" and, as a result, the general perception of academics that migration studies are an insignificant field of study.[10] Except for a small group of researchers in the field of migration or overseas emigration, there simply is not much enthusiasm for developing migration studies. Similarly, few people value—and advocate for the need to collect, organize, and reprint— immigration-related documents left in the town halls in emigrants' prefectures, such as directories, personal correspondence, local newspaper and magazine articles, letters from America such as *Amerika dayori*, and consular reports held at diplomatic archives, among others. Although people in the Hiroshima, Yamaguchi, and Okinawa prefectures, known for high rates of emigration, make efforts to collect these materials, they are slow to classify and organize them and have not made them publicly available to researchers. Furthermore, there is no serious attempt to house these documentary records as compilations of resources in public libraries to aid migration studies. A small number of public libraries, such as the National Diet Library and the emigration collection (*imin shiryōshū*) of the Wakayama Civic Library, make emigration collections available to the public. However, the majority of repositories have not even seriously discussed implementing plans to do so.[11]

It requires tremendous effort and persistence to conduct migration studies in Japan today. For example, as far as I know, hardly any handy Japanese-language documents or catalogs of articles with commentaries are available for researchers.[12] When researchers search the index of documents, theses, and articles, documents labeled *emigration* or *overseas migration* are classified under *population*. If researchers want to conduct more refined searches, such as "Japanese who are ineligible to be naturalized," "Japanese Americans' structural assimilation," "education issues for Nisei and Sansei," and "Japanese Americans as an ethnic group," they need patience and time to guess the most relevant subjects to search for, extract all the descriptions in the classified items, and collect the scattered theses. Therefore, one is required to spend a long time preparing before the actual research begins. Many important documents might be missed even after such careful pre-research preparation.

It is strongly desirable to prepare an environment in Japan that will allow scholars to develop more productive research in migration and emigration studies and gain higher respect for their research. I would like to stress that one of the important first steps is to create indexes of documentary records with commentaries and to compile and reprint materials.

Two Areas within Migration Studies: An Evaluation of Nikkei Research Resource Collections in America

With a growing demand for Japanese American studies, American researchers in the 1960s enthusiastically began cultivating new research in their respective fields. As they began reexamining documentary records and materials, scholars realized that they would need to explore materials that had not been identified by researchers and began seriously discussing potential methodologies and approaches to unearth them. At that time, however, most of the documents useful to Japanese migration or Japanese American studies stored at universities and public libraries were too focused on specific topics, while the cutting-edge and breakthrough documents that researchers were seeking were almost impossible to find. Japanese-language documents, in particular, were not available at most public libraries, with the exception of large libraries with abundant collections of "Japanese studies"–related documents such as the Library of Congress or Bancroft Library at the University of California–Berkeley.

Against this backdrop, the University of California–Los Angeles (UCLA) began the Japanese American Research Project (JARP) in 1963. Its ambitious purpose was to conduct a nationwide historical study, conduct sociological surveys of Japanese Americans in the United States (three generations: the Issei, Nisei, and Sansei) through interviews, and collect all available related documents essential to Japanese American studies in both Japanese and English, including newspaper and magazine articles, records of churches and other organizations, personal correspondence, and diaries.[13] Simultaneously, projects to collect materials for Japanese American studies were in progress regionally by the University of Hawai'i and the University of Washington.[14] After UCLA completed cataloging its collections, they became available for research in the 1970s, significantly improving the quality and standards of Japanese American studies in the United States.

The current JARP collection at the UCLA library, which Yuji Ichioka expanded to include collections of diaries and personal correspondence (including the Abiko family, Karl Yoneda, and Edison Uno papers), was considered one of the largest and most valuable collections of its kind in the United States. It has dramatically expanded to be more comprehensive and richer since its foundation.[15] Researchers on immigration and Japanese American studies from both Japan and the United States immediately began showing interest in the JARP collection, but after they organized, categorized, analyzed, and evaluated the documents carefully, in particular the Japanese materials, it became clear that they faced unexpected and potentially serious problems. I will present main summaries of these issues below.

First, it is well known that the Great Fire caused by the 1906 San Francisco earthquake burned down and destroyed San Francisco's Japantown. Perhaps even more devastating to Japanese American researchers was that the fire also destroyed most of the valuable documents, such as newspaper articles, records, letters, and diaries owned by Japanese residents. Although researchers who categorized the JARP collection at UCLA noticed the paucity of records related to Japanese residents in California from the 1890s, they did not fully recognize how serious the circumstances could be. Research of the JARP collection concluded that the destruction of Japantown in 1906 created a gap in history for Japanese residents in the continental United States that was difficult to restore.

As I will explain in detail later, the destroyed documents were valuable records not only of Japanese residents directly affected in the San Francisco Bay Area, including Alameda and Oakland, but also of Japanese farmworkers based in San Francisco and working in Northern and Central California. Thus, the destruction of those documents in Japantown meant that the records of daily life, working conditions, and the joys and sorrows of Japanese residents that may have been recorded in diaries were permanently erased from history. Although it may sound like an exaggeration, the 1906 Great Fire in San Francisco deprived us of at least one chapter of Japanese American history. I will discuss the details later in this paper.

The destruction of records in 1906 caused another unexpected problem. As the Japanese population on the West Coast grew and formed communities of Japanese migrants after the 1900s, they began work on what is known as *Zaibei Nihonjin shi* (History of Japanese in America). When this kind of project was conducted in California, the history of early Japanese migrants was divided into two categories; *dekasegi shosei* (schoolboys), who settled in the Bay Area around 1885 and increased in number yearly, and *dekasegi rōdōsha* (migrant laborers), who arrived on the West Coast, especially California, after 1890. The history of early Japanese migrants plays an important chapter in *Zaibei Nihonjin shi*, and it is fine to fill the gap of the lost textual records by interviewing survivors and recording their memories. There is nothing wrong about compiling a history in this way.

Historians can write a unique history and enhance the credibility of the underlying sources if they carefully select the interviewees. The problem stems from editing and, in some cases, revising the original narrations and from the random selection and growing number of interviewees over time. Over the process of compiling multiple histories of Japanese in the United States and other similar publications, this type of oral history was prone to change with each iteration. In some cases, the narration of an old man was edited multiple times and became exaggerated or even developed into a tale far from the original narration.

Worse yet, the survey interviews were not limited to the early gap in history. Issei writers (those in the first generation of Japanese Americans), who edited several regional Japanese histories and other related publications, valued the retrospective stories of their fellow Issei, with whom they shared hardship. As a result, many of their memories were included in the history of Japanese in America without close investigation. In 1940, a year before the Pacific War broke out, the Jiseki Hozonkai (Preservation Committee of Footsteps) established by the Zaibei Nihonjinkai (Japanese Association of America) compiled these locally published Japanese histories and other anniversary publications into its *Zaibei Nihonjin shi* (History of Japanese in America).[16] Although this *Zaibei Nihonjin shi*, which offers rich content, has been regarded as one of the most valuable resources for researchers of Japanese American studies, its mosaic inclusion of both historical facts and tales is similar to that of the many other regional publications of Japanese history. Since *Zaibei Nihonjin shi* covers Japanese residents, namely Japanese immigrants, across the entire continental United States, its [negative] influence would be deeper and more widespread if it was misused or the trustworthiness of its resources was carelessly investigated. Needless to say, I have no intention of criticizing the editors of *Zaibei Nihonjin shi* or downplaying its value as reference material. Nonetheless, I should emphasize that researchers need to predict where pitfalls might lie.

Second, tragedy appears to repeat itself. Thirty-six years after the 1906 San Francisco earthquake, nearly 120,000 Japanese Issei and their families residing on the West Coast were faced with an unimaginable event: they were removed from their residences and forced to relocate to incarceration camps, pursuant to President Roosevelt's Executive Order 9066, issued soon after the Pacific War broke out. Nearly 90 percent of the Japanese and their American-born descendants in the continental United States resided in areas affected by the executive order, where many Issei had lived and raised their families for more than twenty or thirty years.[17] The total number of Issei and their families forced to move to "relocation centers" exceeded 110,000. They were allowed to take only belongings that would fit into two pieces of baggage. Under these conditions, one can imagine how materials valuable to researchers were lost in the process of the forced removal and incarceration. Now, half a century later, many Issei who experienced that historical event have died, and there is no way of accurately knowing what kinds of personal records or documents were lost. As time passes, however, researchers are likely to increasingly recognize the importance of such losses.

Later, I will explain more about the documents and other materials that have been confirmed as missing. Here, I would like to examine the lasting impact on research caused by the loss or dispersal of materials owned by individuals, organizations, and churches as a result of Japanese immigrants and Nikkei being relocated to incarceration camps.

First, we need to examine the types of documents that have survived. In the wake of the San Francisco earthquake on April 18, 1906, its victims had no time to think about what belongings needed to be saved. Although the Executive Order 9066 of February 1942 must have been just as shocking as the earthquake to the victims, we can assume that they had time to select valuable belongings to bring with them to the incarceration camps. How, then, did they select what to take with them?

Although what I describe here is just a conjecture without documentary support, I am convinced that this is close to what happened. In 1942, what position did the Issei occupy and in what kind of psychological state were they? Anti-Japanese sentiment among Americans undeniably existed, and US-Japan relations increasingly deteriorated through the 1930s until the outbreak of the US-Japan War, although this decade did not witness repeated harassment from overt racial hatred or strong anti-Japanese movements as did the 1910s or early 1920s. After the Japanese attack on Pearl Harbor, which was criticized as a disgraceful surprise attack, the Japanese Issei, overnight, became enemy aliens in the United States, for they could not obtain US citizenship on the basis of their being ineligible for naturalization. If the Issei lived in neighborhoods where anti-Japanese sentiment was intense, they worried about their safety. After the US-Japan War began, many

Issei, their families, and Japanese groups and organizations, including *Nihonjinkai* (Japanese associations), Japanese Chambers of Commerce, and *kenjinkai* (prefectural associations), likely attempted to burn, bury, or throw into the sea documents that might be taken as evidence of their loyalty to Japan, their motherland and new enemy nation. It became clear through postwar research interviews that their foremost criterion for selecting potentially dangerous documents was anything written in the Japanese language.[18] In some cases, they destroyed materials randomly. The same research interviews suggest that, to the dismay of historians, some documents that might have been considered unfavorable or inconvenient to Japanese individuals and organizations were also destroyed.[19]

The negative impact of the US-Japan War and the Japanese Americans' forced removal and incarceration became even worse in the postwar period. The leadership of Japanese communities switched from the Issei to the Nisei (the second generation), who demonstrated absolute loyalty to the United States as American citizens. The Issei, on the other hand, found themselves without the protection of the Japanese government but were still suspected of a hidden loyalty to Japan, a militaristic nation that had invaded China and thereby worsened the US-Japan relationship. Nisei leaders in the 1930s—particularly after 1937, when the second Sino-Japanese War broke out—sharply criticized the Issei for leading Nikkei communities to support Japan with fundraising activities and continuing to show their loyalty as Japanese citizens.[20] After World War II this Nisei attitude was clearly demonstrated to the Issei, whose emotional anchor, Japan, was defeated and became occupied by the Allied forces. Many postwar Issei, particularly those who had been in the incarceration camps, lost their spirit when arguing against the Nisei's accusations and criticisms. To protect themselves, they withdrew from publicly speaking about past experiences, or even tried to hide them, fearing that they might be found responsible for the deterioration in the US-Japan relationship in the 1930s.[21]

Coincidentally about the same time, UCLA began the Japanese American Research Project, or JARP, collecting documents and materials that reflected the Issei's sentiments. Many personal documents, regarded as valuable on the basis of their large number and wide variety, were donated by devout Issei members of mainly white Christian churches who were released from the incarceration camps before other Issei because of pleas for mercy from white ministers and church members. Some of them, regarded as dangerous left-wingers by the Japanese government in the 1930s, actively collaborated with the US military during the war. These Issei could boast that they had nothing to do with the dark past of the 1930s—a topic other Issei avoided.[22]

However, the personal documents, diaries, and records from the interwar period of the late 1920s to 1941 of respected Issei community leaders, including the chairmen and secretaries of central or regional Japanese associations, were unfortunately not included in the JARP collection. The Nisei, who took over community leadership positions from the Issei during the interwar period, wrote and published many Japanese American histories and memoirs, attempting to explain their own perspectives.[23] The Issei leaders' personal records or memoirs from the 1930s, however, were not published. Since many Issei were already deceased, their criticisms of the Nisei could no longer be heard. The Issei's silence, caused by different circumstances from the 1906 San Francisco earthquake, probably created another gap in Japanese American history. I suggest that researchers of Japanese American studies, historians in particular, pay careful attention while evaluating, analyzing, studying, and investigating materials of the interwar period.

Third, although not directly related to missing documents, the loss and dispersal of large volumes of historical documents is considered to have indirectly led to the following phenomenon. As I mentioned before, some editors of regional Japanese histories and similar publications used interviews and memoirs to complement the lack of textual records. These compilers' reliance on so-called *magobiki* (secondhand citations or excerpts from other works) is often pointed out as a bad habit. I suggest here one of the possible reasons why *magobiki* were common in publications related to Nikkei communities. In local Japanese communities, projects about Japanese histories or other commemorative publications had a limited number of Issei editors. Those who were considered for selection were in most cases *bunpitsuka* (writers), and many were working as editors or reporters at Japanese-language newspapers. Some of the newspaper publishers with larger circulations, such as Nichi-Bei Shinbunsha or Shin Sekai Shinbunsha in San Francisco and Rafu Shinpōsha in Los Angeles, often edited their own *nenkan* (yearbooks) or regional Japanese histories.[24] The same Issei writers or newspaper companies often published multiple editions of similar publications. In such cases, *magobiki* were probably natural and unavoidable when the same editors republished chapters, sentences, or excerpts of articles from previous publications.

The issue here is the use of previously published passages without citing original sources. When excerpts from a publication edited by a different editor are used in the compilation of a regional history, it is not a problem if the sources are clearly indicated. However, citations were not given in prewar publications in Japanese communities. Writers rather commonly wrote sentences using excerpts from multiple books, and editors would further edit them without citation—an act that would not be possible to defend from accusations of plagiarism. One can imagine that if each regional community had edited its Japanese history once every ten years, we would have had increasingly more untrustworthy publications. Fortunately, however, the irony here is that limited funds and staff for editing in overseas Japanese communities generally prevented the publishing of more than one volume. Therefore, uncontrollable situations did not happen.

Zaibei Nihonjin shi (History of Japanese in America), published by the Japanese Association of America, explains its editorial process at the end of the book:

> For the publication of *Zaibei Nihonjin shi*, Zaibei Nihonjin Jiseki Hozonkai (Preservation Committee of Japanese Footsteps in America) was founded. To collect historical materials, they requested regional research reports from across North America. The Jiseki Hozonkai editors, consisting of two editorial committee members—historian Fujiga Kōichi and the former president of Hokubei Chōhōsha, Nagata Shigeru—and the chief editor and former executive of Nichi-Bei Shinbunsha, Shimanai Yoshinobu, were dispatched across California and other states to gather information by collecting historical materials and holding meetings with seniors. Furthermore, regional Japanese associations, Japanese-language schools, and Japanese churches were asked to collaborate on this landmark publication.[25]

The above statement describing the research method turned out to be *tatemae* (a public position) and not *honne* (a real intention), however. Abe Toyoharu, one of the editors in chief, stated, "While editing, I came across some misinterpretations and unreliable materials. I thought it would be better to title the publication *Nihonjin shi shiryō shū* (Collection of Japanese history materials) rather than a complete *Zaibei Nihonjin shi*." However, this was a difficult task to accomplish in just six months. He admitted that the thousand-page publication was completed in that incredibly short period of time.[26] The chief Issei writers who had edited regional Japanese history publications participated in this project, making it safe to assume that *magobiki* was practiced in the process.

How, then, should scholars evaluate postwar publications on Japanese American history? The credibility of publications in Hawai'i versus the continental United States varies widely. *Hawai Nihonjin iminshi* (A history of Japanese immigrants in Hawai'i), published in 1964 and edited by the Hawai Nihonjin Iminshi Kankō Iinkai, and *Hawai no Nihonjin Nikkeijin no rekishi, jōkan* (The history of Japanese and Japanese Americans in Hawai'i, upper volume), published in 1986 and edited by Watanabe Reizō, have high levels of credibility because researchers were involved in the editing and provided annotations.[27] On the other hand, for the publications in the continental United States, the prewar editorial inclusion of *magobiki* was still commonly practiced. Moreover, in some publications in Los Angeles, editors revised or deleted parts that might have been regarded as unfavorable to postwar Nikkei communities, without giving due consideration to their act.[28] One reason these sources are less trustworthy could have been the loss of a massive number of records owing to the community's forced removal and incarceration. One of these postwar Japanese American history publications, *Beikoku Nikkeijin hyakunenshi* (One hundred years of Japanese American history), edited by Katō Shin'ichi of Shin Nichi-Bei Shinbunsha in 1961, commemorated the hundredth anniversary of US-Japan amity.[29] This volume was published in a large quantity for the purpose of distributing it to the thousands of Issei that were listed in the appendix, titled *Zaibei Nihonjin hatten jinshiroku* (Directory of Japanese Americans). The appendix was sold to those who had contributed to the development of their communities and to their families. There was a rumor that the sales of that publication saved Shin Nichi-Bei Shinbunsha from filing for bankruptcy.[30] Many Japanese researchers used this publication, citing it frequently because it was relatively easier to acquire in postwar Japan than other documents. For prewar studies of Japanese or Japanese communities in America, however, one should carefully avoid using these kinds of postwar publications, which could lead to serious errors unless scholars can closely examine and verify the facts and contents by referencing other materials or documents.

Some may contend that my argument so far is based only on my analysis of Japanese-language materials in the JARP collection at UCLA. Keep in mind, however, that the volume of documents necessary for Japanese American studies in both the United States and Japan became extremely limited due to their loss or dispersal caused by the 1906 San Francisco earthquake and the community's forced removal and incarceration after the breakout of the Pacific War.[31] Prewar publications of regional Japanese histories published by Japanese communities in America are primary materials that every researcher of Nikkei studies needs to review. Therefore, it is important to be fully aware of the decisions, processes, and procedures that governed their editing and the nature of their hidden flaws. Even a witness at a trial can give false testimony. Witnesses to historic events are in an even more casual position and can freely add their opinions and embellish their testimony liberally. If this type of retelling of a historical account is repeated several times with *magobiki*, and revised via the editors' points of view, how horrifying can the mainstream narrative possibly become? To prevent this kind of situation, researchers need to pay careful attention in selecting, evaluating, and studying these historical documents.

The Great Fire in San Francisco and Its Aftereffect

On April 18, 1906, right after a huge earthquake hit San Francisco and its surrounding areas, a fire destroyed most of the city. Who were the Japanese who resided in the city of San Francisco and the San Francisco Bay Area at the time?[32]

Japanese migrant laborers began arriving in the continental United States around 1890. About five years earlier, so-called *dekasegi shosei* (schoolboys), who subsidized their school expenses by engaging in domestic labor, came to America. Until the first half of 1892, those *dekasegi shosei* and other laborers landed at the port of San Francisco. As if in response to their arrival, "anti-yellow" racial sentiments spread throughout the Bay Area. In 1891, when a new immigration act was enacted, inspections by US government officials became stricter at the San Francisco port, causing a dramatic increase in the number of Japanese passengers who were denied disembarkation. As a result, many migrant laborers changed their point of entry to the Victoria port (opened for transnational navigation around the second half of 1892) in Vancouver, British Canada, after which they crossed the border and entered the United States via Washington, where immigration inspection was not yet as strict as in San Francisco. Thus, some Japanese began settling in cities in the Northwest, including Seattle and Tacoma in Washington and Portland in Oregon.[33] Nonetheless, many Japanese who entered the United States from the British territory of Canada later moved even farther south; by the 1890s, most Japanese migrant laborers on the West Coast worked near the San Francisco Bay Area and engaged in seasonal work in fruit farming or other types of agriculture.[34]

"Beikoku junkai kakuchi shōkyō narabini zairyū honpōjin jōtai" (a regional site-survey report on the business status of Japanese residents in America) was issued by the consulate of Japan in San Francisco on May 15, 1895. It stated that there were approximately 7,000 Japanese residents in the consulate's geographic area. For this survey report, "the consular officers were dispatched in seven areas in Southern California, two areas in Northern California, one area in Oregon, two areas in Washington . . . totaling more than ten areas in three states." It was also reported that there were approximately 600 Japanese residents in seven cities in Southern California, including Fresno and Los Angeles, approximately 2,400 in San Francisco and its surrounding areas, 1,650 in Sacramento, 450 in Vacaville, 400 in Portland, Oregon, and 500 in both Seattle and Tacoma in Washington. Therefore, Japanese residents in the San Francisco Bay Area, Sacramento, and Vacaville were estimated to have accounted for more than 60 percent of the 7,000 Japanese residents in California.[35]

Furthermore, according to a US Census Bureau survey in 1900, 24,326 Japanese were living in the continental United States; 18,269 of them, about 75 percent, resided in three West Coast states: California, Oregon, and Washington.[36] In addition, according to the survey by the Japanese consulate, 11,451 Japanese resided in San Francisco, accounting for 45 percent of the 25,638 Japanese residents in California, with 1,466 Japanese residents in three nearby cities, Alameda, Oakland, and Berkeley, at the end of 1904.[37] Therefore, we can conclude that more than half of the Japanese residents in California resided in the San Francisco Bay Area, where the 1906 San Francisco earthquake hit and caused enormous damage. A survey conducted in late 1904 reported seven Japanese doctors, six Japanese dentists, four bookstores, twenty-two barbers, sixteen clothing stores, twelve public bathhouses, eleven Western restaurants, thirty-five Japanese restaurants, eight fresh-produce stores, and fifty-two other Japanese-related stores in the Japanese residential areas in San Francisco. Serving the many Japanese seasonal migrant laborers working on fruit and other agricultural farms were eight employment agencies, sixty-one boardinghouses and lodgings, nine billiard rooms, ten archery galleries, and four *geiko* (geisha) and *maiko* (apprentice geisha). In the Japanese residential area were eight newspaper and magazine publishers, two banks, twenty-six Japanese associations and organizations including *kenjinkai* (prefectural associations), and eleven Japanese trading company offices.[38]

As one can see from the above explanation, at the time of the 1906 San Francisco earthquake, Japantown, the base of Japanese immigrant life and activities, had already been established, serving as a place of comfort for *dōhō* (compatriots), featuring restaurants, eateries, and entertainment centers. Not only were there Japanese residents of the San Francisco Bay Area present but, during the farming off-season, Japanese migrant laborers working in the fruit and agricultural farms of Vacaville and Sacramento in Northern California and Fresno, Salinas, and Watsonville in Central California came to Japantown for comfort and rest while looking for or preparing for jobs during the next farming season.[39] Therefore, we can assume that San Francisco's Japantown was where information and records of the Japanese *dekasegi* laborers' lives, experiences, and jobs were stored during the early stages of the formation of the Japanese immigrant community. The Great Earthquake hit San Francisco at 5:12 a.m., April 18, 1906. "The entire city was covered by an inferno and its facilities destroyed. As far as the eye could see, there was nothing but burnt ruins. . . . Our fellow Japanese victims reached 10,000 in number."[40] As a result, almost all public and personal records concerning Japanese immigrants were incinerated. The lost documents included those of *Shinsekai* and *Nichi-Bei shinbun*, Japanese-language newspapers published in San Francisco. Both newspapers continued publishing until the forced removal and incarceration of Japanese Americans residing on the West Coast, beginning in April 1942. Although these newspapers had a strong influence on the Japanese immigrant communities and became essential materials for the study of Nikkei communities, few issues published before 1906 have survived today.[41]

The loss of valuable documents caused by the natural disaster was enormous and truly regrettable for researchers. Additionally, not only did the Great Earthquake in 1906 cause an invaluable loss of records, but it also left aftereffects we cannot ignore, as in the case of the Idaho incident.

The "Idaho Incident," a Rewritten History

Descriptions of the *"Aidaho haikan jiken"* in various publications of regional Japanese history inadvertently confused two different actual incidents. In many cases, they were instances of folklore dramatized with yellow-journalism-like sensational content; they are not considered credible renderings of the events as verified by historical materials.

The first Idaho incident started in July 1892, when one of the Japanese migrant laborers who did track maintenance for the Union Pacific Railroad Company near Nampa, Idaho, was diagnosed with smallpox. A group of white workers who believed they had lost their jobs to the Japanese became strongly dissatisfied with the railroad company, turning hostile against the Japanese railroad workers and attacking them. As a result, the Japanese workers were forced out of six towns, including Nampa, Mountain Home, and Caldwell. This marked the first anti-Japanese incident in the continental United States in which Japanese workers were attacked by armed mobs. Chinda Sutemi, the Japanese consul in San Francisco, considering this a serious matter, requested that the governor of Idaho and the head of police in Nampa investigate the causes of the incident and explain the measures taken to deal with its effects. He then reported the details of this incident to Enomoto Takeaki, the minister of foreign affairs.[42] After receiving the report, Enomoto sent a telegraph message to Chinda, instructing him to make an official visit to the crime scene of the Idaho incident to conduct an investigation on-site and report the details.[43] Consul Chinda's *fukumeisho* (report) included a *gushinsho* (detailed report) by Tanaka Chūshichi, the labor contractor who provided the Union Pacific Railroad Company in Idaho with Japanese migrant laborers and managed their camps. It also appended other related materials, including copies of the letters from Chinda to the governor and the head of police and clippings of English-language newspapers. His report was titled "Beikoku Aidaho-shū Yunion Pashifikku Tetsudō kōji ni jūjiseru honpōjin rōdōsha hōchiku jiken no tame Chinda Ryōji shucchō no ken" (The case of Consul Chinda's official trip about the banishment of Japanese migrant laborers working with the Union Pacific Railroad Company in Idaho, United States) and was stored in the Diplomatic Archives of the Ministry of Foreign Affairs of Japan.[44] Chinda's *fukumeisho* described in detail the cause and development of this anti-Japanese incident, and the state and local police's policies for dealing with it, as well as the conditions of the Japanese migrant laborers and the terms of their employment with the railroad company. The detailed appendix report sent from Tanaka to Enomoto, the minister of foreign affairs, contained statistics and information about the working conditions, wages, management policy of the camps, and other conditions of the Japanese migrant laborers engaged in maintaining the Union Pacific Railroad Company's tracks.[45]

Chinda addressed the status of Japanese migrant laborers employed by the Union Pacific Railroad Company in his report as follows:

> The right track part of the railroad in the State of Idaho, where Japanese migrant laborers were employed, was named the Union Pacific Railroad, whose railroad line started from the territories of Wyoming, extended through the State of Idaho, and ended in Portland, Oregon. In addition to the main line, the Union Pacific Railroad owned many supporting lines in the surrounding states, and thus was considered one of the three largest railroad companies

in the western United States, along with the South Pacific Coast Railroad and the Northern Pacific Railway.

The right side of the main lines, the one starting from Granville in the territories of Wyoming and ending in Huntington, Oregon, was built by Japanese migrant laborers, and its extension was 543 miles long. . . . Japanese migrant laborers started working on the railroad construction last October in 1891; at that time the workers numbered only in the tens. By April or May of this year 1892, however, the number had increased dramatically, to more than four hundred. . . .

Before the hiring of Japanese migrant laborers, Italians and Irish workers were employed. Since they were not local workers, however, they wandered aimlessly, quit frequently, and sowed discord. Since they had notorious habits of drinking and gambling and did not work industriously on railroad construction, the troubled railroad company tried hiring Japanese migrant laborers instead. Although there were inconveniences in language communication, they were obedient and hard workers. Because they were so different from the former workers, the company ended up firing the white workers and employing Japanese workers instead. Among the employed Japanese migrant laborers, natives of Hiroshima prefecture comprised the majority; others were natives of Wakayama, Kumamoto, and Okayama prefectures. Eight or nine out of ten workers were farmers; there might have been some sailors and gamblers there as well, although their number was small. After the company fired the sailors and gamblers, they decided to hire only genuine workers. Those workers all arrived in Canada first. . . . Those who landed in the San Francisco port and came here for jobs were very rare. . . .

Although the workers' wage was a dollar and twenty-five cents a day, ten cents was deducted as a fee for the Remington Johnson company and labor office, the labor contractor for railroad laborers. Therefore, they actually received a dollar and fifteen cents a day. They worked ten hours a day; in the case of overtime, two hours of extra work was considered one day of work and paid accordingly. Thus, they had no trouble making ends meet and were even able to have enough left over for saving.[46]

Tanaka Chūshichi, the intermediary who arranged the Japanese workers' contracts, submitted a *gushinsho* (detailed report) to Consul Chinda, in which he explained in detail how Japanese migrant laborers began to work on maintaining the Union Pacific Railroad Company's tracks in Idaho:

> The initial encounter with the group was made in early September last year (1891), when Tanaka Chūshichi, a native of Niigata prefecture, and Harada Fusatarō and Mizubayashi Jinzō, both natives of Shizuoka prefecture, traveled together and met "Asai," a Chinese contractor for projects by the Idaho division of the Union Pacific Railroad Company. Having agreed upon a contract to provide laborers, they recruited Japanese migrant laborers in various places. Although the aim was to start the project in October, fewer than eighty workers had been recruited by last April (1892) and thus it seemed hopeless to continue the project. Asai, as a sly Chinese man, however, planned to make his fortune by imposing heavy profits on the supply of clothes and foods for Japanese laborers by deducting 70 percent of their wages for those items. Because the Japanese workers no longer could stand this oppression, they finally went on strike. Asai abrogated the relationship and was replaced by Tanaka, who cleaned up the mess, gained the company's trust, and increased the number of workers to what we see today.[47]

Although both documents are rare and valuable historical materials, few researchers would use them, likely for the following reasons: The second Idaho incident, the so-called *Aidaho haikan jiken*, occurred in 1894. This *haikan jiken* had no connection to the exclusionary activity in 1892, for it actually took place in San Francisco, not in Idaho. It was reported that two Japanese-language newspapers in San Francisco, *Sōkō*, Aikoku Dōmei's (Patriotic League) organ paper, and its competitor newspaper, *Kinmon nippō*, were considered to be deeply involved.[48] Organizations such as Aikoku Dōmei and Enseisha, organized by the *Jiyū minken-ha shosei* (schoolboys belonging to the Freedom and People's Rights Movement) residing in San Francisco, were reported to be involved with the second Idaho incident as well.[49] It is impossible to verify, however, because the related documents were destroyed in the Great Fire caused by the 1906 San Francisco earthquake. The only remaining record related to this *haikan jiken* is *Aidaho jiken haikan shimatsu* (1894), which was compiled by Sōkō Hyōron, Enseisha, and Kinmon Nippōsha from articles in a San Francisco–based Japanese-language newspaper and which attacked and defamed Tanaka Chūshichi, the central figure of this incident, who supplied Japanese migrant laborers to the Union Pacific Railroad Company.[50] Tanaka's achievement of contracting many Japanese migrant laborers for the railroad company's track maintenance project was widely recognized. As early as 1894, when the *haikan jiken* occurred, there was a different version of how he supplied Japanese laborers. That later version, which implied the involvement of Tanaka's mistress described in *Aidaho jiken haikan shimatsu*, became widely accepted as the true story among Japanese residents in the United States.

In the past, railroad construction in the region of Idaho was mainly done by white and Chinese workers; not until 1891 did Japanese migrant laborers enter that field.

A man commonly known as Daishin ran a prostitution business in Portland. Onani, his wife, had a client called Asei from Nanking. He was a labor contractor that extensively contracted Chinese workers for railroad construction. At that time, the jobless Tanaka was a client of Daishin, acting as a stooge for his brothel. He started talking to Asei after being introduced by Onani, the wife of Daishin. Asei procured women with Onani.

Because Asei thought Tanaka was smart enough to be useful, he placed a few Japanese laborers with him that he selected from the brothel's guests and hired them under his supervision. Tanaka then brought Japanese workers for the first time to Idaho to work on railroad construction (September 1891). Thus, Tanaka went to work under Asei, although he was not competent enough to receive as much profit as he would have liked.

After making strenuous efforts to become free from Asei, Tanaka became independent enough to lead Japanese laborers himself. This worked smoothly, and, within several months, the number of Japanese workers he led reached more than three hundred. Since it was not possible for him to manage all the Japanese laborers, he hired Asano Hiroshi, who agreed to work under his supervision. He assigned responsibilities to three people (from Aikoku Dōmei, the Patriotic League), including Asano, had them do their jobs, and supervised their work. He acted like the *Sō tsuibushi* [a governmental officer who had rights over political and military affairs] of the entire Japanese migrant laborer workforce.

Currently, Tanaka has about four hundred Japanese migrant laborers working under him. He is the governor general of Japanese laborers and several assistants, including Asano Hiroshi and Ōsawa Kiichirō. He can do anything he wants to do. He is no longer acting like the stooge of the brothel that he used to be.[51]

In *Aidaho jiken haikan shimatsu*, Tanaka Chūshichi was described as an uneducated ex-sailor who, by luck, became successful as an intermediary agent for migrant laborers, receiving hundreds of dollars in fees every month. "He indulged in luxuries, spent earned money in the red-light district, kept a mistress and lived in a most extravagant way. He neglected to pay workers, and even spent their savings, which led to the banishment incident called the *haikan jiken*."[52]

This embellished, humorously exaggerated scenario persisted for the second Idaho incident of 1894 and seemed branded into the memories of Japanese residing in the United States. Therefore, the more significant Idaho incident in 1892, the first anti-Japanese incident, was either forgotten or confused with the *haikan jiken*. For example, a false theory spread that Consul Chinda took an official trip to Idaho, not for the on-site investigation of anti-Japanese activity but to investigate Tanaka's "embezzlement." In 1894, not long after the *haikan jiken*, *Rokkī to dōhō*, edited by Iida Shirō and published by the Japanese-language newspaper publisher Rokkī Jihōsha in Salt Lake City, Utah—near the site of the first Idaho incident in which Japanese migrant laborers were banished—stated that "as the word about the *haikan jiken* spread in San Francisco, Consul Chinda was compelled to patrol Idaho and subsequently clean up Tanaka's debts."[53] Moreover, *Rokkī to dōhō* added the following fiction. In *Aidaho jiken haikan shimatsu*'s account, "the wife of Daishin, who ran a prostitution business in Portland, introduced Tanaka, one of their clients, to Asei, an intermediary contractor for Chinese railroad workers." In *Rokkī to dōhō*, however, it was rewritten as follows:

> The current Oregon Short Line Railroad used to be a part of the Union Pacific Railway. There was a powerful Chinese foreman named Asei. He was well connected with Largo (a labor contractor for railroad construction workers) and later replaced Remington as a managing contractor. When Asei came to Pocatello and contacted Largo, he began coveting the profits and controlling the Chinese coolie workers.
>
> Asei, consorting in a Japanese brothel in Ogden, Utah, met with the wife of Tanaka Chūshichi around 1891. He finally took her with him to Rock Springs, his base, and made her his mistress. Tanaka was happy to see Asei employ eight hundred workers, whom he supervised for the railroad and coal mining work, which greatly expanded his profits. As Tanaka became happily acquainted with Asei, his wife's lover, he sank into dependence on them. He persuaded Asei through her that he would like to provide Japanese migrant laborers for the railroad company. Asei agreed. Tanaka went to Portland and recruited more than forty migrant laborers.
>
> Although Japanese migrant laborers on the coast only made sixty-seven cents a day, Tanaka told them to pay thirty dollars per month. It must have sounded like the gospel to the workers; he had so many applicants. Here, you could see how pitiful the situation was.[54]

The editor of *Zaibei Nihonjin shi* published a compilation of various prewar regional Japanese histories and, as previously cited, collected various versions of the Idaho incident. He also, however, confused the two Idaho incidents with the erroneous descriptions that had been handed down.

Aidaho Haikan Jiken

Following the Chinese Exclusion Act, as the power of Chinese migrant laborers diminished, many Japanese immigrants settled in the intermountain areas including Idaho, Utah, west of Lawrence in Wyoming, east of Elko in Nevada, and an area in western

Colorado, and were mainly employed by the railroad or the mining companies.

At that time, there was an influential intermediary agent that provided railroad companies with workers named Tanaka Chūshichi. All three hundred Japanese migrant laborers obediently followed his orders. Later, his administration of homeland remittance, which began to appear suspicious, together with objections against Tanaka that erupted inside the company, triggered a call for his firing. The case escalated to the point that it became a major issue among Japanese in America; two newspapers in San Francisco, *Kinmon* and *Sōkō*, began arguing with one another on this issue and Consul Chinda Sutemi traveled to the intermountain area. This event agitated the Japanese and demonstrated the nature of "wild west" society, which included many unrefined hot-blooded men (the social order of Japanese communities had not yet been established).

Although Tanaka was an uneducated ex-sailor, he quickly seized the opportunity. He was already living in Ogden before other Japanese settled in the intermountain areas. The Oregon Short Line Railroad at that time was a part of the Union Pacific Railway. The head of the eight hundred Chinese workers in the company was Asē, who lived in Rock Springs. He visited Ogden frequently and became acquainted with the wife of Tanaka, previously mentioned. In 1891 Tanaka, through his wife, convinced Asē to hire Japanese migrant laborers. . . .

Tanaka's activities were based in Nampa, Idaho, around 1891. When one of his subordinates contracted smallpox, foreign farmers around the area picked up their weapons and together tried to banish the Japanese workers. Tanaka, by spreading his fortune wisely, succeeded in preventing that and was able to survive the incident. The Japanese migrant laborers under Tanaka then numbered over three hundred. Tanaka, along with adviser Katsunuma, held absolute power over them. . . . Tanaka's reputation of being as mighty as a king spread to San Francisco, luring transient Japanese students in San Francisco to follow Tanaka into the intermountain areas. Although the students were good with words, they lacked execution. Wherever they were, there was trouble, ensuring sufficient conditions to trigger *haikan jiken* as described herein.

Tanaka's clerk, . . . who kept in touch with the Sōkō Aikoku Dōmei [Japanese Patriotic League, San Francisco], frowned on his subordinates. Tanaka dealt with many of his subordinates' remittances to Japan by himself and was thus able to siphon off their money for himself. His dishonesty, however, was exposed, and one of his subordinates who suffered from the loss reported it to the newly created *Kinmon nippō*, appealing for public discussion. The *Sōkō* publication issued by the Aikoku Dōmei dealt with that issue and opposed *Kinmon nippō*, resulting in a heated war of words, the so-called *Aidaho haikan jiken*. When public opinion turned turbulent, Consul Chinda took a trip to Idaho to investigate the case. Tanaka admitted his fault and reorganized his debts, 15,000 dollars in total, from which Remington, his supervisor, paid 1,200 dollars, while the rest remained as his own personal debts. Thus, the problem was eased.[55]

The Idaho incident was only one example of rewritten histories hidden in texts of various Japanese histories. To study this period, efforts should be made to supplement other materials in Japan, such as the consular reports in the Diplomatic Archives of the Ministry of Foreign Affairs of Japan, or "News from America" magazine articles that were not affected by the destructive 1906 San Francisco earthquake.[56]

Missing and Confiscated Documents Due to the Forced Removal and Incarceration

I already discussed the effect of missing or dispersed records and documents caused by the forced removal and incarceration of Japanese and US citizens of Japanese ancestry. Here, I will only discuss those documents that are deemed important.

Personal Papers of the Leaders of Japanese Communities   Immediately after the US-Japan War broke out, following the Japanese attack on Pearl Harbor, approximately 1,200 Issei leaders who had been kept under surveillance as a possible national security threat were arrested and incarcerated at detention centers by the Federal Bureau of Investigation (FBI) and the intelligence bureaus of the army and navy.[57] Many of them were executive members at central or local Japanese associations; Japanese-language schoolteachers; priests of Buddhist churches and Shinto shrines; publishers, editors, and reporters of Japanese-language newspapers; and directors of Japanese groups and organizations, including the *kenjinkai* (prefectural associations). Moreover, Issei fishermen from California's coastal fisheries were also detained because they were familiar with the US Navy's coastal defense facilities. As these Issei were arrested, household searches were conducted, and many books, diaries, letters, documents, business records, and photo collections were confiscated as evidence.[58]

Akahori Masaru, the donor of the Akahori family papers—considered one of the most valuable collections of documents in quality and quantity in the JARP collection at UCLA—served as an editor in chief for *Taihoku nippō* in Seattle when the war broke out. He was arrested as one of the "dangerous" Issei on December 7, 1941. I met with him when he donated the Akahori family papers and had the opportunity to listen to his story in detail. He explained how those papers were returned to him after the war.

During the war, he was moved around to several detention stations. After the war ended, he was finally released, and he settled in Los Angeles for a new life. When he inquired whether he could reacquire his books, diaries, and letters that were confiscated by the FBI, he was instructed to set up a date and time and collect them in person. He went to the designated warehouse, where they returned everything they had confiscated. In the warehouse, small piles of books, documents, and records were stored in several places, and each pile was marked with its owner's name. As he recognized many names of his friends or acquaintances, he recommended at every opportunity that they contact the FBI quickly and reacquire their confiscated materials. However, as leaders of Japanese communities, they still had fresh memories of bearing the brunt of attacks from anti-Japanese advocates immediately after the war. Most of them hesitated to meet with the FBI, who had arrested and cross-examined them, and declined to voluntarily reacquire the personal documents that may have been the source of their arrests. Akahori said that for those reasons, it was likely that very few Issei actually went to the warehouse to reacquire their belongings.[59]

We can probably conclude from Akahori's interview that his hypothesis was correct, since among the detained leaders, Akahori was the only donor of personal papers, with the exception of one or two donors of smaller collections of postwar records. Setting aside the question of why these documents were left uncollected, researchers should recognize the severe reality that Issei leaders' personal papers, which are essential for the study of the 1930s, have not been preserved.

The Records of the Zaibei Nihonjinkai (Japanese Association of America) and Those Collected by the Jiseki Hozonkai (Preservation Committee of Footsteps)   Among all the records in UCLA's JARP collection, those of the various *Nihonjinkai* may be considered the most valuable. They include records, letters, and collections of documents, and—particularly important—minutes, from central organizations in each region, such as Taiheiyō Engan Nihonjinkai Kyōgikai (Pacific Coast Japanese Associations Deliberative Council), Nanka Chūō Nihonjinkai (Central Japanese Association of Southern California), and Aidaho-shū Nihonjinkai Rengō Kyōgikai (United Japanese Association of Idaho) and the regional Japanese associations in the western states, such as [Rafu] Rosuanzerusu Nihonjinkai (Japanese Association of Los Angeles), Sanchūbu Nihonjinkai (Intermountain Japanese Association [Ogden, Utah]), Kawashimo Nihonjinkai (Japanese Association of Walnut Grove [California]).[60] Unfortunately, however, the records of Zaibei Nihonjinkai, a prewar nationwide organization whose activities and events were vital to the Japanese in America, are not included in UCLA's collection.

I was involved in UCLA's JARP as a researcher and curator from its foundation in 1963 until 1973. During those ten years, I asked former directors of the prewar Zaibei Nihonjinkai if any of their minutes, letters, accounting ledgers, or directories survived, and if so, who owned them. None of them, however, provided me with clear answers. One individual disclosed the following rumor: In April 1942, when the forced removal of Japanese and US citizens of Japanese ancestry began, records, documents, and other related materials from Zaibei Nihonjinkai and books and materials that had been collected by Jiseki Hozonkai for the 1940 *Zaibei Nihonjin shi* (History of Japanese in America) were stored in the basement of a house owned by Zaibei Nihonjinkai in San Francisco's Japantown. After the war, the Zaibei Nihonjinkai members returned to San Francisco, opened the door to the basement, and found all the stored materials soaked in water. Since the damage was too extensive to restore, they had to discard them. This was the explanation given to me why the materials collected by Nihonjinkai and Jiseki Hozonkai disappeared from the historical record.[61]

However, an important question still remains. Zaibei Nihonjinkai played the most central role among the organizations in Japanese communities in the United States. Moreover, since it maintained a close relationship with the Japanese government through the consulates, the FBI regarded it as the Japanese government's agent before the war broke out. Its executives, including the chairman, were arrested and detained as posing a national security risk immediately after the Japanese attack on Pearl Harbor. Just like the aforementioned Akahori case, their private residences were also searched, so the Zaibei Nihonjinkai office would also have been the target of an FBI house search. In fact, it was reported that the records of Rafu Nihonjinkai (Japanese Association of Los Angeles) and Chūō Nihonjinkai (Central Japanese Association), which were donated to UCLA's JARP, were confiscated at the beginning of the war and returned to the organizations afterward.[62] If true, it would be inconceivable that the Zaibei Nihonjinkai office, which served as the foremost Japanese organization, could have avoided a search and seizure of its records and papers.

Whatever the reasons, the records of Zaibei Nihonjinkai and the Jiseki Hozonkai collection were never found, even half a century after the war ended. We must assume that they were lost or destroyed. It is a great loss to researchers.

Collections of Documents of Nikkei Migration in North America: Background

For a holistic study of Japanese immigrants in North America, it is desirable to investigate and analyze Japanese migration patterns over the border (the Pacific Ocean) as a chain of causes and effects from international and interdisciplinary perspectives. Currently, however, researchers in both the United States and Japan are independently studying the history of immigration in their own fields. One group is focused on the homeland of immigrants. In the area of Japanese emigration to North America, researchers primarily aim to discover and analyze the conditions and circumstances related to Japan and so-called *shutsuimin* (emigrants), including their living conditions, socioeconomic status, motivations and reasons for leaving their homeland, and circumstances during their journey. The other group targets immigrant countries, including Hawai'i, the continental United States, and Canada, and they specifically study those governments' immigration policies, economies, social and political environments, anti-Japanese sentiments and movements, the immigrants' economic activities, community formation and assimilation, and Nisei issues within each country or region. These studies—*Nikkei imin* (Japanese immigration) or *Nikkeijin* (Japanese American) studies—are conducted by researchers in their respective fields within the framework of American studies. Thus, although research activities have developed separately, the research itself is closely related. As I explained earlier, it is ideal to study research materials written in both English and Japanese for any specialized field of study.

Therefore, the goal of compiling reprinted reference materials is to select documents that cover a wide range of fields and many subjects in English and Japanese. Because these documents are dispersed among various libraries in Japan and America, however, it would be very difficult, if not impossible, to do so with limited time. Thus, English-language documents were excluded from my compilation.

I should also point out that I limited the geographical selection of documents related to Japanese immigrants for reprint to the continental United States, with few exceptions. Although Hawai'i became part of the United States in the twentieth century after being annexed in 1898, Japanese emigration to the Hawaiian islands began in 1885 when Hawai'i was an independent nation. When studying the history of Japanese immigrants or residents living on the Hawaiian islands, we should consider Hawai'i a separate region from the continental United States because of a few crucial differences. Otherwise, various problems could develop. A similar consideration was applied to immigration in British Canada.

I will cite some examples. Japanese emigration across the Pacific Ocean began in the late nineteenth century, when Japanese migrant laborers began arriving in the Kingdom of Hawai'i as contract laborers for sugar plantations in 1885, five years earlier than they arrived in the continental United States. On the other hand, the United States, which annexed the Hawaiian islands in 1898, had been enforcing the Labor Contract Act since 1885, which prohibited contract laborers (including government-sponsored migrants) from entering the country. Therefore, Japanese who left Japan for the continental United States as contract laborers with the help of emigration companies or agencies around 1890 (like those who emigrated to the Kingdom of Hawai'i) were prohibited from entering the United States by US immigration officers.

Furthermore, the Chinese Exclusion Act of 1882 banned Chinese entry as immigrants to the United States. As an extension of the anti-Chinese movement, local American residents started expressing the same hatred and contempt toward Japanese migrant laborers, who were increasing in number on the West Coast at the beginning of the 1890s. On the other hand, in the Kingdom of Hawai'i, it was not until the second half of the 1890s when similar anti-Japanese sentiment toward Japanese migrant laborers became directed toward Japanese residents of Hawai'i, coinciding with the debate over the possible annexation of the kingdom by the United States.

The history of Japanese emigration to North America and Hawai'i may appear to demonstrate similar patterns, such as the timing of emigration from the middle Meiji to the Taisho eras (approximately 1885 to 1926), racial discrimination by whites, and the eventual limitation of immigration in Canada and prohibition in the United States. However, the fundamental issues concerning Japanese immigration and Japanese American studies—including the political environment, immigration policies, employment status, living conditions, exclusionary sentiments, the formation of immigrant communities, assimilation, and other topics—are essentially different in each location, such as the Hawaiian islands (Kingdom of Hawai'i), the continental United States, and British Canada. This suggests potential research problems could occur if these migration studies were considered uniform across regions. Until researchers can conduct extensive studies of all three regions, it may be best to focus on their own regional studies for now. This is why I limited my research focus to the continental United States.

*"Collection of Documents of Nikkei Migration," North America, Volume 1: Migration History in North America (*Tsūshi, *the General History of Japan)*

The fundamental work concerning migration studies used widely in Japan is *Hōjin kaigai hattenshi*, jō, ge by Irie Toraji (Ida Shoten, 1942). Since it was published after the outbreak of the Pacific War, and the author was an advocate of expansionistic overseas development, such views are repeated throughout. His descriptions of the historical facts, however, are valuable references that are based on abundant materials, including *Ryōji hōkoku* (consular reports) at the Diplomatic Archives of the Ministry of Foreign Affairs of Japan. Although this book was once difficult to obtain, after Hara Shobō reprinted it in 1981 as *Meiji hyakunenshi sōsho*, it became easy to access. A similar *tsūshi* (general history of Japan) published in Nikkei communities in America was *Zaibei Nihonjin shi*. It was compiled by the Zaibei Nihonjin Jiseki Hozonkai (Preservation Committee of Footsteps), which was founded in 1940 as part of the celebration commemorating the 2,600th year of the founding of Japan. The *Zaibei Nihonjin shi* was difficult to obtain in the United States until PMC Shuppan reprinted it in 1984. Although it does contain some erroneous descriptions due to *magobiki*, a methodology I explained earlier, its abundant records cannot be obtained from any other Japanese history texts. For example, many valuable statistics about Japanese residing in the United States that are based on consular reports such as *Tsūshō isan* and *Kanpō* are included but cannot be found elsewhere. However, sources for those statistics are not cited. Thus, the work, though highly valued as a reference, requires cross-examining and scrutinizing its details.

As one of the early publications on the history of Japanese in the United States, Katō Jūshirō's *Zaibei dōhō hattenshi* (Hakubunkan, 1908) focused on Japanese residing in the Pacific Northwest (Washington and Oregon), where he was working as a newspaper reporter. Another significant publication was Torai Jun'ichi's *Hokubei Nihonjin sōran* (Chūōdō Shobō, 1914). In addition to those *tsūshi*, other equally or even more valuable publications include *taikan* (literally, large books), anniversary publications by newspaper companies, and other publications issued by business organizations such as Nihonjin Shōgyō Kaigisho. Although there is no catalog that covers all these publications, some examples include Shin Sekai Shinbunsha, comp., *Panama Taiheiyō bankoku dai hakurankai, dai 1* (1912); Nanka Kaki Shijō Kabushiki Kaisha, comp., *Kashū Nihonjin kaengyō hattenshi* (1929); Nichi-Bei Shinbunsha, comp., *Nichi-Bei taikan* (1939); and Murai Kō, *Zaibei Nihonjin sangyō sōran* (Beikoku Sangyō Nippōsha, 1940). Containing abundant statistics, they are useful references for examining the historical facts in *Zaibei Nihonjin shi*.

Other valuable materials for reference include publications by churches and Japanese-language schools, such as Hokka Nihongo Gakuen Kyōkai, comp., *Beikoku Kashū Nihongo Gakuen enkakushi* (1930); Murano Takaaki, *Bukkyō kaigai dendōshi* (Hokubeizan Zenshūji, 1933); and Fujiga Yoichi, *Hokka Kirisuto Kyōkai binran* (Hokka Kirisuto Kyōkai Dōmei, 1936).

One of the most valuable postwar materials is Fujioka Shirō's *Ayumi no ato* (Ayumi no Ato Kankō Kōenkai, 1957). The author compiled and published the articles he contributed to *Rafu shinpō* in Los Angeles, based on information he gathered as a reporter and editor at *Taihoku nippō* (The Great Northern Daily News), *Nichi-Bei shinbun* (The Japanese-American News), and from reader submissions during his long career. *Ayumi no ato* contains some rare articles that no other documents discuss, including the story of Yamaoka Ototaka, a contractor for Japanese migrant laborers in Seattle. Yamaoka bribed government officials in the Shizuoka and Niigata prefectures, had them forge Japanese passports, and then smuggled migrant laborers from Japan in 1899 and 1900. Although I was initially planning to include this book for reprint, it was excluded because it was the only postwar publication among the selected documents.

One of the *tsūshi* published after the war was Shin Nichi-Bei Shinbunsha, comp., *Beikoku Nikkeijin hyakunenshi: zaibei Nikkeijin hatten jinshiroku* (1961). For publications on Japanese Americans residing in Southern California, Nanka Nikkeijin Shōgyō Kaigisho, comp., *Minami Kashū Nihonjin shi* (1952) and *Minami Kashū Nihonjin shi, kōhen* (Nanka Nikkeijin Shōgyō Kaigisho, 1957) are available. Although they may be valuable publications, we should exercise caution until their content is fully analyzed and examined.

This collection of documents on Japanese American emigration to North America includes Fujiga Yoichi's *Nichi-Bei kankei zai Beikoku Nihonjin hatten shiyō* (Beikoku Seisho Kyōkai Nihonjinbu, 1927), which was reprinted as *tsūshi*. Although it may be closer to a chronological table than a *tsūshi*, I decided to include it because the author painstakingly collected historical facts over many years. Particularly valuable are the detailed and rare descriptions of the organizations established in early Japanese communities in the Bay Area and other regions of Northern California, including rosters of *dekasegi shosei* (schoolboys), before the 1906 San Francisco earthquake, as well as the Fukuinkai (Gospel Society) and Aikoku Dōmei (Patriotic League) with their organization rosters. Another reprinted *tsūshi* is *Beikoku Chūō Nihonjinkai shi* (1940). Empirical research on central and regional Japanese associations has not been published in either the United States or Japan. The main reason for this, as I explained earlier, might be that these associations' records have been lost. The editor of *Beikoku Chūō Nihonjinkai shi* was Fujioka Shirō, the active editor in chief of *Rafu shinpō*, a daily newspaper in Los Angeles with the second-largest circulation, after *Nichi-Bei shinbun* in San Francisco, of all Japanese newspapers in the United States in the 1920s and 1930s. Fujioka was also selected as the chairman and executive of the Central Japanese Association in Southern California. He was a highly respected writer of the Nikkei community, similar to Washizu "Shakuma" Bunzō, the author of *Zaibei Nihonjin shikan* (Shinpōsha, 1930). Fujioka also published *Minzoku hatten no senkusha* (Dōbunsha, 1927), which compiled the articles of *Rafu shinpō* in a similar way to *Ayumi no ato*. *Beikoku Chūō Nihonjinkai shi* drew on the minutes and other records of the Central Japanese Association and is considered a highly valuable primary source.

The "Encouragement Theory" of Migration and Emigration

Although it is not clear who started promoting Japanese emigration to America, it is well known that Fukuzawa Yukichi, an intellectual leader of Japan's westernization movement during the Meiji era, showed an early interest in Western colonization and overseas development. For example, he mentioned the Western concept of *jiyūshugiteki shokumin* (liberal colonization) in *Seiyō jijō, shohen*, published in

1866. Before zeal for overseas expansion became widespread in the Meiji 20s (starting from 1887), he insisted that Japanese should expand overseas, particularly to the United States.[63] In the article "Beikoku wa shishi no sumika nari," published in the *Jiji shinpō* in 1883, he praised the United States, stating that "people in American society were superior to their European ancestors, and the scarcity of indolent people in the country was without parallel in the world."[64] In the next article, titled "Ijūron no ben" (lecture on migration), he encouraged emigration to the United States as follows: "For people in the prime of their lives, strong but suffering from lowly occupations, making every effort to earn a living throughout the year but failing, they should depart their hometowns with determination, overcome homesickness, study abroad, plan for success, and someday, return home with great honor in the finest clothes."[65]

Thus, at the beginning of the Meiji era, theories of migration and overseas expansion were introduced to Japan as byproducts of the spread of Western thought, particularly that of liberal economic philosophy. In the Meiji 20s (starting from 1887), migration and overseas expansion were not discussed as a systemized economic theory. Instead, *imin* (immigration and emigration), *shokumin* (colonization or expansion), and *kaigai dekasegi* (overseas migration for work) were studied independently by scholars as measures for the government of a modern nation to consider. They were linked to specific matters such as a population increase, food shortages, the spread of poverty and distress, and trade expansion.

Therefore, because terminologies such as *shokumin*, *imin*, *kaigai hatten* (overseas expansion), and *kaigai dekasegi* were not strictly defined, there were many cases where the terms *imin* (emigration) and *dekasegi* (temporarily working away from home) were used interchangeably in the same publication.[66]

The theories of *shokumin* and *kaigai ijū* (overseas migration), which were introduced around this time, discussed these measures as suitable for the poor and disgruntled, who under the circumstances would be deemed "surplus population" and who should migrate from Japan to selected countries and regions. Furthermore, those theories insisted that *kaigai ijū* and *dekasegi* were important to the national welfare and—underscoring their necessity—would benefit not only emigrants but also the emigrant nations and their people, as shown by the success of advanced European nations and their colonial histories. For example, Taguchi Ukichi, who introduced the concept of *jiyūshugi shokumin* (liberal colonization) to Japan, insisted that "the forty million fellow Japanese were already suffering from a lack of wealth in their country." He argued Japan should pour its surplus population into fertile lands, therefore accomplishing *Nan'yō keiryaku* (South Sea plan). He stated that Japanese expansion to the South Sea islands would "bring national prestige, expand trade" and improve the national defense. He said that from a national security standpoint, "by increasing the size of the South Sea fleets, trade there would improve. By planting our people on the islands, we would increase traffic and the frequency of trade between Japan and the Philippine islands." [67]

Moreover, influenced by Friedrich List's *shokumin* idea, Wakayama Norikazu considered Mexico the most suitable country for Japanese resettlement. Regarding the profits gained, he explained, "These days, poor, disappointed samurai are actively agitating ignorant people and causing political trouble. . . . Farmers and craftsmen currently also have difficulty making their ends meet. . . . If we persuade them to emigrate or engage in agriculture or mining work, it will dramatically decrease the unrest in our country." [68] Shiga Shigetaka's *Nan'yō jiji* (Maruzen Shōsha Shoten, 1887) and Tsuneya Seifuku's *Kaigai shokuminron* (Hakubunsha, 1891), along with other promoters of *kaigai dekasegi*, encouraged "lower-class people" living in poor conditions to be engaged in *dekasegi* in the Hawaiian islands, the South Sea islands, or South America to save their livelihood.

Among the emigration theorists in the mid-Meiji era, the only one that encouraged *dekasegi* to the United States was Mutō Sanji, the author of *Beikoku ijūron* (Maruzen Shōsha Shoten, 1887). Mutō was surprised by "the bravery of Chinese people competing against the white people" when he was studying on the West Coast. He based the book on "his research on Chinese immigrants in his limited spare time during his studies" and published it after his return to Japan. [69] Mutō found that nearly 20 percent of Chinese migrant laborers who came to America became successful businessmen, and the amount of profit they took back to their homeland was too substantial to ignore. Even low-wage migrant laborers could make truly huge amounts of money in one year. According to his study, "if their average wages were one yen per day, since they worked at least ten months out of a year, their yearly wages would be 260 yen." Furthermore, according to the US government statistics, since 104,000 Chinese migrant laborers were working in California, "the sum of their wages would be an estimated 27,040,000 yen." He emphasized this was a truly remarkable large amount. He proceeded to note that "the languages, clothes, and cuisines of the Orientals are different from the whites, so Chinese and Japanese would be nearly alike. However, our Chinese neighbors emigrate to the unfamiliar land of America and compete against the whites for their share of fortune; there is no reason why our fellow Japanese could not migrate to America, just like the Chinese do." He suggested that the government should establish *imin kaisha* (emigration companies) and other systems to encourage workers to migrate to the United States.[70]

Papers related to *ijū shokumin*, *imin*, and *kaigai dekasegi* in the mid-Meiji era include Torii Akita, "Ijūron," in *Tōkyō keizai zasshi*, 21-kan 514-gō (March 29, 1890), 397–402; Koshimura Shigeru, "Nihon shokuminron 1, 2," in *Tōkyō keizai zasshi*, 22-kan 546-gō (November 8, 1890), 652–55 and 22-kan 548-gō (November 22, 1890), 733–38; Itagaki Taisuke, "Shokumin seiryaku," in *Shokumin Kyōkai hōkoku*, 30-gō (October 1895), 1–8; Shiga Shigetaka, "Tanken oyobi ijū no hōshin," in *Taiyō*, 1-kan 10-gō (October 5, 1895), 1811–15; and Nakane Hisashi, "Shokuminron," in *Taiyō*, 2-kan 5-gō (March 5, 1896), 1131–37.

Although these authors, for various reasons, recommended *ijū shokumin*, *imin*, and *kaigai dekasegi* to different destinations, including the South Sea islands (Taguchi), Hawai'i and the South Sea islands (Shiga), and North America (Mutō), they all assumed that the targeted population for migration were "low class" or "the dissatisfied": those who had trouble paying for clothes, food, and living costs in Japan or those who would potentially cause occasional social instability in Japanese society. However, these arguments were mere idealistic dogmas, promoting what Japan should do after its modernization. For example, Taguchi's proposal was to create colonies on the South Sea islands by increasing the size of fleets in this region to improve trade. Shiga's proposal was to "give jobs to the low class of Japanese society, teach such ignorant people disciplined labor law, and send people in Japan who are too poor to buy clothes, food, and houses overseas to repatriate funds to Japan and increase Japan's capital." [71] But this large-scale migration to resolve the issue of "population surplus" in Japan was impossible to execute in the 1890s. Even the most seemingly realistic argument, Mutō's *Beikoku ijūron*, which was based on his research during his stay in America as a *dekasegi shosei*, should also be judged unrealistic. His proposal to increase the emigration of migrant laborers to the West Coast of the United States was problematic and could have instigated further issues, given the rising anti-Asian sentiment.[72] Although Mutō's *Beikoku ijūron* is a significant document, it was already included in *Mutō Sanji zenshū dai 1-kan* (Shinjusha, 1963), 237–92. Instead, I selected Tsuneya Seifuku's *Kaigai shokumin-ron* to be reprinted as part of the "Collection of Documents of Nikkei Migration," North America, volume 1.

How do the theories of *imin* and *shokumin* of the late Meiji era, particularly after the Russo-Japanese War, compare with the theories written during the mid-Meiji era? A major difference is that Japanese migration was considered a threat to the friendly US-Japan relationship of the late Meiji era, when a substantial number of Japanese people were already residing in the Hawaiian islands and the United States. Since around 1884–85, encouraged by Japan's intellectual leaders, including Fukuzawa Yukichi, the so-called *toshu kūken no dekasegi shosei* (empty-handed schoolboys), enlightened by the idea of going to America and studying while working, had already begun appearing in the United States. Simultaneously, *kan'yaku imin* (government contract *dekasegi* laborers) were arriving in the Hawaiian Islands in 1885 in response to strong requests made by the Kingdom of Hawai'i and the owners of sugar plantations. Moreover, beginning about 1890, some of the *kan'yaku imin* who finished the three years on their labor contract planned to move from Hawai'i to the continental United States, where they heard working conditions and wages were better. Furthermore, by that time, overseas *imin* brokers were already in operation in Japan, sending migrant laborers to ports in San Francisco and elsewhere.

Radical anti-Asian sentiment stemming from racial prejudice toward Asian or "yellow race" laborers was strong in the western United States, particularly in the San Francisco Bay Area. The federal government had already passed and enacted the Chinese Exclusion Act in 1882, a discriminatory law that excluded Chinese from entering the country for ten years. By the early 1890s, when Japanese migrant laborers began appearing on the US West Coast, they could no longer escape the contagious effect of the anti-Chinese movement, experiencing harassment and exclusionist activities. Pursuant to the Immigration Act of 1891, the US Bureau of Immigration within the Treasury Department enforced immigration inspections at each port. The new act allowed the immigration officers to deny entry to Japanese *dekasegi* laborers on the basis of their being "impoverished" or "contract laborers." Local "yellow journalism" newspapers reported these incidents sensationally. Moreover, white American workers and residents in the western United States conducted anti-Japanese activities, targeting migrant laborers, occasionally expelling them with arms.[73]

In the second half of the 1890s, the anti-Japanese movement intensified, corresponding with the arrival of Japanese migrant laborers in the United States. In 1895, when the Sino-Japanese War ended, Japanese migration, which had been temporarily halted during the war, resumed on the West Coast. Widespread unemployment in the western United States, due to an economic recession beginning in 1893, aggravated anti-Japanese sentiment further; the Japanese were willing to work longer hours for lower wages than white laborers in farming, railroad construction, and mining.[74]

In August 1900, seriously concerned about the intensified anti-Japanese movement on the West Coast, the Japanese government voluntarily halted Japanese *dekasegi* laborers' migration to the United States until anti-Japanese activities subsided. Moreover, the attacks on Japanese by white residents in the western United States, which had caused the Japanese government to enforce such a drastic measure, provoked Japanese anger in the early twentieth century. The anti-Japanese movement in the 1890s was targeted only toward Japanese *dekasegi* laborers in the United States. Just like the Chinese migrant laborers, who were banned from entering the United States by the Chinese Exclusion Act of 1882, they were criticized as "low-wage contract laborers" just like Chinese "coolies" because they were just as ignorant and unrefined and willing to lead miserable lives and work for low wages that American laborers would not tolerate. However, anti-Japanese sentiment in the early 1900s, drawn from white supremacist ideology, targeted the Japanese as an ethnicity: white Americans of European ancestry claimed they were superior from eugenic and anthropological perspectives, and that the developed European civilizations in the past centuries were superior to Oriental civilizations, which were, on the other hand, stagnant and showed no signs of progress. Thus, anti-Japanese sentiment became an insult to the Japanese people as a whole, who came to represent the inferior Oriental civilization and were unfit for American culture, society, and religion. Therefore, their immigration to the United States was unacceptable, just like the migrant laborers who worked in the western United States.[75]

Separate from these developments in the United States, Japan came to advocate its own *bōchō shisō* (expansionist ideology), following the early theories of *shokumin* and *kaigai ijū*. Tokutomi "Sohō" Iichirō advocated it in *Kokumin no tomo*. *Bōchō shisō* rose in popularity and, in the opinion of the Japanese people, represented a "new, successfully modernized Japan." [76] Thus, as the Japanese increasingly became competitive with the great Western powers, they expected to enjoy an equal relationship with those powers as a reward for the past efforts and sacrifices they had made. Reflecting this rising nationalistic sentiment, arguments concerning *ijū* (migration) and *kaigai hatten* (overseas expansion) called for compromises on the immigration policies of American and European governments and their people. For example, Takahashi Sakue defined the new US-Japan relationship in the introduction of *Nichi-Bei no shinkankei* as follows:

> Japanese people respect America and feel indebted to it. For a while, we looked up to America as if they were our own uncles. That feeling is still deep-rooted in the mind of the Japanese people. But after a while, the child grew up to be a strong man that fought against its neighbors and won. Now he is equal to his uncle, and changing of the old relationship of uncle and nephew to a new deep friendship is inevitable.[77]

From this perspective, Takahashi insisted that immigration issues in America not only were the individual problems of Japanese migrants but also involved the Japanese nation's sovereign rights.

Abe Isoo, a Christian socialist, is considered to have held an opposite ideological view from that of Takahashi Sakue. He, too, criticized the persistent anti-Japanese movement in America that intensified in the early twentieth century and emphasized that the anti-Japanese movement stemming from racial prejudice was not only wrong but negatively affected other Americans economically, stating that Japanese laborers were essential to California's economy. Furthermore, Abe encouraged Japanese emigration to the western United States to build a "new Japan" there:

> Since only sixty thousand people of Japanese ancestry live on the West Coast, some may argue that it is an exaggeration to call it a new Japan. The number of Japanese there, however, will never stop growing. If Japan's government enacts the right policy, and the US government does not object to our immigration, our population would reach sixty thousand in no more than several years, and six million within twenty to thirty years. The US Pacific coast has enough land for twenty to thirty million people. Moreover, if it were to have a similar population density to Japan's, even eighty or ninety million could live there. I would see no inconvenience if we, Japan, send six million of our fellow Japanese there. Depending on the determination of our government and our people, building a new Japan on the other side of the Pacific will never be a difficult task. I must endorse the future creation of a new Japan.[78]

In addition to *Nichi-Bei no shinkankei* and *Hokubei no shin Nihon* (reprinted in "Collection of Documents of Nikkei Migration," North America, volume 1), the following texts encouraged *ijū*, *kaigai ijū shōreiron* (theory of encouraging overseas migration) in the early twentieth century. Ōkawahira Takamitsu's *Nihon iminron* (Bunbudō, 1905) maintained that emigration for Japanese laborers was a necessity and discussed ways to encourage them to leave, regardless of the destination. Tōgō Minoru, in *Nihon shokuminron* (Bunbudō, 1906), suggested that, from an agricultural economics perspective, Japanese people should emigrate to Korea, Taiwan, and Manchuria to establish colonies after the Russo-Japanese War. Okunomiya Kenshi, in

Hokubei iminron (Tōkyōdō, 1903), discussed emigration to North America.

Tobei Annai *(Guides for Going to America)*

If the theories of *shokumin* and *ijū* were commonly considered mostly idealistic and abstract, the *tobei annai* would be their more practical counterpart. As manuals for travelers and emigrants, they focused on the actual specifics of the destination and the experiences of travelers. The authors explained in detail everything from the reasons for emigration to North America and its expected benefits and experiences, to every possible situational scenario. Among the *tobei annai*, some authors even published letters or correspondence from Japanese residing in the United States that described their actual lives, their employment, wages and payment methods, working hours, locations, and so on. As I explained earlier, many of the materials essential to the research of early Japanese migrants were lost in the Great Fire of San Francisco. Among the extremely limited surviving documents, these *tobei annai* provide valuable detailed descriptions that no other materials mention. In addition to abundant information on the daily life and the working conditions of early immigrants, they also include material about the clothes and belongings to pack, the costs of transportation and the amount of cash to carry, the daily life, hardships, and common mistakes on ships, customs inspections upon entry to the United States, thorough advice for cases of denied entry detention, a lodging guide after arriving, and so on.[79]

Some of the earliest publications of *tobei annai* include Akamine Seichirō, *Beikoku ima fushigi* (Jitsugakukai Eigakkō, 1887) and Ishida Kumajirō, *Kitare Nihonjin: ichimei Sōkō tabi annai* (Kaishindō, 1887), which are included in the *Nikkei imin shiryōshū* ("Collection of Documents of Nikkei Migration," North America, volume 1). As Hayashi Tadasu explained in *Batsu*, Akamine's *Beikoku ima fushigi* contains documents relating the author's own experience and hearsay during his five-year stay in San Francisco. Other than the short and seemingly offensive descriptions of Japanese migrants residing in San Francisco, the book is made up of rare descriptions of San Francisco, including some of Chinatown, and a summary of the history and geography of California.[80] Although these descriptions are rare, after I read them carefully, some statements made me suspicious about whether the author truly believed that "Japan's future in the advancement of civilization, enlightenment, trade, industry, fortune, and prosperity, was most strongly related to laborers in California."[81]

The author of *Kitare Nihonjin* called himself a *Beikoku Sōkō gū Shūyū Sanjin*, an easygoing traveler in San Francisco. In this *tobei annai*, he stated that he was disappointed in Japan's being too small and cramped. "More than 37 million Japanese found nowhere to go in small Japan and were suffering from the poor economy"; he suggested they should migrate to "the noble American and European nations, where the wages were higher than those in Japan." There, they can "engage in business and devote themselves to hard work." After five to ten years, they will finally be able to return home "in fine clothes with honor."[82] The contents of this book are different from those in *Beikoku ima fushigi*, adding detailed and practical descriptions of *shosei* experiences and daily life in San Francisco, travel procedures, preparation and costs, advice while on the ship, information about universities in the United States, and so on.

There was a longer-than-ten-year hiatus of *tobei annai* publications after the late 1880s, when *Beikoku ima fushigi* and *Kitare Nihonjin* were published. In August 1900, the Japanese government temporarily halted issuing passports for Japanese migrant laborers heading to the continental United States. They then strictly controlled the flow of Japanese *dekasegi* laborers to British Canada, and finally tightened passport inspections for those wishing to travel to the United States to study or conduct business. As a result, obtaining passports for the United States became extremely difficult, although the desire for traveling to the United States continued to grow. To address this issue, the publications of *tobei annai* and other related guidebooks resurged for people who desired to go to the United States, particularly students without much money, offering "off-the-beaten-path advice" for passport applications, travel preparations, life aboard ships, immigration inspections, procedures after landing, and so on.

Among the many *tobei annai* published in the early twentieth century, "Collection of Documents of Nikkei Migration," North America, volume 1, contains the reprints of Katayama Sen's *Tobei annai* (Rōdō Shinbunsha, 1901); Shimanuki Hyōdayū's *Tobei annai taizen* (Chūyōdō, 1901); Shimizu Tsurusaburō's *Beikoku rōdō benran* (Matsuda Jinzaburō, 1902); Iijima Eitarō's *Beikoku tokō annai* (Hakubunkan, 1902); and Yoshimura Daijirō's *Tobei seigyō no tebiki* (Okajima Shoten, 1903). These authors, except for Shimanuki Hyōdayū, all lived part of their lives in America. Katayama Sen, who later played a significant role in the Japan Communist Party movement, lived in America as a student for twelve years, from 1884 to 1896. He established *Tobei Kyōkai* and issued the *Tobei zasshi* in 1902 to promote and assist Japanese coming to America. In addition to *Tobei annai*, he published *Zoku tobei annai* (Tobei Kyōkai, 1902), *Shin tobei* (Rōdō Shinbunsha, 1904), and *Tobei no hiketsu* (Tobei Kyōkai, 1906). Katayama provided prospective Japanese students with useful instructions, such as travel preparation for the United States, advice for the onboard journey, postlanding life, and job opportunities.

Iijima Eitarō, a student at Stanford University, provided an introduction to American universities (including women's colleges) to Japanese students, including information on admissions procedures and qualifications, classes, and the daily life of students. Other publications, such as *Tobei annai taizen*, *Beikoku rōdō benran*, and *Tobei seigyō no tebiki*, were for a broader category of Japanese travelers to America. While *Tobei seigyō no tebiki* explained labor market trends, job opportunities, and life for workers, *Beikoku rōdō benran* (literally, handbook) added quick cooking recipes, manuals for daily English conversation, instructions on how to write letters, and on how to keep track of personal accounting. Besides *Tobei annai taizen*, Shimanuki Hyōdayū, who later founded the Rikkōkai (an organization that played a significant role in Japanese emigration to Latin America), issued *Saishin tobeisaku* (Nihon Rikkōkai, 1904) and *Shin Tobeihō* (Hakubunkan, 1911) for travelers to the United States.

Other *tobei annai* included Shūkō Akihiro, *Kaigai kugaku annai* (Hakuhōdō, 1904); Amano Torasaburō, *Tobei rashin* (Tōkyō Keiseisha); Ishizuka Iozō, *Genkon tobei annai* (Ishizuka Shoten, 1903); Iwasaki Katsusaburō, *Saishin tobei annai* (Daigakkan, 1904); Kawamura Tetsutarō, *Saishin katsudō hokubei jigyō annai* (Hakubunkan, 1906); Kimura Yoshigorō and Inoue Tanebumi, *Saikin seikaku Hawai tokō annai* (Hakubunkan, 1907); Kitazawa Toranosuke and Narusawa

Kinbē, *Shinsen tobei annai* (Naigai Shuppan Kyōkai, 1905); Ichiyanagi
Shōan, *Tobei no shiori* (jihi shuppan, 1901); Umeda Matajirō, *Zaibei
no kugakusei oyobi rōdōsha* (Jitsugyō no Tomosha, 1909); Watanabe
Kanjirō, *Kaigai dekasegi annai* (Naigai Shuppan Kyōkai, 1902);
Watanabe Shirō, *Kaigai risshin no tebiki* (1902); and Yamane Goichi,
Saikin tobei annai (Tobei Zasshisha, 1904).

"Collection of Documents of Nikkei Migration," North America, Volume 2: Regional Histories of Japanese

I previously examined US regional histories of Japanese in detail,
including the methodology and process of their compilation, publication, and editing. Moreover, I have already discussed what researchers
should cautiously understand when referring to those histories, and
what the historical value of similar publications as research materials might be, because exaggerations drawn from an elderly's reminis-
cences and memoirs, and repeated *magobiki*, devalued their credibility.
Therefore, I will avoid repeating that information here. The only
thing I have to add to the general description of regional histories of
Japanese is that most publications contain a directory of the names
and profiles of significant people in an appendix. Often the appendix
makes up a sizable portion of the books and, in some cases, more than
half. These are very valuable references for Japanese migration and
Nikkei studies scholars, although they will often find it frustrating to
deal with obscure spellings of names or unspecified hometown prefectures or villages. The only *jinmeiroku* (directory) that covers the entire
West Coast is *Zaibei Nihonjin jinmei jiten*, compiled by Nichi-Bei
Shinbunsha (1922). Even this publication, however, is by no means
comprehensive; if we exclude the Japanese residing in California, there
are more people who are not listed than those who are. One should
also exercise caution when reading selective biographies and achievements as a person's profile, since the editors often introduced selection
and evaluation bias.

When selecting regional histories of Japanese to add to the
"Collection of Documents of Nikkei Migration," North America, volume 2, I attempted to find the most valuable materials for research,
particularly the oldest editions published, on the histories and experiences of Japanese residing in California, the Pacific Northwest

(Washington and Oregon), and the Rocky Mountain regions (Idaho, Utah, Wyoming, and Colorado). The original books for reprint, however, were scattered in US and Japanese libraries, making it difficult to access them to make copies. Even when accessible, the books sometimes suffered from severe damage. Thus, the project did not always proceed as smoothly as I had planned. Moreover, I could not proceed with some valuable publications, such as Takeuchi Kōjirō's *Beikoku seihokubu Nihon iminshi* (Taihoku Nippōsha, 1929), which another publisher had already scheduled for reprinting.[83] I thought about substituting other material, but I was not able to select an appropriate replacement. As a result, the Northwest regions of the Pacific Coast were not included in the collection.

Important literature for the studies of Japanese residing in California includes Kanai Shigeo and Itō Banshō, *Hokubei no Nihonjin* (Kanai Tsūyaku Jimusho, 1909); Kashiwamura Keikoku, *Hokubei tōsa taikan dai 1* (Ryūbundō, 1911); and Ichihashi Makoto, *Kashū no Nihonjin* (Ichihashi Makoto, 1916). Although these titles refer to *Hokubei* (North America), their texts focus on California, describing its geography, residential areas, and histories of Japanese residing in the United States, including profiles of Japanese community leaders. For information on Northern California, where early Japanese settled, got jobs, and formed Japanese communities, refer to Hokka Nihonjinkai, comp., *Hokka Nihonjin hattenshi* (1922); Maruyama Chikuma, *Agun dōhō taisei ichiran* (Shinsekai Shinbunsha, 1908); Merisubiru Chihō Nihonjinkai, *Hokka yongun Nihonjin hattenshi* (1932); and Ōhashi Kanzō, *Hokubei Kashū Sutakuton dōhōshi* (Sushi Nihonjinkai, 1937). Among these books, *Hokka yongun Nihonjin hattenshi*, edited by Merisubiru Nihonjinkai, describes the history of Japanese living in four districts in Northern California (Yuba, Sutter, Butte, and Colusa), who began working at fruit or agricultural farms in the 1890s. Maruyama Chikuma's *Agun dōhō taisei ichiran*, reprinted in "Collection of Documents of Nikkei Migration," North America, volume 2, is a 130-page booklet that illustrates the history of the Japanese residents in three cities in Alameda County: Oakland, Berkeley, and Alameda. I selected Maruyama's booklet for reprint considering that the year of the publication was 1908, two years after the San Francisco earthquake, and its publisher was Shinsekai Shinbunsha. The publisher issued a daily paper in Nikkei communities before *Nichi-Bei shinbun* was started and moved its office to Oakland after having suffered huge damages from the earthquake.

Although a large number of Japanese resided in Southern California just before and after the war, surprisingly, the regional histories of Japanese are limited in this region, with two exceptions: Saka Hisagorō's *Santa Maria Heigen Nihonjin shi* (Gadarūpu Nihonjinkai, 1936) and Takeuchi Kōsuke's *Sanpidoro dōhō hattenroku* (1937). The former is about the history of the plains of Santa Maria, once the center of Japanese agricultural development in Southern California, and the latter deals with the history of Japanese fishermen communities in San Pedro, a suburb of Los Angeles and a central site for development of the Japanese fishing industry. Saka's work was selected for reprinting at this time, although they are both essential documents for the research of prewar Japanese communities.

In Southern California, Los Angeles in particular was the primary center of Japanese residents. There, Rafu Shinpōsha and Beikoku Sangyō Nippōsha compiled and published *nenkan, taikan,* and other anniversary publications. In addition, Nihonjin Shōkō Kaigisho (Japanese Chamber of Commerce), Nanka Hana Ichiba (Southern California Flower Market), and Nanka Nihonjin Kirisutokyō Renmei (Japanese Christian Church Federation of Southern California) issued similar history-related publications. Besides the previously mentioned regional histories, many prefectural associations in Southern California issued their own *kenjinkai shi* (histories of prefectural associations). I suspect that no publications such as *Rafu Nihonjin shi* or *Minami Kashū Nihonjin shi* were published before the war because many publications like these were available.

After the war, as if to make up for their absence in the prewar era, many regional histories of Japanese were compiled for a certain time. These included the histories issued by Nanka Nikkeijin Shōgyō Kaigisho—*Minami Kashū Nihonjin shi* (1956); *Minami Kashū Nihonjin shi,* volume 3 (1957); and *Minami Kashū Nihonjin nanajūnenshi* (1960)—as well as *Beikoku Nikkeijin hyakunenshi: zaibei Nikkeijin hatten jinshiroku,* compiled by Shin Nichi-Bei Shinbunsha. *Minami Kashū Nihonjin shi* (1956), a chronicle based on newspaper articles, which began its compilation before the war, is considered one of the most valuable references published after the war. However, it is desirable to avoid using other materials for studying the history of Japanese residing in the United States if close examination of the historical facts is difficult.[84]

In addition to Takeuchi's *Beikoku seihokubu Nihon iminshi*, publications from the Pacific Northwest include the following: Ishioka Hikoichi, *Nihonjin jijō* (jihi shuppan, 1907); Beikoku Seihokubu Renraku Nihonjinkai, comp., *Beikoku seihokubu zairyū Nihonjin hatten ryakushi* (1921); Takoma Nihonjinkai, comp., *Takoma shōkai* (1922); Takoma Shūhōsha, comp., *Takoma-shi oyobi chihō Nihonjin shi* (1941); and Yakima Nihonjinkai, comp., *Yakima Heigen Nihonjin shi* (1935).

For documents concerning the history of Japanese residing in the Rocky Mountains, refer to Suzuki Mutsuhiko et al., *Intā maunten dōhō hattatsushi* (Denbā Shinpōsha, 1910); *Rokkī to dōhō*, ed., *Rokkī Jihō hensan kyoku* (Rokkī Jihōsha, 1912); and Rokkī Jihōsha, comp., *Sanchūbu to Nihonjin* (1925). *Intā maunten dōhō hattatsushi* was among the earliest publications of regional histories of Japanese, describing the lives of Japanese laborers residing in Colorado, Utah, Wyoming, Nebraska, and Kansas. The second half of the book, which details the experiences of Japanese contract laborers working for railroad and mining companies, is a valuable reference. The descriptions of the early lives of Japanese laborers in Colorado and Utah and the geographic distribution of Japanese workers in *Sanchūbu to Nihonjin* are important. The directory with profiles near the end of the book is also valuable.

I explained earlier that I limited the regional histories of Japanese to the continental United States for the reprint of the "Collection of Documents of Nikkei Migration." As a result of this regional limitation, it became harder to grasp the entire picture of Japanese migration to North America. Therefore, in order to supplement this collection as much as possible, I decided to add one *tsūshi* each on Japanese who settled in Hawai'i and Canada, and selected Kihara Ryūkichi, *Hawai Nihonjin shi* (Bunseisha, 1935) and Nakayama Jinshirō, *Kanada no hōko* (jihi shuppan, 1921). Both are considered trustworthy and valuable materials, particularly *Kanada no hōko*, which is a 2,036-page masterwork.

Although the title of Mizutani Shōzō, *Nyūyōku Nihonjin hatten-shi* (Nyūyōku Nihonjinkai, 1921) indicates its content as "Japanese development history" in general, its value is more substantial for studies of US-Japan trade history. This work, once difficult to obtain, was reprinted by PMC Shuppan in 1984.

Zaibei Kenjinshi *(History of Prefectural Associations in America)*

Despite the number of publications titled *Zaibei kenjinshi*, their purposes and editing methods varied, making it difficult to collectively evaluate their value as research materials. Three reprinted books, however, are valuable for their statistics and are trustworthy about historical facts directly related to emigrants from the Hiroshima, Kumamoto, and Fukuoka prefectures, which are always among the top six prefectures of ancestry for Japanese emigrants to the continental United States.[85] These are Takeda Jun'ichi, *Zaibei Hiroshima kenjinshi* (Zaibei Hiroshima Kenjinshi Hakkōjo, 1929); Nakamura Masatoshi and Mukaeda Katsuma, *Zaibei no Higojin* (Nanka Kumamoto Kaigai Kyōkai, 1931); and Hirohata Tsunegorō, *Zaibei Fukuoka kenjin to jigyō* (Zaibei Fukuoka Kenjin to Jigyō Hensan Jimusho, 1936). The only major drawback is that the sources are not indicated. Perhaps more important is the *jinmeiroku* (directory), which contains pertinent information about the Issei, including the addresses of their hometowns in Japan, the dates of their arrival, their addresses, their occupations, and their family structures in America at the time of publication. These directories are often the most important part of *kenjinshi* and are considered valuable materials for studies such as social ecology.

Other *kenjinshi* include Furukawa Eiji, *Minami Kashū to Kagoshima kenjin* (Nihon Keisatsu Shinbunsha, 1920); Hirose Shurei, *Zaibei Kōshūjin funtō gojūnenshi* (Nanka Yamanashi Kaigai Kyōkai, 1934); Kaihara Sakae, *Kashū Hiroshima kenjin hattenshi* (Yorozu Shoten, 1916); Kazahaya Katsuichi, *Minami Kashū Okayama kenjin hattenshi* (Minami Kashū Okayama Kenjin Hattenshi Hensanjo, 1955); Mie Kenjin Hokubei Hattenshi Hensan Iinkai, ed., *Mie kenjin Hokubei hattenshi* (Mie-ken Kaigai Kyōkai, 1966); Mizutani Bangaku, *Hokubei Aichi kenjinshi* (Aichi Kenjinkai 1920); Nanka Fukui Kenjinkai, comp., *Nanka Fukui kenjin gojūnenshi* (1953); Oka Naoki, *Hokubei no Kōchi kenjin* (jihi shuppan, 1921); Satō Yasuji, *Kashū to Fukushima kenjin*,

Nanka hen (Kashū Fukushima Kenjin Hattenshi Hensanjo, 1929); Senoo Manrō, *Ōshū Hiroshima kenjin hattenshi* (Senoo Manrō, 1916); Tomimoto Iwao, *Zaibei Wakayama kenjin hattenshi* (jihi shuppan, 1915); Tsuyuki Sōzō, *Shōwa seidai zaibei Kanagawa kenjin* (Zaibei Kanagawa Kenjinsha, 1934); Tsuyuki Sōzō, *Zaibei Kanagawa kenjin* (Zaibei Kanagawa Kenjinsha, 1915); and Yatsu Riichirō, *Zaibei Miyagi kenjinshi* (Zaibei Miyagi Kenjinshi Hensan Jimusho, 1933). Most of them were published in Southern California and focused on the Issei residing there. The reason *kenjinshi* were not published in Northern California or the Pacific Northwest is, unfortunately, still unknown.

Documents and Directories Related to North American Immigrants (Meiji and Taishō Eras)

The Collection of Documents at the Diplomatic Archives of the Ministry of Foreign Affairs of Japan

Most of the records on *dekasegi shosei*, students who engaged in domestic work in the San Francisco Bay Area, and Japanese migrant seasonal workers at fruit and other agricultural farms in Central and Northern California were destroyed by the 1906 Great Fire in San Francisco. Therefore, it is a well-known fact that the diplomatic documents about the *dekasegi shosei* in the Diplomatic Archives of the Ministry of Foreign Affairs of Japan are essential materials for studies about Japanese emigration to the continental United States during the Meiji era. Many researchers know, however, that using these materials efficiently requires a large amount of time and patience.

The Diplomatic Archives compiled *Gaimushō Gaikō Shiryōkan*'s *Gaimushō kiroku sōmokuroku*, 3-kan (Hara Shobō, 1992), which simplified the search for the appropriate files of historical documents stored there. However, to read an individual report or document, one must physically retrieve the file and peruse all the documents, page by page, to find it. While that may simply be what it takes to conduct research, reading consular reports written in *sōsho* (cursive) in the Meiji era would be a tremendous burden for American researchers and others.

Considering the reasons mentioned above, I decided to create a catalog of the letters, telegraphs, reports, *gushinsho* (detailed reports),

instructions, and document attachments, among others, for reference filed in "Zaibei honpōjin no jōkyō narabini tobeisha torishimari
kankei zassan," 2-kan (May 1888–February 1894).[86] Later items are
in "Hokubei Gasshūkoku ni oite honpōjin tokō seigen oyobi haiseki
ikken," 19-kan (April 1891–April 1912). Many important consular
reports and related documents were reprinted in *Nihon gaikō bunsho*
(foreign diplomatic documents of Japan), compiled by the Ministry
of Foreign Affairs.[87] We closely examined and compared the collection of documents in the Diplomatic Archives with the reprints in
gaikō bunsho. Surprisingly, in many cases, I noticed that some rare
and valuable reports from the archives were excluded from the reprint,
including lengthy detailed reports and records of important incidents.
In addition, English letters and clippings from local English-language
newspapers, which are compiled in an appendix and used as a reference
for reports by the consul, were omitted in most *gaikō bunsho* from
the Meiji era. In order to conduct comprehensive research, one must
understand that it is essential to navigate the files of historical materials
thoroughly and patiently.

Besides the "Zaibei honpōjin" and "Hokubei Gasshūkoku" catalogs, some useful *gaikō bunsho* on the Japanese who arrived in North
America in the Meiji era include "Meiji Imin Kabushiki Kaisha gyōmujō
no jikkyō chōsa narabini dō kaisha yori Bikutoria oyobi Hawai tō
e dekaseginin boshū tokō ikken," "Hawai imin Beikoku tokō kinshi
ikken," "Hokubei Gasshūkoku beisakuchi e Nihonjin ijū torishimari
zakken," and "Beikoku Aidaho-shū Yunion Pashifikku Tetsudō kōji ni
jūjiseru honpōjin rōdōsha hōchiku jiken chōsa no tame Chinda Ryōji
shucchō ikken."[88] In addition, the Ministry of Foreign Affairs' policy
concerning the issuance of passports to control emigration, and the
related instructions for local offices, are filed in "Ryoken hōki oyobi
dō hōki torishimari tetsuzuki ni kansuru kunrei shirei narabini ryoken
kafu tetsuzuki torishimari zakken."

Ryōji Hōkoku *(Consular Reports) Published in* Kanpō *(the Official Gazette) and* Tsūshō Isan

Japanese consulates in San Francisco and Vancouver regularly sent
special reports titled "Beikoku junkai kaku chihō shōkyō narabini

zairyū hōjin jōtai" or "Honpō dekaseginin no jōkyō" to Gaimushō Tsūshōkyoku (the Trade Bureau, Ministry of Foreign Affairs). These materials, which contain valuable statistics, were reprinted not in *gaikō bunsho*, but in *Kanpō* or *Tsūshō isan*, which Gaimushō Tsūshōkyoku edited.[89] The microfilm version, *Maikurofirumuban Ryōji hōkoku shiryō shūroku mokuroku*, edited by Tsunoyama Sakae and Takashima Masaaki, has made searching through consular reports easier. However, each issue of *Tsūshō isan* contained many Japanese consular reports from around the world, categorized by topic, such as "immigrants." For example, it is quite time-consuming to find the specific items related to people who migrated to the United States from the "emigration" category. Thus, I created a catalog of items that I considered to be important, although it is not comprehensive.

I have already mentioned that consular reports in *Kanpō* and *Tsūshō isan* were not included in the *Nihon gaikō bunsho*. Moreover, by comparing these reports with the ones that were selected for the *Nihon gaikō bunsho*, I noticed that the content and nature of the reports were different. Those that were selected for the *Nihon gaikō bunsho* were mainly about matters and conditions that affected US-Japan diplomatic issues. These included the refusal to admit Japanese passengers, the movement against Japanese migrant laborers, trends of anti-Japanese sentiment, the US government's immigration policy, and requests to limit the number of emigrants from Japan. On the other hand, reports not selected for the *Nihon gaikō bunsho*—as suggested by the topics— were mostly closely related to the migrants' actual life experiences, their living conditions, their employment status and business conditions, statistics regarding their occupations, the situation of Japanese migrant laborers during the recession, and the population of Japanese residing in each area in the United States. The reports that were published contain valuable information and data for researchers. Since both are *gaikō bunsho* (foreign diplomatic documents), it is important for researchers of Japanese emigration to thoroughly search and examine all the consular reports and records in *Kanpō*, *Tsūshō isan*, and *Nihon gaikō bunsho*. For research based on statistical materials published in *Kanpō*, refer to Yoshida Hideo, "Meiji shonen no Hawai dekasegi, jō, ge" in *Takushoku ronsō dai 3-kan dai 2-gō* (October 1941), 1–53 and *dai 3-kan, dai 3-gō* (December 1941), 1–34 (later published in Yoshida Hideo, *Nihon jinkōron no shiteki kenkyū* [Kawade Shobō, 1944], *dai 6-shō*, 437–509).

Theses and Magazine Articles

One of the most challenging tasks in searching through materials is finding the appropriate documents from a list of titles in a catalog of magazine articles. However, as I have repeated, documents related to early migrants in the United States, including those on *dekasegi shosei* and migrant laborers, have been lost. Therefore, efforts to search for letters, reports, and contributed articles that may have been sent to Japan have become an essential part of scholarly pursuit.

Instead of individually selecting essential theses and articles from a catalog, I selected magazines that were most likely to contain relevant papers and articles, and subsequently decided to make a catalog after gathering the contents related to migration studies. For every title, I compiled a catalog containing its contents. The selected magazines were *Chūō kōron*, *Jitsugyō no Nihon*, *Kokumin no tomo*, *Mita jitsugyōkai*, *Nihonjin*, *Ajia*, *Nihon oyobi Nihonjin*, *Taiyō*, *Shokumin kyōkai hōkoku*, and *Shokumin jihō*. Although I also began working on *Tōkyō keizai zasshi* and *Tōyō keizai zasshi*, that catalog has not yet been completed. For each magazine, the articles I selected were limited to the Meiji and Taishō eras.

The magazines *Nihonjin*, *Ajia*, *Nihon oyobi Nihonjin*, and *Jitsugyō no sekai*, which were retitled because of publication bans, featured many articles and reports written by *shosei* and other Japanese residing in America. Some of them are valuable. If we could expand our search to include local newspapers and magazines, more new materials would become available for study.

Notes

1. In American immigration studies, Maldwyn Allen Jones, *American Immigration*, 2nd ed. (Chicago: University of Chicago Press, 1992) is basic and useful. For the study of racial prejudice by white Americans, Howard Zinn, *A People's History of the United States* (New York: Harper & Row, 1980), and Alexander Saxton, *The Rise and Fall of the White Republic: Class Politics and Mass Culture in Nineteenth-Century America* (New York: Verso, 1990), are

interesting. The Japanese-language edition of Zinn is *Minshū no Amerika shi, jō, chū, ge,* ed. Saruya Kaname, trans. Tomita Torao, Hirano Takashi, and Yui Daizaburō (TBS Buritanika, 1993).

2. Important post–World War II research includes the following: Edna Bonacich and John Modell, *The Economic Basis of Ethnic Solidarity: Small Business in the Japanese American Community* (Berkeley: University of California Press, 1980); F. Hilary Conroy, *Japanese Frontier in Hawaii 1868–1869* (Berkeley: University of California Press, 1953); Roger Daniels, *Politics of Prejudice: The Anti-Japanese Movement in California and the Struggle for Japanese Exclusion* (Berkeley: University of California Press, 1962); Roger Daniels, *Concentration Camps USA: Japanese Americans and World War II* (Hinsdale, IL: Dryden Press, 1971); Roger Daniels and Harry H. L. Kitano, *American Racism: Exploration of the Nature of Prejudice* (Englewood Cliffs, NJ: Prentice-Hall, 1970); Richard Drinnon, *Keeper of Concentration Camps: Dillon S. Myer and American Racism* (Berkeley: University of California Press, 1987); Bill Hosokawa, *Nisei: The Quiet American* (New York: William Morrow, 1969); Yuji Ichioka, *The Issei: The World of the First Generation Japanese Immigrants, 1885–1924* (New York: Free Press, 1988); Peter Irons, *Justice at War* (New York: Oxford University Press, 1983); Masakazu Iwata, *Planted in Good Soil: A History of the Issei in United States Agriculture,* 2 vols. (New York: Peter Lang, 1992); Gene Levine and Colbert Rhodes, *The Japanese American Community: A Three-Generation Study* (New York: Praeger, 1981); Ivan H. Light, *Ethnic Enterprise in America: Business and Welfare among Chinese, Japanese, and Blacks* (Berkeley: University of California Press, 1972); John Modell, *The Economics and Politics of Racial Accommodation: The Japanese of Los Angeles, 1900–1942* (Urbana: University of Illinois Press, 1977): Alan Takeo Moriyama, *Imingaisha: Japanese Emigration Companies and Hawai'i, 1894–1908* (Honolulu: University of Hawai'i Press, 1985); Sandra C. Taylor, *Advocate of Understanding: Sidney Gulick and the Search for Peace with Japan* (Kent, OH: Kent State University Press, 1984); Michi Weglyn, *Years of Infamy* (New York: William Morrow, 1976); Robert A. Wilson and Bill Hosokawa, *East to America: A History of the Japanese in the United States* (New York: William Morrow, 1980). Although a considerable number of books have been translated into Japanese, those titles are omitted. The basic materials for pre–World War II studies were Yamato Ichihashi, *Japanese in the United States: A Critical Study of the Problems of the Japanese Immigrants and Their Children* (Stanford, CA: Stanford University Press, 1932). In addition, valuable studies of expansionism in both Japan and America and the US-Japan relationship are by Akira Iriye, *Pacific Estrangement: Japanese and American Expansion, 1897–1911* (Cambridge, MA: Harvard University Press, 1972).

3. One of the most active researchers in this field is Ronald Takaki. His most representative work is *Strangers from a Different Shore: A History of Asian Americans* (New York: Penguin Group, 1989). Other references are Roger Daniels, *Asian America: Chinese and Japanese in the United States since 1850* (Seattle: University of Washington Press, 1988); Roger Daniels, Sandra Taylor, and Harry H. L. Kitano, eds., *Japanese Americans: From Relocation to Redress* (Salt Lake City: University of Utah Press, 1988); Stephen S. Fugita and David J. O'Brien, *Japanese American Ethnicity: The Persistence of Community* (Seattle: University of Washington Press, 1991); Harry H. L. Kitano, *Japanese Americans: The Evolution of a Subculture* (Englewood Cliffs, NJ: Prentice-Hall, 1969); Harry H. L. Kitano, *Race Relations*

(Englewood Cliffs: Prentice-Hall, 1974); Stanford M. Lyman, *The Asian in North America* (Santa Barbara, CA: Clio Press, 1979); Minako K. Maykovich, *Japanese American Identity Dilemma* (Tokyo: Waseda University Press, 1972); Darrel Montero, *Japanese Americans: Changing Patterns of Ethnic Affiliation over Three Generations* (Boulder, CO: Westview Press, 1980); Dennis Ogawa, *From Japs to Japanese: The Evolution of Japanese American Stereotypes* (Berkeley, CA: McCutchan, 1971); Daniel I. Okimoto, *American in Disguise* (New York and Tokyo: Walker/Weatherhill, 1971); William Peterson, *Japanese Americans: Oppression and Success* (Washington, DC: University Press of America, 1971).

4. Both Ichioka and Iwata used Japanese-language materials from the JARP collection at the University Research Library, University of California–Los Angeles. For reference to this collection and materials, please refer to Yuji Ichioka, Yasuo Sakata, Nobuya Tsuchida, and Eri Yasuhara, comps., *A Buried Past: An Annotated Bibliography of the Japanese American Research Project Collection* (Berkeley: University of California Press, 1974), and Yasuo Sakata, comp., *Fading Footsteps of the Issei: An Annotated Check List of the Manuscript Holdings of the Japanese American Research Project Collection* (Los Angeles: Asian American Studies Center, UCLA, and Japanese American National Museum, 1992).

5. The main literature of prewar Japanese emigration is contained in Irie Toraji, *Hōjin kaigai hattenshi*, jō, ge (Ida Shoten, 1942) and *Meiji hyakunenshi sōsho*, vol. 303 (reprinted by Hara Shobō, 1981). Because it was published after the Second World War began, the author's expansionistic perspective was expressed throughout. It is a valuable reference, however, because the descriptions were based on diplomatic documents of the Ministry of Foreign Affairs of Japan. For the study of the overseas expansion theory in the Meiji era, refer to Kuroda Kenichi, *Nihon shokumin shisō shi* (Kōbundō, 1942). The study of *kan'yaku imin* (government-sponsored immigration) in Hawai'i is in Yoshida Hideo, *Nihon jinkōron no shiteki kenkyū* (Kawade Shobō, 1944), the first research based on the consular reports (published in *Kanpō*) and government records. For postwar emigration studies, both Ishikawa Yūki and Kodama Masaaki have been actively researching for more than twenty years, focusing on emigration from prefectures, including Hiroshima, Yamaguchi (Ishikawa and Kodama), and Okinawa (Ishikawa), based on a detailed analysis of the materials. They were also involved in the compilation and writing of *Hiroshima-ken ijūshi: tsūshi hen* and *shiryō hen*, ed. Hiroshima prefecture (Daiichi Hōki Shuppansha, 1993 and 1991). I will not list their research papers because there are so many. Kodama Masaaki, *Nihon iminshi kenkyū josetsu* (Tansuisha, 1991) analyzes emigration to Hawai'i, the continental United States, and Australia and the role of *imin kaisha* (emigration companies) during the Meiji era. Regarding *ken iminshi* (the prefectural history of emigration), besides *Hiroshima-ken ijūshi*, previously cited, *Wakayama-ken iminshi* (Wakayama prefecture, 1957); *Kaigai imin ga boson ni oyoboshita eikyō: Wakayama-ken Hidaka-gun Mio-mura jittai chōsa*, ed. Fukutake Tadashi (Mainichi Shinbunsha Jinkō Mondai Chōsakai, 1953); *Amerika-mura: imin sōshutsuson no jittai*, ed. Fukutake Tadashi (Tōkyō Daigaku Shuppankai, 1953); "Kotō iminmura no kenkyū" in the special issue of Ritsumeikan Daigaku, *Jinbun Kagaku Kenkyūjo kiyō* 14 (January 1964) are valuable. For studies on Japanese immigration to Hawai'i and North America, refer to Shimaoka Hiroshi, *Hawai imin no rekishi* (Kokusho Kankōkai, 1983); Tamura Norio, *Amerika no Nihongo shinbun* (Shinchōsha, 1991); *Beikoku shoki no Nihongo shinbun*, ed. Tamura Norio and Shiramizu Shigehiko (Keisō

Shobō, 1986); *Japanīzu Amerikan: Ijū kara jiritsu e no ayumi,* ed. Togami Sōken (Mineruva Shobō, 1986); Doi Yatarō, *Yamaguchi-ken Ōshima-gun Hawai iminshi* (Matsuno Shoten, 1980); *Hokubei Nihonjin Kirisutokyō undōshi,* ed. Dōshisha Daigaku Jinbun Kagaku Kenkyūjo (PMC Shuppan, 1991); *Imin no Nihon kaiki undō,* ed. Maeyama Takashi (Nihon Hōsō Shuppan Kyōkai, 1982); *Hawai no shinbōnin: Meiji Fukushima imin no kojinshi,* ed. Maeyama Takashi (Ochanomizu Shobō, 1986); Murayama Yūzō, *Amerika ni ikita Nihonjin imin: Nikkei Issei no hikari to kage* (Tōyō Keizai Shinpōsha, 1989); Yagasaki Noritaka, *Imin nōgyō: Kariforunia no Nihonjin imin shakai* (Kokon Shoin, 1992); Wakatsuki Yasuo, *Hainichi no rekishi : Amerika ni okeru Nihonjin imin* (Chūō Kōronsha, 1972); Yoshida Tadao, *Hainichi iminhō no kiseki: 21-seiki no Nichi-Bei kankei no genten* (Keizai Ōraisha, 1983). For immigration studies in Canada, the useful references are Shinpo Mitsuru, *Jinshuteki sabetsu to henken: Rironteki kōsatsu to Kanada no jirei* (Iwanami Shoten, 1972); *Ishi o mote owareru gotoku: Nikkei Kanadajin shakaishi* (Tairiku Nippōsha, 1975); *Nihon no imin: Nikkei Kanadajin ni mirareta haiseki to tekiō* (Hyōronsha, 1977); *Kanada Nihonjin imin monogatari* (Tsukiji Shokan, 1986); *Umi o watatta Nihon no mura,* ed. Gamō Masao (Chūō Kōronsha, 1962); and *Kanada no Nihongo shinbun,* ed. Shinpo Mitsuru, Tamura Norio, and Shiramizu Shigehiko (PMC Shuppan, 1991). Refer to Karl Yoneda, *Zaibei Nihonjin rōdōsha no rekishi* (Shin Nippon Shuppansha, 1967) for histories of the Japanese American labor movement in America.

6. Wakatsuki Yasuo, *Hatten tojōkoku e no ijū no kenkyū: Boribia ni okeru Nihon imin* (Tamagawa Daigaku Shuppanbu, 1987); Togami, *Japanīzu Amerikan*; and Maeyama, *Imin no Nihon kaiki undō* are good examples. Moreover, Asada Sadao's thesis in *Kōza, Nihon to Amerika dai 3-kan,* ed. Ōhashi Kenzaburō, Katō Hidetoshi, and Saitō Makoto (Nagumodō, 1969) is valuable research, for it considers immigration issues in light of the United States and Japan's relationship.

7. Kimura Kenji, *Senzenki Nihon imingaku no kiseki,* 10. This was an excerpt sent by the author, but the journal title and the publication date were not included.

8. For more about the "yellow peril" theorists in the United States and Japan during the so-called war scare period, from the late 1900s until the 1910s, when the jingoists warned against the threat of war between the two countries, refer to Iriye, *Pacific Estrangement*; Shōichi Saeki, "Images of the United States as a Hypothetical Enemy" in *Mutual Images: Essays in American-Japanese Relations,* ed. Akira Iriye (Cambridge, MA: Harvard University Press, 1975), 100–114 (*Nihon to Amerika: aitekoku no imēji kenkyū,* ed. Katō Hidetoshi and Kamei Shunsuke [Nihon Gakujutsu Shinkōkai, 1977]). Furthermore, for a background on the legal process of *Gaijin tochihō* (California Alien Land Law) or *Hainichi iminhō* (Immigration Act of 1924), refer to Daniels, *The Politics of Prejudice* and Ichioka, *The Issei* (*Issei: reimeiki Amerika imin no monogatari,* trans. Tomita Torao, Kumei Teruko, and Shinoda Satae [Tōsui Shobō, 1992]); and Yoshida, *Hainichi iminhō no kiseki.*

9. Regarding anti-Japanese issues, the California Alien Land Law, and the Immigration Act of 1924, refer to Akamatsu Hiromi, *Gunjin no mitaru hainichi to taibeisaku* (Nisshindō, 1924); Arima Sumikiyo, *Beikoku no hainichi* (Keiseisha Shoten, 1922); Ōishi Kiichi, *Nichi-Bei mondai jitsuryoku kaiketsusaku* (Sankōdō, 1916); Ōyama Ujirō, *Taiheiyō no higan* (Hōchi Shinbunsha, 1925); Suzuki Saburō, *Hainichi mondai no shinsō* (Ōsaka Mainichi Shinbunsha, 1924); Chiba Toyoharu, *Hainichi mondai kōgai* (Nichi-Beisha, 1913); Tsunashima Kakichi, *Hainichi*

mondai to Kirisuto kyōto (Keiseisha Shoten, 1916); Nakajima Kurō, *Taibei Nisshi imin mondai no kaibō* (Ganshōdō, 1924); Matsueda Shōji, *Beikoku hainichi no jissō* (Dai Nihon Yūbenkai, 1925). In addition, many papers were published in the *Gaikō jihō*. Refer to Ichioka et al., *A Buried Past,* 50–68, and Kimura, *Senzenki Nihon imingaku no kiseki,* 20–28. Some examples of Issei themselves dealing with these issues include *Hokubei Gasshūkoku Arizona-shū hainichi jiken* (Arizona Nihonjinkai, 1934); Okumura Takie, *Hainichi yobō keihatsu undō* (1922); and Washizu "Shakuma" Bunzō, *Zaibei Nihonjin shikan* (Rafu Shinpōsha, 1930). Regarding Nisei issues, refer to Aoyagi Ikutarō, *Zaigai hōjin dainisei mondai, dai 1-shū* (Imin Mondai Kenkyūkai, 1940); *Dainisei to kokuseki mondai, dainisei sōsho, dai 3-shū* , ed. Nihon Beifu Kyōkai (Runbini Shuppan, 1938); Shishimoto Hachirō, *Nikkei shimin o kataru: Amerika umare no Nihonjin* (Shōkasha, 1934); Yamada Tatsumi, *Kaigai dainisei mondai* (Kibundō Shoten, 1936); Yamada Tatsumi, *Kaigai dainisei mondai* (Kōbundō Shobō, 1936); Yamashita Sōen, *Nikkei shimin no Nihon ryūgaku jijō* (Bunseidō, 1935); and Yamashita Sōen, *Nichi-Bei o tsunagu mono* (Bunseidō, 1938). Shishimoto and Yamashita discuss issues from the Issei's point of view. One example of Nisei issues, from a new perspective, is Yuji Ichioka, "A Study in Dualism: James Sakamoto and the Japanese American Courier, 1928–1942," *Amerasia Journal* 13 (1986–87), 49–81. For criticism of the bridge theory of the relationship between the United States and Japan, useful readings are Ichioka Yuji, "Dainisei mondai 1902–1941: Nisei no shōrai to kyōiku ni kanshite henkasuru Issei no tenbō to kenkai no rekishiteki kōsatsu," trans. Sakata Yasuo in *Hokubei Nihonjin Kirisutokyō undōshi,* ed. Dōshisha Daigaku Jinbun Kagaku Kenkyūjo (PMC Shuppan, 1991), 731–84.

10. In 1969, while studying in Japan for a year as a fellowship recipient of the Japanese American Research Project of University of California–Los Angeles, I was repeatedly asked questions such as, "If you are studying US history at an American university, why are you researching topics like Japanese emigration?" I still remember my frustration. In "Kinō no tabi," Shimizu Ikutarō's traveler's journal contributed to *Bungei shunjū*, he described Japanese immigrants he had met in various places in America as follows: "They are called Issei. I knew the old phrase 'venturing overseas,' as a child. However, if I am to speak truthfully, the majority of them were dropouts of old and poor Japan. They are still struggling with poverty, labor, and prejudice after having migrated to the foreign land. During the war, they were forcefully removed, their houses and properties confiscated, and sent to incarceration camps" (*Bungei shunjū*, series 54, no. 3, March 1976, 146–47). If even Shimizu held this prejudice against the Japanese immigrants, I thought it was not surprising that the general public looked down on them.

11. For Japanese-language documents in the emigration reference room in Wakayama City Library, refer to *Wakayama Shimin Toshokan imin shiryō mokuroku,* ed. Kyōto Daigaku Iminshi Kenkyūkai and Wakayama Shimin Toshokan (Wakayama Shimin Toshokan Imin Shiryōshitsu, 1985). For materials about Hiroshima and Okinawa prefectures, refer to *Hiroshima-ken ijūshi, shiryō hen,* ed. Hiroshima-ken, and *Kunigami-son kaigai iminshi, shiryō hen,* ed. Kunigami-son Kaigai Iminshi Hensan Iinkai (Kunigami-son Yakuba, 1992).

12. Readings in this topic include Kumei Teruko and Iino Masako, "Nihon ni okeru Nihonjin imin Nikkei Amerika kenkyū I, II" in *Tōkyō Daigaku Amerika Kenkyū Shiryō Sentā nenpō* 13 (1990), 18–54. Moreover, useful catalogs to read for prewar documentation and papers include *Keizai hōritsu bunken mokuroku*

(Hōbunkan, 1927) and *Keizai hōritsu bunken mokuroku, dai 2-shū,* ed. Kōbe Kōtō Shōgyō Gakkō Shōgyō Kenkyūjo (Hōbunkan, 1931); *Hōsei keizai shakai ronbun sōran,* ed. Amano Keitarō (Tōkō Shoin, 1927); *Hōsei, keizai shakai ronbun sōran, tsui hen* (Tōkō Shoin, 1928); Honjō Eijirō, *Nihon keizai bunken, dai 1-kan* through *dai 6-kan* (Nihon Hyōronsha, 1953–69); Kokushō Iwao and Kikuta Tarō, *Keizai chirigaku bunken sōran* (Sōbunkaku, 1937); *Nihon jinkō mondai kenkyū dai 3-shū* and *Jinkō mondai bunken, zoku,* ed. Ueda Teijirō (Kyōchōkai, 1937); and *Hōbun jinkō kankei bunken narabini shiryō kaidai: Fu, jinkō kankei ronbun mokuroku,* ed. Naikaku Tōkeikyoku (Naikaku Tōkeikyoku, 1951). For documents about Japan's emigration from a diplomatic point of view, refer to *Nihon gaikōshi kankei bunken mokuroku,* ed. Hanabusa Nagamichi (Keiō Daigaku Hōgaku Kenkyūkai, 1961); for the *Ryōji hōkoku* (consular reports) refer to *Kanpō* or *Tsūshō isan, Maikurofirumu-ban ryōji hōkoku shiryō shūroku mokuroku,* ed. Kadoyama Sakae and Takashima Masaaki (Yūshōdō Firumu Shuppan, 1983). *Shokumin Kyōkai hōkoku, kaisetsu, sōmokuji, sakuin* (Fuji Shuppan, 1987) is also valuable. In America, more than ten catalogs of specific topics, including a catalog of master's theses and description catalogs for the documents for Nikkei immigration studies, were compiled, such as Orpha Cummings and Helen E. Hennefrund, *Bibliography on the Japanese in American Agriculture, United States Department of Agriculture Bibliographic Bulletin No. 3* (Washington, DC: Government Printing Office, 1943); Edward N. Barnhart, *Japanese American Evacuation and Resettlement* (Berkeley: University of California, General Library, 1958); William W. Lum, *Asians in America: A Bibliography of Master's Theses* (Davis: University of California, 1970). For those documents, refer to Ichioka et al., *A Buried Past,* 13–14.

13. For UCLA's Japanese American Research Project collection, refer to Ichioka et al., "Introduction" in *A Buried Past,* 11–13, and Sakata, "Introduction" in *Fading Footsteps of the Issei,* 11–14.

14. For the documents in the collection of Nikkei studies, refer to Ichioka et al., *A Buried Past* and Sakata, *Fading Footsteps of the Issei.* For the University of Hawai'i library collection, refer to Matsuda Mitsugu, *The Japanese in Hawai'i: An Annotated Bibliography of Japanese Americans,* rev. Dennis M. Ogawa with Jerry Y. Fujioka (Honolulu: Social Sciences and Linguistics Institute, University of Hawai'i, 1975). The Burke (Edward M. Burke) Collection in the University of Washington library in Seattle contains the records of Hokubei Nihonjinkai (Japanese Association of North America), founded in 1912 via the merger of Shiatoru Nihonjinkai (Japanese Association in Seattle) and Washinton-shū Nihonjinkai (Japanese Association in Washington State), and Hokubei Nihonjin Shōgyō Kaigisho (the Japanese Chamber of Commerce of Northern California), founded in 1931 via the merger of Shiatoru Nihonjin Shōgyō Kaigisho (Japanese Chamber of Commerce in Seattle) and Hokubei Nihonjinkai. Unfortunately, the catalog has not yet been published though it is available at the library.

15. For newly added personal papers, refer to Yuji Ichioka, "Foreword" in *Fading Footsteps of the Issei,* ed. Sakata, xii–xiv and 43.

16. *Zaibei Nihonjin shi* (Zaibei Nihonjinkai, 1940). A volume of 1,293 pages, *Zaibei Nihonjin shi* has historical descriptions and is full of writings on history, unlike many of this type of publication, which typically devotes half of the volume to personal profiles and directories. This compilation was one of the Zaibei Nihonjinkai's projects to celebrate the 2,600th anniversary of the founding of

Japan. It established the Zaibei Nihonjin Jiseki Hozonkai, inviting Satō Toshihito, the Japanese consul general in San Francisco, to be the honorary president (ibid., "Shuppan keika," 1290).

17. Dorothy Thomas, *Salvage* (Berkeley: University of California Press, 1952), Statistical Appendix, 571–626.

18. Issei Interview Survey Questionnaire Schedules, Japanese American Research Project Collection, University Research Library, University of California–Los Angeles. From here on, I will refer to this as the UCLA JARP Collection.

19. Ibid. For example, the *Zaibei Nihonjin shi*'s list, 534–51, of publications in prewar America includes Suzuki Eishirō, *Ankoku no Rafu* (1913). However, the book has not yet been found.

20. Sakata Yasuo, "Conflicting Identities: Issei and Nisei in the 1930s," *Osaka Gakuin University International Colloquium* (1991), 133–160.

21. As an instructor for survey interviewers of Issei for the UCLA JARP Collection, I read the whole "Interview Questionnaire Schedule," which contains seventy-three pages and 1,135 items in total. The Issei interviewees, the subjects of the survey, were selected randomly. Many of them did not answer or hesitated to answer the questions concerning the interwar period. Moreover, some of the Issei refused to be interviewed when asked if they experienced any anti-Japanese activities and protested, saying, "Why do you have to dig out the past?"

22. For personal papers and their donors, refer to Sakata, *Fading Footsteps of the Issei,* 23–122.

23. For example, Hosokawa, *Nisei: The Quiet American;* Frank F. Chuman, *The Bamboo People: The Law and the Japanese Americans* (Del Mar, CA: Publisher's Inc., 1976); Bill Hosokawa, "JACL" in *Quest of Justice* (New York: William Morrow, 1982); Mike Masaoka (with Bill Hosokawa), *They Call Me Moses Masaoka: An American Saga* (New York: William Morrow, 1987).

24. For Japanese-language newspapers published in America, refer to Tamura Norio, *Amerika no Nihongo shinbun* (Shinchōsha, 1991); Ebihara Hachirō, *Kaigai hōji shinbun zasshishi* (Gakuji Shoin, 1936), and *Zaibei Nihonjin shi* (Zaibei Nihonjinkai), 505–52.

25. Ibid., 1290–91.

26. Ibid., 1289.

27. Hawai Nihonjin Iminshi Kankō Iinkai, ed., *Hawai Nihonjin iminshi: Hawai kan'yaku ijū 75-nen kinen* (Hawai Nikkeijin Rengō Kyōkai, 1964); and Watanabe, ed., *Hawai no Nihonjin Nikkeijin no rekishi: Nihonjin Hawai kan'yaku imin hyakunensai kinen, jōkan* (Hawai Hōchisha, 1986). The subsequent volume has not yet been published.

28. As a researcher for the Japanese American Research Project (JARP) at UCLA, I conducted interviews for oral histories in addition to survey interviews. These were statements from the editors of Japanese-language newspapers, who were also involved in the publication of *nenkan* (yearbooks) and *Nihonjin shi* (Japanese histories).

29. *Beikoku Nikkeijin hyakunenshi: zaibei Nikkeijin hatten jinshiroku* (Shin Nichi-Bei Shinbunsha, 1961). Katō Shin'ichi, the editor, published a separate volume with supplementary descriptions in Japan. Katō Shin'ichi, *Amerika imin hyakunenshi, jō, chū, ge* (Jiji Tsūshinsha, 1962).

30. Abiko Kyūtarō, the former owner of Nichi-Bei Shinbunsha, explained in a letter to his uncle that the publication of *nenkan* became a source of income

for the company. "Since running a newspaper company is sort of a hobby business, as revenue increases, so do expenses. Therefore, I don't consider revenue as profits. . . . Regarding newspaper business, I think the model that generates most success in revenue is *nenkan*. Even though the yearly profit of daily newspapers is about $25,000, costs such as printing machines and other expenses are increasing, and I could almost say there is no cash left. This year's annual revenue is approximately $3,000. If you estimate $1,500 for all the miscellaneous expenses, including fees for editing, compilation, and printing materials, and deduct it from the revenue, I estimate that the remaining $1,500 might be pure profit. The *nenkan* published by Nichi-Beisha last year was unique at the time, establishing a reputation for the company. Other newspaper companies or individuals would not be able to replicate this" (letter from Abiko Kyūtarō to his uncle on January 9, 1906, the Abiko Family Papers, UCLA JARP Collection). Although this letter was written in 1906, Akahori Masaru, the former chief editor of the *Taihoku nippō* in Seattle, told me that it was normal practice, even in the 1930s, for newspaper companies to issue directories or *nenkan* to rebuild the companies' finances. He also said that with directories in particular, the newspaper company collected fees from every individual listed in the directory in advance and applied it to the cost of compilation and publishing. Therefore, the sales from the publication became pure profit. About two-thirds of *Beikoku Nikkeijin hyakunenshi*, edited by Shin Nichi-Bei Shinbunsha, which totaled nearly eight hundred pages, was made up of *Zaibei Nikkeijin hatten jinshiroku*. When I interviewed Kido Saburō, the owner of Shin Nichi-Bei Shinbunsha, he said that it was a profitable project.

31. Documents were also lost in Japan. For example, Washizu "Shakuma" Bunzō, a writer in a Japanese community already involved in editing and publishing a Japanese-language newspaper and *Agohazushi,* a humorous magazine in the 1890s, returned to Japan before the war, carrying valuable documents with him. While living in Tokyo, however, all the documents in his possession were burnt in an air raid (according to Sado Takuhei, his grandson). For the *Agohazushi,* refer to Washizu "Shakuma" Bunzō, "Wagahai no Beikoku seikatsu," 68–70; "Shinbun kisha seikatsu no koto," 1–3; "Wagahai no Beikoku seikatsu," 71; "Agohazushi no seinen, Noguchi (Yonejirō) to Takahashi (Kosen)"; "Wagahai no Beikoku seikatsu," 72–73; "Yamada Dongyū no koto," *Nichi-Bei shinbun* (September 18 to 23, 1924); and Ebihara, *Kaigai hōji shinbun zasshishi.*

32. For the Issei's experiences of the 1906 San Francisco earthquake, refer to Hei Iwao (Ninomiya Risaku), "Nijūhachinenkan no yo ga kaiko-chinbun-kidan, naka ni wa taisetsuna shiryō mo" 55, *Shinsekai* (September 7, 1931). Ninomiya, a former newspaperman in Japan, arrived in America in November 1902. At the time of the earthquake, he was staying at a hotel in Vacaville and then rushed into San Francisco. The subtitles of the articles included "The morning of San Francisco earthquake, I was shocked and jumped to my feet," "The station was filled with anxious people," "Crossing the bloody sea and entering the flaming town," and "Poor fire protections turned the earthquake into an inferno."

33. For the *dekasegi shosei*'s arrival in the United States, refer to Sakata Yasuo, "Datsu-a no shishi to tozasareta hakusekijin no rakuen: Minkenha shosei to Beikoku ni okeru ōshoku jinshu haiseki . . ."; *Beikoku shoki no Nihongo shinbun,* ed. Tamura Norio and Shiramizu Shigehiko, 47–193; and "Jiyū minkenki ni okeru Sōkō wangan chiku no katsudō," ed. Arai Katsuhiro and Tamura Norio in *Tōkyō Keizai Daigaku jinbun shizen kagaku ronshū* dai 65-kan (December 5, 1983).

34. For *dekasegi rōdōsha* (migrant laborer) passages to the West Coast of the continental United States, refer to the reports of the Japanese consulates general in San Francisco and Vancouver in "Zaibei honpōjin no jōkyō narabini tobeisha torishimari kankei zassan" and "Hokubei Gasshūkoku ni oite honpōjin tokō seigen oyobi haiseki ikken" held at the Gaimushō Gaikō Shiryōkan (Diplomatic Archives of the Ministry of Foreign Affairs of Japan). These important reports are referred to as "Honpōjin no Beikoku imin narabini haiseki kankei ikken" and "Honpōjin no Kanada imin narabini haiseki kankei ikken" in *Nihon gaikō bunsho* nos. 24–28, ed. Gaimushō (Nihon Kokusai Rengō Kyōkai, 1952–53). Hereafter, I will indicate *Nihon gaikō bunsho*, ed. Gaimushō as *Gaikō bunsho*. [The digital collection of *Nihon gaikō bunsho* is now available at https://www.mofa.go.jp/mofaj/annai/honsho/shiryo/archives/mokuji.html.]

35. "Beikoku junkai kaku chihō shōkyō narabini zairū honpōjin no jōkyō" (the consular report of San Francisco dated April 20, 1895) in *Tsūshō isan dai 17-gō*, ed. Gaimushō Tsūshōkyoku (May 15, 1895), 3–13.

36. Ichihashi, *Japanese in the United States*, 94.

37. "Hokubei Gasshūkoku Sōkō oyobi sono fukin zaijū honpōjin" from a late December 1904 survey (the consular report of San Francisco on April 20, 1905) in *Tsūshō isan dai 66-gō* (November 18, 1905), ed. Gaimushō Tsūshōkyoku, 24–27. This is included in the first yearbook, *Zaibei Nihonjin nenkan dai 1* (Nichi-Bei Shinbunsha, 1905), 160–62, as charts explaining the number of Japanese residents in California and the professions of Japanese residents in San Francisco at the end of 1904. (For Nichi-Bei Shinbunsha's *Zaibei Nihonjin nenkan dai 1*, refer to the text of Abiko Kyūtarō's letter to his uncle cited in endnote 30.) These statistical tables are also shown in *Zaibei Nihonjin shi*, 76–77 as "Zaikashū honpōjin bunpu ichiran" (a list of distribution charts of Japanese residents in California) from the 1904 year-end survey, and "Zaibei hōjin shokugyō bunpu ichiran" (a list of the occupation distribution of Japanese residents in America), from the end of 1904.

38. "Zaibei hōjin shokugyō bunpu ichiran," a 1904 year-end survey in *Zaibei Nihonjin shi*, 74–75.

39. Valuable historical materials that illustrate Japanese people's lives in San Francisco at this time are Hei Iwao (Ninomiya Risaku), "Nijūhachinenkan no yo ga kaiko-chinbun-kidan, naka ni wa taisetsuna shiryō mo," 1–97, in the *Shinsekai* (issued between June 25 and October 31, 1931); Washizu "Shakuma" Bunzō, "Wagahai no Beikoku seikatsu," 1–132, in the Sōkō *Nichi-Bei shinbun* (issued between July 10, 1924, and January 23, 1925). For brief descriptions, refer to *Zaibei Nihonjin shi*, 81.

40. See note 32.

41. For the history of the *Shinsekai*, *Nichi-Bei shinbun*, and the consequences of the 1906 San Francisco earthquake, refer to *Zaibei Nihonjin shi*, 505–24. The materials that survived the earthquake were reproduced as microfilms.

42. Kimitsu dai 18-gō Meiji 25-nen 8-gatsu 4-ka zai Sōkō Ryōji Chinda Sutemi yori Gaimu Daijin Enomoto Takeaki ate, "Tōkoku Aidaho-shū ni oite tasū no Nihonjin hōchikuseraretaru ken guhin" in "Beikoku Aidaho-shū Yunion Pashifikku Tetsudō kōji ni jūjiseru honpōjin rōdōsha hōchiku jiken no tame Chinda Ryōji shucchō no ken" (July–September 1892) and *Gaikō bunsho*, no. 25, 718–21.

43. Densō dai 102-gō Meiji 25-nen 8-gatsu 22-nichi Gaimu Daijin Mutsu Munemitsu yori Sōkō Ryōji Chinda Sutemi ate, "Aidaho-shū Namupa hoka nikasho e shucchō kata denshin kunrei no ken" in "Beikoku Aidaho-shū Yunion

Pashifikku Tetsudō kōji ni jūjiseru honpōjin rōdōsha hōchiku jiken no tame Chinda Ryōji shucchō no ken" (July–September 1892) and *Gaikō bunsho,* no. 25, 724.

44. Among the reports, related documents, and newspaper articles of "Beikoku Aidaho-shū Yunion Pashifikku Tetsudō kōji ni jūjiseru honpōjin rōdōsha hōchiku jiken no tame Chinda Ryōji shucchō no ken" (July–September 1892), only three reports, made up of the statements in endnotes 42 and 43, along with Kimitsu dai 21-gō, Meiji 25-nen 9-gatsu 17-nichi, Chinda yori Mutsu ate, "Aidaho-shū shucchō hōkoku no ken" are recorded in *Gaikō bunsho* no. 25. Other important, valuable, and lengthy reports, such as Chinda's *Fukumeisho,* Tanaka Chūshichi's *Gushinsho,* and related English-language documents or newspaper articles were omitted, reason unknown.

45. "Tanaka Chūshichi gushinsho" in Kimitsu dai 22-gō, Meiji 25-nen 9-gatsu 27-nichi, Chinda yori Mutsu ate, "Aidaho-shū shucchō torishimari fukumeisho sōfu no ken," Fuzokusho daiichi, Chinda Sutemi, "Aidaho-shū shucchō torishirabe fukumeisho," Fuzokusho daini, "Bōdō Nihonjin rōdōsha hōchiku jiken jōkyō hōkokusho"; and "Beikoku Aidaho-shū Yunion Pashifikku Tetsudō kōji ni jūjiseru honpōjin rōdōsha hōchiku jiken no tame Chinda Ryōji shucchō no ken" (July–September 1892). As I mentioned previously, these are not included in the *Gaikō bunsho,* no. 25.

46. Kimitsu dai-22 gō, Meiji 25-nen 9-gatsu 27-nichi, Chinda yori Mutsu ate, "Aidaho-shū shucchō torishimari fukumeisho sōfu no ken," Fuzokusho dai 1, "Aidaho-shū shucchō torishirabe fukumeisho."

47. Ibid., Fuzokusho dai 3, "Tanaka Chūshichi gushinsho" (Meiji 25-nen 9-gatsu 15-nichi).

48. For *Sōkō* and *Kinmon nippō,* refer to Washizu "Shakuma" Bunzō, "Rekishi enmetsu no tan 53, Shinbun zasshi no konjaku, odorokubeki genron kikan" in *Nichi-Bei shinbun* issued on May 29, 1922; ibid., 54, "Shinbun zasshi no konjaku, seikatsu no soaku dai 1" in *Nichi-Bei shinbun* issued on May 30, 1922; and Ebihara, *Kaigai hōji shinbun zasshishi.*

49. For the activities of *Jiyū minkenha shosei* (schoolboys involved in the Freedom and People's Rights Movement) in the San Francisco Bay Area, refer to *Jiyū minkenki no Sōkō wangan chiku no katsudō,* ed. Arai Katsuhiro and Tamura Norio; Arai Katsuhiro, *Jiyū minkenki no tobei hōjin katsudōshi (jo); Beikoku shoki no Nihongo shinbun,* ed. Tamura and Shiramizu, 233–56; and "Jiyū minkenki ni okeru zaibei zaifu Nihonjin no kenri ishiki" in *Kokuritsu Rekishi Minzoku Hakubutsukan kenkyū hōkoku dai 35-gō* (November 1991), 545–98. For the reference of Enseisha and its publication of *Ensei,* refer to Ariyama Teruo, *Zasshi "Ensei" no genron katsudō: 1890-nendai San Furanshisuko ni okeru "yūshi" no kiseki; Beikoku shoki no Nihongo shinbun,* ed. Tamura and Shiramizu, 257–79. For *minkenha shosei* and yellow peril movements in America, refer to Sakata, *Datsu-a no shishi to tozasareta hakusekijin no rakuen,* and *Beikoku shoki no Nihongo shinbun,* ed. Tamura and Shiramizu. For the Sōkō Fukuinkai (Gospel Society, San Francisco), organized by many Christian *shosei,* refer to *Fukuinkai enkaku shiryō,* ed. Fumikura Heizaburō, held in the UCLA JARP Collection (refer to Sakata, *Fading Footsteps of the Issei,* 151); currently more Sōkō Fukuinkai–related research is being conducted by the Institute for Study of Humanities and Social Sciences, Doshisha University. The other organizations and groups, including Aikoku Dōmeikai (Japanese Patriotic League), Dōshūkai, and Kirisutokyō Seinenkai are mentioned in Washizu, *Rekishi enmetsu no tan*; Ebihara, *Kaigai hōji shinbun zasshishi; Nichi-Bei kankei zai Beikoku Nihonjin hatten shiyō,* ed. Fujiga Yoichi (Beikoku Seisho Kyōkai Nihonjinbu, 1927); and *Nikkei imin shiryōshū dai*

1-kan, Hokubei hen, reprint (Nihon Tosho Sentā, 1991). This area, however, has not been well researched.

50. This book is included in a list of books published in Nikkei communities in the United States mentioned in *Zaibei Nihonjin shi.* The description of *Aidaho haikan jiken* in another book mentioned this book as a reference. As far as I know, however, no universities, public libraries in the United States, or libraries in Japan hold that book. The book is considered as most likely having been lost. Fortunately, there is a passage from the book quoted regarding the *Aidaho jiken haikan shimatsu* in Washizu "Shakuma" Bunzō, "Wagahai no Beikoku seikatsu," 103; "Shosei jidai kara rōdōsha jidai e, tetsudō ninpu no bokkō 2, Tanaka Chūshichi no koto" in *Nichi-Bei shinbun* issued on December 14, 1924.

51. Ibid.

52. Ibid.

53. "Dai 2-hen dōhō hattenshi, dai 2-shō, tetsudō to dōhō" in *Rokkī to dōhō,* ed. Rokkī Jihō Henshūkyoku (Iida Shirō) (Rokkī Jihōsha, 1912), 4–8.

54. Ibid., 4.

55. *Zaibei Nihonjin shi,* 61–64.

56. Refer to the materials in the Gaimushō Gaikō Shiryōkan.

57. Bob Kumamoto, "The Search for Spies: The American Counterintelligence and the Japanese Community, 1931–1942," *Amerasia Journal* 6 (1979), 45–75; Jere Takahashi, "Japanese American Responses to Race Relations: The Formation of Nisei Perspectives," *Amerasia Journal* 9 (12), 29–57; and Roger Daniels, "Japanese America, 1930–1941: An Ethnic Community in the Great Depression," *Journal of the West* 24 (1985), 35–49.

58. Sakata, *Fading Footsteps of the Issei,* Akahori Family Papers, 25–51.

59. A conversation with Mr. Akahori from Sakata's personal notes.

60. For details on *Nihonjinkai* records, refer to Sakata, *Fading Footsteps of the Issei,* Japanese Associations, 131–42.

61. Sakata's personal notes.

62. Ibid.

63. Fukuzawa Yukichi, "Seiyō jijō, shohen" (Shōkodō, 1866) in *Fukuzawa Yukichi zenshū,* dai 9-kan (Iwanami Shoten, 1958), 275–608.

64. "Beikoku wa shishi no sumika nari" in *Jiji shinpō,* March 25, 1884; *Fukuzawa Yukichi zenshū,* dai 9-kan, 442–44.

65. "Ijūron no ben" in *Jiji shinpō,* April 12, 1884 gō; *Fukuzawa Yukichi zenshū,* dai 9-kan, 458.

66. For the difference of analytical concepts between *ijū* and *dekasegi* in studies of Japanese emigration history, refer to Sakata Yasuo, "Fubyōdō jōyaku to Amerika dekasegi" in *Hokubei Nihonjin Kirisutokyō undōshi,* ed. Dōshisha Daigaku Jinbun Kagaku Kenkyūjo (PMC Shuppan, 1991), 681–85, and pages 115–18 of chapter 2 of this volume, and Sakata Yasuo, "Nihonjin Amerika dekasegi no chiikisei no ichi kōsatsu (II)," *Ōsaka Gakuin Daigaku kokusaigaku ronshū dai 1-kan, dai 2-gō* (March 1991), 164–71.

67. Taguchi Ukichi, "Nan'yō keiryakuron" in *Tōkyō keizai zasshi* (1890); Kuroda Jōichi, *Nihon shokumin shisōshi* (Kōbundō, 1942), 223.

68. A Letter to Ōkuma Shigenobu, the minister of foreign affairs, in 1889. See Kuroda, *Nihon shokumin shisōshi,* 229–30.

69. Mutō Sanji, *Beikoku ijūron* (Maruzen Shōsha Shoten, 1887); *Mutō Sanji zenshū dai 1-kan* (Shinjusha, 1963), 273–92.

70. Mutō Sanji, *Beikoku ijūron*, 257, 277, and 279.

71. Shiga Shigetaka, "Hawai zairyū Nihon ijūmin" in *Nan'yō jiji* (Maruzen Shōsha Shoten, 1887), 176–95.

72. Refer to Sakata Yasuo, "Shōtotsuten e mukau kidō: Meijiki ni okeru Nihonjin no Amerika dekasegi (II)," in *Ōsaka Gakuin Daigaku kokusaigaku ronshū dai 3-kan, dai 2-gō* (December 1992), 49–61, and pages 185–94 of chapter 4 of this volume.

73. For example, refer to Kimitsu dai 18-gō, Meiji 25-nen 8-gatsu 4-ka, Chinda yori Enomoto ate, "Tōkoku Aidaho-shū ni oite tasū no Nihonjin hōchikuseraretaru ken guhin"; "Beikoku Aidaho-shū Yunion Pashifikku Tetsudō kōji ni jūjiseru honpōjin rōdōsha hōchiku jiken no tame Chinda Ryōji shucchō no ken" (July–September 1892) held at the Gaimushō Gaikō Shiryōkan; *Gaikō bunsho*, no. 25, 718–21; and Kōshin dai 25-gō, Meiji 26-nen 4-gatsu 6-ka, Zai Sōkō Ryōji Chinda Sutemi yori Gaimu Jikan Hayashi Tadasu ate, "Zaibei honpōjin tetsudō kōfu hakugai ni kanshi jōhō sōfu no ken" (Fuzokusho 1), Kakukō dai 11-gō utsushi, Meiji 26-nen 4-gatsu 6-ka, Chinda Ryōji yori Tokumei Zenken Kōshi Tateno Gōzō ate, "Dōjō no ken ni tsuki hōkoku" (Fuzokusho 4), Meiji 26-nen 3-gatsu 31-nichi, Tetsudō kōfu ukeoinin Ban Shinzaburō gushinsho, "Minami Taiheiyō Tetsudō shūgyō Nihon kōfu sōnan no ken" in *Gaikō bunsho*, no. 26, 710–19.

74. For example, refer to the *San Francisco Bulletin*, May 15, 1885; Kimitsu dai 1-gō, Meiji 28-nen 6-gatsu 12-nichi, Zai Sōkō Ryōji Kamiya Saburō yori Gaimu Daijin Rinji Dairi Saionji Kinmochi ate, "Sōkō shinbun Nihon dekasegi ni kansuru kiji o keisaishite sendōteki kōgekiron o shōdōshi hikite Gasshūkoku imin kensaku chihō ni shucchōshi honpō rōdōsha ni tsuki rōdō keiyaku no zonhi o torishirabetaru ken ni tsuki gushin"; "Hokubei Gasshūkoku ni okeru honpōjin seigen oyobi haiseki kankei ichiran dai 1" held at the Gaimushō Gaikō Shiryōkan. This article in the *Bulletin* criticized Japanese *dekasegi* laborers, stating that they were low-wage laborers who survived on only forty cents per day just like coolies.

75. "Japanese people were by no means wealthy . . . even today, while half the population is leading miserable impoverished lives, the other half is, to state without an exaggeration, still poor as well. That is not surprising at all. History shows that Japan's population has grown so much, to the point that even thirty years ago Japan ran out of land to grow their food. Therefore, many Japanese are barely scraping by, severely economizing on their food. Infanticide is a common practice. Starvation frequently occurred. Epidemics and sexually transmitted diseases are widespread in every region, even today leaving traces in their bodies. . . . In this country, only a small number of people are well-mannered. . . . Ninety-five percent of Japanese immigrants to America are 'coolies' or similar poor farmers." "Immigration of Japanese," a report submitted by the commissioner general of immigration, May 15, 1900: US Congress, H.R. Doc. No. 686, 56th Cong., 1st Sess. (Washington, DC: Government Printing Office, 1900).

76. Akira Iriye, *Pacific Estrangement: Japanese and American Expansion, 1897–1911* (Cambridge, MA: Harvard University Press, 1972), 43–45.

77. Takahashi Sakue, *Nichi-Bei no shinkankei* (Shimizu Shoten, 1910), 2–3.

78. Abe Isoo, *Hokubei no shin Nihon* (Hakubunkan, 1905), 119.

79. For *tobei annai*, refer to Imai (Kumei) Teruko, "Meijiki ni okeru tobei-netsu to tobei annaisho oyobi tobei zasshi" in *Tsudajuku Daigaku kiyō* dai 16-gō (March 1984), 305–42.

80. Akamine Seichirō, *Beikoku ima fushigi* (Jitsugakukai Eigakkō, 1886), 20–25.

81. "It is admirable that the government of the United States publicly permitted the prostitution business. If prostitutes are prohibited from conducting their prosperous illegal sales, it is much worse not to hunt evil women that lead young men astray in the mountains of the hell. Even though having a mistress is taboo in the United States, there are quite a few people who, by cleverly skirting the public eyes and the law, keep mistresses. There are many people who play around with mistresses and lovers under the mask of visiting temples" (Akamine, *Beikoku ima fushigi*, 61–62).

82. Ishida Kumajirō, *Kitare Nihonjin: ichimei Sōkō tabi annai* (Kaishindō, 1886), 4.

83. Takeuchi Kōjirō, *Beikoku seihokubu Nihon iminshi*, 2-satsu, Fukkokuban (Yūshōdō, 1994).

84. The descriptions about the war and postwar periods, such as relocation during the war, may have been evaluated differently.

85. There are no accurate statistics detailing Japanese emigration statistics by prefecture. There are two kinds of charts in yearbooks and other materials issued by Japanese-language newspapers in the United States. One estimates the prefectures that produced most Japanese emigrants on the basis of the statistics of origin places of passengers; the other estimates it from the amount of money emigrants sent to their hometowns. Takeda Jun'ichi, "1925-nendo kenbetsu sōkindaka hyō" in *Zaibei Hiroshima kenjinshi* (Zaibei Hiroshima Kenjinshi Hakkōjo, 1929), 32–33, lists the ranking from the top: Hiroshima, Wakayama, Okayama, Fukuoka, Yamaguchi, Kumamoto, Shizuoka, Mie, Shiga, Kagoshima, Fukushima, Fukui, Tottori, and Ehime.

86. The titles are different from the first volume and the second volume. The title of the first volume is "Zaibei honpōjin no jōkyō narabini tobeisha torishimari kankei zassan" and the second volume is titled "Zaibei honpōjin no jōkyō narabini tobeisha torishimari kankei zakken."

87. These reports are included in "Hokubei ni oite honpō imin seigen narabini haiseki no ken" in *Nihon gaikō bunsho*.

88. Refer to the account under the subheading "The 'Idaho Incident,' a Rewritten History," in this chapter.

89. Among the consular reports, the earlier serial publications on commerce and trade are collected in annually published *Meiji 14-nen Tsūshō isan* (July 1882), ed. Gaimushō Kirokukyoku. From 1883, they were compiled into two publications a year. Starting from 1883, these were published twice a year. Continuing the genre, starting from 1886, *Tsūshō isan* were published as *Tsūshō hōkoku* several times a year until the publication ended in December 1889. Afterward, from January 1890, the column of *Tsūshō hōkoku* began publishing in *Kanpō*. In addition, in January 1894, the Trade Bureau of the Ministry of Foreign Affairs started compiling and publishing *Tsūshō isan* once a month, in which *Tsūshō hōkoku* were included (refer to Tsunoyama Sakae, *Kaisetsu, Ryōji hōkoku shiryō*; and *Maikurofirumuban Ryōji hōkoku shiryō shūroku mokuroku*, ed. Tsunoyama Sakae and Takashima Masaaki [Yūshōdō Firumu Shuppan, 1983], 9–10). These *Tsūshō hōkoku* included consular reports on living conditions, economic activities, and population statistics of Japanese residing overseas. Furthermore, emigration was under the supervision of Gaimushō Tsūshōkyoku. These *Ryōji hōkoku shiryō* regarding commerce and trade were reprinted and made available as microfilm.

CHAPTER 2

Unequal Treaties and Japanese Migrant Workers in the United States

About 150 Japanese overseas migrant workers—so-called *gannen-mono* (named after the first year of Meiji, or *gannen*, and the term for person, *mono*)—sailed to Hawaiʻi in 1868. The second major Japanese overseas labor migration took another seventeen years: the first government overseas contract workers, about 940 of them, were dispatched from Yokohama to Hawaiʻi in January 1885.[1] It has been suggested that during these seventeen years the Meiji government did not permit or condone Japanese overseas migration; no one, however, has provided a convincing explanation of why that was the case.[2] In other words, these seventeen years have been considered a period not worthy of serious study in Japanese emigration history. There does exist research on *gannenmono* contract workers in Hawaiʻi, but there has been no research relating to these two events in the context of Japanese history during the Meiji era.

In discussions about Japanese overseas emigration in the Meiji era, I would argue that this pre-1885 era is analogous to "prehistory." It is true that Japanese people generally did not migrate overseas during this period. For example, according to immigration statistics from the US government, fewer than five Japanese people entered the country annually between 1874 and 1880.[3] This statistical evidence, however, does not indicate a lack of historical importance.

This paper was translated from Sakata Yasuo, "Fubyōdō jōyaku to Amerika dekasegi," in *Hokubei Nihonjin Kirisutokyō undōshi*, ed. Dōshisha Daigaku Jinbun Kagaku Kenkyūjo (Tokyo: PMC Shuppan, 1991), 627–703.

It may also be said that research until now has not focused on the relationship between the overseas *dekasegi* laborers in the early Meiji era and the unequal treaties at the time. For example, one of the unequal treaties, the *Kaizei yakusho* (Tariff Convention), signed in 1866, allowed Japanese to travel overseas for the first time after the closed-door policy of the pre-Meiji *bakufu* (Tokugawa shogunate) government. Scholars have not given this serious consideration. In addition, it is a little-known fact that Article VIII of the 1858 *Nichi-Ei shūkō tsūshō jōyaku* (Anglo-Japanese Treaty of Amity and Commerce) stipulated that subjects and citizens of the treaty countries could hire Japanese people for any purpose and would not be subject to Japanese law at open ports.[4]

The stipulations for the hiring of Japanese workers in the unequal treaties meant that foreign residents could hire Japanese in open ports without restrictions. Moreover, the treaty guaranteed that Japanese could travel overseas. Therefore, it would be difficult, if not impossible, for the Japanese government, in particular the pre-Meiji *bakufu* government that had signed the unequal treaties, to legally prevent Japanese being hired by foreigners to be taken out of the country. It was in this context that the overseas travel of *gannenmono* to Hawai'i occurred. Therefore, the conditions would have been ripe for another *gannenmono* incident, even if not to the same horrific degree as that of the "coolie trade" in China or the situation of the contracted laborers in the British West Indies. It was fortunate for the Meiji government, before and after the Restoration, that such a series of events did not occur.

In this article, I aim to shed light on the understudied relationship between the unequal treaties and Japanese migrant workers in the early Meiji era—a significant area in the history of Japanese emigration to the United States. In addition, I aim to explain the influences behind the Japanese emigration to the United States during the middle and late Meiji era. In doing so, I hope to explain the reasons why Japanese migration stopped until the arrival in Hawai'i of the officially government-contracted *dekasegi* (working away from home) laborers, why Japanese migration to Hawai'i took the form of contract labor, and why the Japanese government implemented regulations to protect the contract *dekasegi* laborers in the name of the *Imin hogohō*

(Emigrant Protection Act), accelerating friction between Japan and the United States. It is important to remember that this timing coincided with the establishment of the Immigration Bureau in the United States, which effectively banned contract migrant workers in the 1890s, making it difficult for Japanese migrant laborers to enter the United States.

The Unequal Treaties and Provisions for the Employment of Japanese People

Townsend Harris and Japanese Servants

In 1856, the first American representative, Townsend Harris, came to Japan to sign the Treaty of Amity and Commerce. As the first representative of a Western government, he opened the first US consulate in Shimoda. By then, the *bakufu* government had already signed a convention with Western nations in 1854 and "opened" the country to foreigners. The Japanese, however, were not ready to welcome foreign dignitaries such as Harris after having suffered the arrival of the black ships of the Perry expedition in 1853. With a two-century gap in negotiating skills vis-à-vis Western countries, officials of the magistrate's office in Shimoda did not have the experience or knowledge that would be useful in interacting with Harris. Even the members of the *bakufu* government who favored the opening of Japan had only limited experience [with the Dutch] in Dejima, Nagasaki, during [the Edo period of] isolationist foreign policy and negotiating with foreign dignitaries after 1852. Therefore, one could hardly expect them to be able to practice Western-style diplomacy or to give a response comprehensible to Western societies. It is not surprising that misunderstandings and friction occurred between the two parties after Harris's landing in Shimoda. One of these disputes was about the hiring of servants.[5]

Harris had requested that the magistrate's office in Shimoda arrange for the employment of two domestic servants, but the magistrates did not know how to reply.[6] On this matter, the magistrate's office needed to receive a judgment from the *bakufu* government; and to begin with, the *bakufu* had considered Harris's landing as temporary.[7] Furthermore, the employing of servants was understood to be possible only under a feudal master-subject relationship. Therefore, the *bakufu* was not willing to entertain Harris's request.

Thus Harris himself had to take care of the household duties, including cooking and cleaning, and became irritated with the magistrate's office. For Harris, a request for domestic servants should have been easily responded to by the next day. A *shihai chōyaku* (official dealing with international relations) at the magistrate's office, Moriyama Takichirō, reported that Harris appeared to be unwell.[8] To add insult to injury, the magistrate's office was planning to deploy guards at the consulate at Gyokusenji Temple in order to "protect" him, which had raised Harris's suspicions.[9]

Harris immediately protested the deployment of guards, for he knew that the role of the guards was to monitor him and was thus a violation of his diplomatic immunity. Immediately after arriving, Harris had explained to the magistrate's office that no one should be allowed to enter his residence.[10] Moreover, monitoring by the guards would mean that the "Deshima prison" (the *bakufu* government's confinement of the Dutch to the small island of Dejima, off the coast of Nagasaki) would be repeated at Shimoda, an idea that he abhorred.[11]

Harris was not the only one to feel that way; many other Western diplomats concerned with the signing of the Treaty of Amity and Commerce had labeled the "Deshima prison" as one of the evils of the Japanese closed-door policy. They felt that they needed to protest strongly against possible restrictive living conditions; otherwise they would succumb to the same insulting fate of the Dutch at Dejima. It was a grave mistake on the part of the magistrate's office to have unnecessarily instigated memories of Dejima, for it led Harris to suspect that the magistrate's office would have any domestic servants that he hired spy on him.[12]

Harris thus became more suspicious of the *bakufu* government's intentions, and his attitude grew increasingly adversarial as the magistrate's office delayed its response to his requests, saying that it was still waiting for an answer from the Tokugawa government. Harris then set a deadline and demanded that the magistrate's office either give him a reasonable reply or give him servants. In the end, although he forcibly obtained two servants from the magistrate's office, the two parties were still not on mutual terms of agreement.[13]

The hiring of servants had the unintended consequence of bringing potentially more serious issues to the surface. The magistrate's office, given the urgent circumstances, supplied servants at the rank of *ashigaru* (low-level samurai allowed to bear arms). Harris, however, did not think that he would need permission from the *bakufu* government when he later wanted those servants to accompany him on an American ship to sail to Hakodate or Shanghai. The bureaucratic red tape further angered Harris, and this incident created a precedent that would trouble the government in the future.[14]

The Nichi-Bei Tsūshō Jōyaku *(Treaty of Amity and Commerce between the United States and the Empire of Japan) and Regulations for the Hiring of Japanese People*

Having had a bitter experience in Shimoda, Harris attempted to resolve the issue by negotiating a treaty that would allow the hiring of Japanese people, despite the concerns of the *bakufu* government. As soon as Harris arrived in Edo (modern-day Tokyo) in October 1857, he handed to the government an English draft of the treaty he had prepared in Shimoda. Article III included this provision: "Americans residing in Japan shall have the right to hire Japanese people as servants or in any capacity." [15]

That clause indicates that Harris tried to have the *bakufu* approve the hiring of Japanese, most likely without the interference of the Japanese government, as a basic privilege given to Americans in Japan. The Japanese translation prepared by the *bakufu* government, however, stipulated that "Americans residing in Japan have permission to hire and transport Japanese to other locations." [16] The translation of the English word *right* into the Japanese word *menkyo* (permission) suggests that the government considered it similar to hiring licensees as stipulated in the *Nichi-Ran tsuika jōyaku* (Japanese-Dutch Supplementary Treaty) signed in August of the same year.[17]

Harris did not accept the idiosyncrasies of the Japanese government's interpretation. The Japanese government would have dealt with more fundamental issues had it understood the essence of the English version. For example, Japanese who were likely to be employed at ports included sailors working on foreign ships as a matter of course. Hiring them would violate the Japanese government's prohibition, a serious issue for the *bakufu* government. For his part, Harris did not consider it a worrisome issue, as he had taken servants out of the country. The consensus among the treaty nations was that the Japanese ban on overseas travel was a violation of the Commerce Treaty and should absolutely be abolished.[18]

At this point, however, few people in the *bakufu* government had thought that opening the country would mean abolishing the longstanding legacy policy of prohibiting Japanese from traveling abroad. As a result, the members of the *bakufu* government discussed specific regulations rather than dealing with the fundamental issue of what the Western government considered to be a "barrier to the successful execution of the Commerce Treaty." They were preoccupied with establishing that Japanese government officials would process applications for the hiring of Japanese by foreigners and that no sword-bearing samurai would be hired by foreigners.[19] This obliviousness revealed a major discrepancy between the two parties.

Perhaps as a result, the different conceptions in the Japanese and English versions of the treaty did not become an issue during the course of the thirteen dialogues between Harris and the *bakufu* government plenipotentiaries.[20] Those negotiations, which involved a cumbersome process of multiple layers of translation from English into Dutch and further into Japanese, might have been why nobody appears to have noticed these differences. Alternatively, one could surmise that the *bakufu* government purposely neglected the issue and thus might have avoided it altogether.

The English version pertaining to the hiring of Japanese in the Treaty of Amity and Commerce was signed without any revisions in June 1858. The Japanese translation noted that it was a process of permission rather than a right, noting that "Americans residing in Japan are permitted to hire *senmin* [lower-class persons] for household duties."[21] It is also important to note that employment was limited to *senmin*.[22] Furthermore, *Kanagawa-kō kisokusho* (Rules Concerning the Kanagawa Port), which the Kanagawa magistrate's office had requested the *rōjū* (Council of Elders) to approve before the Yokohama port was opened in July 1859, stipulated that the hiring of *senmin* was within the jurisdiction of Japanese government officials.[23]

The Anglo-Japanese Treaty of Amity and Commerce
and the Hiring Clause: Ulterior Motives

The Anglo-Japanese Treaty of Amity and Commerce was signed on July 18, 1858, pushing the Japanese commitment even further beyond the Japanese government's understanding, when the British government delegate, Lord Elgin, arrived in Japan after signing the Commerce Treaty with Qing delegates in Tientsin (Tianjin). By then, the Japanese government had already signed commerce treaties with the United States, the Netherlands, and Russia. It has been pointed out that the Anglo-Japanese Treaty was modeled after the US-Japan Treaty, and the two differed very little in key provisions. However, this assessment does not evaluate the differences between the two treaties in the clause concerning the employment of Japanese.[24] The clause of Japanese employment became a separate article in the Anglo-Japanese Treaty as opposed to its inclusion within Article III in the US-Japan Treaty. The Japanese translation said that a British subject residing in Japan could have no restriction on hiring *senmin* for various purposes; the English translation said that "the Japanese Government will place no restriction whatever upon the employment, by British subjects, of Japanese in any lawful capacity."[25] As one can see, this article was completely different from the stipulation in the US-Japan Treaty.

It is hard to imagine that the *bakufu* government made a concession that changed *permission* to *no restriction*. The Japanese version of the Anglo-Japanese Treaty is similar to that of the US-Japan Treaty, saying that the Japanese government would not obstruct the employment procedure under the jurisdiction of the Japanese officials, which can mean in the Japanese language that the Japanese procedure would not be inhibited and that the matter would remain under the jurisdiction of Japanese officials. This interpretation probably reflected the Japanese plenipotentiary's idea of "permission." The English, in contrary, left no room for the *bakufu* government to make such an interpretation, insisting on the notion of placing "no restriction whatever" on the hiring of Japanese employees.

In actuality, the British determination to drive the *bakufu* into a corner was hidden in Article VIII. One can surmise that the real purpose of inserting the provision of hiring Japanese into the Anglo-Japanese

Treaty was to annul the closed-door policy, particularly the banning of overseas travel by the Japanese. The comparison between the two treaties reveals that Article VIII of the Anglo-Japanese Treaty is a copy of Article XIII of the Tientsin Treaty that Lord Elgin had negotiated with the Qing Court in 1858. It simply replaced *Chinese* with *Japanese*: "The Chinese Government will place no restriction whatever upon the employment, by British subjects, of Chinese in any lawful capacity."[26]

Why did Lord Elgin negotiate to include this hiring clause in the Tientsin Treaty? Like the *bakufu* government, the Qing Court had banned Chinese from traveling abroad, and their return after emigration and long-term sojourns overseas since 1721 was under penalty of death. The Qing Court also did not intend to remove or abolish the travel ban even after it opened five ports for trade with four Western countries subsequent to its defeat in the Opium War and the signing of the Nanjing Treaty in 1842. After the Arrow War that started in 1856, Lord Elgin, instructed by the British government and backed by the British and French navies, inserted Article XIII of the Treaty of Tientsin signed in 1858, forcing the Qing Court to recognize the realities of opening the country and allowing Chinese travel overseas.[27] I would argue that both Article XIII and Article VIII of the 1858 Anglo-Japanese Treaty of Amity and Commerce reflected similar intentions of the British government, given their identical language.

Let's turn to China to explain the historical background in more detail.

Unequal Treaties and Government Approval of Overseas Contract Workers: A Case Study in China

The Coolie Trade

The European colonies in the West Indies and South Africa, particularly the British colonies, where slavery was abolished in 1833, suffered severe labor shortages in the 1840s. The European powers had hoped for massive migration by the Chinese—who were believed to have suffered poverty under a tyrannical rule—once China opened its doors in 1842. The Qing Court, however, did not abolish the travel ban, and traveling to South America and the West Indies would have been difficult given the high cost and long distance. As a result, Chinese migration to the colonies was not as large as had been hoped.[28]

Some colonies, however, lacking prospects for economic improvement, expressed a strong desire for the migration of slavelike laborers who were willing to work for minimum wages under adverse conditions. Against this backdrop, the illegal "coolie trade" began at Chinese ports, with Amoy (Xiamen) becoming the center of activities beginning in 1845.[29]

The coolie trade peaked in the first half of the 1850s, but, as reported by the British governor of Hong Kong, John Bowring, it was indistinguishable from a slave trade.[30] Chinese crimps hired by foreign trading posts would collect "coolies" and transport them to barracoons, or slave barracks. These crimps often forcibly recruited workers through means such as blackmail and abduction to meet the demand for labor. It would have been almost impossible to escape from the guarded barracoons; according to Hosea Morse, "their clothes were stripped away and coded destinations were painted on their chests, such as C for Cuba, P for Peru, and S for Sandwich Islands (the South Georgia and the South Sandwich Islands)."[31] Occasionally the victims in transport would revolt on the ship and murder the captain and crew.

Despite the risks involved, due to the large profitability of the coolie trade, nearly all the foreign trading companies were involved, led by Tait & Co.[32] Many ships under British and United States flags were used to transport coolies, and the British and US governments and their diplomats at first turned a blind eye to the criticism of the trade as evil or atrocious, stating that the shipment or transportation of coolies did not conflict with their laws. Instead they criticized the Chinese local officials' corruption for not controlling the illegal acts by Chinese recruiting agents.[33]

That, however, was just an excuse. Although Chinese police sometimes arrested Chinese coolie-recruiting agents, foreign trading houses such as Tait & Co. had the agents released from the police in the name of diplomatic immunity. Therefore, the agents came to behave so ruthlessly that they would recruit coolies openly during the day. As a result, Chinese residents could no longer feel secure in Amoy and the neighboring towns because British trading houses were the most aggressive in coolie recruitment. Frequent murders of British soldiers and sailors by Chinese can be attributed to these rising anti-British sentiments. Ministers and consuls, who had until that point turned a blind eye to the trade, began to advocate stricter control to the British government.[34]

The inhumane behavior among the British residing in Chinese ports, the slavelike working conditions, and the maltreatment of coolie workers in Peru and Cuba soon became known in Britain. Public opinion that culminated in the establishment of an antislavery law in the British colonies in 1833 thus resurfaced. The public sharply criticized the government for not regulating the coolie trade. By 1855, the British government had enacted the Chinese Passenger Act, requiring British ships carrying Chinese from any Chinese open port to dock in Hong Kong for inspection. As a result, by the second half of the 1850s it had become difficult to take coolies directly from Chinese open ports, so the trade flourished in Macau, a Portuguese territory. The coolie recruiters, however, moved from Amoy to Canton (Guangdong) located near Macau, further fueling anti-British sentiment that had never fizzled out after the Opium War.[35]

The Labor Shortage in British Colonies and the British Government's Policy toward Chinese Migrant Workers

The British government, in particular the Ministry for Immigration, was sympathetic to the colonizers of the British West Indies regarding their labor shortage in sugar plantations, but they could not ignore public opinion and had thus strictly forbidden coolie workers to be transported to those colonies. By the second half of the 1840s, many sugar plantations had become bankrupt. Against that backdrop, by the beginning of the 1850s, the British government and the colonial governments had begun to exchange opinions on how to institutionalize the importation of Chinese contract workers and what types of measurements should be taken to avoid the practice of the coolie trade. By the mid-1850s they had reached a consensus that the Qing Court had to permit overseas travel by Chinese and allow recruiters authorized by the British government to openly recruit contract workers.[36]

Although the transportation of coolies from Chinese open ports had become difficult, the coolie recruiters still engaged in illegal practices.

In addition, by the second half of the 1850s Canton, near the dispatch-ing port of Macau, replaced Amoy as the supply center of coolie labor-ers. The British were frequently attacked in Shanghai and Canton, the center of British trade in China. The British minister and consuls resid-ing in China strongly hoped that the coolie trade would end. To accom-plish that, as a first step they wanted the Qing Court to allow overseas travel by Chinese and to ban or institute stricter regulations on the coolie trade. Despite differences in the exact plans and in their rea-soning, the government officials in British colonies and the diplomats residing in China were united on that front. The Qing Court, which had refused to face the reality of opening the country and banned Chinese overseas travel, however, did not acknowledge the practice of the illegal coolie trade and turned a blind eye to it. Judging from the court's previous obstinacy, the British had no prospect of persuading it to permit Chinese overseas travel or regulating the coolie trade through diplomatic routes.[37]

The Occupation of Canton and Overseas Contract Workers

The Arrow Incident and the subsequent Second Opium War gave the British an opportunity to threaten the Qing Court with their power, demanding that the court accept their conditions. The Arrow Incident occurred on October 8, 1856, when Chinese soldiers came on board the *Arrow*, a Chinese-owned Hong Kong ship with a British-Irish cap-tain and Chinese crew members, and demanded that the British flag be rolled down. The soldiers abducted twelve Chinese crew members who were suspected of piracy. After this incident, negotiations fell through between Harry Parkes, the British consul at Canton, and Imperial Commissioner and Viceroy of Liangguag Ye Mingchen. The British Navy launched a military action on October 29 and temporarily occu-pied the Zongli Yamen, the Qing Court body in charge of foreign pol-icy. The British government, having accepted the decision made by its diplomats, dispatched 5,000 troops led by Lord Elgin, plenipotentiary, despite the opposition of the House of Commons. The French gov-ernment also decided to dispatch troops to China led by Baron Jean-Baptiste Louis Gros, plenipotentiary. On December 12, 1857, a British and French alliance declared war and occupied Canton by December 29 and captured Ye Mingchen.[38]

In Canton, having been isolated by the central government in Beijing due to its occupation by foreign powers, British consul Rutherford Alcock and the British commissioner of the allied forces, Harry Parkes, demanded that Governor Bo Gui announce the banning of coolie recruitment on April 9, 1859. This announcement included a clause that implied that Chinese employed by foreigners would be officially allowed to travel abroad.[39] The true purpose of this declaration was to institutionalize the transportation of contract laborers to the West Indies. The British intention is clearly displayed in a letter from Alcock to Governor Bowring:

> By this proclamation, a step has been taken on the part of the Chinese high authorities of extremely [*sic*] significance in regard to the free emigration of labourers from China, which has now been legalized. Out of a great evil, therefore, a greater good has come, and an advantage has been gained in the interests of all Colonies requiring labour, which, but for these occurrences, might have been sought for in vain.[40]

This announcement of the British government forced Chinese officials in occupied Canton to make the announcement without the Qing Court's approval. One has to say that the British demonstrated an arrogant attitude in announcing that the "free immigration of laborers . . . has now been legalized." Immediately after that declaration was issued, a sugar plantation agent in the West Indies applied to Bo Gui to establish an emigration house to recruit contract laborers. Parkes wrote in a report addressed to the Ministry of Foreign Affairs and dated November 13, 1859, that "they have established an institution to send contract laborers to the West Indies following the approval of the Canton government."[41] British minister Frederick Bruce told Lord Russel that Parkes had made a meaningful social contribution. With this, Parkes predicted that Chinese overseas migration would begin.[42] Bruce also mentioned that the establishment of contract laborers would make the "malpractice and inhumane treatment of coolie trade a thing of the past." Both Parkes and Bruce treated China as if it were British territory.[43]

Trade Treaties and the Approval of Overseas Travel

The Qing Court in Beijing still refused to negotiate trade treaties even after the occupation of Canton by the British and French allied forces after the Second Opium War. The French forces that were stationed in Canton took military action in Beijing and occupied the Taku Forts in April 1858. This action forced the Qing Court to begin negotiations with Lord Elgin in Tianjin, and finally the Treaty of Tientsin was signed on June 26, 1858.[44] Lord Elgin, who was instructed to have the Qing Court remove the ban of Chinese overseas travel, departed from Britain. Elgin, however, judged that the timing was not right for this negotiation; he wanted to make sure that the Qing Court would include a clause related to employment in the treaty (aiming to control the coolie trade in occupied Canton) and to have the Qing Court allow overseas travel (Article XIII).[45]

The remaining issue was when the British should make the Qing Court legalize overseas travel. The timing came unexpectedly early. The Qing Court rejected the British and French representatives from entering Beijing to ratify the Tientsin Treaty. The British and French navies were dispatched to the Taku Forts but were attacked and dispelled in August 1860. Then the negotiation in Tianjin fell apart; forty officials, including Parkes, the British commissioner of the allied forces, were captured and taken to Beijing. To retaliate, Britain and France sent a 20,000-man army to enter Beijing and plunder and destroy the Old Summer Palace. The emperor escaped to a remote palace in Rehe province, but Prince Gong, who had stayed in Beijing, received an ultimatum from the allied forces, and signed the Peking Convention with Lord Elgin and Baron Gros.[46] Some scholars explain that Article V, signed on October 24 and commonly called the Emigration Clause, legalized Chinese travel overseas.[47]

Article V, however, clearly states that "Chinese, in choosing to take service in British Colonies or other parts beyond sea, are at perfect liberty to enter into engagements with British subjects for that purpose, and to ship themselves and their families on board any British vessels."[48] Its true purpose was to make the Qing Court approve, in the form of treaty provisions, the recruitment and shipment of contract laborers to plantations in the West Indies. The official authorization of Chinese travel abroad is nothing but a side product of these negotiations.

The Approval of Overseas Travel in Japan

The Convention of Peking and Its Influence in Japan

Perhaps Lord Elgin was planning to implement an article in Japan pertaining to employment similar to the Convention of Peking.[49] When the Treaty of Amity and Commerce between the United States and Japan was signed, one could predict a similar fate for Japan. Westerners were already aware that even if the *bakufu* government opened Japanese ports to Western countries, it would continue to feel no sense of urgency for immediately abolishing its long-standing isolation policy or promoting overseas trade. The dispute over Article VIII of the Anglo-Japanese Treaty, which occurred in June 1859 immediately after the ports were opened, had already demonstrated that the *bakufu* government had no intention of changing its policy.

British minister Alcock (the former consul general), who took over the negotiations from Harris, the US minister, brought "gunboat diplomacy" to the British Far East. A veteran diplomat in opening Chinese ports, he aided Commissioner Parkes and the British consul general in Canton when the system of Chinese contract laborers was established in occupied Canton. Alcock, who despised the *bakufu* officials—who, like the Qing bureaucrats, would not abandon outdated practices—went to Japan determined to confront these officials with whatever it took.[50] If the British colonies had strongly demanded Japanese laborers just as they had with the Chinese, the *bakufu* government would have been forced to permit the travel of Japanese contract laborers overseas. The *bakufu* government, however, was able to avoid the Qing Court's fate.

What was fortunate for Japan was that the demand for low-wage laborers was already being met by the Chinese at Chinese ports, probably including the demand for sailors on British ships. Consequently, the recruitment and transportation of contract laborers did not become a diplomatic issue in Japan.

Daily needs in Japan, however, created disputes in Japan between Westerners and *bakufu* officials. Many traditional Japanese practices puzzled the Westerners. These included the system of *shinōkōshō* (which set the four social classes as samurai, peasants, artisans, and merchants) and the employment of domestic servants and *niageninpu* (cargo-delivery staff) through *kuchiiregyō* (middlemen). In addition, immediately after the opening of ports, most Japanese wanted to avoid contact with Westerners. Even without the *bakufu* officials' interference, employing Japanese at the open ports would have been a frustrating nuisance for Westerners. On top of that, the *bakufu* government would not alter its policy that government officials should be in charge of employment. As a result, Westerners at open ports could not employ Japanese as they wished, an inconvenient situation for them. Therefore, at a meeting in Kanagawa, Westerners residing in Japan discussed the violation of Article VIII, and they strongly wanted to remove the old law and outdated practice, considering it a trade barrier.[51]

Stipulation of Japanese Employment and the Bakufu's Perspective

In June 1859, as expected, servants employed by ministers and consuls general of the treaty nations boarded ships immediately after the opening of the Kanagawa port. Even as trade with foreign countries began, the *bakufu* did not change its principal policy of forbidding Japanese from boarding foreign ships, and the treaty nations did not know how to respond.[52]

As expected, the foreign magistrate decided it would be impossible to prevent the ministers and consuls general, in particular, from hiring *senmin*, as the treaty clearly stipulated it. There was concern, however, that Japanese traveling overseas without permission would cause Japan to suffer negative consequences. The foreign magistrate submitted a recommendation to the *rōjū*: Those who wished to employ Japanese should submit a certificate to the minister; otherwise they would be fined regardless of the social status of the employed. Sailors, who were free to travel only within Japan, were also to be prohibited from traveling overseas. Harris, who had taken *ashigaru* (low-level samurai or foot soldiers) out of the country without receiving permission, would have been upset again had he heard that recommendation.[53]

In addition, British consul general Alcock went to the *rōjū* in October 1859, demanding to have samurai accompany him because foreigners were being attacked by *jōi rōnin* (anti-foreigner masterless samurai). Alcock specified that his attendants should be "Japanese of relatively high status and well cultivated, preferably the sons of officials." In addition, he said, "my security attendants should exemplify my respectful position as Consul General in Japan. He will be compensated or paid for his exclusive duty to me without any restrictions." [54] The specific conditions stated in Alcock's correspondence would have been unimaginable during the Edo period (1603–1868), for example, "two servants dressed like samurai and carrying swords," or sons of *hatamoto* (samurai directly working for the shogunate) and *gokenin* (direct vassals of the shogunate) working for foreigners as bodyguards and compensated for their duties.

In this case as well, the Japanese foreign magistrate, noting the example of Harris in Shimoda having been presented with two *ashigaru* from the magistrate's office as servants, decided that he would be unable to deny a request for samurai from ministers and consuls general. However, the accounting *kanjō bugyō* (magistrates) opposed this proposal, saying that samurai, once employed, would become a foreigner's servant, forming a master-servant relationship. Furthermore, they emphasized that even if Japan was obliged to supply servants to foreigners, it had to make sure that the foreign parties understood that it was a temporary hire. In addition, *metsuke* (inspectors) were absolutely opposed to this plan, saying that allowing a low-class servant to wear two swords would be egregious because carrying two swords was considered to be the most important way of protecting oneself and one's master. They criticized the careless action of the Shimoda magistrate for allowing Harris to take Japanese servants out of the country, "causing permanent damage." [55] Alcock, however, did not take their arguments seriously.

The *hyōteisho* (High Court) discussed another case, the punishment of the *yūjo* (prostitute) Hananoka in Nagasaki, who was forced to drink Western alcohol by a Frenchman on a ship. She became so intoxicated that she did not notice when the ship left for Shanghai. She was sentenced to five months in prison, and the *hyōteisho* sent her cross-examination report to the French consulate in Nagasaki. [56]

Growing Dissatisfaction among Foreign Residents in Japan

Foreigners residing in Japanese open ports naturally wished to employ Japanese freely; however, Japanese employment was under the jurisdiction of *bakufu* officials. The *unjōsho*, a *bakufu* body that collected transportation taxes, strictly adhered to the *Kanagawa-kō kisokusho* (Rules Concerning the Kanagawa Port) regarding the hiring of *senmin* by foreigners. Westerners couldn't tolerate their intervention.[57] Alcock called this attitude absurd, since the American missionaries could hire two Japanese women as servants only after paying an exorbitant amount of money to a brothel. In addition, Alcock pointed out that Japanese government officials pocketed half the requested money, implying that Japanese officials were corrupt just like Chinese bureaucrats.[58]

Reverting to pretreaty conditions of Japanese employment by foreigners was not up to the *hyōteisho* court. In fact, the conditions deteriorated every year. The foreign ministers made firm protests many times in 1860 against government intervention in the employment of Japanese by foreigners. They argued to the *rōjū* that the *unjōsho's* intervention in Japanese employment was a violation of Article VIII of the Anglo-Japanese Treaty, which guaranteed the ability of foreigners to hire Japanese without any restrictions. The foreign ministers criticized not only the inflexibility of the *bakufu* officials but also the traditional Japanese *oyakata* (master-apprentice) system.[59] What the treaty countries requested was freedom of employment, but the *bakufu* government clearly did not understand what "employment at liberty" meant.

The London Protocol (1862) and Freedom of Employment

Alcock was not satisfied with the *bakufu* government's not recognizing its obligation to adhere to the treaties and attempting to negate its responsibilities by making an excuse at every possible occasion. Alcock also was aware that the Japanese political and economic situations were not stable and that strong demands to resolve outstanding issues might trigger the collapse of the ailing *bakufu's* central government."[60]

Therefore, when the *bakufu* government was in no condition to open the Kobe and Niigata ports and the cities of Edo and Osaka to foreigners as stipulated by the *Ansei no gokakoku jōyaku* (Ansei Five-Power

Treaties), Alcock recommended that the United Kingdom government accept the *bakufu* government's postponement request. In exchange for accepting the request, Alcock decided that he would ensure that the *bakufu* government would adhere to the treaties and remove trade barriers.[61]

By the end of 1862, the *bakufu* government had dispatched delegates to the United Kingdom and France to negotiate directly, as Alcock had recommended. The London Protocol stipulated that they would specifically do away with six articles, including Article II, regarding the *bakufu* intervention in Japanese employment by foreigners. As translated, the Japanese lines read: "Refusal on the hire of craftsmen, and more particularly on the hire of carpenters, boatmen, coolies, teachers, and servants of whatever denomination" is to be removed.

On the other hand, the English version reads: "All restrictions on labor, and more particularly on the hire of carpenters, boatmen, coolies, teachers, and servants of whatever denomination" are to be abolished.

The differences between the Japanese and English versions are clear.[62] The *bakufu* delegates accepted the London Protocol; however, what enraged Alcock was that they proposed conducting hiring practices as usual, an unacceptable proposal to Western countries.[63] The *bakufu* government did not want to concede on this matter, perhaps creating its ambiguous Japanese translation. But in the end, by agreeing to sign this protocol, the *bakufu* government was past the point of no return in allowing foreigners to hire Japanese.

The New Tariff Convention and Approval of Japanese Travel Abroad

The British minister in Shanghai, Parkes, replaced Alcock as the minister in Japan after the latter returned to Britain after the successful attack on Shimonoseki in the Chōshū Domain by Britain, the United States, the Netherlands, and France. Parkes had been in China from the age of thirteen and fought in the Opium War, later serving as a translator at the consulate and as consul himself for more than twenty years altogether. He was appointed as a British commissioner of the allied forces in Canton, then occupied by Britain and France, and worked closely with Alcock during the Arrow War. With this background,

Parkes was an experienced diplomat and, known as a "port-opening diplomat," became a capable successor to Alcock.[64]

The British government had expected Harris to settle a tariff issue: that is, to convince the *bakufu* government to revise the tax clauses of the Ansei Treaties and accept the ad valorem tax rate of 5 percent, as had already been done with the Qing Court to resolve a source of British discontent. Similarly, the British government strongly hoped that the *bakufu* government would adhere to the London Protocol.[65] Parkes's experience in China served him well. He had persuaded Governor Bo Gui to approve Chinese travel abroad and used the same strategy in negotiating with the *bakufu* government to abolish the closed-door policy and allow Japanese travel abroad.

First, Parkes demanded that the *bakufu* government issue notices on the first *gomen no inshō* (passports) on April 9, 1866.

> Those who apply to travel abroad, or to study or conduct commerce, will be permitted after they submit their applications. After their application, they will have to acquire a passport, which requires full information: the name of applicant; method of arrival to destination; the reason; the country, and then they will have to submit the application to the master. Farmers, craftsmen, and merchants will have to go to their local magistrate office, *daikan* (local governor), and their *ryōshu* (feudal lord), and their *jitō* (property manager). Those who try to travel abroad without a passport will be severely punished and reprimanded.[66]

Two months later, the agreement to revise tariff regulations was signed on May 13. Parkes made the *bakufu* government approve and insert the provision in Article X of *Kaizei yakusho* (Tariff Convention of 1866):

> [As announced by the Japanese government, once having obtained a passport,] all Japanese subjects may travel to any foreign country for purposes of study or trade. They may also accept employment in any capacity on board the vessels of any nation having a treaty with Japan. Japanese in the employ of foreigners may obtain

government passports to go abroad on application to the governor of any open port.

Furthermore, Article IX approves the principle of free trade, stipulating that Japanese were at liberty to travel abroad or trade with foreigners at the open ports.[67] Parkes confidently reported to the foreign minister, Lord Clarendon: "Article IX and X . . . will enable Japan and her people to share freely in the commerce of the world, to the complete abandonment of their old exclusive policy." He declared that the most important provision was not the revision of tariffs but the agreement on Articles IX and X, which stipulated that Japanese were permitted to travel abroad and guaranteed free trade.[68]

It took the British government more than twenty years to gain this type of concession in China, having cost multiple military engagements and naval wars. In Japan, on the other hand, it took only six years to have the Japanese sign the London Protocol. This was certainly an achievement for Parkes, but perhaps not on the part of the *bakufu* government.

Unwelcome Interference

Beginning in 1860, the *bakufu* government sent missions to the United States and other countries to ratify treaties. Other Japanese, albeit a small number, did sneak out of Japan. However, without the aggressive persuasion of Parkes, who had waged a war in Canton using the Arrow Incident as an excuse, the *bakufu* government would not have officially permitted Japanese travel abroad as early as 1866 in the form of an irrevocable announcement approved by the treaty countries. In fact, the *bakufu* government had been hesitant to sign the Tariff Convention because of Articles IX and X. Even after the signing, the *bakufu* would not issue passports, prompting Parkes to send a letter to the government on September 19, demanding immediate action. The *bakufu* government then realized it could no longer delay issuing passports, so it sent a sample passport to the ministers of treaty nations ten days later, on September 29, saying it was ready to give passports to the applicants who had applied.[69] It had been nearly half a year since the proclamation was announced, indicating that the *bakufu* government had only grudgingly adhered to the convention.

Some people certainly benefited from the new "open" travel regulations; however, surprisingly few were Japanese. Government passport records in open ports from 1866 and 1867 show that those who were issued passports were mostly employed by foreigners as acrobats, other performers, and "those for hire." [70] It was the foreigners who were aiming to take Japanese out of Japan for a specific purpose, rather than Japanese leaving Japan of their own accord, who benefited. One must say it was unfortunate that Japanese travel abroad was approved by way of unequal treaties in the name of free trade favorable only to the developed nations of mid-nineteenth-century East Asia.

Parkes reported to Lord Clarendon that the enactment of the Tariff Convention would allow the "freest commercial and social intercourse with foreigners at open ports." He expected that the Japanese government, appearing to have serious concerns about Japan's future, would take a more progressive approach. He further reported that having observed the conservative attitude of the *bakufu* government, in common with other "oriental potentates," he would add a "close-watchfulness combined with persuasion" to make sure that the Japanese government adhered to Articles IX and X.[71] The purpose of what Parkes, known as a skillful diplomat in East Asia open ports, called "patient persuasion" should be self-explanatory. His ultimate concern was the British national benefit and economic development rather than the profit or progress of the Japanese.

By the beginning of the Meiji era, the Japanese government could no longer directly exercise control over Japanese travel abroad at departing ports, without worrying about the treaty countries' reaction. As indicated in the negotiation between treaty nations and the *bakufu* government, even when a situation intolerable to the Japanese government would arise, such as the abuse of Japanese contract laborers abroad, a temporary banning of Japanese travel would be criticized as a violation of the treaty. Such a ban would result in an insufficient supply of sailors at Japanese open ports. Even Parkes wouldn't have been able to oppose the enactment of Japanese law controlling overseas travel, since it would be regarded as interfering with Japanese politics. Meiji diplomatic history, however, demonstrates that Parkes was not willing to allow a regulation unfavorable to the interests of Britain and its subjects. For example, in March 1876, Parkes protested that *Gaikokusen norikomi kisoku* (regulations about boarding foreign ships) enacted by the *daijōkan* (Grand Council of State) forbade Japanese from boarding foreign ships and forcibly negotiated with Foreign Minister Terashima Munenori to end them.[72] With this arrangement, Japanese inadvertently found themselves compelled to thankfully attribute their freedom to travel abroad to the foreigners' unwelcome interference in domestic politics.

The Passport System and Regulations on Overseas Dekasegi Laborers

The Japanese government enjoyed one advantage over the Chinese: it had established a passport system as a prerequisite for Japanese travel abroad, which was stipulated in the Tariff Convention. Article IX required the Japanese government to issue passports to applicants who were hired by subjects and citizens of treaty countries residing at open ports before they could accompany their foreign masters abroad. Furthermore, the treaty countries acknowledged this requirement. This served as a barrier against abuses of the privileges enjoyed by the treaty nations.

To some degree the Japanese government could prevent foreigners from abusing the Japanese official approval of overseas travel by requiring passport applicants to enter into a labor contract with the foreign employer, and set the services to be paid, the working conditions, and the arrangement of a return journey, before their departure.[73] The treaty nations did not object to the passport system as long as it did not harm their own interests. Fortunately, the demand for low-wage labor had been met by the Chinese and there was no imminent need for a large-scale transport of Japanese labor. Therefore, the Japanese government could avoid the lamentable situation in which the Chinese government found itself as it tried to control the recruitment and overseas transportation of workers, although both governments faced difficulties.

The Japanese government used the passport system as an example when it modeled a new system after that of the United States and Europe but included its own interpretations. The *bakufu* government understood the *inshō* (passport) to be a permit, one granted to Japanese to leave the designated homeland of their *koseki* (family register) or *jinbetsu* (individual registration) but requiring them to return after their business was done. Needless to say, Japanese as emigrants living permanently overseas was beyond the *bakufu*'s imagination.[74] The back of the passport clearly indicated the *bakufu*'s view, saying that Japanese should not overstay in a foreign country, acquire citizenship abroad, or affiliate with foreign religions.[75]

The passport also indicated that the Japanese government meant to protect Japanese overseas, although in practice this was difficult and hence useless: "It is requested that authorities of any government, . . . in case of need, give him lawful aid and protection."[76] The *bakufu* government attempted to interpret overseas travel by those engaged in lower-class or menial work as a type of the familiar *dekasegi*.[77] Therefore, it is not surprising that the *bakufu* government treated the Japanese going overseas in a fashion similar to those going to work in Edo or Osaka. Japanese were required to return to Japan regardless of their destination after their *dekasegi* was over. Foreign employers who took Japanese out of the country, therefore, were expected to bring them back; overseas travel was something the Japanese government officials would grant permission for and supervise rather than a decision made by individuals at liberty to do so. Had Harris known this, he would have been disgusted. At this point, however, it was probably impossible for the Japanese to break tradition and understand the essence of emigration. This difference in perspectives, nonetheless, helped them rein in foreigners' self-interest.

Although it is not clear what the *bakufu*'s intentions and perception of the passport system were at the time of the Tariff Convention, suffice it to say that the *bakufu* government laid the groundwork for the later Meiji government by not making a full concession to Parkes.

The Failed Recruitment of Contract Laborers at Japanese Open Ports

The Gannenmono *Incident*

The *gannenmono* incident occurred in 1868. That year, the Boshin War started in February, when the Meiji government dispatched troops from the Tōseigun (Eastern expedition army) in Kyoto to suppress the remaining parts of the *bakufu* government; by early March the troops approached Edo. The open port of Yokohama, still under the jurisdiction of the Yokohama *bakufu* office, was under threat of this new government force. Foreign troops stationed in Yokohama, under the leadership of the representatives of the treaty nations, who declared neutral positions, were protecting the port.[78] Minister Parkes requested that the Meiji government immediately dispatch a high official in charge of foreign affairs to Yokohama. At the same time, he requested that the *bakufu* magistrate officers in Kanagawa, Mizuno Yoshiyuki and Yorita Morikatsu, stay in Yokohama until the government officials arrived. The Meiji government established the Yokohama Court and appointed Higashikuze Michitomi as governor general together with Nabeshima Naohiro, his deputy, who both arrived on April 16 on an English ship. By April 20 they had completed the bureaucratic transfer from the Kanagawa magistrate's office.[79] With this, Yokohama was placed under the jurisdiction of the Meiji government.

During this time, Eugene Van Reed, an American residing in Yokohama, was working with Japanese agents to recruit Japanese laborers for a Kingdom of Hawai'i sugar plantation. At the beginning of April, Van Reed, having applied for passports earlier in the year, received a letter of passport issuance from the Kanagawa magistrate's office. But by the time he prepared for the departure of the approximately 150 Japanese contract laborers on the chartered ship *Scioto*, the bureaucratic transfer of power was taking place between the magistrate's office and the Yokohama Court. As a result, Van Reed had to reapply for all the passports at the Yokohama port.[80]

Having heard the situation from Van Reed, the Yokohama Court requested the return of the already issued passports and rejected their reissuance on the grounds that there was no treaty between Japan and the Kingdom of Hawai'i. Van Reed then dispatched Japanese laborers to Hawai'i on April 25 without passports from the Meiji government.

The Yokohama Court's *kumigashira* (division heads), Itō Iwaichirō and Takagi Shigehisazaemon, protested Van Reed's actions when they learned about the ship's departure. Van Reed, for his part, criticized the court for not endorsing the permission granted by the Kanagawa magistrate's office or allowing the issuance of new passports, and requested that the matter be judged at the meeting of treaty nations' ministers. The Yokohama Court, now under the jurisdiction of the new Meiji government, could not ignore this incident; Higashizuke and Nabeshima of the Yokohama Court sent a letter to the US minister, Robert B. Van

Valkenburgh, informing him of the incident and requesting his attention to the subject.[81]

The details of Van Reed's recruitment of Japanese laborers, the
results of the incident, and the arrival of the Japanese laborers in
Hawai'i have already been studied and published in both Japan and
the United States.[82] I would only like to add that negotiations after
the incident focused on the shipment of laborers without passports
issued by the Meiji government. On the basis of Article IX of the Tariff
Convention, this is the only point on which the Japanese government
could accuse Van Reed of wrongdoing. Despite the Japanese government's wish, the trial of Van Reed's case was not possible at the open
port protected by the unequal treaties, for trials by consuls were only
nominal, and in reality open ports were not under the jurisdiction of
Japanese law.[83]

The Japanese Contract Laborers Who Were Sent to Guam

The *gannenmono* incident attracted a considerable amount of government and media attention. For example, *Chūgai shinpō* derided it as a
"quasi-slave trade" event.[84] Besides the *gannenmono* incident workers,
another group of Japanese was sent to Guam in 1868. Approximately
forty Japanese contract laborers who were recruited at Yokohama
sailed to Guam in April of that year. This incident was brought to light
three years later when a British schooner, the *Wanderer*, rescued four
stranded Japanese and took them back to Japan from Guam. Later,
a Russian Navy ship and an American ship took back the remaining
twenty-four survivors to Japan from Guam. Having investigated them,
the Meiji government discovered that forty-two Japanese laborers, of
which eleven died and one was missing, had been shipped to Guam
immediately before the departure of the *gannenmono*.[85]

The government investigation report noted that these Japanese
laborers were said to have been recruited by the Prussian trading house
Rottmann & Wilmann to farm in Guam for three years. The forty-two
Japanese were issued passports from the Kanagawa magistrate's office
and boarded the Prussian ship the *Emmy Trader* on April 7. The signed
contract stipulated that each laborer was to be paid four *ryō* (taels);
half that, however, was retained by the governor general of Guam for
medical and return-trip expenses. While farming at Tantano on the

island of Guam, ten laborers became ill and died. The Japanese laborers petitioned the governor general, saying that they were not receiving their payments on a regular basis and were mistreated by the managers. They were subsequently fired in August 1870. Their request for the return of the deposit was never granted. In addition, [the governor general] did not mediate to arrange a return ship and told the Japanese to find one on their own. With the help of generous local residents, they avoided starvation by eating nuts and taro roots.[86] Fortunately, no other incidents related to contract laborers occurred after these in the first year of the Meiji era.

Why Further Incidents Did Not Occur

It was probably not surprising that the *gannenmono* and Guam incidents occurred, given the Japanese hiring clause of the Treaty of Amity and Commerce, the lawless conditions of the open ports under the unequal treaties, and the demand for contract laborers overseas. Recruiting and transporting contract laborers was not in violation of the laws of the treaty countries and was beyond the control of Japanese law.

So why didn't a similar incident happen? The following conditions are considered the main reasons. Press reports of this incident as being similar to those in "coolie" and "slave" trades made people perceive the recruitment of contract laborers at open ports as unscrupulous acts, without realizing that such acts were permitted. Had Van Reed been British and had he sought advice from Parkes, he would have realized that Article VIII of the Anglo-Japanese Treaty allowed him to recruit and hire Japanese at will. In fact, there was nothing to be condemned about Van Reed's contract with the laborers and their recruitment. Fortunately for Japan, the country's open ports were unlike the Chinese ports, in that the British lower-class residents there, who were regarded as "trash" by elites such as Alcock and Ernest Satow, did not follow Van Reed's attempt to make money out of recruiting laborers.[87] One should not overlook the importance of having the precedent of coolie trade in China's open ports.

Given that the hiring clause of the Anglo-Japanese Treaty did not become an issue, the Meiji government gained an advantageous position. Furthermore, Parkes and other diplomats of treaty nations had high expectations of the Meiji government, which had successfully

resolved incidents that began under the *bakufu* government, whose
polices and attitude were the targets of criticism and attack by treaty
nations and their diplomats.[88] The Meiji government protested the Van
Reed case, emphasizing his treaty violation; that is, he had shipped
Japanese without passports to a nontreaty nation for his own profit.[89]
The representative of the treaty nations did not argue against the Meiji
government's accusations.

The Gannenmono *Incident and the US Minister*

As mentioned earlier, the fact that Van Reed was American, not
British, was very fortunate for the Japanese government. US minister
Van Valkenburgh was not an experienced diplomat, unlike British minister Parkes, and the US consulate did not have a Japanese interpreter.[90]
Van Valkenburgh was not knowledgeable about the Japanese situation,
having been stationed in Japan for only a year and a half. Furthermore,
he acted independently and avoided collaboration with Parkes, who
was regarded as the leader of the treaty nations.[91] Consequently, foreign consulates other than the United States' treated the *gannenmono*
incident as beyond the realm of their consideration, partly because the
US government had an official interest in the Kingdom of Hawai'i, the
destination of the *gannenmono*. In other words, the other foreign consuls concluded that the incident was not of interest to the treaty nations
and residents at open ports. Against this backdrop, the Meiji government did not have to negotiate with all the treaty nations, particularly
the British and Parkes, although Van Reed had hoped to have a meeting
with the other ministers.[92]

Van Valkenburgh somewhat misguidedly criticized the Meiji government for the Yokohama Court's failure to stop the *Scioto* ship. But needless to say, stopping British ships at open ports governed by the unequal
treaties at the end of the Edo period was impossible.[93] Van Valkenburgh
further stressed that the *gannenmono* incident was outside the jurisdiction of the US consulate, given that it did not violate US laws.[94]

However, in his report to Secretary of State William Seward, Van
Valkenburgh mentioned that the Act to Prohibit the Coolie Trade in
China, enacted by the US Congress on February 19, 1862, should also
be applied to Japan.[95] He had informed the Americans in Japanese
open ports of this on May 26, 1868, and received approval. His report

shows that he was concerned that the recruitment of overseas labor in Japanese open ports might develop into another coolie trade. Van Valkenburgh added that the Japanese government opposed Japanese laborers being dispatched overseas, such as in the *gannenmono* incident, and was making an effort to prevent another incident.[96] Van Valkenburgh's edict, therefore, was in line with the intentions of the Japanese government. This edict was considered to have stopped Americans at Japanese open ports from engaging in practices similar to those of the coolie trade.

The Treaty Nations' Responses to the Firm Position of the Japanese Government

The *gannenmono* incident was not a welcome development for the Meiji government. It took more than three years to resolve the situation, including the dispatching of an envoy to Hawaiʻi. Through this process the Meiji government demonstrated to the treaty nations that it was opposed to sending Japanese contract laborers overseas and thus would not easily issue passports. That the treaty nations acknowledged this and did not protest was a fortunate development, given that the government could not control Japanese travel overseas, particularly immediately after the establishment of Meiji government. The demand for contract laborers was met by Chinese with an ample supply, fortunately for the Japanese but not for the Chinese.

Against this backdrop, the *gannenmono* incident was the last large-scale recruitment of Japanese contract laborers at open ports. In 1868, however, several inquiries were made to the Japanese government from overseas, requesting a government response to invitations of Japanese contract laborers. In 1870, the Japanese diplomatic record shows that an American named Gartner made a request to the Ministry of Foreign Affairs through the US consulate for the hiring of 250 Japanese *ninsoku* (laborers) to work at a sugarcane plantation in Louisiana for five years. The conditions were the following:

1. Accommodations, land, tools, firewood, and food are supplied with a monthly wage of seven Spanish dollar silver coins.

2. Interpreters will be hired for fifty dollars a month and a US officer will be hired as a manager.

3. Wages are transferred to the manager at the end of the month.

4. Travel expenses are supplied.

Of course, the Ministry of Foreign Affairs declined.[97]

Dutch minister Van der Hoeven sent a request to the Minister of Foreign Affairs Sawa Nobuyoshi, saying that he would like to hire five hundred Japanese mercenaries to be dispatched to the territories of the Netherlands. Sawa's response: "Our country traditionally does not have such a system, and since the Meiji Restoration we have been studying the political systems of civil governments, and we have already compared systems abroad and are currently discussing this issue. Therefore, it is impossible to accommodate your request." His explanation was difficult for the Dutch to understand but did demonstrate the Japanese government's unwillingness to send Japanese abroad for hire.[98]

The Final Gesture: The Maria Luz Ship Incident

By 1872 it was widely known that the Meiji government was absolutely opposed to the recruitment of Japanese contract laborers overseas at open ports and that it would decisively deal with incidents regarding overseas travel. In the *Maria Luz* incident, the government demonstrated its determination to not allow the inhumane coolie trade within Japanese territorial waters.

The *Maria Luz*, a Peruvian transport ship "loaded with coolies," stopped for repair at the Yokohama port in July 1872 on the way from Macao to Peru. The 231 Chinese coolies on board "suffered from malnutrition and physical abuse, cramped into confined spaces, and forced to cut their queue hairstyle." When the ship was being repaired, some coolies jumped into the sea, hoping to be rescued by a nearby British Navy ship. Instead, they were returned to the *Maria Luz* after having been rescued and attended to. Since similar incidents continued, the British admiral attempted to investigate the situation, but the captain of the *Maria Luz* declined his inquiries. The admiral then requested that the Japanese Ministry of Foreign Affairs, through the British consulate, investigate the situation, saying "such behavior occurring in the Japanese territories was a disgrace to its government." [99]

The Ministry of Foreign Affairs dispatched *Daijō* Hanabusa Yoshimoto to Yokohama and requested that the Kanagawa prefecture government "severely investigate" the incident. The Kanagawa Court discovered, after questioning the captain and the passengers, that the Chinese passengers were without doubt "coolies" and treated unfairly on the ship. The Chinese passengers were hoping to return to China, and the Kanagawa Court decided to grant their request. The captain was ordered to not sail from Yokohama. The Peruvian government dispatched envoys to the Japanese government, objecting that its decision was inappropriate. The two nations convened multiple times but could not agree on a resolution, instead deciding to ask the emperor of Russia, Alexander II, to mediate. In June 1875, Alexander's judgment was that the Japanese government took the right course of action. [100]

In October 1872, the Meiji government enacted the *Jinshin baibai kinshirei* (ban on human trafficking) to strictly prohibit "the abusive treatment of lifetime or termed servants at the hands of their masters, condemning such practices as inhumane." [101] The Meiji government took advantage of a clause in this edict, which regulated the term for domestic servants hired by foreigners to a maximum of one year and applied it to Japanese overseas stay. [102] This certainly made it more difficult for foreigners to take Japanese hires out of the country after October 1872.

"Disgraceful" Japanese in Foreign Countries: Absolute Guarantee of Return Home

Troupes of Light Entertainers Deserted in a Foreign Land

After the *gannenmono* incident, the large-scale recruitment of *dekasegi* laborers for overseas hire stopped, as the Meiji government wished. However, the *Kōkai jinmei saikan* (directory of sea voyagers) of the Ministry of Foreign Affairs indicates that the overseas travel of Japanese light entertainers and domestic servants continued, albeit in a small number. [103]

In the early years of the Meiji era, the government could hardly keep up with the large number of domestic issues to solve and tariff treaties to negotiate. Evidently, it did not have the capacity to be concerned about the Japanese taken by foreigners abroad. The Japanese government at that time did not have diplomats stationed overseas and thus had no way of knowing the conduct and conditions of Japanese abroad until 1872, when the government established an official overseas diplomatic presence. Terashima Munenori had been dispatched as the envoy extraordinary and minister plenipotentiary to London.[104] He reported the devastating conditions of Japanese hired by foreigners abroad, explaining that the light entertainer Yoshigorō and four other men and women were issued passports on September 30, 1869.[105] According to Terashima's report, after the troupe arrived, the foreign employer decamped, and they were stranded in London. They did not have the means to return home and could not work. They managed to avoid starvation by leading beggar-like lives. As soon as they learned Terashima was posted in London, they made a request to borrow money for a return trip. As Tershima's investigation suggested, many other Japanese appeared to have suffered similar situations.

The Japanese consulate was not equipped with funds to lend to these stranded Japanese citizens. Terashima originally thought that helping Yoshigorō and his troupe would induce similar cases and decided to leave the case alone. Their passports, however, stated that Japanese citizens were entitled to request help. Terashima calculated that if such a request were made to a foreign government, particularly in Britain, where Japanese diplomats were already stationed, it would harm the Japanese government's standing with other nations. After considering pros and cons, and consulting with the Iwakura Mission (a Japanese delegation of scholars and statesmen in 1871–1873) during their US tour, Terashima decided to lend money to the Yoshigorō troupe so they could return home.

After reporting this incident, Terashima recommended several measures: private individuals who applied for a passport should be required to make a return-travel deposit at the Ministry of Foreign Affairs or prefectural government for the equivalent of a lower-class cabin fare. When they safely returned to Japan, the deposited amount would be returned to the applicants. Those who requested help at a consulate would have those expenses deducted from their deposit. He also recommended that foreigners who wished to take their Japanese employees abroad should make a similar deposit.

The Requirement for Passport Issuance for Overseas
Japanese Hired by Foreigners in Early Meiji

The Meiji government did pay some attention to the hiring of Japanese by foreigners and devised measures, albeit insufficient, to deal with foreseeable issues. After having established wage and employment terms with an Argentine employer, members of another light entertainment troupe and their families applied at the Tokyo prefectural government for passports to travel to the United States. Lacking previous experience, unlike the Kanagawa prefectural government, the Tokyo prefectural government made an inquiry to the Ministry of Foreign Affairs as to whether the ministry would issue a passport after the initial investigation of each applicant's profession, debt, birthplace, and physical characteristics, among other traits. The ministry notified the governments of Tokyo and other prefectures with open ports such as Hokkaido, Niigata, Kanagawa, Osaka, and Nagasaki that if the following conditions were met, a passport should be issued:

1. The name of the foreign employer, among others, and travel arrangements for the departure and return, must be provided.
2. The destination and duration of the contract must be clear.
3. The applicants or their relatives must have a procedure to receive expenses and fees that need to be paid.
4. In the case of lost properties while abroad, the applicants may borrow money from a foreigner; however, the applicants must be able to return the money.
5. Those who are low-level or menial laborers employed by foreigners must clarify the wages and procedure of returning home.
6. If merchants and aforementioned applicants borrow money from foreigners and return to Japan, they shall return the money themselves. Or, if they are to source the money from a town or village, the agreement from the guarantor and other documentation must be included.[106]

These requirements indicate that the Ministry of Foreign Affairs instructed applicants on how to deal with borrowing money while abroad, but it did not provide instructions for how to procure travel funds in case they were stranded in a foreign country.

Travel Abroad with "Low-Class" Japanese and the Gesture of the New Nation

It is commonly thought that the Meiji government was making an effort to not let "low-class" citizens such as light performers and servants spoil the image of Japan, as opposed to having an interest in rescuing a small number of stranded Japanese abroad. The government probably had Americans and Europeans in mind because they looked down on the Japanese and on the Japanese government as "half open." [107] Terashima's report clearly demonstrates that his main concern was not the stranded entertainers but rather the Western contempt they would face had they sought protection from the British government.[108]

The government and intellectual leaders in early Meiji made a tremendous effort to complete the Restoration under the flag of *bunmei kaika* (the Civilization and Enlightenment movement), to westernize the nation, and to have the nation's progress acknowledged by Westerners, who emphasized their cultural superiority.

The most effective measure to deal with the situation was to prohibit travel abroad by those who could bring shame to Japan's image. But as long as the unequal treaties remained in place, preventing citizens, particularly those who were hired by foreigners, from traveling abroad would violate those treaties and was thus impossible. Therefore, government officials unanimously agreed that no Japanese should be allowed to leave the country without a guarantee of returning home.[109] Although the "progressive" clauses of the Tariff Convention officially allowed Japanese to travel abroad, ironically, in the early Meiji era, the government's highest priority was likely to have Japanese return home. The passport system introduced in this convention thus became a useful tool for the Meiji government to address this issue.

Overseas Dekasegi *and the Guaranteed Return Home*

Given the low status of Japanese hired by foreigners, Terashima's proposal to have them make a security deposit with a government institution for their return trip was difficult to implement. The alternative proposal was to have foreign employers issue certificates or contracts that guaranteed their return and their travel expenses, at the time of the passport application. The confidence gained by having treaty nations acknowledge the Meiji government's handling of the *Maria Luz* incident was likely a catalyst for the government's bold decision in 1872.

Just immediately after Terashima's report arrived at the Ministry of Foreign Affairs on October 19, 1872, the Kanagawa prefectural government reported to the ministry that a Frenchman named Pascal had hired twelve light entertainers and applied for passports so they could perform for two years in England.[110] By that time issuing passports was part of the routine work of the Kanagawa prefectural government. Therefore, the letter from Kanagawa was a mere report rather than a request for approval. After finding no problems with their application, the Kanagawa prefectural government issued passports in exchange for the usual (nominal) guarantor's certificate, which stipulated that the government's requirement had been met. The new *Daijō* Yanagihara Sakimitsu, however, sent a letter to Kanagawa governor Ōe Taku, explaining the new policy of the Ministry of Foreign Affairs, directing it to Pascal's application, and instructing the Kanagawa prefectural office to issue passports in accordance with the Terashima notification.[111]

Yanagihara requested that if the troupe had not yet departed from Japan, Pascal should guarantee paying their return trip or have the consul general certify that Pascal would assume the guarantor role. Yanagihara explained that the traditional guarantee by Japanese would have no bearing in a foreign country and instead instructed that future passport applications have a certificate from the foreign employer to guarantee the return trip.[112] If the latter was deemed insufficient, Yanagihara added that employers should have the consul guarantee that employers would fulfill these responsibilities.

Certificate for Return Trip by the Consulate General's Seal

The convention in Japan was to have the applicant designate a guarantor if he or she did not meet all the requirements. The officials in the prefectural government knew, however, that these were nominal guarantors without qualifications. Therefore, they feared that guarantee certificates by foreign employers would also be only nominal and end up being just a piece of paper. To address this issue, they proposed requiring foreign employers to submit certificates stamped by the consul general.[113]

In response to the letter from the Kanagawa prefectural government, officials explained the issues associated with the guarantors. The first issue with the applicants (domestic servants, women, and sailors) hired by foreigners in Yokohama is that many of them were found to lack a proper *koseki* (family register), even after investigation. On their passport applications, they put guarantors down as unspecified acquaintances. Even if those Japanese were sent home for legitimate reasons, they could not rely on their guarantors of thin resources to pay for the return trip or to repay loans. They recommended that two guarantors' certificates be issued by the foreign employer to guarantee the payment of travel expenses and to assume all the responsibilities while abroad. According to their recommendation, two copies of these certificates were required and stamped by the consul general. One was retained by the prefectural government office; the other would accompany the passport applicant throughout his or her travels. The certificate that the traveler carried would be proof of a guarantee to Japanese ministers, consuls, or a local court if they were to issue a petition against the employee. The Ministry of Foreign Affairs accepted the recommendation from Kanagawa and notified the other government offices at open ports of this procedure, including the fact that the passport application should be made through the consulate office, rather than the Japanese government office directly.[114] This notification was signed by the *shō* (vice minister) of the Ministry of Foreign Affairs, Yamaguchi Naoyoshi, on November 19, 1873.

The Contract Labor System and *Dekasegi* of the Middle Meiji Era

The Establishment of a Labor System and Its Significance

The notification issued by the Ministry of Foreign Affairs in 1873 played an important role in the history of Japanese overseas migration. In essence, the government established a prototype of the contract labor system by requesting a security deposit from the guarantor or an emigration agent who escrowed a written oath or security deposit, thus guaranteeing the return of *dekasegi* laborers to Japan and their rescue in case of an emergency.

The notification from 1873 required proof of the certificate of guarantee as part of the process of applying for a passport (in the form of *inshō*, or passport, prior to 1876). Those requirements meant that no Japanese contract laborers would be going abroad unless they had been hired by foreigners. Therefore, one can determine that the intention of the Meiji government was to establish a kind of contract-labor system, because the certificate of guarantee assumed that the foreign employer and the Japanese employee entered into a contract.[115]

There is one important difference between the labor contract required for a passport application and the contract used for a laborer who had worked in Hawai'i or Guam in 1868. The former required the absolute guarantee of a return trip and the assumption of liability in case of an emergency. In this paper, I call the system of *dekasegi* laborers based on these contracts the "contract *dekasegi* system," differentiating it from the system of contract laborers commonly seen in the second half of the nineteenth century.[116]

The contract agreement for overseas laborers typically included clauses that covered items such as working conditions, the term of the contract, wages, measures taken in the case of illness or accident, and anti-abuse protection.[117] As in the case of Chinese coolie laborers in the British West Indies, and the *gannenmono* recruited to work in Hawai'i, however, many of these contracts were often regarded as a way to solicit recruits for overseas labor. The ultimate aim of the employers and their recruiting agent was to make a profit from the laborers, not to protect their welfare.[118] Sending laborers back to their home country was not considered in typical employment contracts.

For their citizens' safe return to their birthplace (where *koseki*, or their family register, was recorded), the government established the contract *dekasegi* system to protect them. It is thought that this system also attempted to prevent the abuse of foreigners in the unequal treaties; in essence, one can argue that the aim of the contract labor system was the opposite of the commonly used system of labor contracts.

However, these reasons may have been the Japanese government's public position, and the ulterior motive may have lain elsewhere. For the purpose of revising the unequal treaties, Japanese government officials and intellectual leaders, who promoted the westernization of Japan, were concerned about the negative impact of "low-class"

Japanese working abroad on the national interest. The Japanese elites' preoccupation was not ameliorated over time, even by the middle Meiji era, when Japanese *dekasegi* migration peaked after *kan'yaku imin* (Japanese government contract laborers) were sent to Hawai'i. The following notification, dated March 1887, from the Ministry of Foreign Affairs was dispatched to the governments of open ports and Hiroshima, Yamaguchi, Fukuoka, and Kumamoto prefectures, which were the main sources of *dekasegi* laborers to Hawai'i:

> As travel in Japan and abroad became more convenient, . . . the number of our citizens who travel abroad has undoubtedly increased. The government should encourage them to open their perspectives, gain knowledge, acquire civilization, promote communication, and encourage industries and trade. There are some Japanese with bad habits among those who travel abroad. . . . they harm our people's honor and are disrespected. They could not avoid being treated like the Chinese. . . . Japanese who are in the professions of light performers, sumo wrestlers, magicians, other performers, and those who want to be hired as fishermen and house servants travel abroad on their own or enter into contracts with foreigners. Next to Japanese who are better controlled, they will expose their low qualities in the foreign land, be treated unkindly by foreigners, and suffer the consequences of being in foreign countries.
>
> Therefore, I hope you understand the situation and would investigate the purpose and travel expenses of the applicants, and if their purpose is not certain or their travel budget is insufficient, you would convince them to give up their plans, or those who are hired by foreigners should apply with the guarantee certificate from the foreign employer. Those who have not entered into complete contract with the employer, you should not issue them passports. Although this procedure would inconvenience these applicants, we should make sure that they would not dishonor the nation as a whole.[119]

Dekasegi *in Middle Meiji*

In 1873, after notification by the Ministry of Foreign Affairs, the effectiveness of the certification system was not tested because the number of Japanese hired by foreigners and traveling abroad substantially declined. (The Ministry of Foreign Affairs holds no record regarding the rescue of stranded Japanese overseas from this period.) After this system was introduced, the Japanese hired by foreigners had difficulty getting passports, which effectively helped the Japanese government control Japanese overseas travel without overtly violating the treaties it had made with other nations. This is a notable side product of the contract *dekasegi* system.

By 1883, ten years after the establishment of the guarantee system, conditions at home and abroad had changed tremendously, and the Japanese government realized that it would be difficult to continue restricting Japanese laborers from going to work abroad and decided to selectively permit overseas *dekasegi*.[120] Nonetheless, the government continued to maintain that *kan'yaku* (Japanese government contract) *dekasegi* was the principle [regulatory model] governing laborers traveling abroad.

The first contract laborers permitted to travel abroad after the *gannenmono* were pearl divers. In May 1883 John Miller, an English resident of Yokohama, having entered into an agreement with Matsuda Makichi in Yokohama, applied for permission to hire thirty-six Japanese pearl divers and helpers, along with one interpreter, to work in the Torres Strait in Australia for two years.[121] The Ministry of Foreign Affairs replied to the office of Kanagawa prefecture, saying that after further investigation it would grant the permit because "the profession required diving techniques, unlike menial laborers, and the size of the party was small. It should be able to fulfill the contract without running into trouble." The government, however, noted that Australia was far away and strictly instructed that "if the employer died or ran into an unforeseeable situation and became bankrupt, or failed to honor the contract, the ministry should determine a guarantor of certainty to assume the employer's responsibilities and have him co-sign the agreement. Kanagawa prefecture should verify its validity with the British consul."[122]

It took until 1885, when the most complete *dekasegi* system, *kan'yaku imin*, was put into practice for contract laborers in Hawai'i. In this case the bilateral agreement between Japan and the Kingdom of Hawai'i stipulated the working conditions, return home, and guarantee of medical treatment in case of emergency.[123] This agreement was probably the most trustworthy type of guarantee. As several other authors have already done so, I will not explain the *kan'yaku imin* system here.[124]

Although later researchers have characterized *kan'yaku imin* as *imin*, they were undoubtedly *dekasegi* laborers, not emigrants. It is well known that the *kan'yaku imin* workers had no intention of settling in Hawai'i for the rest of their lives. This was also the view of the Meiji government, which did not consider the possibility that *dekasegi* laborers would become permanent settlers. According to the agreement, those who wished to stay after the expiration of the three-year contract could make their own decision.[125] The Japanese government, however, unwittingly accepted the request of the Hawai'i government that this clause be included in the agreement.[126] Senda Sadaaki, the Hiroshima governor, reminded the contract laborers in a memorandum that their purpose for going to Hawai'i was to return to Japan with wealth and pride by saving money and accumulating property.[127] Senda's remarks most likely reflected the Japanese government's true intent. The security deposit of savings of 25 percent, in which Minister of Foreign Affairs Inoue Kaoru showed a strong interest, was also established as a measure to make sure the *dekasegi* laborers would return to Japan.[128] Needless to say, the bilateral agreement guaranteed the safe return for those who wished to return home.

The *kan'yaku imin* system was planned as a measure to help financially troubled farmers affected by Prime Minister Matsukata's austerity measures so workers could make a fortune in a short period of time overseas and turn around the family fortune. Only a limited number of *kan'yaku imin* eventually settled in Hawai'i permanently; the majority decided not to do so.[129] Therefore, *kan'yaku imin* were bewildered by the criticism of generations in the second half of the twentieth century that they were transient *dekasegi* laborers without a commitment to settle permanently.[130] The later generations neglected the historical fact that the Japanese government did not allow laborers to travel abroad without an underlying commitment to return home.

The System of Keiyaku Dekasegi *and the*
Imin Hogohō *(Emigrant Protection Act)*

The Meiji government's policy requesting the guarantee of the *dekasegi* laborers' return trip was not revised even by the early 1890s, when the Shokumin Kyōkai (transplantation or colonial association) was established.[131] After 1890 the *imin kaisha* (emigration companies) and *imin* recruiting agents replaced foreign employers and began to recruit *dekasegi* laborers and arrange their trips abroad.[132] No regulation, however, controlled the for-profit activity. As a result, the recruiting agents would often not perform their duties, by neglecting dangerous situations for laborers abroad, beguiling *dekasegi* laborers with various benefits, and acting exclusively for their own interest.[133] The Japanese recruiters, therefore, followed the steps of foreign employers at the beginning of the Meiji era.

Concerned about the situation, the Meiji government enacted regulations (*imin hogo kisoku, chokurei dai-42 gō*) to protect the emigrants and control the activities of emigration agents in April 1894.[134] To further strengthen the rights of emigrants and the duties of emigration recruiting agents, control the relationships between the two parties, and manage the security deposit, the Meiji government enacted the *imin hogohō shikō saisoku* (details regarding the Emigrant Protection Act), Ministry of Foreign Affairs order number 3.[135]

The word *imin* (emigrant) in this regulation is a misnomer; it should be called *dekasegi* protections or *dekasegi* regulations. Those regulations and acts defined *imin* as those who travel abroad to work.[136] In addition, the detailed regulations narrowly defined laborers as those who worked in "farming, cultivation, pasturing, fishery, mining, manufacturing, civil engineering, transportation, and construction" or as "domestic servants engaged in cooking, laundry, sewing, serving, and attending to the sick."[137] Thus, the *imin* narrowly defined in these regulations apparently do not differ from those *dekasegi* laborers engaging in low-end work. In other words, the government simply called the *dekasegi* laborers a different name, *imin*. Furthermore, Sections 6, 7, 8, and 9 of *Imin hogo kisoku* and Articles 10 and 13 of *Imin hogohō* stipulate that the *imin* recruiting agents must "place deposits with the local government officials and arrange the return travel or rescue for the sick and those in other emergency situations" after receiving the permit from the local government.[138] The *jiyū imin* who went abroad without an *imin* recruiting agent were required to list guarantors and submit a certificate of guarantee in their application (Section 2 of *Imin hogohō shikō saisoku*). The guarantors and the *imin* recruiting agents, therefore, carried similar responsibilities. In summary, these two laws simply legalized the existing contract *dekasegi* system, rather than setting forth a new government measure on *dekasegi* laborers abroad.[139]

The Keiyaku Dekasegi *System and* Dekasegi *Laborers Traveling to the United States*

In the early Meiji era, the Japanese government did not consider the possibility that laborers would travel to work in the continental United States.[140] Even the *dekasegi* laborers in Hawai'i did not seem to intend to work in the United States when the *kan'yaku imin* began in 1885. By 1892, however, the *dekasegi* laborers in Hawai'i continued to travel to the West Coast after finishing their three-year contract, having discovered better opportunities there than in Hawai'i. Beginning in 1892, the number of *dekasegi* laborers arriving in the United States from Hawai'i increased exponentially.[141] In addition, around 1890, *imin* recruiting agents began sending laborers to the West Coast. Unfortunately, the timing coincided with the proclamation of the Foran Act (Alien Contract Labor Law), under which the nature of Japanese contract labor would come into question.

The Foran Act, enacted in February 1885, prohibited foreign contract laborers from working in the United States.[142] The nature of the contract and guarantee certificate required by the Meiji government differed substantially from the type of labor contract prohibited by the act. They were intended to guarantee the laborers' return to Japan, rather than to support their immigration. As discussed earlier, the Japanese government did not encourage emigration; rather, they discouraged it. However, the Japanese system and policies were misunderstood by local officials in the United States. Many Japanese laborers who came to the United States were denied entry because of the contract of guarantee they carried from Japan, which was interpreted as a violation of the Foran Act.[143]

Even more unfortunate for Japanese arriving in the United States, the 1891 Immigration Act allowed the newly established US Immigration

Bureau to deny the entry of "undesirable" foreign citizens and to conduct immigration examinations at ports.[144] This is when the US policy was changing from being "open" to controlling immigration on the basis of race or country of origin.[145] Furthermore, even after the 1882 Chinese Exclusion Act was enacted, anti-Asian sentiment remained unabated, so the exclusionists' focus shifted to Japanese as an increasing number of Japanese laborers arrived on the West Coast. For Japanese laborers, entering the United States became even more difficult.[146]

Despite these events in the United States, the Meiji government did not attempt to review the *dekasegi* policy. By the late 1880s the Japanese government did not have a reason to fear that the treaty nations would claim a violation of treaties even if the government tried to halt Japanese laborers attempting to travel to the United States. The US government would have welcomed such a controlling measure by the Meiji government, but it did not take this measure.[147] I speculate that the Japanese government was not willing to suspend the flow of *dekasegi* laborers abroad voluntarily before the anticipated amendment of the unequal treaties, as the passage covering Japanese employment or hire was an indirect cause of the long-standing friction between the two countries.

Even after the Meiji government received a report that anti-Japanese sentiment was on the rise on the West Coast, it took the government until August 1900 to temporarily stop *dekasegi* laborers from traveling to the United States.[148] It was not a coincidence that the amendment of unequal treaties was then within reach and that the Treaty of Commerce and Navigation between Japan and the United States had been enacted one year earlier.[149] From this point, the Meiji government policy shifted its focus from *dekasegi* to emigrants. At the same time, however, there was too large a gap to fill between the two nations on the issue of immigration.

By the beginning of the twentieth century, Japanese believed that Japan had modernized and had joined the Great Powers. They sent selected Japanese to enter the United States on an equal footing with European immigrants instead of sending more *dekasegi* laborers. By that time, however, anti-Asian sentiment went beyond lower-class Japanese laborers. Americans attempted to exclude the Japanese as a whole as undesirable aliens. In the twentieth century, the Japanese government and the Japanese could not ignore this demeaning situation, and the issue of immigration developed into a serious matter beyond diplomatic negotiation.[150]

Conclusion

Immigrants and Dekasegi *Laborers*

Throughout this paper I have suggested that *imin* (immigration and emigration) and *dekasegi* (temporarily working away from home) have distinct purposes and patterns of mobilization. Here, I would like to once again clarify the differences between them.

Scholars of Japanese migration studies of the Meiji era often consider these two terms synonymous. Sometimes they combine the two words into *dekasegi-imin*. On the other hand, *immigrant*, the English word for *imin*, is defined in Webster's dictionary as "a person who comes to a country to take up permanent residence."[151] Therefore, strictly speaking, the term *immigrant* refers to an individual who is moving with a clear intent to take permanent residence. Prior the 1880s, before the entry of so-called new immigrants [from Southern and Eastern Europe], it is known that most immigrants were coming to the United States to settle permanently.[152] In this context, the term *immigration* implies that immigrants would have reason to terminate their relationship with their mother country and seek to settle permanently in a foreign country.

However, *dekasegi* laborers did not necessarily intend to settle permanently, nor did they always endure hardships in Japan that caused them to leave their homeland. These laborers intended to return home, as their destinations were temporary places to sojourn; once their purpose had been completed, they would need to have a homeland to welcome them back. The destination for a *dekasegi* worker is not a new frontier for permanent settlement but a place to make money to return home with prestige and fortune. Furthermore, the economic conditions of the home country that would induce *dekasegi* laborers to leave should be temporary, as opposed to long-lasting conditions that would induce emigrants to settle permanently elsewhere. If the latter was the case, *dekasegi* laborers would not have a reason to return home.

The Japanese migration abroad of *dekasegi* laborers was not unidirectional, the way it was observed to be among European emigrants in the first half of the nineteenth century. Japanese *dekasegi* constitutes a pattern of mobilization that is defined as a temporary sojourn and an eventual return home. In the case of emigration, an emigrant's dreams and wishes are expected to be fulfilled in a new country; whereas in the case of *dekasegi*, the new country is considered a temporary site for economic activities, and the laborers' goals and wishes are expected to eventually be fulfilled in the motherland. As I have demonstrated, the terms *imin* and *dekasegi* cannot be synonymous, since they encompass different motives, intentions, purposes, and behaviors. Therefore, combining the two terms into *dekasegi-imin* would invite confusion if not properly defined.

The Study of Dekasegi and Immigration: The History of Overseas Migration and Nikkei

Japanese who moved to the United States during the middle and late Meiji era ended up staying in the United States or extending their stay. By virtue of their decisions, their descendants became Nikkei, citizens of new countries with Japanese ancestry.

Japanese *dekasegi* laborers predominantly moved to the United States, Canada, and Brazil. Those countries recognized every citizen, other than the Native Americans, as descendants of immigrants.[153] The Hawaiian islands, where many Nikkei live, was an independent kingdom until 1898, when it was absorbed into the United States, and nonnative Hawaiian residents are all immigrants or their descendants.

Modern American historians emphasize the United States as a country of immigrants, of which Americans are proud, as symbolized by the Statue of Liberty and the "immigrants' paradise" legend.[154] As a result, scholars who study Japanese American history or immigration history may be confused by the idea that the Japanese were immigrants from the beginning. For example, the *gannenmono* who traveled to work in Hawai'i were often considered as the beginning of Japanese immigration.[155]

Certainly, no one can deny that the Issei became permanent settlers, regardless of their naturalization status, and the Nikkei community has played an important role in the immigrant society. Therefore, writing the history of Issei and their descendants living in American society means writing about Japanese immigration history. However, I argue that the use of the incorrect term *imin* to refer to the initial wave of *dekasegi* laborers to the United States is a falsification of history, not dissimilar to rewriting history. The history of Japanese going to the United States is the history of *dekasegi*, not emigration history.

The fact that the Issei became immigrants indicates a significant historical process that we cannot afford to overlook. It is a process by which the *dekasegi* laborers were transformed into immigrants when they decided to settle in the United States or extend their stay. Therefore, the transformation took place in the Americas, and the reasons and causes should be explored in the context and history of the United States. Judging from or knowing their original conditions or intentions when they left Japan, it is hard to surmise how and why they stayed in the Americas. For this reason, the study of the emigrants' motives and causes of leaving Japan should be conducted separately from the study of their transformation into immigrants. I suggest that this [difference] has kept migration researchers from studying the factors behind Japanese decisions to stay in the Americas.[156]

The history of Japanese migration to the Americas consists of three periods. First came the *dekasegi* period, when Japanese crossed the Pacific and sojourned in the United States and Hawai'i. Second came the transition period, when the Japanese began to change into immigrants, distinct from *dekasegi* laborers. Third came the *imin* period, when they became immigrants or permanent residents. To gain a holistic understanding of Japanese immigration, it is necessary to study these three periods independently and investigate the internal relationships among them. I suggest that the traditional methodologies of studying Japanese immigration have conflated these three distinct periods, which would erroneously cite parts that do not fit into a preconceived singular history as exceptional conditions or reasons.[157]

An example of amalgamation of three distinct periods of Japanese emigration is the previously widely accepted simplistic "emigration push" theory that poverty was the cause of Japanese overseas emigration. That incorrect interpretation stems from defining *dekasegi* laborers as immigrants. In contrast, the theory did apply to many cases of emigration from Western Europe, where hardships in the homeland were the direct cause of people deciding to emigrate to a new frontier (for example, the potato famine in Ireland being the direct cause of Irish emigration in 1845–46).

We cannot, however, apply this case to Japan, and it would be a mistake to try to find economic, political, or social causes in Japan that would have reduced Japanese to emigrants. The ultimate purpose of *dekasegi* workers was to return home and use the money they earned overseas to improve their economic condition and the living standard of themselves and their families. I suggest that the fact that few people from the Tōhoku region (the northeastern part of Japan that at the time had suffered from relatively worse economic conditions than many other parts of the country) applied to become *kan'yaku imin* (government contract laborers) to Hawai'i supports my thesis.[158] The argument that Japanese overseas emigration stemmed from poverty is not well supported by the historical record.

Agenda of Future Studies

This paper focused on the overseas *dekasegi* system of the Japanese government and its policies during the early to middle Meiji era. Future studies should include analyses of immigration theories introduced to Japan from the West, their relationship with Japanese emigration policy, and their impact on the encouragement of emigration by private-sector leaders during the Meiji era. This discussion is outside the scope of this paper and will be explored on another occasion.[159]

Notes

1. The numbers of *gannenmono* (arrivals in the first year of Meiji) and *kan'yaku imin* (Japanese government contract laborers) are somewhat different in the records of the United States and Japan. Therefore, the numbers I use here are estimated totals. Furthermore, the Meiji government permitted thirty-six contract laborers and an interpreter to work in Australia for non-Japanese before *kan'yaku imin* began. Refer to pages 99–100 in this chapter.

2. See, for example, "The Japanese Government refused until 1894 to permit the emigration of its laborers" in Yamato Ichihashi, *Japanese in the United States* (Stanford, CA: Stanford University Press, 1932), 5. However, Ichihashi did not provide an explanation. For studies in Japan, Irie Toraji, who supported Japan's overseas expansion, criticized the Meiji government for its weak-kneed diplomacy. See *Hōjin kaigai hattenshi, jōkan, fukkoku-ban* (Hara Shobō, 1981), 3–4.

3. Before 1903, when US law was amended to require an accurate list of passengers, US immigration statistics reported only passengers in steerage as immigrants. Passenger ship companies were supposed to query potential immigrant passengers. Questions included whether they had contagious diseases, stayed in almshouses, or were psychotic. Since some of these questions were considered too rude to ask first- and second-class passengers, some passenger ship companies refused to ask them. Therefore, the immigration statistics before 1903 are not accurate. See US Bureau of the Census, *Historical Statistics of the United States, Colonial Times to 1957* (Washington, DC: Government Printing Office, 1960), 49, and US Senate, *Regulations of Immigration: Report of the Committee of Immigration,* S. Doc. No. 62, 57th Cong., 2nd Sess., 1902, 100–104. Furthermore, in the 1870s during the mass migration of Chinese to America, some Japanese who arrived there were likely to have been mistaken for Chinese. The reason I cited inaccurate statistics here is that some English-language studies tried to prove that the Japanese government did not permit Japanese laborers' entry into America, such as Ichihashi, *Japanese in the United States,* and Roger Daniels, *The Politics of Prejudice: The Anti-Japanese Movement in California and the Struggle for Japanese Exclusion* (Berkeley: University of California Press, 1962). They probably did so because other than these statistics, there was a dearth of materials that showed a limited number of emigrants to the United States. For US immigration statistics, refer to Sakata Yasuo, "19-seiki kōhan ni Amerika ni tokōshita Nihonjin to 'imin tōkei'— itsuwaru sūji—" in *Kirisutokyō shakai mondai kenkyū* dai 38-gō, (Dōshisha Daigaku Jinbun Kagaku Kenkyūjo, March 1990), 51–102.

4. Refer to sections 1 ("The Unequal Treaties and Provisions for the Employment of Japanese People") and 3 ("The Approval of Overseas Travel in Japan") in this chapter.

5. Refer to Ishii Takashi, *Nihon kaikōshi* (Yoshikawa Kōbunkan, 1972), and *The Complete Journal of Townsend Harris, First American Consul General and Minister to Japan* (New York: Japan Society, New York, 1930). The most frequently used historical materials include *Dai Nihon komonjo: Bakumatsu gaikō kankei monjo,* vols. 14–30 (Tōkyō Teikoku Daigaku Bungakubu Shiryō Hensanjo, 1922–60) and microfilm copies of the records in the National Archives, No. 133: Dispatches from the United States Ministers to Japan, vols. 1–2 (March 17, 1855–December 31, 1959). From here on I will cite these historical materials as *Bakumatsu gaikō kankei monjo* and "Minister's Dispatches."

6. *The Complete Journal of Townsend Harris,* 230–31; *Bakumatsu gaikō kankei monjo,* vol. 14, 715–19; and Hizuka Tatsu, *Yokohama kaikō gojūnenshi, jōkan* (Yokohama Shōgyō Kaigisho, 1909), 270–71.

7. *Nihon kaikōshi,* 212–13, and *Bakumatsu gaikō kankei monjo,* vol. 14, 526–27.

8. *Bakumatsu gaikō kankei monjo,* vol. 14, 717.

9. *The Complete Journal of Townsend Harris,* 214–15.

10. *Bakumatsu gaikō kankei monjo,* vol. 14, 531, and *The Complete Journal of Townsend Harris,* 221.

11. Commodore Perry did not include Nagasaki on the list of potential open ports when he negotiated at the Kanagawa Convention. The reason is as follows: "Since the Nagasaki government is accustomed to dealing with the obsequious Dutch, he thought, that if Americans were to establish a port in Nagasaki, the Japanese may force Americans to obey them more than they are willing to do" (Ishii, *Nihon kaikōshi,* 94).

12. Laurence Oliphant, who visited Japan as a personal secretary of the Earl of Elgin, spoke cynically, saying, "People who can live in Dejima must be misanthropes who do not mind living alone in lighthouses in remote islands." See Laurence Oliphant, *Narrative of the Earl of Elgin's Mission to China and Japan, 1857–1859* (Edinburgh: William Blackwood and Sons, 1859), vol. 2, 11–12. Rutherford Alcock, the first British consul general (later British minister) to Japan, criticized the Dejima prison and the obsequious Dutch most critically, saying that the Dutch "held to this foot of earth with desperate tenacity, nothing daunted by a prison life; and such a series of vexations and indignities as only an Oriental race like the Chinese or Japanese could have the ingenuity to devise; or the patience to put into execution for two centuries, without cessation or intermission." See Rutherford Alcock, *The Capital of the Tycoon: A Narrative of Three Years' Residence in Japan* (London: Longman, Green, Longman, Roberts & Green, 1863), vol. 1, 74.

13. *The Complete Journal of Townsend Harris*, 231–35.

14. Refer to pages 75–77 in this chapter.

15. *The Complete Journal of Townsend Harris*, 499, and "Minister's Dispatches," vol. 1.

16. For the Japanese-language translation of a draft of the Treaty of Amity and Commerce, refer to *Bakumatsu gaikō kankei monjo*, vol. 18, 522–41.

17. For the Japanese-language translation of the Japanese-Dutch Supplementary Treaty, refer to *Bakumatsu gaikō kankei monjo*, vol. 17, 409–27, and its English-language translation, W. G. Beasley, ed., *Select Documents on Japanese Foreign Policy, 1853–1868* (London: Oxford University Press, 1960), 149–55. In addition, this treaty and the Edo *bakufu*'s intentions refer to Ishii, *Nihon kaikōshi*, 190–204 and 261–65.

18. Alcock, *The Capital of the Tycoon*, vol. 1, chap. 10, 202–33.

19. Refer to pages 75–77 in this chapter.

20. Japan's side of the negotiation is recorded in *Bakumatsu gaikō kankei monjo*, vol. 14. For Harris's records, refer to *The Complete Journal of Townsend Harris* and "Minister's Dispatches," vol. 1.

21. *Bakumatsu gaikō kankei monjo*, vol. 20, 474–93. For English-language texts, refer to "Minister's Dispatches," vol. 2, and Beasley, *Select Documents on Japanese Foreign Policy*, 183–89.

22. The Japanese-language translation of the treaty's draft that Harris handed to the Edo *bakufu* initially stated for Americans to "employ Japanese as servants." However, in the final treaty, the word *Japanese* was replaced with *senmin* (the lower class). In this case, *senmin* probably means people holding menial occupations, juxtaposed against the samurai at the top of the caste system. In the early years of the Meiji era, the Ministry of Foreign Affairs also used the word *senmin* to describe servants of foreigners who traveled abroad with them (refer to page 94 in this chapter).

23. *Bakumatsu gaikō kankei monjo*, vol. 22, 122–26.

24. Ishii, *Nihon kaikōshi*, 371–82, and Grace Fox, *Britain and Japan, 1858–1883* (Oxford University Press, 1969), 42–45.

25. *Bakumatsu gaikō kankei monjo*, vol. 20, 791–810. For an English-language translation, refer to Fox, *Britain and Japan*, appendix 1, 555–65.

26. William F. Mayers, ed., *Treaties between the Empire of China and Foreign Powers, Together with Regulations for the Conduct of Foreign Trade, Etc.* (Shanghai: North China Herald Office, 1897), 11–20.

27. Refer to Banno Masataka, *Kindai Chūgoku seiji gaikōshi* (Tōkyō Daigaku Shuppankai, 1973); W. G. Costin, *Great Britain and China, 1833–1860* (Oxford: Oxford University Press, 1968); John K. Fairbank, *Trade and Diplomacy on the China Coast: The Opening of the Treaty Ports, 1842–1854* (Cambridge, MA: Harvard University Press, 1953); Banno Masataka, *China and the West, 1858–1861: The Origins of the Tsungli Yamen* (Cambridge, MA: Harvard University Press, 1964); and pages 73–75 in this chapter. Furthermore, for the Qing dynasty's overseas travel ban, refer to Robert L. Irick, *Ch'ing Policy toward the Coolie Trade, 1847–1878* (Taipei, Taiwan: Chinese Materials Center, 1982), 11–15.

28. For the Chinese "coolie trade," refer to Persia C. Campbell, *Chinese Coolie Emigration to Countries within the British Empire* (London: P. S. King & Son, 1923); Irick, Ch'ing Policy toward the Coolie Trade, and Costin, *Great Britain and China*, 168–76.

29. Campbell, *Chinese Coolie Emigration*, 94–96.

30. Cited in Bowring to Malmesbury, December 24, 1852, and Costin, *Great Britain and China*, 171. Irick cited the advertising of an auction simultaneously selling Chinese women and a mule in a newspaper from Havana, Cuba, as follows:

FOR SALE
A Chinese girl with two daughters, one 12–13 years and the other 5–6 years, useful for whatever you may desire. Also one mule . . .

(*Diario de la Habana,* June 12, 1847).
Also refer to Irick, *Ch'ing Policy toward the Coolie Trade,* 1.

31. Hosea B. Morse, *The International Relations of the Chinese Empire* (London: Longmans, Green, 1918), vol. 2, 166–76; and Irick, *Ch'ing Policy toward the Coolie Trade,* 32–43.

32. In the early 1850s, crimps were paid twenty-five to thirty dollars per person (no such records exist for the late 1840s). Coolies who were sent to auctions were sold for between two hundred and four hundred dollars (according to Morse, *The International Relations of the Chinese Empire,* vol. 2, 170). In addition, it is reported that the USS *Wakefield* (AP-21) spent fourteen thousand dollars to transport coolies worth a combined sales price of forty-five thousand dollars to Cuba. See M. Foster Farley, "The Chinese Coolie Trade, 1845–1875," *Journal of Asian and African Studies* 3: 3–4 (July and October 1968), 259.

33. Syme, Muir & Co., a British company, was a major player in the coolie trade in Xiamen. However, the most notorious company might be Tait & Co. Its president, James Tait, had served as the British consul in Spain in 1846, in Holland in 1851, and in Portugal in 1852. He abused his authority and made tremendous profits from the coolie trade. He even sent young children; on one British ship in 1855, the eldest was an eight-year-old girl. The British consul who discovered this trade could not do anything because Tait was the consul of three countries and the crimps involved had Spanish and Portuguese nationalities as well. Furthermore, John Connolly served as the British consul in France while being engaged in the coolie trade. Charles W. Bradley, an American consular agent, was an employee of Tait & Co. I assume British ministers could do nothing to stop the trade (Fairbank, *Trade and Diplomacy,* 213–14; Campbell, *Chinese Coolie Emigration,* 96, and Costin, *Great Britain and China,* 174).

34. Refer to Costin, *Great Britain and China*, 168–76, and *Parliamentary Papers*, 1852–1853, vol. 68, "Correspondence with the Superintendent of Chinese Trade upon the subject of the emigration from that country."

35. Refer to Campbell, *Chinese Coolie Emigration*, 101–19, and *Parliamentary Papers*, 1860, vol. 69, "Correspondence respecting emigration from Canton."

36. Campbell, *Chinese Coolie Emigration*, 86–117, and *Parliamentary Papers*, 1852–1853, vol. 63, "Dispatches relative to Chinese immigrants introduced into British Guiana and Trinidad," 1857–1858, vol. 63; "Correspondence on emigration from Hong Kong and the Chinese Empire to the British West Indies and foreign countries," 1857–1858, and vol. 41; and "Letters and papers relative to emigration from China to British Guiana and Trinidad."

37. Irick, *Ch'ing Policy toward the Coolie Trade*, 81–89.

38. Refer to Banno, *Kindai Chūgoku seiji gaikōshi*, 234–40.

39. Proclamation by Straubenzee, major-general of the British troops in China, April 7, 1859; proclamation by Pih-kwei, governor of the Province of Kwangtung, April 9, 1859; and proclamation by Choo, acting chief magistrate of the District of Nan-hai, and Hwang, chief magistrate of the District of Pwanyu, April 6, 1859; and *Parliamentary Papers*, 1860, vol. 69, "Correspondence respecting emigration from Canton." Also refer to Irick, *Ch'ing Policy toward the Coolie Trade*, 89–101.

40. Alcock to Bowring, April 12, 1859, *Parliamentary Papers*, 1860, vol. 69, "Correspondence respecting emigration from Canton."

41. Campbell, *Chinese Coolie Emigration*, 121–24.

42. Parkes to Bruce, April 11, 1859, *Parliamentary Papers*, 1860, vol. 69, "Correspondence respecting emigration from Canton."

43. Bruce to Malmesbury, May 3, in ibid.

44. Banno, *Kindai Chūgoku seiji gaikōshi*, 240–41.

45. Campbell, *Chinese Coolie Emigration*, 116–17.

46. Banno, *Kindai Chūgoku seiji gaikōshi*, 250–55.

47. For example, refer to Irick, *Ch'ing Policy toward the Coolie Trade*, 148–50.

48. The English-language text of the Convention of Peking between Britain and the Qing Empire is reprinted in Mayers, *Treaties between the Empire of China and Foreign Powers*, 8–10.

49. Laurence Oliphant, a personal secretary of the earl of Elgin, was concerned that British unilateral demand would result in problems without an understanding of Asian cultures, habits, and ethics (Oliphant, *Elgin's Mission*, vol. 2, 243–44).

50. Refer to Fairbank, *Trade and Diplomacy on the China Coast*, 162–63 and 172–75; and Alcock, *The Capital of the Tycoon*, vol. 2, 329–30.

51. Refer to *Parliamentary Papers*, "Correspondence respecting affairs in Japan," 1861, vol. 67; 1862, vol. 64; 1863, vol. 74. For example, Abel Anthony James Gower, a British diplomat, sent a letter to Francis Howard Vyse, the British consul at the time, dated September 5, 1862, complaining about the employment of Japanese.

52. Gaikoku bugyō Kanagawa bugyō narabini gunkan bugyō Mizuno Chikugonokami Tadanori jōshinsho, rōjū ate, "Oranda shōnin Nagasaki e kozukai ren'etsu no ken," Ansei 6-nen 9-gatsu 21-nichi, in *Bakumatsu gaikō kankei monjo*, vol. 27, 193–96.

53. Gaikoku bugyō shokan, Hakodate bugyō ate, "Eikoku tsūbenkan Hakodate e Nihonjin meshitsukai ren'etsu no ken"; Ansei 6-nen 9-gatsu 1-nichi; and Nagasaki

bugyō ukagaisho, rōjū ate, "Ranjin no Nihonjin meshitsukai ren'etsu no ken," Ansei 6-nen 9-gatsu 27-nichi, in *Bakumatsu gaikō kankei monjo*, vol. 27, 8–10 and 261–72.

54. Refer to Eikoku Sōryōji Ōrukokku shokan, rōjū ate, "Bushi fuhō ni tsuki torihakarai kata no ken," Ansei 6-nen 10-gatsu 14-ka, in *Bakumatsu gaikō kankei monjo*, vol. 28, 202–12. This English-language text is from a letter from R. Alcock, the British consul general, to the Japanese minister of foreign affairs, October 27, 1859, in *Bakumatsu gaikō kankei monjo*, vol. 28, Documents in European Languages, no. 16, 22–28.

55. Gaikoku bugyō Kanagawa bugyō narabini gunkan bugyō Mizuno Chikugonokami Tadanori ukagaisho, rōjū ate, "Gaikokujin taitō no mono yatoiire no ken," Ansei 6-nen 9-gatsu, in *Bakumatsu gaikō kankei monjo*, vol. 27, 312–17.

56. Nagasaki bugyō shokan, Fukkoku fuku ryōji Meruro ate, "Futsujin Nihon fujin o Shanhai e tsuredashi no ken," Ansei 6-nen 10-gatsu, in *Bakumatsu gaikō kankei monjo*, vol. 28, 57–58, 122–24, and 170–78.

57. For the *Unjōsho* (government office in charge of transportation taxes), refer to *Yokohama shishi* dai 2-kan (Yokohama-shi, 1959), 231–38.

58. Alcock, *The Capital of the Tycoon*, vol. 1, 354.

59. "Minutes of a conference held in Yokohama, February 22, 1861, between Messrs. Alcock and de Bellecourt and Sakai Okinosuke," Encl. 3, Alcock to Russel, March 3, 1861, *Parliamentary Papers*, 1861, vol. 66, 433–41; and Ishii, *Meiji ishin no kokusaiteki kankyō, zōtei*, 132–33.

60. Ishii, *Meiji ishin no kokusaiteki kankyō, zōtei*, 55–104.

61. Ibid., 105–15, and Beasley, *Select Documents on Japanese Foreign Policy*, 208–224.

62. Ishii, *Meiji ishin no kokusaiteki kankyō, zōtei*, 115–38. The English-language text of "Rondon Oboegaki" (London Protocol) is cited in Beasley, *Select Documents on Japanese Foreign Policy*, 216–17.

63. Ishii, *Meiji ishin no kokusaiteki kankyō, zōtei*, 120.

64. For Parkes's career in China, refer to Stanley Lane-Poole, *The Life of Sir Harry Parkes, K.C.B., G.C.M.G., Sometime Her Majesty's Minister to China and Japan*, vol. 1, *Consul in China* (London: Macmillan, 1894). For his reputation as a diplomat in China's open ports, refer to Fairbank, *Trade and Diplomacy on the China Coast*, 174–75.

65. Fox, *Britain and Japan*, 160–64.

66. *Ishin shiryō kōyō* dai 6-kan (Meguro Shoten, 1943), 403, and Irie Toraji, *Meiji nanshinshikō* (Ida Shoten, 1943), 314. The text of the proclamation is recorded in "Kaikoku kigen" dai 48-shō ("Kaikoku kigen" dai 5-kan, in *Katsu Kaishū zenshū* 19 [Kōdansha, 1875], 639–40). A. L. C. Portman, an acting minister of the embassy of the United States in Japan, sent a copy of a letter he received from *rōjū* to William Seward, the secretary of state of the United States. In the letter he reported that Japan's *inshō seido* (passport system) was established and that he was pleased, stating, "Another barrier of Japanese isolation has been removed" (Portman to Seward, June 1, 1866, "Minister's Dispatches," vol. 7).

67. The Japanese-language text of Kaizei yakusho (the revised version of the Japanese Commercial Tariff) is included in *Nihon gaikō nenpyō narabini shuyō bunsho, jōkan*, ed. Gaimushō (Hara Shobō, 1965), 28–31. The English-language text is in *Parliamentary Papers*, 1867, vol. 74, "Correspondence respecting the revision of the Japanese Commercial Tariff," 1 and 381–84.

68. Parkes to Clarendon, July 16, 1866, *Parliamentary Papers,* "Correspondence respecting the revision of the Japanese Commercial Tariff," 387–90.

69. Keiō 2-nen 9-gatsu 19-nichi (October 27, 1866), "Eikoku Kōshi 'Parkes' bakufu ni chōshi, sumiyakani kaigai tokōsha ni ryokōken o hakkōsuru no kakushō o en koto o motomu. Tsuide nijūkunichi bakufu, ryokōken o seiteishite, Ei, Bei, Ran, Ro nado shokoku shishin ni ichōsu" in *Ishin shiryō kōyō dai 6-kan,* 628, and Van Valkenburgh to Seward, November 10, 1866, "Minister's Dispatches," vol. 7.

70. Refer to "Kyū seifu no setsumenjō mōshiuke no mono seimei shirabe" held at the Gaimushō Gaikō Shiryōkan (Diplomatic Archives of the Ministry of Foreign Affairs of Japan).

71. Parkes to Clarendon, July 16, 1866, in *Parliamentary Papers,* "Correspondence respecting the revision of the Japanese Commercial Tariff," 389.

72. "Gaikokusen norikomi kisoku ni taishi Eikoku kōshi kōgi ikken" in *Dai Nihon gaikō bunsho dai 9-kan,* ed. Gaimushō Chōsabu (Nihon Kokusai Kyōkai, 1940), 732–82.

73. Refer to pages 89–90 in this chapter.

74. For example, the Edo *bakufu*'s *Ofure* (proclamation) in March 1843 stated that from then on, village people must not close their residency, move to Edo, or register for the Edo census. If village carpenters, plasterers, woodworkers, etc., needed to leave their residence and move into shops or other people's residences in Edo to work temporarily, they had to set an exact return date. They had to apply and receive permission from local officials. If they applied to the *daikan* (magistrate), *ryōshu* (landlord), and *jitō* (land administrator), they had to receive joint signatures from village officials. Additionally, if their residence was in the territory controlled by the *daikan,* they needed permission from the *tedai* (low-ranking provincial government officials); otherwise, if it was private property, they needed a license in the form of *kerai okugaki ingyō* (official verification seals). When leaving for Edo, they had to present the licenses to the masters of their residence in Edo. Furthermore, they had to inform their village officials where and with whom they would reside in Edo. Once the term expired, they had to go home at once. If they left their home again, they had to follow the same procedures. See "Tokugawa kinrei kō" 6-chitsu (Shihōshō, 1895), 534–35. It is interesting to compare this with the proclamation from April 1866.

75. "Bakufu irai hakkyū kaigai yuki menjō oyobi kaigai ryoken ruishū" held at the Gaimushō Gaikō Shiryōkan and Irie, *Meiji nanshinshi kō,* 3–4.

76. "Bakufu irai hakkyū kaigai yuki menjō oyobi kaigai ryoken ruishū."

77. I will explain more details on the difference between *dekasegi* and *imin* later (refer to pages 105–6 in this chapter). Also refer to "Nihonjin Amerika dekasegi no chiikisei no ichi kōsatsu (II)" in *Ōsaka Gakuin Daigaku, Kokusaigaku ronshū 1-kan, dai 2-gō* (March 1991), 164–71.

78. *Yokohama shishi dai 3-kan jō* (Yokohama-shi, 1961), 1–11.

79. *Dai Nihon gaikō monjo dai 1-kan, dai 1-satsu* (Nihon Kokusai Kyōkai, 1936), 536–38 and 571–72; *Ishin shiryō kōyō dai 8-kan,* 354–55, 365, 416, and 479–80; and Van Valkenburgh to Seward, April 19, 1968, "Minister's Dispatches," vol. 10.

80. For background on this incident, refer to *Dai Nihon gaikō monjo dai 1-kan.* More recent references are Watanabe Reizō, *Hawai no Nihonjin Nikkeijin no rekishi, jōkan* (Honolulu, Hawai Hōchisha, 1986), 68–165, and Masaji Marumoto, "'First Year' Immigrants to Hawaii & Eugene Van Reed," in *East across the*

Pacific, ed. F. Hilary Conroy and T. Scott Miyakawa (Santa Barbara, CA: Clio Press, 1972), 5–39. The new government's negotiation records are in "Beishō Uenrīto fusei no kyodō shimatsusho," considered the official position of Meiji government on this incident, in *Dai Nihon gaikō monjo dai 2-kan, dai 1-satsu,* 421–25.

81. Higashikuze Michitomi oyobi Nabeshima Naohiro shokan Van Vorukenbāgu ate, "Hawai dekaseginin mumenkyo shukkō no koto ni tsuki Amerikajin Van Rīdo torishirabe kata yōkyū no ken" in *Dai Nihon gaikō monjo dai 1-kan, dai 1-satsu,* 645–46.

82. In addition to endnote 3, for the Japanese-language documents refer to Shimaoka Hiroshi, *Hawai imin no rekishi: shintenchi o motometa kunan no michi* (Kokusho Kankōkai, 1978) and Imai Teruko, "Gannenmono imin mumenkyo Hawai tokō mondai ni tsuite no ichi kōsatsu" in *Tsudajuku Daigaku kiyō dai 11-gō* (March 1979), 37–66. For English, refer to F. Hilary Conroy, *The Japanese Frontier in Hawai'i, 1868–1898* (Berkeley: University of California Press, 1953).

83. "The right of exemption from the law of Japan is alone a reality; the other condition of the extraterritoriality clause is too much of a fiction." Quoted in Alcock, *The Capital of the Tycoon,* vol. 2, 368.

84. *Shinbun shūsei Meiji hennenshi dai 1-kan* (Shinbun Shūsei Meiji Hennenshi Hensankai, 1934), 45.

85. *Dai Nihon gaikō monjo dai 4-kan,* 570–73.

86. Ibid., 573–78.

87. Alcock, *The Capital of the Tycoon,* vol. 2, 365–66, and Ernest Satow, *A Diplomat in Japan* (Rutland, VT: Charles E. Tuttle, 1983), 25–26.

88. Fox, *Britain and Japan,* 227–30.

89. "Higashikuze Michitomi oyobi Nabeshima Naohiro shokan, Van Vorukenbāgu ate, Hawai dekaseginin mumenkyo shukkō no yue o motte Amerikajin Van Rīdo o kokugai ni taikyo seshimuru ni tsuki kyōgi no ken," Keiō 4-nen 4-gatsu 26-nichi, in *Dai Nihon gaikō monjo dai 1-kan, dai 1-satsu,* 741–42.

90. Payson J. Treat, *Diplomatic Relations between the United States and Japan, 1853–1895,* vol. 1 (*1853–1875*) (Stanford, CA: Stanford University Press, 1932), 281–82.

91. Ibid., 306–35.

92. Van Rīdo shokan, Itō Iwaichirō narabini Takagi Shigehisazaemon ate, "Hawai dekaseginin no kikoku hoshō ni kanshi kakkoku kōshi kaigō subeki mune tsūchi no ken," April 23, 1868; Itō Iwaichirō narabini Takagi Shigehisazaemon shokan Van Rīdo ate, "Hawai dekaseginin ni kanshi kakkoku kōshi kaigi no shidai tsūhō kata yōkyū no ken," Keiō 4-nen 4-gatsu 24-ka; and Van Rīdo shokan, Terashima Tōzō ate, "Hawai dekaseginin kyoka ni tsuki daisangoku no kōshi ni iken o motomuru koto fukanaru mune tsūchi no ken," Keiō 4-nen 4-gatsu 24-ka in *Dai Nihon gaikō monjo dai 1-kan, dai 1-satsu,* 615 and 618–21.

93. Van Valkenburgh to Higashikuze and Date, April 8, 1869, in *Dai Nihon gaikō monjo dai 2-kan, dai 1-satsu,* 364–67.

94. Ibid., 510–16.

95. Van Valkenburgh to Seward, May 20, 1868 in "Minister's Dispatches," vol. 10.

96. "This government entirely disapproves of the shipment of their people in any other capacity than as voluntary emigrants; they will be able, no doubt, to

prevent similar shipments in future" (Van Valkenburgh to Seward, May 20, 1868, in "Minister's Dispatches," vol. 10).

97. "Amerikajin Karutoneru Nihon ninsoku yatoiiretaki mune mōshiire no ken," in *Kaigai ijū dekasegi zakken*, held at the Gaimushō Gaikō Shiryōkan.

98. "Orandakoku seifu yori honpōjin o heishi ni hennyū shitaki mune mōshiire no ken" in *Hōjin hiyō zakken*, held at the Gaimushō Gaikō Shiryōkan.

99. R. G. Watson to Soejima Taneomi, August 3, 1872; Soejima Taneomi shokan, Ōe Taku ate, "Mariya Rūsu Gō jōkyaku gyakutai jiken shikyū torishirabe no ue hōkoku kata shirei no ken," Meiji 5-nen 7-gatsu 1-nichi; and "Soejima Gaimukyō to Eikoku Rinji Dairi Kōshi to no taiwasho," Meiji 5-nen 7-gatsu 3-ka, in *Dai Nihon gaikō monjo dai 5-kan*, 415–27.

100. For the Japanese records, refer to "Perūkoku fūhansen Mariya Rūsu Gō ni kansuru ken" in *Dai Nihon gaikō monjo dai 5-kan*, 412–545. For the US government's diplomatic documents, refer to *Foreign Relations of the United States, 1973* (Washington, DC: Government Printing Office, 1973), vol. 1, 524–630.

101. "Meiji 5-nen fukoku dai 295-gō," Meiji 5-nen 10-gatsu 2-ka, in *Hōrei zensho*, Meiji 5-nen, vol. 1 (Naikaku Kanpōkyoku, 1889), 200–201.

102. Asada Gaimu Kōshin Kyokuchō shokan, Kanagawa kenrei ate, "Hokugō shinju ryōsai sensuifu no ken ni tsuki kaitō no ken," chū, in *Nihon gaikō bunsho dai 16-kan*, 441–42.

103. "Kaikōjō ni oite inshō fuyo kaigaiyuki jinmei hyō"; "Kaigaiyuki menjō hyō"; Kōkainin meisaikan"; "Kōkainin meisaibo"; and "Kaikōjō oyobi kaku fuken kaigai ryoken fuyo seimei shirabe" held at the Gaimushō Gaikō Shiryōkan. In 1876, the name *inshō* was replaced with *ryoken*; thus, these records were about issuing *inshō*.

104. "Nihon gaikō nenpyō narabini shuyō bunsho," jōkan, nenpyō, 69.

105. "Zaiei Terashima Dai Benmushi yori no kōshin bassui" in "Kaigaiyuki menjō enkaku narabi tesūryō" held at the Gaimushō Gaikō Shiryōkan. Since this is an excerpt, the date is not clear. Since Terashima was seconded in England on April 23, 1872, it must have been written later than this date.

106. "Gaikokujin ni hiyō kaigaiyuki negaide sōrōsetsu menjō watashi kata no gi," Meiji 2-nen 10-gatsu 12-nichi and "Kaigaiyuki negaide sōrōsha kadokado toritadashi kata no gi tasshi," Meiji 2-nen 10-gatsu 15-nichi in "Kaigaiyuki menjō enkaku narabini tesūryō."

107. Terashima advised the Japanese government to change the text in *inshō* for Japanese hired by foreigners and traveling abroad as follows: "Japanese with *inshō* can request assistance with immigration issues. Naturally, the Japanese government must make arrangement with foreign governments, and compensate these governments to help Japanese nationals . . . when the inconveniences as mentioned above happen. Therefore, we should change the text of *inshō* for public officials and private citizens by deleting the requirement of mutual aid from overseas *inshō*, and significantly simplify it." The minister of foreign affairs accepted this suggestion, prepared two types of passports, and sent those drafts to each minister. Refer to "Kaigaiyuki menjō enkaku narabini tesūryō."

108. The government officials and intellectual leaders were concerned over the negative image of Japan caused by lower-class Japanese abroad from the early to the middle Meiji era. Refer to pages 98–99 in this chapter; Sakata Yasuo, "Datsu-a no shishi to tozasareta hakusekijin no rakuen in *Beikoku shoki no Nihongo shinbun*, ed. Tamura Norio and Shiramizu Shigehiko (Keisō Shobō, 1986), 58–62.

109. Refer to "Kaigaiyuki menjō enkaku narabini tesūryō."

110. Ibid., Kanagawa-ken shokan, Gaimushō ate, "Karuwazashi kaigaiyuki no gi," Meiji 5-nen 10-gatsu 19-nichi.

111. Ibid., Yanagihara Sakimitsu shokan, Ōe Taku ate, "Karuwazashi kaigaiyuki no gi ni tsuki tasshi," Meiji 5-nen 10-gatsu 20-ka.

112. Ibid.

113. Kanagawa-ken sanji shokan, gaimukyō ate, "Kakkokujin meshitsukai kozukai suifu kaigaiyuki hikiukenin nashi no setsu torihakarai ukagai," Meiji 6-nen 11-gatsu 11-nichi, in *Kaigai yuki menjō hakkō ikken.*

114. Ibid., Gaimushō shokan, Kanagawa-ken sanji ate, "Kakkokujin meshitsukai kozukai suifu kaigaiyuki hikiukenin nashi no setsu torihakarai kata kaitō," Meiji 11-nen 11-gatsu 19-nichi. See also Gaimushō shokan, Ōsaka-fu chiji narabini Hyōgo-ken Nagasaki-ken chiji ate, "Kakkokujin meshitsukai kozukai suifu kaigaiyuki hikiukenin nashi no setsu torihakarai kata tasshi," Meiji 11-nen 11-gatsu 19-nichi.

115. Federal government officials denied the Japanese entry into the ports of the West Coast in the 1890s on the basis of the Foran Act, enacted by the US Congress on February 26, 1885. This regulation defines contract laborers as workers who made labor contracts via a third party, including employers and contractors, before leaving their countries to work in the United States. See *Reports of the Immigration Commission*, vol. 39, Immigration Legislation (Washington, DC: Government Printing Office, 1911, 125–26).

116. It is known that Chinese immigrants, just like Japanese immigrants, did not intend to settle in the United States for good when they migrated. Therefore, they should also be considered migrant laborers. Some researchers differentiate Chinese immigrants to the United States, Australia, and New Zealand from Chinese migrant laborers sent to the West Indies or coolies sent to Peru or Cuba. The immigrants to the United States, Australia, and New Zealand were part of the "credit ticket system," in which migrant laborers borrowed money for the passage from employers or contractors under the condition that they work overseas for a certain amount of time. Refer to Campbell, *Chinese Coolie Emigration.*

117. The contracts of *gannenmono* also required an advance payment for trip preparation, an agreement of the duration, the wage, the payment methods, and allowances in case of sickness. Refer to Watanabe, *Hawai no Nihonjin Nikkeijin no rekishi, jōkan*, 127–28.

118. In the British territory of the West Indies, the British government discussed and introduced contract laborers instead of illegal coolies. Although the British government had originally presumed that the "contract *dekasegi* system" would prevent the abuse of workers, the owners of sugarcane plantations in the colonies examined the system for importing Chinese laborers and wanted it to be established there. Refer to Campbell, *Chinese Coolie Emigration,* 86–160.

119. Gaimushō tasshi, kaikō jōken narabini Hiroshima, Yamaguchi, Fukuoka, Kumamoto-ken ate, Meiji 20-nen 3-gatsu 7-ka, in "Kaigai ryoken kisoku narabini sono toriatsukai tetsuzuki seitei oyobi kaisei ikken," held at the Gaimushō Gaikō Shiryōkan.

120. Detailed research of this period has not been published. Refer to Conroy, *The Japanese Frontier in Hawai'i*, 54–64.

121. Oki Morikata Kanagawa Kenrei shokan, Asada Tokunori Gaimushō Kōshin Kyokuchō ate, "Hokugō nite shinju ryōsai no tame honpō sensuifu yatoiire

toiawase ni kanshi shōkai no ken," Meiji 16-nen 5-gatsu 3-ka, in *Nihon gaikō bunsho dai 16-kan*, 440–41.

122. Asada Tokunori shokan, Oki Morikata ate, "Hokugō shinju ryōsai no tame honpō sensuifu no ken ni tsuki saikaitō no ken" in *Nihon gaikō bunsho dai 16-kan*, 440–49. The problem occurred as expected. For this, refer to "Hokugō ni oite shinju ryōsai no tame honpō sensuifu hiyō tokō ikken," in *Nihon gaikō bunsho dai 17-kan*, 475–90, and *dai 18-kan*, 518–47.

123. Two English-language texts can be found in Doi Yatarō, *Yamaguchi-ken Ōshima-gun Hawai iminshi* (Matsuno Shoten, 1980), 10–13 and 35–37. "Yakujōsho sōan" was the draft for an official contract for emigration to Hawai'i; it was published in the *Bōchō shinbun* in November 1884. The second, "Yakujōsho," was signed by Robert Irwin, the Hawaiian king's special commissioner and special agent of the Bureau of Immigration, with the first *zuii tokōjin* (voluntary passengers) on the ship the *City of Tokio*, which left the port of Yokohama in January 1885. Also, a *Tokō jōyaku* (formal immigration treaty between Hawai'i and Japan) for Japanese *zuii dekasegi* (voluntary migrant laborers) was recorded in *Nihon gaikō bunsho dai 19-kan*, 462–65. This treaty was signed between Inoue Kaoru, the minister of foreign affairs, and Robert Irwin in Tokyo on January 28, 1886.

124. One of the most interesting Japanese-language studies is Doi, *Yamaguchi-ken Ōshima-gun Hawai iminshi*. For an English-language text, refer to Conroy, *The Japanese Frontier in Hawai'i*. One recent publication in Hawai'i regarding *Nikkeijin* is *Hawai Nihonjin iminshi* (Hawai Nikkeijin Rengō Kyōkai, 1964), published for the commemoration of the 75th anniversary of *kan'yaku imin*. (*Hawai Nihonjin Nikkeijin no rekishi, gekan,* for the commemoration of the 100th anniversary of *kan'yaku imin*, has not yet been published.) For historical materials, refer to "Nihon jinmin Hawaikoku e dekasegi ikken," in *Nihon gaikō bunsho* at the Gaimushō Gaikō Shiryōkan.

125. For example, although the word *dekasegi* is often used in this publication, similar to Doi's *Hawai iminshi*, the title says *iminshi* (immigration history). In addition, the contradictory words *dekasegi imin* are often used in other research publications. At that time, in Japanese literature and government documents, the words *dekasegi* or *dekaseginin* (people who go *dekasegi*) were regularly used; the word *imin* was rarely used and limited to translations, such as *iminkyoku* (immigration bureau). I will explain later the definitions of *dekasegi* and *imin* and their different contexts in historical studies. Refer to pages 105–7 in this text, and Sakata, "Nihonjin Amerika dekasegi no chiikisei no kenkyū (II)," 164–71.

126. Doi, *Yamaguchi-ken Ōshima-gun Hawai iminshi*, 11.

127. "Dekasegi shuisho," Meiji 17-nen 12 gatsu, is held at Yamaguchi-ken Ōshima-gun Kuga-mura Yakuba. An excerpt follows: "If one saves money from working, it is not very difficult to save more than four hundred yen in three years. However, if he does not save diligently or study hard, and instead eats extravagantly and leads a lazy life, he will fall into debt. *Tokō dekasegi*, a venture that requires investment, might instead cause him trouble. He must try to live moderately." Furthermore, the *kunji* (instructions) that Nabeshima Miki, the governor of the Hiroshima prefecture, gave to *dekaseginin* reads: "If one performs three good years' labor and builds a fortune, he should come back to his hometown immediately after his term expires. Take care of yourself." In addition, "*dekasegisha* [people who go *dekasegi*] must never forget that they are citizens of the Empire of Japan and will not bring shame to Japan."

128. Irie, *Hōjin kaigai hattenshi, jōkan*, 59.

129. Out of the first ten groups of *dekaseginin* (9,413 people in total) who arrived in Hawai'i between 1885 and 1889, 62.95 percent (525 people) of the first group (834 people) and 51.14 percent (537 people) of the tenth group (1,050 people) had returned to Japan by the end of 1897. The death rate in the same period was about 10 percent and the rate of the *dekaseginin* who moved to the continental United States was 7 percent. Furthermore, by the end of 1897, 18.58 percent of the first group stayed in Hawai'i, while the ratio was much higher, at 34.5 percent, of the tenth group. Thus, within ten years, two out of three *dekaseginin* returned to Japan. (*Kanagawa-ken tōkeisho*, Meiji 20-nendo, 21-nendo, 22 and 3-nendo, 24, 5 and 6-nendo, 27-nendo, and 28-nendo.) The research conducted by Yoshida Hideo further supports that many *dekaseginin* returned to Japan. See Yoshida Hideo, "Meiji shonen no Hawai dekasegi, jō" in *Takushoku ronsō dai 3-kan, 2-gō* (October 1941), 276–79.

130. *Hawai Nihonjin iminshi*, 119.

131. "Shokumin Kyōkai setsuritsu no keika," in *Shokumin Kyōkai hōkoku dai 1-gō* (April 1893), 102–21.

132. Refer to "Zaibei honpōjin no jōkyō narabini tobeisha torishimari zakken"; "Hokubei Gasshūkoku ni oite honpōjin tokō seigen oyobi haiseki ikken, ichi"; and "Meiji Imin Kabushiki Kaisha gyōmujō no jikkyō chōsa narabini dō kaisha yori Bikutoria oyobi Hawai nado e dekaseginin boshū tokō ikken," held at the Gaimushō Gaikō Shiryōkan. For *dekaseginin* who were recruited to Hawai'i by *imin kaisha* (emigration companies), refer to Alan T. Moriyama, *Imingaisha: Japanese Emigration Companies and Hawaii, 1894–1908* (Honolulu: University of Hawai'i Press, 1985).

133. Mutsu Munemitsu Gaimu Daijin oyobi Inoue Kaoru Naimu Daijin shokan, Itō Hirobumi Naikaku Sōri Daijin ate, "Imin hogo kisoku seitei ni tsuki kakugi yōsei no ken," Meiji 27-nen 2-gatsu 12-nichi, in *Nihon gaikō bunsho dai 27-kan*, 618–19.

134. Chokurei dai 42-gō, "Imin hogo kisoku" and "Imin hogo kisoku shikō saisoku" are recorded as "Migi Mutsu, Inoue shokan fuki 1" in *Nihon gaikō bunsho dai 27-kan*, 619–22.

135. Saionji Kinmochi Gaimu Daijin shokan, Itō Hirobumi ate, "Imin hogohō kitei ni tsuki kakugi seikyū no ken," dated January 4, 1896, fuzokusho narabini fuki 1 oyobi 2, in *Nihon gaikō bunsho dai 29-kan*, 976–85.

136. *Nihon gaikō bunsho dai 27-kan*, 621, and *dai 29-kan*, 978.

137. Ibid., *dai 29-kan*, 981.

138. Ibid., *dai 27-kan*, 620, and *dai 29-kan*, 983.

139. Ibid., *dai 29-kan*, 981.

140. In this period, the United States was idealized as a model nation of highly civilized people. To Japanese government officials and intellectual leaders, it would have been unimaginable to send *dekaseginin* that would disgrace themselves in public in such a country. Refer to Kamei Shunsuke, *Jiyū no seichi: Nihonjin no Amerika* (Kenkyūsha Shuppan, 1978).

141. According to a report by Fujii Saburō, Japanese consul general in Hawai'i, the number of Japanese who moved to the continental United States from Hawai'i was only 19 in 1891. The following year, 1892, however, it dramatically increased, to 499. He theorized that "in 1892, an unidentified American came to Hawai'i and persuaded Japanese *dekaseginin*, including those whose term had already expired,

to move to the continental United States for work. He told them he received the information that wages were higher there" (Yoshida, *Meiji shonen no Hawai dekasegi*, jō, 279).

142. Reports of the Immigration Commission, Volume 39, Immigration Legislation, 125–26; and Maldwyn A. Jones, *American Immigration* (Chicago: University of Chicago Press, 1960), 250–52.

143. For example, Chū-Bei Kōshi Tateno Gōzō shokan, Gaimu Daijin Aoki Shūzō ate, "Sōkō ni oite Nihonjin yonmei jōriku kinshi no ken," Meiji 24-nen 4-gatsu 30-nichi; and Sōkō Ryōji Chinda Sutemi shokan, Gaimu Daijin Aoki Shūzō ate, "Honpō tokōsha jōriku kyozetsu no ken." Meiji 24-nen 5-gatsu 7-ka in *Nihon gaikō bunsho dai 24-kan*, 478–87.

144. Implemented on April 1, 1891. Article VII of the 1891 act created the Office of Superintendent of Immigration. Refer to *Reports of the Immigration Commission, Volume 39, Immigration Legislation*, 98–100. For background on how the US government restricted immigration after the 1880s, refer to Jones, *American Immigration*, 247–77.

145. Sōkō Ryōji Chinda Sutemi shokan, "Gaimu Daijin Aoki Shūzō ate, Beikoku imin shinkisei shikō ni tsuki honpōjin tokō torishimari kata ni kanshi jōshin no ken," Meiji 24-nen 4-gatsu 25-nichi in *Nihon gaikō bunsho dai 24-kan*, 463–76. After 1906, immigration inspection was implemented at the Canada-US and the Mexico-US borders, in addition to immigration inspection at ports in the United States. Refer to Sakata, "'19-seiki kōhan ni Amerika ni tokōshita Nihonjin to 'imin tōkei,'" 66–67.

146. Sakata, "Datsu-a no shishi," 88–151.

147. When Mutsu Munemitsu, the minister of foreign affairs, was preparing preliminary negotiations for a revision of the treaty with the United States, the United States agreed that revision was prudent. It said, however, that any revision of the treaty should not apply to Article I, which protects US citizens' freedom of entry, travel, residency, and the complete protection of their bodies and assets. This was because the domestic political situation, one where Chinese migrant laborers had been banned from immigration since 1882, was anti-Asian. See *Jōyaku kaisei keika gaiyō*, ed. Nihon Gakujutsu Shinkōkai (Nihon Kokusai Rengō Kyōkai, 1950), 402–5.

148. Sō 659, Gaimu Daijin Aoki Shūzō kunrei, kaku fuken chiji ate, "Hokubei Gasshūkoku oyobi Kanada imin tokō kinji kata kunrei no ken," Meiji 33-nen 8-gatsu futsuka; and Den 22, Gaimu Daijin Aoki Shūzō kunrei, Chū-Bei Kōshi Takahira Kogorō ate, "Hokkayuki imin tōbun no aida sashitomeraretaru ni tsuki ninchi no hōjin haisekiron jokyo kata ni zensho subeki mune kunrei no ken," Meiji 33-nen 8-gatsu 2-ka, in "Hokubei Gasshūkoku ni oite honpōjin tokō seigen oyobi haiseki ikken, 3," 1428–32. For background, refer to "Hokubei Gasshūkoku ni oite honpōjin tokō seigen oyobi haiseki ikken, 3," 1287–1427; and "Beikoku ni oite honpōjin imin seigen no ken" in *Nihon gaikō bunsho dai 33-kan*, 405–61.

149. The Treaty of Commerce and Navigation was signed on November 22, 1894. Its Article XIX stipulates, "This treaty shall go into operation on the 17th of July, 1899." See *Compilation of Treaties in Force: Prepared under Act of July 7, 1898* (Washington, DC: Government Printing Office, 1899), 352–59.

150. I will save this subject for another paper.

151. This definition was the same in the mid-nineteenth century. Refer to *Dr. Webster's Complete Dictionary of the English Language . . . thoroughly*

Revised and Improved, Volume 1, comp. Chauncey A. Goodrich and Noah Porter (London: Bell and Daldy 1864), 660, for an example.

152. For "new immigrants" and the "intransigency" argued by the advocates of immigration restriction, refer to Jones, *American Immigration*, 177–82.

153. "The population of the United States today, except for the Indians, consists entirely of immigrants and of the descendants of immigrants" (ibid., 1).

154. For example, see Oscar Handlin, *The Uprooted: The Epic Story of the Great Migrations That Made American People* (New York: Grosset & Dunlap, 1951): "Once I thought to write a history of the immigrants in America. Then I discovered that the immigrants were American history" (page 3); and Jones, *American Immigration*: "Immigration, which was America's *raison d'être*, has been the most persistent and the most pervasive influence in the development. The whole history of the United States during the past three and a half centuries has been molded by successive waves of immigrants who responded to the lure of the New World and whose labors, together with those of their descendants, have transformed an almost empty continent into the world's most powerful nation" (page 1).

155. For example, Kihara Ryūkichi, *Hawai Nihonjin shi* (Bunseisha, 1935), 397.

156. For English-language literature, only Yosaburo Yoshida, "Sources and Causes of Japanese Immigration," *Annals of the American Academy of Political Science* 34 (September 1909), 159–62, is available. For the current studies of Japanese migration and emigration in Japan, refer to Sakata, "Nihonjin Amerika dekasegi no chiikisei no ichi kōsatsu (I)–(III)" in *Ōsaka Gakuin Daigaku, Kokusaigaku ronshū dai 1-kan, dai 1-gō* (November 1990), *dai 1-kan, dai 2-gō* (March 1991), and *dai 2-kan, dai 1-gō* (October 1991).

157. For example, one sociologist wrote as follows: "I often encountered Japanese and their descendants in not only Brazil but also other countries in Latin America and the United States. I immediately understood that they could be divided into multiple categories. First, the people called *Issei*. I thought of a glorified saying 'venturing overseas.' Although it may sound rude, the majority of them have fallen off from the old, poor Japan" (Shimizu Ikutarō, "Kinō no tabi 1," in *Bungei shunjū*, 54, no. 3, March 1976, 146–47). For the relationship between migration and poverty, refer to Sakata, "Nihonjin Amerika dekasegi no chiikisei no ichi kōsatsu (II)," 155–63.

158. Among the 29,196 *kan'yaku imin* who arrived in Hawai'i between 1885 and 1894, six were Tōhoku natives (one from Aomori, one from Fukushima, two from Iwate, and two from Miyagi). Refer to *Kanagawa-ken tōkeisho*, Meiji 18-nendo–28-nendo.

159. Refer to Sakata, "Datsu-a no shishi," 65–87.

CHAPTER 3

On a Collision Course

The Migration of Japanese *Dekasegi* Laborers to the United States during the Meiji Era (I)

"The United States is composed of immigrants. Men and women immigrate to this country in search of wealth, nobility, and prosperity. Everybody is active, both physically and mentally, giving an unparalleled vigor to this country. There is no question about the United States' wealth and success." [1] This account was published in the March 25, 1884, issue of *Jiji shinpō*. It was part of the article titled "Beikoku wa shishi no sumika nari" (The United States is the home of the ambitious), written by Fukuzawa Yukichi, who encouraged Japanese schoolboys to emigrate to the United States. Also, two years later in 1886, a Japanese man residing in San Francisco named Shūyū Sanjin wrote the following in the *Kitare Nihonjin: ichimei Sōkō tabi annai* (Come, Japanese: Travel guide of San Francisco):

> Instead of staying in Japan, where you could make only a limited achievement in a claustrophobic society, it would not be difficult to become wealthy and return to Japan in glory if one would devote oneself to business pursuits for five to ten years in the civilized

This paper was translated from Sakata Yasuo, "Shōtotsuten e mukau kidō: Meiji ki ni okeru Nihonjin no Amerika dekasegi" (On a Collision Course: The Migration of Japanese *Dekasegi* Laborers to the United States during the Meiji Era) (I), *Ōsaka Gakuin Daigaku Kokusaigaku ronshū 3-kan, 1-gō* (1992). The author intended to refine this article at a later date.

world of the United States or Europe, where wages are higher. Today the center of civilization is the United States; it is a newly opened land where abundant unexplored lands are still available. These enterprises are plentiful as if they are waiting for the ambitious to come. Some thirty-one thousand brothers and sisters, you should have a bigger purpose and be resolved to lay your bones in a grave and create a second new Japan in the United States. One could have equal rights with the white people and gladly let them know that the Japanese do not deserve contempt. Furthermore, these achievements would undoubtedly bring prestige and the public good to the people of the Japanese government.[2]

This brave promotion of Japanese emigration would have dumbfounded the American anti-Japanese advocates if they had heard it. Encouraged by these pro-emigration statements, poor *shosei* (schoolboys) who were studying in Tokyo started traveling to San Francisco in the mid-1880s.[3] Their purpose was to continue studying while they worked as houseboys. In early 1889, Ozaki Yukio, who stopped by San Francisco during his grand tour of Europe and the United States, wrote that *dekasegi* (temporarily working away from home while going to school) students in San Francisco numbered approximately two thousand. This was written in the *Kenbunki* (travelogue) sent to *Hōchi shinbun*.[4]

By the mid-1880s, when Japanese schoolboys, encouraged by Fukuzawa and other intellectual leaders of the *bunmei kaika* (Civilization and Enlightenment movement) in Japan, began to reside in the San Francisco Bay Area, the US government had already enacted the Chinese Exclusion Act in May 1882. By this law, the entry of Chinese laborers to the United States as immigrants was barred for ten years. The Chinese, who were regarded as undesirable aliens, were exclusively targeted. The restrictive period under this statute was extended twice in 1892 and 1902, and finally, the law as amended in 1904 prohibited the immigration of the Chinese to the United States. The golden door was shut firmly for the Chinese.[5] Moreover, Chinese laborers residing in the United States also became the target of racial harassment and exclusion and, at times, even physical abuse and lynching.[6]

At this point, however, Japanese intellectual leaders who had encouraged schoolboys to study in the United States, along with Japanese students on the West Coast, did not even consider that Japanese, though thought of as "Orientals" like the Chinese, would be placed in the same category as "Chinamen" laborers, who were despised and thus subjected to restriction and exclusion in the United States—an immigrants' paradise.[7] These leaders convinced themselves of this and advocated as such. On the opposing side of their self-righteous notion that they were different was a narcissistic confidence in the *datsu-a ron* (the idea to promote Japanese westernization, or de-Asianization), despite its geographical location in Asia.[8] Furthermore, they held an absolute trust in the generosity of American citizens, full of the spirit of independence in the sacred land of liberty, the United States being one of the models the Meiji government based its westernization on.[9]

Around this time, one of the Japanese residing in the United States looked down on and criticized the Chinese as the Americans did, instead of worrying about his own future:

["Chinamen" residing in San Francisco] number 25,000: 4,000 are contract laborers and factory workers, 5,000 are house servants, 3,000 are laundry operators, shopkeepers and small-scale merchants, and others are vagrants. Chinese women in San Francisco number 2,000, of which eight to nine out of ten are prostitutes. The renowned Chinatown was once proud and clean, adorned with temples and inns; its every corner was without dust. However, storms came and American flowers have wilted over time. Chinatown deteriorated and became a bizarre scene, with yellow papers written with Chinese characters posted on the storefronts. Perhaps pork stores or opium smoking creates a distinctly terrible rotten smell. . . . It is not a joy to see women's faces; they are dressed like men, wearing trousers. It's a sorry scene to observe them behaving as if they are beauties. The Chinese in the United States suffer from extreme contempt by the Americans. Even though many state governments have enacted laws to prevent them from becoming US citizens or marrying white people, they don't care about this treatment and are willing to work like slaves as their ultimate goal is to earn money and return to China.[10]

Published in the *Ai Koku*, the paper of the organization Sōkō Nihonjin Aikoku Dōmei (San Francisco Japanese Patriotic League), formed by schoolboys living in the San Francisco Bay Area as part of the *jiyū minken undō* (Freedom and People's Rights Movement in Japan), an article stated: "The Chinese residing in the United States represent the lower classes of the Chinese people, while the Japanese residing in the United States represent the upper class of the Japanese. This is the first factor. The Chinese are old-fashioned and unwilling to change, in disagreement with the United States. The Japanese are progressive and in harmony with the United States. This is the second factor. These two elements are distinct and should call for attention." [11] This article emphasized that the Japanese in the United States were "de-Asianized upper-class citizens" and probably recognized by Americans as such.

However, anti-Japanese sentiment spread to the general Japanese population, despite optimistic predictions. In San Francisco, Consul General Chinda Sutemi reported the following to Foreign Minister Enomoto Takeaki on May 10, 1892:

It's a lamentable situation that some Americans driven by racial prejudice tried to exclude the Japanese, just as they did the Chinese. The number of Japanese laborers and travelers who arrive in the United States is more than ever before. Since April 1, 1892, those who came directly from Japanese ports and those who came from Hawai'i and British Canada numbered together 500. This large wave of Japanese migration has alarmed American workers, making them afraid that it would cause chaos in the labor market. Various newspapers in San Francisco published a series of articles regarding the issue of Japanese people coming to the United States, speculating that the Japanese government was encouraging laborers to move to the United States, aiming to expand its overseas colonization (*Examiner*, April 25), and that they aim to topple white superiority (*Examiner*, April 28). They are arguing that after the Chinese, it is the Japanese laborers that should be excluded from the United States . . . and are featuring the Japanese people's economic status and the shortcomings of their daily practice (*Morning Call* and *Bulletin*, May 4). The articles are alarming the American public in the Bay Area, and we cannot afford overlooking them. . . .

I hope you observe the American sentiment against the Japanese in this country.[12]

In the 1890s, the Japanese, who had considered themselves equal to Westerners, realized the undeniable fact that they were subject to the US government's immigration restrictions and American discrimination and were greatly shocked.[13]

Even today, after over a century, the factors causing similar confusion still exist in this immigrant country, though the situation and background are different. The reason is that the United States has two contradictory aspects. One is the idealized notion—which American citizens take every chance to exert—of an immigrant nation that stresses the United States as an asylum for the "huddled masses," as exemplified in Emma Lazarus's poem.[14] On the other hand, the reality of exclusion and the immigration restrictions of certain ethnic groups in the latter half of the nineteenth to the first half of the twentieth century is clearly recognizable.[15] Furthermore, the exclusionists were themselves descendants of immigrants. It is confusing for researchers to reconcile these two contradictory images of the United States when they try to analyze the intentions and purposes of implementing policies to restrict the immigration of a certain group or "race," or when they try to examine the prejudice of American citizens against certain groups on the grounds of ethnic idiosyncrasies.

Was the United States an immigrants' paradise for European citizens only—white Anglo-Saxons who constituted the American mainstream in the first half of the nineteenth century—as has been suggested by some historians?[16] The erection of the Statue of Liberty in 1886, only four years after the Chinese Exclusion Act, in New York Harbor, where European immigrants landed, seems to suggest that this might have been the case.[17] Should we feel chagrin that the Statue of Liberty is smiling only toward Europe?

Theses That Attempt to Explain the Contradiction

The "Regional Conspiracy" Thesis

During the pre–World War II period, scholars have primarily discussed two theses in various scholarly publications to explain the large gap between the idealized image and the reality of the United States as an immigrant nation. One is the regional conspiracy thesis, which suggests the exclusionist activities against the Chinese and Japanese were geographically limited to California or the West Coast. It stresses the fact that racially discriminatory and exclusionist demagogues fueled activities driven from a narrow-minded perspective, disregarding the founding fathers' principles and the interests of the nation as a whole.[18] The fundamental idea for this comes from Mary Coolidge, who first proposed the "California conspiracy thesis" in her publication *Chinese Immigration*:

> The clamor of an alien class [Irish] in a single State [California]— taken up by politicians for their own ends—was sufficient to change the policy of a nation and to commit the United States to race discrimination at variance with our own professed theories of government, and so irrevocably that it has become an established tradition.[19]

Coolidge's thesis was largely accepted as convincing for more than half a century. After sixty years, in 1969, Stuart Miller questioned for the first time this monolithic perspective being used to explain America's exclusion and persecution of the Chinese. In his meticulous study, Miller proved that the derogatory image of "Chinamen"—as ignorant, pig-headed, filthy, unsanitary, crafty, immoral, and pigtailed—which was thought to have developed among the general American public after its direct witness of working-class Chinese laborers arriving in the United States in the latter half of the nineteenth century—actually originated before Chinese immigration to the United States began in 1848. American missionaries, diplomatic agents, and traders had visited China and spread their perceptions through letters and reports sent home, especially on the East Coast. Miller demonstrated the flaw in Coolidge's suggestion that racial discrimination was restricted to Californians.[20] Today, scholars seldom rely on Coolidge's California conspiracy thesis alone. However, the distorted concentration of anti-Chinese exclusion movements on the West Coast is still emphasized as a historical fact. One prominent immigration scholar, Oscar Handlin, takes the position that the Chinese-exclusion movement was regional.[21]

As Roger Daniels explains, "the anti-Japanese campaign was mainly a tail to the anti-Chinese kite," bearing a strong relationship between the two.[22] As a result, the study of anti-Japanese exclusion is often drawn from the regional conspiracy thesis. In his scholarly book, *Japanese in the United States: A Critical Study of the Problems of the Japanese Immigrants and Their Children*, valued even after World War II as the only English-language scholarly publication regarding the Japanese in the United States, Yamato Ichihashi emphasized that "the Japanese in the United States inherited the prejudice against the Chinese."[23] He concluded that the anti-Japanese movement was largely confined to the West.[24] This regionalized point of view dominated the study of the Japanese-exclusion movement for a long time.

The "Undesirable Lower-Class Immigrant" Thesis

The California conspiracy thesis attempted to explain the activities of Americans that contradicted the American founding principles and US government policies, while the next thesis focused on the immigrants, attempting to prove that Chinese and Japanese *dekasegi* laborers were "unsavory" in comparison with European immigrants. This thesis was useful for exclusionists in criticizing the Chinese and Japanese and was actually used in that way. The essence of this thesis was that because the Chinese and Japanese in the United States were "ignorant, unrefined, and poor-looking" transient *dekasegi* laborers in the eyes of civilized American citizens, and because they did not abide by the necessary practices to become part of American society and insisted on maintaining their motherland's foreign culture and customs, they were therefore incapable of becoming US citizens. This "undesirable lower-class immigrant" thesis stressed the aspect of the immigrants' unassimilability as a race—their inability to assimilate even into America's melting pot—and was the main reasoning behind the restrictive immigration policies exclusively targeting them.

Naturally, while exclusionists made utmost effort to prove that Japanese laborers were similar to Chinese laborers in being unassimilable and undesirable immigrants for America, those who were critical of the anti-Japanese exclusion tried to explain that though the Japanese and Chinese were of the same race, the Japanese possessed different qualities as citizens of the nation. One of the latter advocates wrote:

The immigration of the Japanese followed that of the Chinese. The whole history of the Japanese has been colored by that fact. The Chinese came to the West under such circumstances that they stood in striking contrast to all other elements in the population. With a different language, with queue and different dress, with no family life, with different customs, and steeled against charges as they were, the reaction against them was strong and immediate when they ceased to be objects of curiosity. . . . As a result of the struggle that ensued they were assigned the inferior place they unprotestingly accepted. The Chinaman was a good loser. Then came the Japanese. They came from the same "quarter of the earth," were of related color, had a similar language, accepted the same economic rank as the Chinese, frequently occupied their bunkhouses, and underbid for work as did the Chinaman. What wonder, though they were vastly different peoples, that the Japanese should be set down as being in the same category as the Chinese? In men's minds they were assigned the same place to begin with. Moreover, it was assumed that they should continue to occupy it. Not to do so was to be regarded as undesirable.[25]

Americans who considered the Japanese to be unassimilable foreigners like the Chinese—believing that they ought to be barred from immigrating to the United States and that those already residing in the country should be excluded from eligibility for US citizenship—were not as sympathetic as this scholar. For example, the following appeared in an article in the *Lincoln Journal*, published in Lincoln, Nebraska:

The Japanese are now coming into San Francisco at the rate of 1,000 every year, and the people are beginning to wonder if it is not to be a repetition of the Chinese evil. The immigrants are of the lowest class, and like the Chinese earn all the money they can and then retire to the land of their fathers with small fortunes. The next war cry of the sand lots will have to do with the summary retirement of the Jap.[26]

Three years later in San Francisco, the purported birthplace of the anti-Japanese movement, an article, derogatory in content, was published:

Undoubtedly these [Japanese] men were in their own country til-
lers of the soil—"hewers of wood and drawers of water." In this
country they intend engaging in the same pursuits. . . . Like their
cousins, the Chinese, they live on little or nothing and need not
what in civilizing life are deemed necessaries, much less luxuries.
For this reason, even if they are out of work for a portion of the
year they still manage to save money. . . . The women here are of
the lowest class, and, like the Chinese women, are imported only
to lead a life of shame. . . . Like the Chinese women, they are held
in bondage and are obliged to turn over their wages of sin to their
masters or importers.[27]

Then, what kind of Japanese laborers arrived in San Francisco
around 1891? The consul general of San Francisco, Chinda Sutemi,
stated the following in his report to the foreign minister:

Two German tramp steamers, the *Remus* and *Pemptos*, arrived in
San Francisco port on April 21 and 22, carrying laborers; approximately 120 from Kumamoto, Nagasaki, Kagoshima, and other
prefectures. The reason so many laborers used these ships was that
they were not regularly scheduled steamships, so their fares are
rather inexpensive, only thirty-five dollars per steerage passenger.
Furthermore, seven months prior to departure, these ship companies advertised for passengers in regional Japanese newspapers.
These laborers have corresponded with their friends in the United
States and have heard that the wages are high there. They took this
opportunity of the low fares to come to the United States. Unlike
the Japanese who arrived previously, eight or nine out of ten of
these laborers were farmers and came to the United States for the
purpose of *dekasegi*. Most likely, they have sold their properties
to pay for the journey, and once they arrive in the United States,
very few of them could support themselves. Many of the passengers
on the *Remus* were poorly dressed and denied landing as it was
thought they would become a burden of the public welfare.[28]

In another report, Chinda stated that simple farm laborers for
dekasegi were beginning to come to the United States in rapidly growing

numbers, in place of schoolboys for study, and recommended that the foreign minister restrict the emigration of "shabby" immigrants who would not qualify and would likely be denied landing due to the newly enacted immigration act.

> In the past, the Japanese who came to the United States had the purpose to study as students. However, the purpose for coming to the United States has completely changed from studying to *dekasegi*. Likewise, the individuals who come to this country are no longer students, but menial laborers who do not speak English or understand American customs. Furthermore, some cannot even write their names. They come here to seek their fortune with limited travel allowances. As soon as they arrive in San Francisco, they have only meager funds to support themselves; many are classified as poor by the recent Immigration Act. San Francisco, being a crossroads of Europeans and Asians, is an important place for Japan to uphold its standing. It is extremely important for the Japanese who come to San Francisco to represent the spirit of Japan and maintain the honor of the nation. The recent arrival of those in undesirable professions, in poor condition and dressed improperly, would likely cause anti-Japanese sentiment among Americans. The Japanese laborers in the pursuit of fortune are likely to be excluded and will unnecessarily provoke a similar situation to the Chinese experience. The Chinese, who became the target of a worldwide discriminatory movement, had a similar start as the Japanese. So, I humbly advise you to monitor the situation of the Japanese coming to San Francisco.[29]

Interestingly, when American criticism toward the Japanese *dekasegi* laborers began to increase and Japanese exclusion was deemed an inevitable reality, self-proclaimed *datsu-a* (de-Asianized) schoolboys and future leaders in the Japanese society in the United States began to ascribe the anti-Japanese exclusion movement to the undesirable lower-class immigrant thesis. One of the Japanese "elites" living in San Francisco wrote the following in an article for the magazine *Nihonjin* in 1893:

The magazine *Ensei* describes the Japanese living on the West Coast: Very few Japanese in the States are supporting themselves. They are mostly schoolboys and farmers. Merchants and businessmen have recently realized that entrepreneurship is profitable and they aspire to make money, but many are not suited to this and fail. It may sound arrogant, but I must say this observation is to the point. The *Chronicle* in San Francisco is not an exception when it comes to attacking the Japanese. The reason behind their anti-Japanese sentiment is that Japanese dress like Americans and follow American customs, and therefore they are misleading the Americans and are even more dangerous than the Chinese. Young Japanese men flirt with young American women and the Japanese prostitutes offend public decency. An increase in the number of Japanese laborers threatens the jobs of Americans. Therefore, the Japanese, together with the Chinese, should be excluded.

The white laborers call the Japanese who haven't been in the states a long time "green Japs." They despise these Japanese as much as or even more than the Chinese.

The Japanese on the West Coast generally suffer from similar situations, reflecting the attitude in various states on the West Coast. That might be due to the Japanese themselves; nonetheless, the Yankees and European immigrants who have just landed in the United States do not understand the true nature of the Japanese.

Many of the white laborers on the West Coast are from Italy, Germany, Ireland, Spain, Russia, and France. Most of them failed in surviving the competition of the East Coast of the United States or in Europe and came to the West Coast in search of fortune. Needless to say, they or their descendants are not well educated and do not know much about Japan. They think that Japan is part of China and that houses in Japan are made of bamboo and so on. They jump to the conclusion that the Japanese are all like those they observe in the United States and imagine Japan in that way, producing a great misunderstanding. The white laborers consider the Japanese as their enemies for jobs. The politicians misjudge Japan as an inferior nation and the Japanese as an inferior race.

Both groups take advantage of the Japanese and want them for their own ambition.[30]

This description, as can be seen, was full of prejudice.

Japanese Prejudice

I will later discuss the condescending view of the "lower-class" Japanese held by Japanese elites, including the intellectual leaders who promoted Japanese emigration to the United States. Here I would like to emphasize that the Japanese residing in the United States, or those who became the Issei, inherited this habit of looking down on early *dekasegi* laborers. According to *Zaibei Nihonjin shi* (History of Japanese in America) compiled by the Jiseki Hozonkai (Preservation Committee of Footsteps) of the Zaibei Nihonjinkai (Japanese Association of America) in 1940:

> The Japanese pioneers, unlike the *dekasegi* laborers, in the United States were not provincial; they possessed relatively large amounts of land, were more or less educated, and had experienced some social activities in Japan. They aspired to do more than make money in the United States. Some came with money, but most were willing to be the pioneers of new frontiers they had dreamed of by working and studying. As the Japanese population in the United States grew, these pioneers played high-level leadership roles in Japanese society in industrial management, organizations, moral guidance, and solving anti-Japanese issues, and maintained the reputation of Japanese society. In comparison, we must consider the fact that the nature of the Japanese society in the US is different from other immigration places centered on purely *dekasegi* laborers.[31]

This *Zaibei Nihonjin shi* was compiled in commemoration of the 2,600th anniversary of the founding of Japan. The publication emphasized that the Japanese in the United States were proof of the overseas expansion of the Yamato race. At the same time, by delineating the Japanese society in the United States from that of immigrants, the publication highlighted the pride of Japanese leaders in this country who repeatedly emphasized that Japanese were different from Chinese and could be equal to Europeans.

As one historian explained:

Japanese leaders believed in the superiority of the Japanese people. In 1913 five prominent leaders ... addressed a revealing letter to Consul General Chinda Sutemi. ... In discussing two immigration bills before Congress, these five men presented their opinion regarding a provision prohibiting the admission of any alien ineligible [for] citizenship. They wrote:

> Of the ten or more immigration bills which have been introduced into Congress, the two most important ones are the Dillingham Bill in the Senate and the Burnett Bill in the House. Both bills contain a provision prohibiting the admission of aliens ineligible [for] citizenship under existing naturalization statutes. This provision has the objective of excluding Japanese and the other Orientals. Among the countries of the Orient, there are those which still cannot claim to rank among the advanced, civilized world powers. That these lesser nations will be treated differentially by American immigration laws is understandable. But since Japan already ranks among the advanced, civilized nations, it is unfair for her to be treated as an inferior country.

This letter expressed the ingrained prejudice of Japanese immigrant leaders. Countries like China and Korea were "inferior nations," in their opinion, whose subjects were unworthy of equal treatment. If the United States elected to discriminate against the people of such nations, that was understandable as well as acceptable. But Japan and its subjects were different. Japan was the equal of the Western powers, and therefore her subjects deserved to be, indeed demanded to be, treated equally. Above all else, Japanese immigrant leaders wanted Japanese immigrants to be treated as European immigrants were. They conceded that the American government had the right to regulate immigration, but they wanted the Japanese immigrant to be placed on the same footing as a European immigrant.[32]

Obviously, hidden behind the pride possessed by leaders of the Japanese in the United States was their prejudice against early *dekasegi* laborers. Compared with early "immigrant" *dekasegi* laborers, who had no intention of settling permanently, and who had many good reasons to be classified as lower-class Japanese, [the editors of] *Zaibei Nihonjin shi* considered themselves to be totally different. One factor supporting this confidence was from American compliments of the Japanese. The quote often referred to was in an op-ed in *The Outlook* issued on January 14, 1911:

> The spread of anti-Chinese sentiment to anti-Japanese sentiment is a natural course of action. It's not about emotion, it's not about suspicion, it's not about debasing Asiatic culture, it's not about education, it's not about cheap labor willing to work for long hours, it's not about inferior living conditions. The nature of the Japanese is brave and honorable. There's nothing inferior about the Japanese compared to European immigrants. However, the American civilization couldn't have developed without the contribution of European immigrants. Although the Orientals, particularly the Japanese, have various excellent virtues, they're not Europeanized citizens by birth. Like Lafcadio Hearn, who has conducted an excellent study of the Japanese culture, and the poet Kipling have clearly stated, by observing the world affairs the Orient is destined to be governed by the Orientals and Europe and United States by the White race. The Oriental exclusion stems from unassimilability.[33]

This op-ed emphasized that the Japanese were unassimilable aliens; therefore, it suggested that restricting the immigration of or barring Japanese entirely was acceptable. Around 1910, when white supremacy was advocated and the anti-Japanese movement peaked, however, this article may be interpreted as one of the few compliments that recognized the Japanese people as "superior."

Former US president Theodore Roosevelt, whom Japanese in the United States respected as their true sympathizer, contributed the following flattering article to *The Outlook*:

The Japanese are a highly civilized people of extraordinary military, artistic, and industrial development; they are proud, warlike, and sensitive. I believe that our people have, what I personally certainly have, a profound and hearty admiration for them; an admiration for their great deeds and great qualities, an ungrudging respect for their national character.[34]

Roosevelt continued:

But this admiration and respect is accompanied by the firm conviction that it is not for the advantage of either country should they settle in mass in the other country. The understanding between the two countries on this point should be on a basis of entire mutuality, and therefore on a basis which I preserve unimpaired the self-respect of each country, and permit each to continue to feel friendly good will for the other. Japan would certainly object to the incoming of masses of American farmers, laborers, and small traders; indeed, the Japanese would object to this at least as strongly as the men of Pacific Coast and Rocky Mountain States object to the incoming in mass of Japanese workmen, agricultural laborers, and men engaged in small trades. The Japanese certainly object to Americans acquiring land in Japan at least as much as the Americans of far Western States object to the Japanese acquiring land on our soil.[35]

As stated above, Roosevelt explained why Japanese laborer immigration should be restricted. The Japanese in the United States, however, blindly valued his "compliment" for many years. One could say that they tried to distance themselves from the epicenter of the problem, fabricating the ground that the "upstanding Japanese"—the true representatives of Japan—were excluded by mistake, and that the real exclusion target was the "lower-class" Japanese. They did this by emphasizing the inappropriately unrefined behavior of the lower-class Japanese.

Explaining the cause of anti-Japanese movement with the lower-class Japanese thesis is not restricted to pre–World War II scholarship. Analyzing the cause of the Immigration Act of 1924, which barred the entry of immigrants from Japan and other Asian countries, post–World War II scholarship suggests the following:

> The reasons behind the anti-Japanese immigration law are multi-faceted and complex. However, one of the causes is undoubtedly the low-quality of Japanese immigrants. Of course, quite a few Japanese immigrants were well educated and of excellent quality. Nonetheless, many immigrants were not ashamed of slurping while eating, spitting and urinating on the street, blowing their noses with their hands, and not being able to speak English or knowing American customs.
>
> The Japanese who live in a foreign country represent Japan. They were diligent and of high moral standing but ignorant of etiquette. For this reason, they were often frowned upon by Americans. And their diligence even accelerated their derision.
>
> Americans can discriminate against the Japanese and deride them if the Japanese are ignorant and incompetent. However, the Japanese in the eyes of Americans had equal or higher capabilities than that of the Whites and were diligent but mysteriously ignorant.
>
> Japanese immigrants' capability and "ignorance"—this was certainly one of the causes leading to the "Japanese exclusion" act.[36]

The lower-class Japanese thesis and the California conspiracy thesis should both be regarded as scapegoatism. In the case of the California conspiracy thesis, only a certain segment of white Americans who had a strong racial prejudice against Asians was considered responsible for the anti-Japanese exclusion. In the lower-class Japanese thesis, the lower-class Japanese laborers were to blame; when comparing Japanese and Chinese arriving and residing in the United States with European immigrants, the Japanese and Chinese were unassimilable and undesirable foreigners. Shifting attention from this fact gave a false sense of relief to some Japanese, that exclusion was not targeting the entire population of Japanese and Chinese. However, it was an unavoidable reality that the Japanese would follow the footsteps of the "Chinaman." Instead of simply discussing why the Japanese *dekasegi* laborers were excluded, researchers of migration studies should examine Japanese prejudice that prevented diplomats in the Ministry of Foreign Affairs, Meiji intellectual leaders, and schoolboys in the United States from grasping the situation.

America as a White Republic

Here we should question America's idealized concept as an asylum for those who have suffered in other countries. For example, Maldwyn Jones argued that this idealized notion continued to exist in the 1880s, when the United States' immigration policy transformed from open doors to restrictive immigration.

> The immigration legislation of 1882–85 did not, it will be noticed, spring from an integrated attempt at restriction. It was devised rather to meet specific, unconnected situations, and those who supported it generally disclaimed any wider restrictive purpose. Thus in 1885 an advocate of the Foran Act (Contract Labor Law) could remark that "this bill in no measure seeks to restrict free immigration; such a proposition would be odious, and, justly so, to the American people." This was undoubtedly true for, as yet, inherited attitudes to immigration had lost little of their potency. Even while giving their assent to the new legislative principle of qualitative exclusion, Americans were at pains to emphasize their devotion both to the asylum concept and to a cosmopolitan ideal of nationality.[37]

Wasn't this interpretation, however, applicable to "Orientals"? It is true that the US government had not started reviewing the open-door policy when Chinese laborers started arriving on the West Coast in the late 1840s and early 1850s.[38] After 1862, against the backdrop of a labor shortage due to the Civil War, the US government, through consulates and other organizations in Europe, promoted the fact that laborers in the United States were earning higher wages and that the Homestead Act made it easier for farmers to own land.[39] In 1864 the

US government enacted an immigration act to encourage European immigrants to come to the United States.[40] Within a few years it was repealed. By the 1870s, when discrimination, abuse, and exclusionist activities were occurring in many parts of the country, Americans demanded a review of the open-door system.[41]

The situation was even more difficult for the Japanese who came after the Chinese Exclusion Act of 1882. The act was significant because it was the first federal act to control immigration, and it marked a historical precedent for the federal government and Congress to single out a particular nationality to be restricted or barred from entry. The spread of the Chinese Exclusion Act to the Japanese was clearly predictable, given that both were "Orientals." In the 1890s Japanese diplomats in the United States tried to prevent this from happening.[42]

In the mid-1880s, when schoolboys intending to study and work in the San Francisco Bay Area started to arrive, and in the early 1890s, when local newspapers began featuring the topic of a surge of Japanese laborers, the reality in the United States had completely changed from what the Japanese had dreamed of before their departure.[43] The real issue here was that Japanese intellectuals, government leaders, and *jiyū minken* schoolboys coming to the United States did not doubt the US capacity as an immigrant nation. Researchers who study Japanese immigrants in the United States should be aware of the duality of the US immigration policy and the issues associated with immigration when the open-door policy was about to end. Without this understanding, scholars would be disregarding the fact that in the Meiji era, Japanese workers going to the United States were not issued passports or allowed to leave the country if they did not intend to be *dekasegi* laborers.[44] Moreover, the conventional misleading view of Japanese immigration, as expressed by the editors of *Zaibei Nihonjin shi*, was that even "pure immigrants" were mistakenly regarded as transient *dekasegi* laborers, and they became the target of exclusionist activities and the anti-Japanese movement.[45]

Immigration History and Racial Prejudice

Post–World War II studies of the Japanese-exclusion movement and exclusionist sentiments in the United States have focused on the strong racist sentiments against Asians and people of color in the late nineteenth and early twentieth centuries, supported by thoroughly studied evidence.[46] The documents establish that Caucasians, particularly Anglo-Saxons, who acknowledged themselves as constituting the mainstream of American society, stressed that they were a superior race on the basis of eugenics and thus had strong racial prejudices and contempt for the Chinese and Japanese, or the so-called yellow race. Furthermore, it is widely understood now that exclusionist behaviors supported by state and local regulations were also driven by racial prejudice. As a result, the study of ethnic minorities, including victimized Asian immigrants, has become an important field in the United States.[47]

One of the most noteworthy studies is Roger Daniels's *The Politics of Prejudice*.[48] Drawing from his meticulous study of historical documents, Daniels demonstrated that those who drove the anti-Japanese movement were in highly valued leadership positions in the American progressivist or labor movements. He argued that one should not easily determine that only demagogues and the yellow press incited the anti-Japanese movement. He emphasized that a historical reality caused by racial prejudice, such as the anti-Japanese movement, happened in the democratic nation of the United States against its founding principles, resulting in the unnecessary deterioration of US-Japan relations.

> The discriminations against the Japanese . . . are clearly blots on the democratic escutcheon which we prize so highly. But the consequences of the anti-Japanese movement were more than moral. The existence of this prejudice helped to poison relations between the United States and Japan. As George F. Kennan has pointed out, in his provocative series of lectures on American Diplomacy, 1900–1950, the "long and unhappy story" of United States–Japanese relationships in this century was constantly worsened by the fact that "we would repeatedly irritate and offend the sensitive Japanese by our immigration policies and the treatment of people of Japanese lineage . . . in this country."[49]

Few researchers would refute Daniels's perspective now. However, he published the results of his study only ten years after the end of World War II. In the mid-1950s many Americans thought that such undemocratic behavior could only be observed in totalitarian countries such as Germany, or in militaristic and imperialist nations such as Japan, and had a hard time accepting his thesis. For these reasons, Daniels's research is very important. Almost thirty years after his publication, American understanding had changed significantly, as the president and Congress officially apologized and offered reparations for the "mistake" of the Japanese American incarceration during World War II.

Future Study Challenges

Needless to say, racial prejudice is an important analytical concept in understanding domestic affairs and incidents, including the background of legal discrimination against the Japanese and the process behind the enactment of federal laws that restricted or banned Japanese immigration. It is obvious, however, that studying racial prejudice alone cannot lead to a full understanding of the background and causes of the "Japanese immigration problem" that led to the US-Japan "war scare" during the late 1900s to 1910s.[50] Not only *dekasegi* laborers and schoolboys in the United States but also intellectual leaders and government officials in Japan who promoted Japanese emigration made a grave misjudgment about the emergency situation and the best ways to deal with it, inviting further aggravation of the bilateral relationship.

To further understand the "Japanese immigration problem," we should not ignore Japan's alienation from the rest of Asia and its claims of superiority over other Asians (*datsu-a*), including the Chinese, who were also the target of exclusionism in the United States. Yuji Ichioka, who was born in Berkeley, California, and incarcerated in a war relocation center, stated the following in *Issei*:

> Japanese immigrants themselves ... were not free of prejudice. Aware of what had happened to Chinese immigrants in the nineteenth century, Japanese immigrant leaders had always dreaded the thought of Japanese exclusion. During the course of the Japanese exclusion movement, the leaders repeatedly said, "We are afraid that we will be excluded as the Chinese have been." Since they themselves had a low opinion of the Chinese people, this was not a pleasant thought to entertain. For their part, anti-Japanese exclusionists always linked Japanese immigration to the past "evils"

of Chinese immigration. To counteract this negative association, Japanese immigrant leaders did everything to disassociate Japanese immigrants from their Chinese counterparts. In the end, however, all of their attempts at disassociation went for naught. For the Japanese people, stigmatized as an equally inferior and undesirable race, were excluded in an identical manner. Japanese immigrant leaders then, reached the inevitable conclusion that "We have been excluded just like the Chinese," which expressed a realization that what they had dreaded for so long had become a horrible reality.[51]

The Japanese leaders in the United States tried to believe that the Americans and the US government would not treat Japan in an unequal fashion as if it were a weaker country in Asia, would not prohibit Japanese from coming to the United States on the basis of unassimilability and undesirability, and would not expel those who were already in the country. This belief was particularly powerful after Japan won the Russo-Japanese War and thus joined the "great powers" of the world. The whites in American society, however, did not accept Japanese idiosyncrasies.

The scholars of migration studies should also pay attention to the large gap in definitions of *immigration* between the Japanese and Americans in the 1880s and 1890s, when many Japanese began to arrive in the United States for the purpose of *dekasegi*.[52] The Japanese officials in the Ministry of Foreign Affairs considered *dekasegi* to be one form of immigration and believed that Japanese entry into the United States as *dekasegi* immigrants would be granted. The anti-Chinese exclusionists, however, argued that the United States should not allow "sojourners" to enter the country, pointing out that it was a characteristic of undesirable immigrants. The Japanese intellectual leaders, however, did not fully grasp the reality in the United States, continued to be allured by an idealized America, and encouraged *dekasegi* emigration. All that gave even more fuel to the attacks against Japanese. Future studies should focus on uncovering historical facts related to both the United States and Japan. In the study of immigration history, reasons cannot exist only on one side.

It is important to review the developments before 1891 when the Office of the Superintendent of Immigration within the Treasury

Department was established and the federal government assumed direct control of inspecting, admitting, denying, and processing all immigrants seeking admission to the United States.[53] This paper discusses measures taken in the United States regarding the Japanese *dekasegi* laborers to the West Coast and the developments and issues associated with their arrival in the 1890s. I will discuss the Japanese reactions and measures in chapter 4.

Immigration Control over "Undesirable" Aliens in the United States

The "Yellow Race" and the "Immigrants' Paradise"

As I pointed out earlier, the idealized United States as an immigrants' paradise changed substantially in the 1880s for "Orientals." One reason was that immigration policies proposed and enacted by Congress and the federal government reflected white Anglo-Saxon prejudice. Those who flaunted their rights of having been in the United States earlier and exerted their racial superiority considered British, Scandinavian, and German immigrants, for example, favorably. These immigrants had ample room to fulfill their dreams. The United States, however, was no longer the immigrants' paradise, even for Caucasians who were regarded as belonging to an undesirable race or nationality on the basis of prejudice, interests, political decisions, and simple dislike. In fact, Chinese laborers, who as members of the "yellow race" were considered one rank below the white race and whose appearance was distinctive, became the target of prejudice and exclusionist behavior by Americans.[54] Very few Americans then, however, pointed out that such acts were wrong. Rather, political scientists concluded that immigration was a domestic issue and that considering racial factors in evaluating whether immigration policies were right or wrong was unavoidable.

> The feeling against the Negroes has forced us to recognize that race feeling is an extremely important political question and may well become a social question. Moreover, we should recognize the fact that the feeling on the Pacific Coast against the Chinese, the Japanese, and the Hindus is not in itself exceptional. A similar feeling against these same races is found in Canada, in Australia, in

South Africa, in every place where these oriental races have come into immediate contact with the white race, and especially when they have come into active competition with it in ordinary labor. We must recognize this feeling, then, as a usual one and one that must be considered when we come to political action. [Although] these races may not be considered in any way inferior to ourselves, it is a fact that they are materially different: that they are not as easily assimilated as are the members of the European races; that they do not readily marry with our people or our people with them. And we should reflect that, short of intermarriage, there is no real amalgamation of races.[55]

It is not an exaggeration to say that the door to the United States was gradually closing on "Orientals" beginning in the 1880s. The 1882 Chinese Exclusion Act indicated one such change. I can point out that the Chinese Exclusion Act had many exceptions from the perspective of immigration law. The US government needed to revise the Burlingame Treaty of 1868 in order to submit to Congress the discriminatory bill targeting a single nationality. The US government took an unusually aggressive approach toward the Qing Court to force a revision of the treaty. The bill included for the first time an immigration restriction on Chinese laborers for ten years. As Coolidge demonstrated, a bill accommodating the interests of a single region in the United States, as demanded by the leaders of the anti-Chinese movement and their supporters in California, was passed in Congress with hardly any opposition.[56]

The First Step toward Chinese Exclusion: Revision of the Burlingame Treaty
The immigration clause in the Burlingame Treaty was considered troublesome for leaders of the anti-Chinese movement. Anson Burlingame (1820–70) was an American diplomat and minister stationed in Beijing from 1862 to 1867. After having retired from his position in November 1867, he was asked to represent the Qing mission at the request of a high official in the Qing dynasty who highly valued Burlingame's personal qualities. Burlingame successfully negotiated the treaty with Secretary of State William Seward, based on the principle of reciprocity, an unusual achievement for an "Oriental" country in the late

nineteenth century—a time when unequal treaties, granting the most-favored-nation treatment exclusively to Western nations, were commonly signed in Asia.[57]

Article V of this treaty stipulated that "the United States of America and the Emperor of China cordially recognize the inherent and inalienable right of man to change his home and allegiance" and "also the mutual advantage of the free migration and emigration of their citizens and subjects respectively from one country to the other for purposes of curiosity, of trade or as permanent residents."[58]

As a principle of international law, domestic regulations and rules will be annulled when in violation of a treaty. The anti-Chinese activists pressured state assemblies in the western states to enact discriminatory rules against the citizens of the Qing Empire; however, if those local acts were challenged in a federal court, they were often struck down.[59] The reasoning behind such federal court decisions was the Burlingame Treaty, in which the citizens of the Qing Empire were guaranteed protection of their rights and privileges equal to the most-favored-nation treatment during their residence, travel, and commercial activities in the United States. As a result, many cases of anti-Chinese regulations were annulled.[60]

The leaders of the anti-Chinese movement on the West Coast were also strongly demanding immigration control of Chinese laborers.[61] Article V of the Burlingame Treaty, however, stood in their way. If anti-Chinese activists managed to persuade members of Congress to submit a bill restricting immigration, support such a bill, and pass it—and if the president did not exercise his veto power—the bill would become federal law. There was no guarantee, however, that this immigration act would have a long life. It was predicted that the Supreme Court would decide that such an act was illegal.

Against this backdrop, anti-Chinese activists focused on revising the Burlingame Treaty in the late 1870s with the government's support.[62] The Chinese Exclusion Act was a campaign promise of both Democrats and Republicans, and thus the government supported revising the treaty. In 1880, US minister George P. Seward, in charge of the negotiations with the Qing Court, was sent home because he made no progress in revising the treaty. To replace Seward, the US government sent three supporters of the anti-Chinese movement to Beijing to negotiate the revision of the Burlingame Treaty: James B. Angell, the president of the University of Michigan, as plenipotentiary, John F. Swift of California, and William H. Trescott of South Carolina. The latter two were members of the mission to support the plenipotentiary. The mission arrived in Beijing in September 1880 and, after five weeks, won the approval of the chief negotiator of the Qing Empire to sign the new treaty.[63]

Article I of the new treaty between the United States and China, signed November 27, 1880, stated:

> Whereas in the opinion of the Government of the United States[,] the coming of Chinese laborers to the United States, or their residence therein, affects or threatens to affect the interests of that country, or to endanger the good order of the said country or any locality within the territory thereof, the Government of China agrees that the Government of the United States may regulate, limit, or suspend such coming or residence, but may not absolutely prohibit.

With this new article, immigration was no longer an unalienable right as stipulated in the Burlingame Treaty but rather a privilege given to certain individuals after consideration of the nation's domestic affairs and issues.[64] Therefore, if certain immigrants were deemed to pose a threat to the interests of the nation or to its citizens, the US government could regulate or suspend immigration.

The Immigration Issue as a Domestic Affair

US government officials and scholars used this treaty to argue for immigration restrictions. An example of this would be former president Roosevelt's statement that every government should control immigration en masse when immigrants were deemed a threat to the lives of its citizens.[65] From this point on, "freedom of immigration" in principle was no longer a universally recognized rule; the acceptance of immigrants was to be considered in light of domestic affairs and only when a problem arose should they depend on diplomatic negotiations to resolve the issue. In 1900, a member of the US Immigration Commission stated the following:

The Governments of China and Japan have really no reason to object to our wishing not to admit the working people of their races in large numbers. As a matter of fact, Americans are not admitted to China or to Japan on even terms with the natives there. They can go into these countries as residents only in very limited communities; they are not permitted to buy land; and they are not admitted to citizenship in those countries. In truth, our country, as a whole, has treated the members, particularly of the Japanese race, more liberally than the Japanese have treated the Americans. The Japanese have been allowed to buy land, in many instances in large tracts; and tho [sic] at the present time we are taking rather active measures to exclude them from coming in large numbers, and in some States are preventing their holding of land, up to date, at any rate, we have treated them more liberally than they have treated us. It may be well argued, then that it is better for them, better for us, better for the civilization of the world at large, that each country, where such fundamental differences exist, attempts to work out its own problems independently, instead of each working them out in the country of the other.[66]

The Chinese Exclusion Act and Its Significance

The president ratified the treaty on May 9, 1881, after the Senate's recommendation on May 5. It became effective on October 5 of the same year. Congress immediately began to discuss the Chinese Immigration Law (commonly known as the Chinese Exclusion Act) and approved it on May 6, 1882. The official title was "An Act to Execute Certain Treaty Stipulations Relating to Chinese," clearly demonstrating that the revision of the Burlingame Treaty made the Chinese Exclusion Act possible.[67]

Article I stipulated that "from and after the passage of this act, and until the expiration of ten years next after the passage of this act, the coming of Chinese laborers to the United States . . . is hereby, suspended, and during such suspension it shall not be lawful for any Chinese laborer to come from any foreign port or place, or having so come to remain within the United States." Article XIV stipulated that "hereafter no state court of the United States shall admit Chinese to citizenship; and all laws in conflict with this act are hereby repealed."[68]

As I mentioned earlier, Jones argued that the principle of the United States to provide an asylum from political, social, economic, and religious persecution was not modified by the passage of the Chinese Exclusion Act. As the reason, he suggested that in the 1870s, the Chinese Exclusion Act was devised "to meet specific, unconnected situations, and those who supported it generally disclaimed any wider restrictive purpose"; thus, immigrant entry from other nations was not restricted entirely.[69] Those who supported Jones's argument stressed that Article II stipulated that individuals such as teachers, students, merchants, travelers, and those who accompany them as household servants, "shall be allowed to go and come of their own free will and accord, and shall be accorded all the rights, privileges, immunities, and exemptions which are accorded to the citizens and subjects of the most favored nation."[70] It should be considered, however, that this stipulation was seldom adhered to.[71]

It is outside the scope of this paper to discuss whether the Chinese Exclusion Act was a revision of the United States' overall immigration policy or if it was temporary legislation to control Chinese laborers' immigration en masse. But the Chinese Exclusion Act had significant consequences on Japanese immigration to the United States. As pointed out earlier, racial considerations were an important criterion in the political decisions regarding immigration in the late nineteenth-century United States.[72] Very few people argued against it in the 1880s and the 1890s.

Therefore, it was predictable that the Chinese Exclusion Act would be considered a precedent for the Japanese, and so it became. The Japanese *dekasegi* laborers' immigration to Hawai'i, however, did not begin until three years later, in 1885. Furthermore, one could not even imagine in 1882 that schoolboys and *dekasegi* laborers would travel to the West Coast. Therefore, few Japanese considered Chinese exclusion as an omen of their future in the United States. Consul General Takahashi Shinkichi in New York submitted a report to the minister of foreign affairs, Yoshida Kiyonari, on February 12, 1884, titled "Regarding Measurements to Prevent Impoverished Japanese from Traveling to New York." He touched on the Chinese Exclusion Act but did not consider it a major issue and suggested that the control of Chinese laborers was an inevitable measure. Regarding sailors and other people of menial professions traveling to the United States, he stated:

> The impoverished citizens including sailors and other menial pro-
> fessionals traveling from Japan to the United States are now being
> gradually hired, and the reason they are coming to New York is to
> work in place of the Chinese laborers who are banned from trav-
> eling to the United States. The Chinese were a target of scorn in
> Europe and the United States, and finally were barred from entry in
> this country. It was conceivable that the United States government
> would try to control their immigration.[73]

An Attempt at "Quality" Control

The Immigration Law of 1882 was passed at the same time as the Chinese Exclusion Act. This immigration law, enacted on August 3, 1882, targeted aliens in general and controlled, restricted, and even barred the entry of aliens who were deemed undesirable: convicts, lunatics, idiots, paupers, or "any persons unable to care for themselves without becoming public charges."[74]

In the 1880s, the Bureau of Immigration was not yet established by the federal government. The immigration authorities of the respective states enforced federal law, and the secretary of the treasury oversaw its execution. He had the power "to enter into contracts with such State commission, board, or officers as may be designated for that purpose by the governor of any State to take charge of the local affairs of immigration in the ports within said State."[75] Therefore, how the act was put into practice varied, depending on the officials at the port. This meant that much of its intended effect could not be fulfilled.

Nine years later, in March, the Immigration Act of 1891 was enacted. The superintendent of immigration was appointed by the federal government; under his supervision immigration officials began inspecting immigrants at ports.[76] This immigration act later gave the white (and prejudiced) superintendent of immigration a tool to prohibit or block Japanese laborers from entering on the basis of their being undesirable aliens, particularly "paupers" and "persons likely to become public charges."

(March 1891, San Francisco Consul General Chinda Sutemi to Foreign Minister Aoki Shūzo) The German ship *Remus* entered San Francisco port carrying about fifty laborers from Kumamoto, Nagasaki, Hiroshima, and other places. Most of the passengers dressed shabbily. The money they carried was smaller than twenty yen at most and might be as little as several tens of sen. They appear to be nothing but the poor. Except for a few who brought financial resources, all the others were barred from landing by the customs officers and detained. Some provided certificates of guarantees, references, and work agreements. Yesterday about thirty people who carried passports were allowed to land. Nine people without passports were detained at Angel Island. They had very little money on them, and, deemed poor, they were barred from landing and put back on the ship to Japan.[77]

The Alien Contract Labor Law and Japanese Dekasegi Laborers

The US Alien Contract Labor Law of 1885 cast another shadow on the prospects of Japanese immigration to the United States. The federal government, under pressure from labor unions, enacted this law. The Alien Contract Labor Law, which is commonly known as the Foran Act, stated:

[Section l] . . . [That] from and after the passage of this act it shall be unlawful for any person, company, partnership or corporation, in any manner whatsoever, to prepay the transportation, or in any way assist or encourage the importation or migration of any alien or aliens, any foreigner or foreigners in the United States, its Territories, or the District of Columbia under contract or agreement, parole or special, express or implied, made previous to the importation or migration of such alien or aliens, foreigner or foreigners, to perform labor or service of any kind in the United States, its Territories, or the District of Columbia.

Section 2. That all contracts or agreements, express or implied, parole or special, which may hereafter be made by and between any person, company, partnership, or corporation and any foreigner or foreigners, alien or aliens, to perform labor or service or having reference to the performance of labor or service by any person in the United States, its Territories, or the District of Colombia, previous to the migration or importation of the person or persons whose labor or service is contracted for into the United States, shall be utterly void and of no effect.[78]

Chinda translated the Alien Contract Labor Law into Japanese (*Gasshūkoku yoyaku rōdosha ijūkinshi jōrei*) and reported it to Japan.[79] This law reflected a strong demand from labor unions that began to be formed in the 1870s.[80] They argued that unlimited acceptance of unskilled alien laborers would lower American laborers' wages, as the westward movement was coming to a halt. This act was a testimony to their strong will to block the entry of unskilled laborers into the United States. It prohibited not only contract laborers who had entered into an agreement with their employers prior to their landing in this country, but also "assisted immigrants" who were given written or oral guarantees of employment or were assisted in finding employment by a third party. It was an unfortunate development for Japanese *dekasegi* laborers that the Alien Contract Labor Law was enacted before their immigration to the United States began.

As I explained earlier, many Japanese *dekasegi* laborers were denied entry in San Francisco based on their status as contract laborers. Chinda reported to the foreign minister in 1891:

Those who were denied entry based on being poor were not many, but more were denied based on being contract laborers. Unfortunately, there were as many as fourteen people who fell into this category. The reason that many were found in violation of the law was that first, the new immigration regulations stipulate that those who carry agreements in documents or oral statements on wages and employment would be subject to the law. Thus, those who came to the United States having a verbal agreement were considered contract laborers. This was not expected by *dekasegi* laborers. When they applied for passports in Japan they were asked if they had employment in the United States; they could not leave the country without having such an arrangement. It was difficult to maintain such a position.[81]

Chinda interviewed those who were denied entry on suspicion of violating the new law. His report suggested that the purpose of American immigration inspectors was to find an excuse to deny them entry.[82]

(Case 1) Kojima Tōkichi, born in February 1868, from 60-banchi, Kurashige-mura, Saeki-gun, Hiroshima-ken: According to the statement he contacted his friend who was working for Mr. Pond in Napa, California. He inquired if it would be easy to find a job there. His friend responded to him that there will be ways to find your way around. So he decided to come to San Francisco and either stay with his friend or ask his friend's employer to hire him. The inspector decided that Tōkichi had entered into a verbal agreement with Mr. Pond by way of his friend's invitation and denied his landing.

(Case 2) Higashiyama Kikujirō, born November 1860, from 174-banchi, Tamura, Naga-gun, Kiino-kuni, Wakayama-ken: According to Kikujirō's statement he had spent a hundred dollars to buy shares of Fuji shōkai, a gardening business in Oakland, California. After landing he intended to go there and work until his English became proficient. After that he would go elsewhere to earn money. Based on this statement the inspector concluded that Kikujirō entered into a contract with Fuji shōkai and therefore was in violation of section 1 of the new law and denied landing.

(Case 3) Okada Kōshirō, from 483-banchi, Jigozen-mura, Saeki-gun, Hiroshima-ken: His younger brother worked for Nagasawa Kanaye in Santa Rosa and earned a high wage. Kōshirō thus decided to come to the United States. Fortunately, a friend, Kuboichi Shintarō, accompanied him to the United States. Kōshirō said he would probably work for Mr. Nagasawa, just like his brother. The inspector therefore decided there was a verbal agreement with Nagasawa for employment. Therefore, Kōshirō was denied landing.

On the West Coast, particularly in San Francisco, the targeted immigrants shifted from the Chinese in the 1870s and 1880s to Japanese laborers in the 1890s. Given this backdrop, immigration inspectors were probably pressured to be stricter with Japanese immigration.

Chinda reported to Enomoto: "The conditions of the labor society in San Francisco are difficult and hostile against Asians. Immigration inspectors are particularly strict dealing with contract laborers. If they see any evidence of that, they are determined to deny their entry." [83] In another report, Chinda wrote: "In the past the US labor society excluded Chinese; recently attention has shifted to our immigrants, and they tend to treat the Chinese and the Japanese in an equal manner, indicating that anti-Japanese sentiment has started rising." [84]

The Japanese, without knowing it, had created a situation that would give the United States a good reason to deny entry: the system of contract labor. From the 1870s, Japanese laborers were required to submit official documents pertaining to overseas employment, such as the form of payment and wages, the financial guarantee of their return travel, and the details of those payments. These were the measures that the Japanese Meiji government authorities had taken to ensure that lower-class Japanese would not run into embarrassing situations, could support themselves overseas, and return home. Furthermore, in the 1880s, in order to obtain emigration permission, *dekasegi* laborers intending to go overseas were required to submit documentation to the government authorities granting passports, such as a certificate of guarantee for their travel expenses to return home, even when they had paid for their outbound journey, and a guarantee in writing that they could decently support themselves, such as a promise by their friends for a job placement or residence sponsorship. [85] Some of these documents or acts of guarantee were possibly regarded as a violation of the Alien Contract Labor Law.

Consul General Chinda reported to Foreign Minister Enomoto saying, "The immigration inspectors are determined to find any evidence of labor contracts, and when Japanese immigrants are questioned by the immigration officers about their purpose in the United States and whether they have a labor contract, the Japanese mistakenly think they need to provide evidence of being contract laborers in order to pass this investigation." Chinda pointed out that the Japanese system was responsible for these immigration denials. [86] The *dekasegi* laborers who went to Hawai'i as "government contract laborers" in 1885 were apparently contract laborers, but the Kingdom of Hawai'i was not yet part of the United States, so it did not become an issue unless a Japanese immigrated to the West Coast.

Coincidentally, Japanese laborers began coming to the US West Coast in the 1890s, one year before immigration inspectors were placed at the ports. Furthermore, *imin kaisha* (emigration companies), established around 1890–91, brokered some laborers to go to the United States.[87] These emigration companies certainly entered into contracts with the *dekasegi* laborers; therefore, nearly all the Japanese *dekasegi* laborers who traveled to the West Coast had some type of documents that might be regarded as labor contracts and thus considered to be in violation of the Contract Labor Law. This Japanese system invited inspectors' misunderstanding.

Chinda to Minister Tateno in January 1892:

Two laborers on the *Gaelic* named Waki and Ōgahara were denied landing because they were deemed to be in violation of the Contract Labor Law. The immigration inspectors investigated Waki, who carried documents stating that he would work for a merchant, Mr. Caracal, in San Francisco, including a specific salary written on the document. The nature of his job was different from a laborer's, but it was classified as a "menial servant"; therefore, he petitioned to be reconsidered. An immigration inspector investigated the facts and determined that he was not in violation of the law. Eventually he was allowed to land.

A man called Ōgahara had a contract to be employed by a tea merchant, Siegfried & Brandenstein Co. He had a document referring to the nature of employment, the salary, and other required items. It took a form of a regular contract, and it had a clause that it was confidential and that the contract should not be disclosed to others. The consulate did not find any argument against the effectiveness of the contract. It's surprising that more entry denials didn't happen.[88]

It is no surprise that Japanese immigrants were often denied entry.

Japanese Dekasegi *Laborers in the United States*

The fact that they were *dekasegi* laborers was another important reason that the Japanese were considered undesirable immigrants. *Dekasegi* laborers were termed as sojourners, or "birds of passage," and were regarded as unwelcome visitors to the United States, where "immigrants" equaled "permanent settlers."[89] Anti-immigrant sentiment on the East Coast was aimed at so-called new immigrants in the 1880s. For example, President Woodrow Wilson, as a historian, published an article in the *History of the American People* in 1902, blaming the new immigrants:

> [The new immigration] consisted of multitudes of men of lowest class from the south of Italy, and men of the meaner sort out of Hungary and Poland, men out of the ranks where there was neither skill nor energy nor any initiative of quick intelligence; and they came in numbers which increased from year to year, as if the countries of the south of Europe were disburdening themselves of the more sordid and hapless elements of their population. . . . The Chinese were more to be desired, as workmen if not as citizens, than most of the coarse crew that came crowding in every year at the eastern ports.[90]

One reason these new immigrants were considered undesirable was that many of the Italians and Greeks came to the United States as sojourners to make money as opposed to settling permanently. Prescott F. Hall, the de facto leader of the Immigration Restriction League in Boston, wrote as follows:

> Not a few of [Greek] immigrants are from rural districts and were, in their own country, agriculturists and shepherds. They are very patriotic and, in most cases, come to this country with the intention of returning; for that reason the immigrants are chiefly men, who leave their women behind to care for the farms and flocks until they return. . . . [There has been] an enormous increase in Italian immigration, mainly from the southern provinces on the mainland and from Sicily. These newer Italians are let out by contract to work on railroads, sewers, and the like. Many go back

and forth according to the state of the labor market. Their standard of living is extremely low, and, owing to their intention of returning to their own country, they are largely indifferent to their circumstances.[91]

The Chinese who were the earlier target of anti-immigrationists were criticized for being *dekasegi* laborers; a rhetorical tool to attack them.[92] Therefore, I would argue that it was almost predictable that the Japanese would fall prey to similar attacks. It was attested by inflammatory newspaper articles that appeared in San Francisco and other areas starting in 1892, claiming that Japanese had no intention of settling in the United States and only came to make money before returning home.

Like the Chinese, they are here for the purpose of acquiring enough money to enable them to end their days in leisure in their native land, and they have no intention of settling down here and making this place their home.[93]

Prescott Hall criticized the Japanese for being poor contract laborers besides being *dekasegi* and demanded that they be excluded just like the Chinese:

The Japanese coolies are brought over largely by "immigration companies" who contract for their labor. Indeed, many of the coolies are of a class which could not come to this country without assistance. . . . In the opinion of some observers, they are more undesirable than the Chinese coolies who were imported in the same way before the passage of the Chinese Exclusion Act. Wages in Japan are about one half of those in the United States, and this stimulus to emigration is aided by the pressure of population in Japan, constantly seeking for new outlets.[94]

If I am to take a bold position, I would argue that many entry denials of Japanese laborers in the 1890s were inevitable; however, as far as I know, no Japanese immigration scholar has pointed out this fact. In the next chapter, in order to understand what was happening on the

Japanese side, I will investigate how Japanese intellectual leaders and promoters of immigration, government officials, and *dekasegi* laborers understood immigration to the United States to be, what *dekasegi* laborers dreamed of achieving when emigrating, and how they attempted to deal with the immigration issues in the United States.

Notes

1. Fukuzawa Yukichi, "Beikoku wa shishi no sumika nari," *Jiji Shinpō* on March 25, 1884, *Fukuzawa Yukichi Zenshū*, dai 9-kan (Iwanami Shoten, 1960), 442–44. Fukuzawa's emphasis of America as a nation of immigrants and the American population consisting of immigrants is interestingly similar to the findings of American scholars in the late twentieth century. For example, "Immigration was America's *raison d'être*" or "the whole history of the United States during the past three and a half centuries has been the history of immigrants." Refer to Oscar Handlin, "Introduction" in *The Americans: A New History of the People of the United States* (Boston: Little, Brown, 1963) and Maldwyn Allen Jones, "Introduction" in *American Immigration* (Chicago: Chicago University Press, 1960).

2. Beikoku Sōkō gū Shūyū Sanjin, Ishida Kumajirō, ed., *Kitare Nihonjin: Sōkō tabi annai* (Kaishindō, 1886); *Nikkei imin shiryōshū, Hokubei hen dai 5-kan* (Nihon Tosho Sentā, 1991).

3. For poor *shosei* who migrated to the San Francisco Bay Area on the West Coast, refer to Sakata Yasuo, "Datsu-a no shishi to tozasareta hakusekijin no rakuen: Minkenha shosei to Beikoku ni okeru ōshoku jinshu haiseki," in *Beikoku shoki no Nihongo shinbun*, ed. Tamura Norio and Shiramizu Shigehiko (Keisō Shobō, 1986), 47–193; Arai Katsuhiro, "Jiyū minkenki ni okeru Sōkō wangan chiku no katsudō," *Tōkyō Keizai Daigaku jinbun shizen kagaku ronshū* 65 (December 1983); Arai Katsuhiro, "Jiyū minkenki no tobei hōjin katsudōshi (jo)," *Beikoku shoki no Nihongo shinbun*, 233–55; Arai Katsuhiro, "Jiyū minkenki ni okeru zaibei zaifu Nihonjin no kenri ishiki," *Kokuritsu Rekishi Minzoku Hakubutsukan kenkyū hōkoku* 35 (November 1991), 545–96.

4. "Beikoku zakkan: Beikoku zairyū Nihonjin," in *Ōbei man'yūki*; *Ozaki Gakudō zenshū dai 3-kan* (Kōronsha, 1955), 344–45. The exact number of *dekasegi shosei* is impossible to estimate. However, the *jōshinsho* (report) from Ōsawa Eizō, the secretary of the San Francisco Gospel Society, sent to Kawakita Toshisuke, the consul general in San Francisco, stated, "Our fellow Japanese residing in San Francisco and surrounded areas number almost four thousand." The total number Ōsawa reported perhaps included Japanese laborers and businessmen residing in San Francisco in addition to *dekasegi shosei*. (Kōshin dai 48-gō Meiji 22-nen 6-gatsu 11-nichi, zai Sōkō Ryōji Kawakita Toshisuke yori Gaimu Daijin Aoki Shūzō ate, "Fukuinkai kanji Ōsawa Eizō jōshinsho sōfu no ken," besshi, jōshinsho, "Zaibei honpōjin no jōkyō narabini tobeisha torishimari zassan 1," held at the Gaimushō Gaikō Shiryōkan [Diplomatic Archives of the Ministry of Foreign Affairs of Japan].)

5. Although it is commonly called the Chinese Exclusion Act, the formal legal title is "An Act to execute certain treaty stipulations relating to Chinese" (22 Stat. L., 58). This law was enacted on May 6, 1882, partly revised on July 5,

1884 (23 Stat. L., 115), extended to ban the entry of laborers on May 5, 1892, for ten more years (27 Stat., 25), and made permanent by further revisions on April 29, 1902 (32 Stat., 176) and extension on April 27, 1904 (33 Stat., 428, Appendix E). Therefore, it is not necessarily wrong to conclude that the first Chinese Exclusion Act in 1882 banned the entry of Chinese laborers to America. For the historical reasons and details of the naming of the Chinese Exclusion Act in 1882, refer to Sakata, "Datsu-a no shishi to tozasareta hakusekijin no rakuen," 104–9, and the section on restriction of residence for undesirable aliens in the United States in this paper. In this paper, the author uses *Shinkoku-jin* (Qing people) referring to the Chinese as a historical term, although he occasional uses the term *Shina-jin* for *Chinaman*, a term Americans used as an insult, where appropriate. [*Shinkoku-jin* was translated as *Chinese* and *Shina-jin* into *Chinaman* in the English translation.] The translator incorporated the original English abstract for clarity.

6. Some English-language research papers on exclusionary activities or racial prejudice toward Chinese laborers include Elmer C. Sandmeyer, *The Anti-Chinese Movement in California* (Urbana: University of Illinois Press, 1973), reprint of the 1939 edition; Stuart C. Miller, *The Unwelcome Immigrant: The American Image of the Chinese, 1785–1882* (Berkeley: University of California Press, 1969); Gunther Barth, *Bitter Strength: A History of the Chinese in the United States, 1850–1870* (Cambridge, MA: Harvard University Press, 1964); Mary Roberts Coolidge, *Chinese Immigration* (New York: Henry Holt, 1909). In addition, refer to Sakata, "Datsu-a no shishi to tozasareta hakusekijin no rakuen," 93–103.

7. Sakata, "Datsu-a no shishi to tozasareta hakusekijin no rakuen," 49 and 110–21. The exceptions were staff at the Ministry of Foreign Affairs, particularly diplomats stationed in the United States who feared that Japanese laborers would be destined to be extremely disgraceful for their mother country, just like the "Chinamen" laborers. For example, Tateno Gōzō, a minister to the United States, demanded that the minister of foreign affairs adopt precautionary measures and stated, "American people are leaning toward enforcing unreasonable immigration restrictions and regulatory issues on the Japanese. Currently, people who support the Japanese immigration regulation are likely to win in Congress soon" (Kimitsu dai 25-gō, Meiji 24-nen 11-gatsu 7-ka, Chūbei Kōshi Tateno Gōzō yori Gaimu Daijin Enomoto Takeaki ate, "Honpō ijūmin seigenhō no seitei no gi ni kanshi arakajime seikun no ken," in *Nihon gaikō bunsho dai 24-kan*, ed. Gaimushō [Nihon Kokusai Rengō Kyōkai, 1952], 513–14). Sutemi Chinda, the consul general in San Francisco, also requested that Japan not send Japanese emigrants who might be barred from entry into the United States (Kimitsu dai 6-gō, Meiji 24-nen 4-gatsu 24-ka, Sanfuranshisuko Ryōji Chinda Sutemi yori Gaimu Daijin Aoki Shūzō ate, "Beikoku imin shin kisoku shikō ni tsuki honpōjin tokō torishimari kata ni kanshi jōshin no ken," in *Nihon gaikō bunsho dai 24-kan*, 463–66).

8. Fukuzawa Yukichi, "Datsu-a ron," *Jiji shinpō*, March 9, 1885, in *Fukuzawa Yukichi zenshū*, dai 10-kan (Iwanami Shoten, 1960), 238–40.

9. Refer to Kamei Shunsuke, *Jiyū no seichi: Nihonjin no Amerika* (Kenkyūsha Shuppan, 1978). The citation is from *Bei-Ō kairan jikki dai 1-hen*, ed. Kume Kunitake (Hakubunsha, 1884), 244.

10. Akamine Seichirō, *Beikoku ima fushigi* (Jitsugakkai Eigakkō, 1886), 43–51. *Nikkei imin shiryōshū hokubei hen dai 5-kan* (Nihon Tosho Sentā, 1991).

11. "Zaibei Nihon minzokuron dai 2" in *Aikoku dai 27-gō*, vol. 2 (April 29, 1892) owned by Arai Katsuhiro. For this newspaper, refer to Arai, "Jiyū minkenki

ni okeru Sōkō wangan chiku no katsudō," and Ebihara Hachirō, *Kaigai hōji shinbun zasshishi* (Gakuji Shoin, 1936), 142–49.

12. Kimitsu dai 14-gō, Meiji 25-nen 5-gatsu 10-ka, Sanfuranshisuko Ryōji Chinda Sutemi yori Gaimu Daijin Enomoto Takeaki ate, "Tokōsha jōriku kyozetsu ni tsuki zensho saretaki mune jōshin no ken," in *Nihon gaikō bunsho dai 25-kan*, 702–3.

13. Sakata, "Datsu-a no shishi to tozasareta hakusekijin no rakuen," 142–49.

14. "Keep, ancient lands, your storied pomp!" cries she
with silent lips, "Give me your tired, your poor,
Your huddled masses yearning to breathe free.
The wretched refuse of your teeming shore.
Send these, the homeless, tempest-toast, to me!
I lift my lamp beside the golden door."

The above poem is cited in Carl Wittke, *We Who Built America*, rev. ed. (Cleveland: Case Western Reserve University, 1964), xi. Emma Lazarus (1849–87), a Jewish American poet, was born in New York. She emphasized the American dream as a second-generation American citizen of immigrant parents. Dumas Malones, ed., *Dictionary of American Biography* (New York: Charles Scribner's Sons), vol. 6, 65–66.

15. A comprehensive research on immigration policy in the United States is limited. Although Robert A. Divine, *American Immigration Policy, 1924–1952* (New Haven, CT: Yale University Press, 1957), is considered representative, there are no detailed studies on the late nineteenth century. Studies on Native American nativism against immigrants include John Higham, *Strangers in the Land: Patterns of American Nativism* (New Brunswick, NJ: Rutgers University Press, 1955); John Higham, "Another Look at Nativism," *Catholic Historical Review* 46 (July 1958): 147–58; and *Nativism, Discrimination, and Images of Immigrants*, ed. George E. Pozzetta, American Immigration and Ethnicity Series, vol. 15 (New York: Garland Publishing, 1991) are useful. For Japanese publications, refer to Akashi Norio, Iino Masako, and Tanaka Masako, *Esunikku Amerika: taminzoku kokka ni okeru tōgō no genjitsu* (Yūhikaku, 1984), particularly, "Kindai Amerika no keisei to esunikku shūdan" in *Esunikku Amerika II*, 81–179. For Chinese laborers, refer to the list in endnote 5. The representative literature on Japanese immigrants are Roger Daniels, *The Politics of Prejudice: The Anti-Japanese Movement in California and the Struggle for Japanese Exclusion* (Berkeley: University of California Press, 1962); Yuji Ichioka, *The Issei: The World of the First Generation Japanese Immigrants, 1885–1924* (New York: Free Press, 1988); and Ichihashi, *Japanese in the United States*. For anti-Japanese movements and incidents in the 1900s, refer to Thomas A. Bailey, *Theodore Roosevelt and the Japanese American Crisis: An Account of the International Complications Arising from the Race Problem on the Pacific Coast* (Stanford, CA: Stanford University Press, 1934) and Raymond A. Esthus, *Theodore Roosevelt and Japan* (Seattle: University of Washington Press, 1966). For Japanese-language literature, refer to Yoshida Tadao, *Hainichi iminhō no kiseki: 21-seiki no Nichi-Bei kankei no genten* (Keizai Ōraisha, 1983).

16. For example, Alexander Saxton, *The Rise and Fall of the White Republic: Class Politics and Mass Culture in Nineteenth-Century America* (London: Verso, 1990).

17. "The dedication ceremonies for the Statue of Liberty in October, 1886, took place, ironically enough, at precisely the time that Americans were beginning seriously to doubt the wisdom of unrestricted immigration" (Jones, *American Immigration*, 247).

18. Miller, *The Unwelcome Immigrant*, 3–15. The first person to suggest the "regional conspiracy thesis" was Mary Roberts Coolidge. Refer to Coolidge, *Chinese Immigration*.

19. Cited in Coolidge, *Chinese Immigration*, 364, and Miller, *The Unwelcome Immigrant*, 4.

20. Miller, *The Unwelcome Immigrant*, 3–15. Regarding the American image of the "Chinaman," refer to Harold Isaacs, *Scratches on Our Minds: American Images of China and India* (New York: 1958).

21. Handlin, *The Americans,* 303–4.

22. Daniels, *The Politics of Prejudice*, 21.

23. Ichihashi, *Japanese in the United States*, 228–29.

24. Ibid., 396.

25. H. A. Mills, *The Japanese Problem in the United States: An Investigation for the Commission in Relation with Japan Appointed by the Federal Council of the Churches of Christ in America* (New York: Macmillan, 1915), 240–41; and Ichihashi, *Japanese in the United States*, 228–29.

26. *Lincoln Journal*, Nebraska, October 12, 1889; dai 88-gō, Meiji 22-nen 11-gatsu 1-nichi, Satsubei Kōshi Mutsu Munemitsu yori Gaimu Daijin Ōkuma Shigenobu ate, "Kashū imin Nihon ni kanshi shinbun kirinuki sōfu no ken," Fuzokusho, "Zaibei honpōjin no jōkyō narabini tobeisha torishimari kankei zassan, 1, Zai-Washinton Kōshikan no bu," held at the Gaimushō Gaikō Shiryōkan.

27. "The Japs," *San Francisco Bulletin,* May 4, 1892; Kimitsu dai 14-gō, Meiji 25-nen 5-gatsu 10-ka, Sanfuranshisuko Ryōji Chinda Sutemi yori Gaimu Daijin Enomoto Takeaki ate, "Tōkōsha jōriku kyozetsu ni tsuki zensho saretaki mune jōshin no ken," Fuzokusho, "Zaibei honpōjin no jōkyō narabini tobeisha torishimari zassan 1, Zai-Sanfuranshisuko Ryōjikan no bu," held at the Gaimushō Gaikō Shiryōkan. This Kimitsu dai 14-gō letter was recorded in *Nihon gaikō bunsho dai 25-kan* (Nihon Kokusai Rengō Kyōkai, 1952) as "Jikō 19 Beikoku ni oite honpō imin seigen narabini haiseki no ken" bunsho 311. The articles of the English-language newspaper were omitted.

28. Kimitsu dai 7-gō, Meiji 24-nen 5-gatsu 7-ka, Sanfuranshisuko Ryōji Chinda Sutemi yori Gaimu Daijin Aoki Shūzō ate, "Honpō tōkōsha jōriku kyohi no ken," in *Nihon gaikō bunsho dai 24-kan*, 480–81, and "Zaibei honpōjin no tobeisha torishimari kankei zassan, 1," held at the Gaimushō Gaikō Shiryōkan.

29. Kimitsu dai 6-gō, Meiji 24-nen 4-gatsu 25-nichi, Sanfuranshisuko Ryōji Chinda Sutemi yori Gaimu Daijin Aoki Shūzō ate, "Beikoku imin shin kisoku shikō ni tsuki honpōjin tōkō torishimari kata ni kanshi jōshin no ken," *Nihon gaikō bunsho dai 24-kan*, 464 and 466; "Zaibei honpōjin no tobeisha torishimari kankei zassan, 1." The new immigration law discussed here was enacted on March 3, 1891. Because immigration inspections began at ports at this time, the inspection for undesirable aliens became even stricter. The author will discuss the details later in this chapter. The English text of this new law and the Japanese-language translation are included in Kimitsu dai 6-gō, 469–76.

30. Nagasawa Setsu, "Hokubei Gasshūkoku Taiheiyō engan ni okeru Nihonjin to Sōkō tōki hakurankai," *Nihonjin dai 1-gō*, November 18, 1893, 15–23. The

Nihonjin was published in April 1888 and banned in June 1891; its title was changed to the *Ajia* to resume its publication. The *Ajia* was banned in July 1894 and was renamed the *Nihonjin* to continue the publication. Nagasawa's above article was published in the *Nihonjin dai 1-gō* after it was renamed.

31. *Zaibei Nihonjin shi* (Zaibei Nihonjinkai, 1940), 32.

32. Ichioka, *The Issei,* 249–50.

33. Washizu "Shakuma" Bunzō, *Zaibei Nihonjin shikan: fu, zaibei zaifu Nihonjin rekishi no minamoto* (Rafu Shinpōsha, 1930), 19. For the same reason, Japanese residing in the United States showed great interest in former president Theodore Roosevelt's article, "The Japanese Question" in *The Outlook,* 92, no. 2 (May 8, 1909).

[Quotation translated into English from the Japanese in the Washizu publication. Shakuma cites the publication date as January 10, 1911. However, *The Outlook* was published weekly, and the correct publication date is likely January 14, 1911. The presumed original English text from this publication is:

Lafcadio Hearn had certainly no anti-Japanese prejudice; and it is Lafcadio Hearn who says: "The Japanese child is as close to you as the European child—perhaps cleaner and sweeter, because infinitely more natural and refined. Cultivate his mind, and the more it is cultivated, the farther you push him from you. . . . As the Oriental thinks naturally to the left where we think to the right, the more you cultivate him, the more he will think in the opposite direction from you." Rudyard Kipling's lines point in the same direction; and few Orientals know the Orient better than does Rudyard Kipling: 'Oh, East is East and West is West, and never the twain shall meet, / Till Earth and Sky stand presently at God's great Judgment Seat.'

"It is better that they should not meet. It is not that the Chinese and the Japanese are inferior races; it is that they are different; and it is better that different men, though frankly recognizing one another as equals in the major qualities of civilization, should have different homes. It is an old adage that no house is large enough for two families. No nation is large enough for two races. The East for the Oriental, the West for the Occidental, with no attempt to keep house together, but free intermingling in international trade, is the true solution of the Oriental problem. This is the solution which the democratic instinct on the Pacific coast has hit upon. And the democratic instinct is right."]

34. Roosevelt, "The Japanese Question," 61–62. Abiko Kyūtarō, a leader of Nikkei communities in the United States and the owner of *Nichi-Bei shinbun* (San Francisco), stated that Japanese residing in the United States must respect and trust Roosevelt in a letter to his uncle on January 9, 1906: "The current president, Roosevelt, is a soldier as well as a literary man. Thus, he is a quite unique president. He often speaks and always fulfills his promises. We the US-residing Japanese fellows feel we should support the greatest president of the age" (from Abiko Kyūtarō to his uncle dated January 9, 1906, Yonako Abiko papers, University Research Library, University of California–Los Angeles). For Abiko Kyūtarō, refer to Ichioka Yuji, "Abiko Kyūtaro: Eijū o shuchō shita Zaibei Nihonjin senkusha," in *Beikoku shoki no Nihongo shinbun,* 195–231.

35. Roosevelt, "The Japanese Question," 61.

36. Yoshida, *Hainichi iminhō no kiseki,* 90–91.

37. Jones, *American Immigration,* 252.

38. Ibid., 92–116.

39. Some were suspicious that the United States government was actively recruiting European immigrants in order to route them to the Union Army (ibid., 173). As explained later in this chapter, the US government entered into a rare commercial treaty with the Qing dynasty, which was given the most-favored-nation treatment. The immigration clauses allowed Chinese laborers free entry into the United States. Akira Iriye explained that this does not mean that Secretary of State William Henry Seward accepted the principle of free immigration but, rather, that he merely wanted to solve the labor shortage immediately after the Civil War. See Akira Iriye, *Across the Pacific: An Inner History of American-East Asian Relations* (New York: Harcourt, Brace, 1967), 29. Shūyū Sanjin, the author of *Kitare Nihonjin* (refer to endnote 2), explained the US government's policy of "homestead," saying, "The US government had originally made uncultivated lands that were not owned by Americans available to people of any nationality." Furthermore, he encouraged immigration to America, saying, "this law should allow Japanese in America to own land and eventually amass huge wealth for their families if they wait patiently for five to ten years, even if they begin penniless (*Kitare Nihonjin*, 6-8). However, it was nearly impossible for Japanese on the West Coast to acquire land by this method in the late 1880s when Shūyū wrote this.

40. Immigration Act, July 4, 1964. Stat. L., Vol. XIII, 385.

41. Jones, *American Immigration*, chap. 9, "The Demand for Restriction, 1882–1924," 247–77.

42. Refer to "Zaibei honpōjin no jōkyō narabini tobeisha torishimari kankei zassan, ichi" and "Hokubei Gasshūkoku ni oite honpōjin tokō seigen oyobi haiseki ikken," 1, 2, held at the Gaimushō Gaikō Shiryōkan, and endnote 6.

43. For example, Kimitsu dai 6-gō, Meiji 24-nen 4-gatsu 24-ka, Sanfuranshisuko Ryōji Chinda Sutemi yori Gaimu Daijin Aoki Shūzō ate, "Beikoku imin shin kisoku shikō ni tsuki honpōjin tokō torishimari kata ni kanshi jōshin no ken," *Nihon gaikō bunsho dai 24-kan*, 463–66.

44. Refer to Sakata Yasuo, "Fubyōdō jōyaku to Amerika dekasegi" in *Hokubei Nihonjin Kirisutokyō undōshi*, ed. Dōshisha Daigaku Jinbun Kagaku Kenkyūjo (PMC Shuppan, 1991) 627–703, and chapter 2 of this volume.

45. Most of the *Zaibei Nihonjin shi* publications, whether prewar or postwar, emphasized this point. Even Ichihashi's *Japanese in the United States*, considered the only authoritative English-language research (a must-read for researchers from its publication in 1932 until today), is not an exception. Before the war, in particular, Japanese people that arrived in the United States were considered immigrants, not migrant laborers.

46. For example, Roger Daniels and Harry H. Kitano, *American Racism: Exploration of the Nature of Prejudice* (Englewood Cliff, NJ: Prentice-Hall, 1970).

47. Refer to Akashi, Iino, and Tanaka, *Esunikku Amerika*.

48. Daniels, *The Politics of Prejudice*. This was submitted as a PhD thesis to the University of California–Los Angeles. It was first published as *University of California Publications in History*, vol. 71, in 1962, and later republished in 1969 by Atheneum.

49. Ibid., 107.

50. Refer to Esthus, *Theodore Roosevelt and Japan*; Bailey, *Theodore Roosevelt and the Japanese American Crisis*; and Shumpei Okamoto, *The Japanese Oligarchy and the Russo-Japanese War* (New York: Columbia University Press, 1970).

51. Ichioka, *The Issei*, 249.

52. Refer to Sakata, "Datsu-a no shishi to tozasareta hakusekijin no rakuen"; Sakata, "Fubyōdō jōyaku to Amerika dekasegi" and chapter 2 of this volume; and Sakata, "Nihonjin Amerika dekasegi no chiikisei no ichi kōsatsu (II)" in Ōsaka Gakuin Daigaku, *Kokusaigaku ronshū dai 1-kan dai 2-gō* (March 1991), 149–71.

53. Immigration Act, March 3, 1891, 26 Stat. L., 1084. Article VIII of this law stipulated the establishment of the Office of the Superintendent of Immigration. This office later became the Bureau of Immigration. [Editor's note: It was March 2, 1895, that the title of the agency head changed from superintendent to commissioner-general of immigration, according to https://www.uscis.gov/history-and-genealogy /our-history/agency-history/origins-federal-immigration-service.]

54. Refer to Sakata, "Datsu-a no shishi to tozasareta hakusekijin no rakuen," 88–109; Sandmeyer, *The Anti-Chinese Movement in California*; and Coolidge, *Chinese Immigration*.

55. Jeremiah W. Jenks and W. Jett Lauck, *The Immigration Problem: A Study of American Immigration Conditions and Needs* (New York: Funk and Wagnalls, 1917), 216–17.

56. "Congress proved sympathetic . . . to the almost complete absence of opposition to the measure," in Jones, *American Immigration,* 249.

57. Refer to Frederick W. Williams, *Anson Burlingame and the First Mission to Foreign Powers* (New York: Charles Scribner's Sons, 1912), 3–160; Miller, *The Unwelcome Immigrant*, 132–34; and Sandmeyer, *The Anti-Chinese Movement in California*, 79–90.

58. US Senate, *Immigration Commission Reports*, vol. 39, *Immigration Legislation* (Washington, DC: Government Printing Office, 1911), 131–32.

59. For example, the Cubic Air Ordinance, a city ordinance issued in San Francisco in 1871, required 500 cubic feet of space for every person residing in a lodging to issue a boarding license. The lower federal courts deemed this law invalid, however. In addition, refer to Sakata, "Datsu-a no shishi to tozasareta hakusekijin no rakuen," 99–101. Furthermore, the Lodging House Law and the Queue Ordinance were enforced by the San Francisco City Council (Sandmeyer, *The Anti-Chinese Movement in California, 62–64*).

60. Ibid., 62–64.

61. Jones, *American Immigration*, 250–51.

62. Ibid., 251.

63. Sandmeyer, *The Anti-Chinese Movement in California*, 90–92.

64. US Senate, Immigration Commission Reports, vol. 39, Immigration Legislation, 131–32.

65. Refer to endnote 34.

66. Jenks and Lauck, *The Immigration Problem*, 217–18.

67. 22 Stat. L., 58; US Senate, Immigration Commission Reports, vol. 39, Immigration Legislation, 132–36; Jones, *American Immigration*, 249–21; and Sandmeyer, *The Anti-Chinese Movement in California*, 90–98.

68. 22 Stat. L., 58.

69. Jones, *American Immigration*, 252.

70. US Senate, Immigration Commission Reports, vol. 39, Immigration Legislation, 131–132.

71. San Francisco was already the center of the anti-Chinese movement. Since most Qing people entered the United States there, further controversy was unavoidable. For example, in 1885 the Qing minister stationed in Washington,

DC, was denied entry in San Francisco because he did not carry a residency certificate, as required by the immigration law. He showed a letter of credence to the president instead and was finally allowed to enter. This disregarded diplomatic custom would be unimaginable today. Sandmeyer, *The Anti-Chinese Movement in California,* 100.

72. For example, Jenks and Lauck, *The Immigration Problem.*

73. Kōshin dai 14-gō, Meiji 17-nen 2-gatsu 13-nichi Nyūyōku Ryōji Takahashi Shinkichi yori Gaimu Daijin Yoshida Kiyonari ate, "Waga kyūmin no Nyūyōku tobei ni taishi bōshisaku kakutei kata gushin no ken," *Nihon gaikō bunsho dai 18-kan,* 106–9.

74. Jones, *American Immigration,* 252; and US Senate, Immigration Commission Reports, vol. 39, Immigration Legislation, 131–32.

75. 18 Stat. L., Pt. 3, 477.

76. Refer to endnote 53.

77. Kimitsu dai 6-gō, Meiji 24-nen 4-gatsu 25-nichi, Sanfuranshisuko Ryōji Chinda Sutemi yori Gaimu Daijin Aoki Shūzō ate "Beikoku imin shin kisoku shikō ni tsuki honpōjin tokō torishimari kata ni kanshi jōshin no ken," *Nihon gaikō bunsho dai 24-kan,* 464.

78. 23 Stat. L., 332.

79. Fuzokusho 1, Gasshūkoku yoyaku rōdōsha ijū kinshi jōrei (the Alien Contract Labor Law) enforced on February 26, 1885, and Kimitsu dai 6-gō, Meiji 24-nen 4-gatsu 25-nichi, Sanfuranshisuko Ryōji Chinda Sutemi yori Gaimu Daijin Aoki Shūzō ate, "Beikoku imin shin kisoku shikō ni tsuki honpōjin tokō torishimari kata ni kanshi jōshin no ken," *Nihon gaikō bunsho dai 24-kan,* 466–67.

80. Jones, *American Immigration,* 251–52.

81. Kimitsu dai 7-gō, Meiji 24-nen 5-gatsu 7-ka, Sanfuranshisuko Ryōji Chinda Sutemi yori Gaimu Daijin Aoki Shūzō ate, "Honpō tokōsha jōriku kyozetsu no ken" in *Nihon gaikō bunsho dai 24-kan,* 480–81.

82. Fuzokusho 2, negō, ibid., 483–84.

83. Kimitsu dai 16-gō, Meiji 24-nen 8-gatsu 11-nichi, Sanfuranshisuko Ryōji Chinda Sutemi yori Gaimu Daijin Enomoto Takeaki ate, "Tobei rōdōsha o shite tōkoku ijūmin shin jōrei no kitei o ryōkai seshime hakaru gi ni tsuki jōshin no ken," *Nihon gaikō bunsho dai 24-kan,* 500.

84. Kimitsu dai 6-gō, Meiji 24-nen 4-gatsu 25-nichi, Sanfuranshisuko Ryōji Chinda Sutemi yori Gaimu Daijin Aoki Shūzō ate, "Beikoku imin shin kisoku shikō ni tsuki honpōjin tokō torishimari kata ni kanshi jōshin no ken," *Nihon gaikō bunsho dai 24-kan,* 465.

85. For details, refer to Sakata, "Fubyōdō jōyaku to Amerika dekasegi," 664–80, and pages 102–15 of chapter 2 of this volume.

86. Kimitsu dai 96-gō, Meiji 24-nen 8-gatsu 11-nichi, Sanfuranshisuko Ryōji Chinda Sutemi yori Gaimu Daijin Enomoto Takeaki ate, "Tobei rōdōsha o shite tōkoku ijūmin shin jōrei no kitei o ryōkai seshime hakaru gi ni tsuki jōshin no ken," *Nihon gaikō bunsho dai 24-kan,* 500–501.

87. Durham White Stevens, counselor of the Japanese legation in the United States, stated in a report to Tateno, the minister, dated October 12, 1891, as follows: "There are unquestionably in Japan at present a number of persons engaged in promoting emigration to the United States simply to obtain the passage money of the immigrant. This seemed to be clear in the case of the steamers 'Remus' and 'Pemptos' and seems to be conclusively proved in the case just reported by

Mr. Chinda of the indigent Japanese landed at Portland. These people have been promised employment in the United States by the agent of the steamer merely to obtain their passage money, there being no intention to fulfill the promise." Refer to Fuzokusho, "Suchībunsu-shi hōkokusho" Kō dai 96-gō, Meiji 24-nen 10-gatsu 14-ka, Zaibei Kōshi Tateno Gōzō yori Gaimu Daijin Enomoto Takeaki ate, "Gasshūkoku Taiheiyō engan shoshū ni dekasegisuru honpōjin ni kanshi Sanjikan Suchībunsu-shi no hōkoku sōtatsu no ken," *Nihon gaikō bunsho dai 24-kan*, 510–13. In regard to *imin kaisha* (emigration companies), see Jikō 18, "Kanada ni oite honpō imin seigen narabini haiseki no ken" and Jikō 19, "Beikoku ni oite honpō imin seigen narabini haiseki no ken," *Nihon gaikō bunsho dai 25-kan*, 652–733; Alan T. Moriyama, *Imingaisha: Japanese Emigration Companies and Hawaii, 1894–1908* (Honolulu: University of Hawaii, 1985); and Sasaki Toshiji, "Yokohama Imin Gōshi Kaisha no Kanada imin sōshutsu" in *Kirisutokyō shakai mondai kenkyū dai 38-gō* (March 1990), 1–50.

88. Fuzokusho 1 kōgō sha, Meiji 25-nen 2-gatsu 10-ka Chinda Ryōji yori Tateno Kōshi ate shokan, "Keiyaku rōdōsha torishimari ni tsuki seikun no ken," Kō dai 16-gō, Meiji 25-nen 3-gatsu 4-ka, Chūbei Kōshi Tateno Gōzō yori Gaimu Daijin Enomoto Takeaki ate "Tokōsha torishimari ni kanshi seikun no ken," *Nihon gaikō bunsho dai 25-kan*, 689–91. For the consular report of Chinda (the consul general in San Francisco) on Japanese travelers who were denied entry to the United States on the suspicion of being contract laborers, refer to Jikō 18, "Honpōjin no Beikoku imin narabini haiseki kankei ikken," *Nihon gaikō bunsho dai 24-kan*, 460–515, and Jikō 19, "Beikoku ni oite honpō imin seigen narabini haiseki no ken," *Nihon gaikō bunsho dai 25-kan*, 683–733.

89. For the difference between immigrants—namely, permanent citizens—and migrant laborers, refer to Sakata, "Fubyōdō jōyaku to Amerika dekasegi," 681–82, and pages 115–16 of chapter 2 of this volume, and Sakata, *Nihonjin Amerika dekasegi no chiikisei no ichi kōsatsu* (II), 149–71. On the criticism and prejudice toward *shin imin* (new immigrants), refer to US Senate, 57th Cong., 2nd Sess., Doc. No. 62, *Regulation of Immigration: Report of the Committee on Immigration, United States Senate, on the Bill (H.R. 12199) to Regulate the Immigration of Aliens into the United States with Statements before the Committee in the First and Second Sessions of the Fifty-Seventh Congress* (Washington, DC: Government Printing Office, 1902); Higham, *Strangers in the Land;* and Pozzetta, ed., *Nativism, Discrimination and Images of Immigrants*, etc.

90. Cited in Woodrow Wilson, *A History of the American People* (New York: Harper, 1902); and Jones, *American Immigration*, 239.

91. Prescott F. Hall, *Immigration and Its Effects upon the United States* (New York: Henry Holt, 1913), 48–49, 54–58. For Hall's "The Immigration Restriction League in Boston," refer to Higham, *Strangers in the Land*, 101–3.

92. For example, Sandmeyer, *The Anti-Chinese Movement in California*, and Coolidge, *Chinese Immigration*.

93. *San Francisco Bulletin*, May 4, 1892. Its sensational headline follows:

THE JAPS
Another Rising Tide of Immigration
The Japanese Colony Increasing Very Rapidly
What the Subjects of the Mikado Do When They Reach California

Their Effect upon the Labor Market
Importation of Women for Immoral Purposes

See Fuzokusho, Kimitsu dai 14-gō, Meiji 25-nen 5-gatsu 10-ka, Sanfuranshisuko Ryōji Chinda Sutemi yori Gaimu Daijin Enomoto Takeaki ate, "Tokōsha jōriku kyozetsu ni tsuki zensho saretaki mune jōshin no ken" and "Hokubei Gasshūkoku ni okeru hōnpojin tokō seigen oyobi haiseki ikken, 1," 241–78, held at the Gaimushō Gaikō Shiryōkan. Even though Kimitsu dai 14-gō is recorded in *Nihon gaikō bunsho dai-25 kan*, a part of *Fuzokusho* (appendix) English-language newspaper articles were omitted.

94. Hall, *Immigration and Its Effects upon the United States*, 59–60.

CHAPTER 4

On a Collision Course

The Migration of Japanese *Dekasegi* Laborers to the United States during the Meiji Era (II)

The Enforcement of the New US Immigration Law and the Incident of "The Denial of Japanese Migrant Laborers' Entry into the United States"

In April 1891 in San Francisco—the center of the anti-Qing people (Chinese) movement—the US federal government, without prior notice, denied entry to more than one hundred Japanese migrant laborers at the port. The consul general of Japan in San Francisco and the Japanese minister residing in Washington, DC, were monitoring anti-Asian sentiment in the United States. They recognized the gravity of this incident, which took place immediately after the enactment of a new immigration law, and reported in detail to the home government.[1] However, even though Japanese diplomats stationed in the United States were concerned about this, many home government officials at first considered it just a temporary incident that they blamed on the "many shabby lower-caste Japanese who arrived in the US." They believed they could solve this problem by temporarily tightening the control of the emigration of poor Japanese migrant laborers. One century later, I can affirm that those Japanese officials' judgment was too optimistic. It is not wrong to point out that the issue of Japanese immigration, one of the factors

---

This paper was translated from Sakata Yasuo, "Shōtotsuten e mukau kidō: Meiji ki ni okeru Nihonjin no Amerika dekasegi" (On a Collision Course: The Migration of Japanese *Dekasegi* Laborers to the United States during the Meiji Era) (II), *Ōsaka Gakuin Daigaku Kokusaigaku ronshū 3-kan, 2-gō* (1992). The author intended to refine this article at a later date.

aggravating the US-Japan relationship in the early twentieth century, started with this 1891 entry denial. Although researchers have not paid particular attention to this incident, it should be reevaluated as one of the most significant events in Japanese-American migration research, and more broadly, in the history of the US-Japan relationship.[2]

The Historical Significance of the Incident

The Japanese government at the time was determined to negotiate treaty revisions with the United States. At the final stage of negotiations, however, the United States took a very strong stand. This incident was deeply connected to the right to regulate and limit immigration by domestic legislation.[3] Furthermore, from the late nineteenth century to the early twentieth century, this incident incited the "yellow peril" movement fomented by sneers at the Japanese claim that "new Japan" had become a world power. Racial prejudice by whites in America was one of the most important factors in deepening the divide between the United States and Japan, the two Pacific countries representing Eastern and Western cultures.[4] However, diplomatic records that have survived clearly show that Japanese government officials, including those in the Ministry of Foreign Affairs, the main office managing Japanese emigration, did not pay much attention to rising anti-Asian sentiment in the United States and its effect on Japanese traveling to America at this time.[5] The Ministry of Foreign Affairs assessed that denying the entry of Japanese after passage of the new immigration law was an isolated event within certain local political and social environments that was triggered by the migration of many lower-class Japanese. Therefore, they failed to seriously consider that the issue of Japanese migrant laborers in America was part of rising anti-Asian sentiment and simply took urgent but ad hoc measures.[6]

It is not appropriate to solely blame the Japanese government officials' sloppy decision. It was not the only cause of the Japanese entry denial in 1891 developing into a more serious immigration problem. In fact, there might have been many other reasons.[7] However, it is true that mismanagement and a lack of interest by Japanese government officials sowed the seeds of future problems. The US government and white American opposition to Japanese migrant laborers working on the West Coast became more uncompromising, stubborn, and dogmatic. This issue of Japanese migrant laborers developed into more serious Japanese immigration problems. In the early twentieth century, these problems became a major factor in widening the gulf between the two countries, so great that a possible Japan-US war was seriously discussed.[8] In fact, George F. Kennan, an American diplomat and historian who famously advocated for a policy of containment of the Soviet Union, suggested in 1951, "We [Americans] would repeatedly irritate and offend the sensitive Japanese by our immigration policies and the treatment of Japanese lineage . . . in this country, indirectly contributing to the breakout of the Pacific War."[9]

Enactment of the New Immigration Law and the Enforcement of Immigration Inspection

Then, what exactly happened in the 1891 incident? As explained in chapter 3, a new immigration law was enacted on March 3, 1891, for the purpose of a general "qualitative restriction" of alien immigration into the United States.[10] For the first time in America's melting pot history, Section 7 of the act created the Office of the Superintendent of Immigration under the jurisdiction of the Department of the Treasury.[11] Moreover, Section 8 established collectors of customs as the main agents to inspect alien passengers on vessels entering US ports. It stated that based on such inspections, entry should be immediately denied to those who were judged to be "undesirable immigrants," including lunatics, paupers, criminals, and contract laborers who were already legally prohibited from entering. Section 8 also stated that "all decisions made by the inspection officers or their assistants touching upon the right of any alien to land, when adverse to such right, shall be final unless appeal be taken to the Superintendent of Immigration." Furthermore, Section 10 stated that "all aliens who may unlawfully come to the United States shall, if practicable, be immediately sent back on the vessel by which they were brought in."[12]

Once an immigration inspector denied aliens entry into the United States, it was impossible for travelers without money or legal knowledge to appeal to immigration inspectors in the Treasury Department in Washington, DC.[13] Therefore, in most cases, passengers who were denied entry had no recourse except to waste all their expenditures, including boat fares, and give up their plans and dreams. They even had to pay for their deportation to Japan. Some migrant laborers were inspired by promotions such as "If you emigrate to a civilized world where wages are higher than your mother country's, get a job, and work hard, then it is not difficult to return home in glory."[14] Nothing was more tragic than penniless migrant laborers intent on success in America but rejected, I would imagine. As explained in private instructions from the Ministry of Foreign Affairs to the prefectural governors, however, since Japanese migrant laborers arriving in the United States in early 1891 had no expectation of these new stricter inspections, not a few had no means to advance or retreat. Therefore, many Japanese migrant laborers were denied entry at once.[15] Presumably, these migrant laborers were then shocked, falling into tragic consequences.

Fair Immigration Law Articles and Its Prejudiced Applications

It is true that, according to the new immigration law, qualitative restrictions of immigrants applied to all aliens.[16] As previously pointed out, it is also true that the law did not generally intend to target certain nationalities based on racial prejudice.[17] However, the interpretation of the articles of the law and its application, and judgments pertaining to violations, were under the jurisdiction of white American immigration officers at each port. In most cases, they were suspected of holding persistent prejudice against the "yellow race." Therefore, it is not a wrong accusation to say that preventing the discriminatory application of articles that targeted specific races or people during immigration inspections at every US port in the late nineteenth century was almost impossible. In areas such as San Francisco, in particular, where the anti-Chinese movement was born, the discriminatory application of the law was demanded by the white residents. As Chinda Sutemi, the consul general of Japan in San Francisco, reported to the foreign minister, "Here in San Francisco, the status of migrant laborers is painful. Amid the [white] residents' opposition against Asian immigration, immigration inspectors carefully search for any proof of illegality and are determined to send them back instantly."[18] For example, a local newspaper antagonistic to Chinese and Japanese migrant laborers published articles inciting anti-Asian sentiment in its community, and admitted that Timothy Guy Phelps, a customs collector at the San Francisco port, supported the Asian-exclusion movement:[19]

Pleasant and polite though the Japanese may be, the people of this country are beginning to look askance at them. The *Call* has shown how greatly on the increase is their immigration to these shores. It has not sounded a false alarm. From every quarter comes proof of the fact that there is danger of our having a Japanese question, just as we have had a Chinese. Of course, the Japanese will never be so objectionable to the moneyed class as are the Chinese. Many people of wealth will not hire Chinese. They do not care to have the filth of Chinatown brought into their homes, but these same people will hire Japanese and be glad to get them, for they will work for little or nothing. The working classes of white people will, however, continue to look upon the Japanese with great distrust and even repugnance. The idea that laborers from Japan are coming here in large numbers under contract is scouted by the Japanese Consul. He says there is nothing in it. Collector Phelps believes that there is a good deal in it. He is getting proof of it, in fact, and has men out looking up the matter. He will make a great stir when he collects all his facts and is ready to give them to the public.[20]

In fact, immigration inspection under the collector Phelps was clearly conducted, by all means necessary, to stop Japanese migrant laborers from entering, and applying the law fairly does not seem to have been even remotely part of his agenda. Chinda also acknowledged that he did not expect a fair execution of the immigration law: "Mr. Phelps, the collector at the port of San Francisco, is generally known for advocating Chinese exclusion, and he naturally seems to want to apply the law most strictly to Japanese immigrants."[21]

Thus, in context with the political and social climate on the West Coast in the early 1890s, the application of the supposedly fair immigration law's prohibition article was abused by "yellow peril" leaders who were determined to exclude the "yellow race" based on prejudice. Through the hands of immigration inspectors, they used it as a rare weapon for Japanese exclusion. Any sensible criticism that this conduct countered America's foundational philosophy of welcoming immigrants was seldom heard on the West Coast. In the early 1890s, Japanese migrant laborers had just started working in America, and the number of Japanese immigrants arriving on US shores exceeded more than one thousand for the first time.[22] In the 1891 incident, approximately one hundred Japanese migrant laborers, or about 10 percent of the arrivals, were denied entry. (A study by Roger Daniels explains the incident in greater detail.)[23]

Mismanagement by Japanese Government Officials

It should be said that mere anti-Japanese sentiment does not adequately define the essence of this incident. As I pointed out previously, Japanese government officials also contributed to this incident for many reasons. For one, officials in the Ministry of Foreign Affairs, other officials, and intellectual leaders, in particular, who were considered the elite in the Meiji era, may have lacked knowledge and understanding of this matter. In other words, they did not yet understand the essence of the immigration problem in the United States, a republic of white people, and the American people's relentless, intense prejudice toward "yellow races" at this time. To the Japanese, emigration to America meant nothing but working overseas for small numbers of poor students and lower-class people aspiring to make a fortune. Only some influential people, including Taguchi Ukichi, advocated Japanese expansion overseas. Thus, perhaps unsurprisingly, Japanese government officials failed to understand that this issue surrounding a small number of emerging Japanese working-class emigrants would become an issue for the entire nation of Japan and its people.[24]

Inattentive Japanese government officials were perplexed at this unexpected incident when more than a hundred migrant laborers arriving in the United States were suddenly denied entry by authorities due to violation of the new immigration law in San Francisco, the city at the center of anti-Chinese movement. A newspaper in San Francisco reported this incident sensationally, and it became obvious that if such incidents continued in the future, the prestige and honor of Japan and its people could be damaged. At this point, the home government accepted the advice of the Japanese diplomats stationed in America, who expressed that this was not a mere incident but a grave situation, and they needed to consider a countermeasure. Even so, the central government office acted only to send internal instructions to the prefectural governors of open ports that had offices issuing passports: "Make the US immigration law known to those who travel to the United States

for the purposes of labor employment. Fully notify [applicants] to prepare appropriate measures in advance to prevent a tragic situation of
entry denial on the grounds of being poor." The measure was pallia-
tive, simply instructing governors to take care of the situation, but it
was far from a permanent solution.[25] Frankly speaking, the Japanese
government did not have the capacity but was simply preoccupied with
keeping up its national appearance.

I might receive some criticism of hindsight for saying this. However,
if the Japanese government had suspended Japanese laborers' migration to America at this early stage, as they did in August 1900 with
long-lasting results, I presume that, at least at this point, the migration
of Japanese laborers to America would not have triggered a serious
diplomatic problem that would eventually threaten the Japan-US relationship.[26] In 1900, the number of Japanese immigrants to America
had already reached more than ten thousand, while in 1891, it was only
approximately one thousand.[27] Back then, I assume the emigration to
America might have been easily and effectively halted. Aside from the
ignorance of Japanese government officials dealing with this matter,
the Japanese government was still unstable right after the Constitution
of the Empire of Japan was promulgated and the first Imperial Diet was
held. In addition, Japan had not recovered from the recession. These
were the circumstances that the Japanese government faced around
1891 that prevented it from taking drastic measures to halt the emigration of migrant laborers to America.

The Concepts of Japanese Emigration Expansionism and
Migrant Laborers Drawn from a Surplus Population

Japanese overseas emigration expansionism was advocated by
Tokutomi (Sohō) Iichirō and others. Tokutomi was a pioneer of the
expansionism that symbolized new Japan and the spirit of this era
from the late 1890s to the early 1900s. *Shokuminron* (discourses about
colonialism) and *kaigai hattenron* (discourses about overseas expansion) were widely introduced in magazines and newspapers, including
Taguchi Ukichi's *Tōkyō keizai zasshi*, *Kokumin no tomo*, published by
Min'yūsha, headed by Tokutomi, and *Jiji shinpō*, related to Fukuzawa
Yukichi. These publications were influential with the younger generation, and the hype of expansionism was escalated among them.[28]

Many expansionists and supporters were also present within government ranks, including Enomoto Takeaki, who established an *iminka* (emigration section) in the Bureau of Commercial Affairs, where paperwork for emigration was conducted while he served as the minister of foreign affairs in 1892. In the following year, 1893, he was selected as chairman of the Shokumin Kyōkai (transplantation or colonial association).[29] Most likely, nobody in the Japanese government advocated halting the migration of laborers to America because this harsh policy may have sparked more criticism and dissatisfaction with the government.

These various concepts for encouraging Japanese emigration overseas were introduced to Japan in 1868 as a Western idea and as a byproduct of liberal economic philosophy, in particular. In the Meiji 20s (starting from 1887), migration and overseas expansion were not discussed as part of a certain systemized economic theory. Instead, *imin* (immigration and emigration), *shokumin* (colonialism or expansion), and *kaigai dekasegi* (overseas migration for work) were studied independently by scholars as government policies that a modern nation should consider. They were linked to specific issues such as population growth, food shortages, the spread of poverty and distress, and trade expansion. Therefore, terminologies such as *shokumin, imin, kaigai dekasegi,* and *kaigai hatten* (overseas expansion) were not strictly defined, and the terms *imin* and *dekasegi* (working abroad) were in many cases used interchangeably even in the same publication.[30]

Discussions on the concepts of *shokumin* and *kaigai ijū* (overseas migration), which were introduced around this time, mostly centered on whether these measures were suitable for the poor and disgruntled, who under the circumstances were deemed "surplus population" and who should emigrate to selected countries and regions. Furthermore, those discourses insisted that *kaigai ijū* and *dekasegi* were important to the national welfare and—underscoring their necessity—would benefit not only emigrants but also the emigrant nation and its people, as demonstrated by the success of advanced European nations and their colonial histories.[31] For example, Taguchi Ukichi, who introduced *jiyū shugi shokumin shisō* (liberal colonization concept) to Japan, insisted that "forty million compatriots were already suffering from a lack of wealth in their country." He argued Japan should pour its surplus population into fertile lands, therefore accomplishing the *Nan'yō keiryaku*

(South Sea plan). He stated that Japanese expansion to the South Sea islands would bring national prestige and improve the national defense. He also said that from a national security standpoint, "the increase of the size of the South Sea fleets would also improve trade. By planting our people on the islands, we would increase traffic and the frequency of trade between Japan and these islands." [32] (Thus, he asserted that *Nan'yō hatten* would bring wealth to the nation.)

Moreover, influenced by Friedrich List's *shokumin* idea, Wakayama Norikazu considered Mexico the most suitable country for Japanese resettlement. He stated in a letter to Ōkuma Shigenobu, the minister of foreign affairs:

> These days, poor, disappointed samurai are actively agitating igno-rant people and causing political trouble. After the promulgation of the Meiji Constitution, in particular, societal outlook appears discouraging. Therefore, troubled people have always caused problems. Agriculture and industry became active in recent years. Railroad construction and other civil engineering projects flour-ished. However, if railway construction diminishes, the troubled people would have free time, and they can go somewhere for a while. If we persuade them to emigrate or engage in agriculture or min-ing work, it will dramatically decrease unrest in our country. . . . If we develop a colony in Mexico and our emigrants reach several millions there, we would gain great power. If we regularly educate them to have resolution and not lose loyalty to the mother country, they would be a great asset. [33]

Shiga Shigetaka's *Nan'yō jiji* and Tsuneya Seifuku's *Kaigai shoku-minron*, along with other promoters of *kaigai dekasegi*, encouraged lower-class people living in poor conditions to be engaged in *dekasegi* in the Hawaiian islands, the South Sea islands, or South America to save their livelihood. [34] In *Nan'yō jiji*, Shiga discussed that through emigration, "lower-class Japanese people would be nourished with adventurous spirit and provided with increased knowledge. [35]

Among the *shokumin* and *imin* discussions, the only one encour-aging *ijū* (emigration) to the United States was Mutō Sanji's *Beikoku ijūron*. Tsuneya explained, "Several years ago, Chinese people were

excluded from the United States, and the property they had managed
for many years seemed to be plundered secretly ... the powerful act
of persecution created more misery to immigrants than the forces of
nature. The misery was greater than nature's wrath." Furthermore,
Mutō emphasized that North America was not suitable for Japanese
immigration: "Emigrants should not be spending efforts to emigrate
to the United States of America and Canada unless they are temporary migrant laborers."[36] Before *shokuminron* and *ijūron*, published in
1887[-1891], started to stir Japanese expansionism, Fukuzawa Yukichi
encouraged young people's emigration to America from the perspective of an intellectual leader of Japan's westernization movement. He
stated, "People in American society are superior to their European
ancestors, and the scarcity of indolent people in the country is without
parallel in the world." He encouraged emigration "for people in the
prime of their lives, strong but suffering from lowly occupations, and
making every effort to earn a living throughout the year in a country
of immigrants."[37] This, however, might be mere unrealistic idealism.
Furthermore, at the same time as the publication of Mutō's *Beikoku
ijūron*, Akamine Seichirō's *Beikoku ima fushigi* and Ishida Kumajirō's
Kitare Nihonjin were published.[38] Even though these books encouraged
Japanese emigration to California, their contents were categorized as
tobei annai (guides for going to America), many of which were published in the Meiji 30s (starting 1897).[39] Therefore, strictly speaking,
they are considered essentially different from the *ijūron* discussed here.

Mutō's *Beikoku ijūron* was written as the young man was traveling to study in America. He was surprised by "the bravery of Chinese
people competing against white people on the West Coast." He based
the book on "his research on Chinese immigrants in his limited spare
time during his studies" and published it after he returned to Japan.[40]
Mutō's description of Chinese people was rare in the sense that it is free
from prejudice or contempt at a time when many Japanese, based on
datsu-a ron (de-Asianization), felt superior to and looked down upon
Chinese. This book is unbiased since it was based on data acquired by
his real-life investigation. In this *ijūron*, Mutō emphasized that nearly
20 percent of the Chinese migrant laborers who came to America
became successful businessmen, and that their activities in America
brought profit to their homeland. He also stated that even low-wage

migrant laborers could make truly huge amounts of money in one year.[41] He proceeded to note that "the languages, clothes, and cuisines of the Orientals are different from the whites, so Chinese and Japanese would be nearly alike. Our Chinese neighbors emigrated to the unfamiliar land of America and compete against whites for their share of fortune; there is no reason why our fellow Japanese could not migrate to America, just as the Chinese do." He suggested that the government and its people together should make efforts for Japanese migrant laborers to emigrate to the United States.[42] This is the essence of Mutō's *Beikoku ijūron*.

Furthermore, Mutō mentioned that some people believed that if white people noticed the shameful gluttonous behavior of Japanese migrant laborers, it would disgrace Japan. Therefore, they thought, lower-class Japanese should not emigrate to America. He laughed and stated cynically, "I have seen disgraceful behaviors from upper-class Japanese who traveled overseas during my study abroad. The idea (of dissuading low-class Japanese from migrating) is very selfish. I don't agree at all." [43] Moreover, he suggested that the Japanese propertied classes should invest in *imin kaisha* (emigration companies) to help the poor who were living hand to mouth and could not afford the travel costs of fifty or sixty yen to emigrate.[44]

Thus, the concepts of *imin* and *shokumin*, around 1887–1890, clearly varied by the destination for emigration or expansion, such as Taguchi's South Sea islands, Wakayama's Mexico, and Shiga's Hawaiian Islands. For various reasons, however, these authors assumed that, without exception, overseas expansion should be carried out by the lower classes or the dissatisfied of the society who could not make ends meet in Japan, and in some cases, could cause social unrest. However, colonizing the South Sea islands "by increasing the size of the South Sea fleets and trade, planting our people on the islands, and increasing the frequency of traffic between Japan and these islands"—these suggestions were unrealistic even in the Meiji 30s (starting 1897), when Japan became recognized as an Asian power, and even more so, one decade earlier, before Japan achieved its goal of revising its treaties. Thus, I assay that the encouragement of worker emigration in discussions of *shokumin* and *ijū*, whatever the destination, was the most realistic proposal for Japan at that time in terms of feasibility. Even Mutō's *Beikoku ijūron*, considered the most realistic, was still potentially problematic because it encouraged migrant laborers to emigrate to the West Coast, where "yellow peril" alarms were rising.[45]

Now, it is difficult to discuss and prove the effect that these concepts of *shokumin* and *ijū* cast on Japanese migrant laborers in America around 1887–1890. Moreover, even if the Japanese laborers' emigration to America was in fact encouraged by overseas expansionists at this time, it is hard to find out now what kinds of policies were discussed. Unfortunately, this field is not yet researched.[46] However, the publication of the concepts of *shokumin* and *ijū* developed expansionistic sentiments among the younger generations at this time. I believe it is correct to point out that the Ministry of Foreign Affairs, the main government office controlling migration, hesitated to take action against the current of the times.

The Reaction on the West Coast to the Japanese Promotion of Emigration to the United States

On the other hand, around 1887–1890 in Japan, the promotion of *kaigai hatten* (overseas expansion) and *dekasegi* (migration for work) naturally caused a negative reaction in America. The causes included the following: Japanese newspapers broadly reported the rise of the expansionist sentiment, discussions, suggestions, and activities of those who advocated *shokumin* and *ijū*. Many of these articles were often translated into English and reprinted by English-language newspapers published in Yokohama. Those English articles were regularly sent by mail boat across the Pacific Ocean to the West Coast, where the anti-Japanese movement was active. For example, the *Japan Weekly Mail* of August 1, 1890, reported that Inagaki Manjirō, the author of *Japan and the Pacific*, recommended that the Ministry of Foreign Affairs establish an *iminka* (emigration section).[47] Also, the *Japan Weekly Mail* of August 15, 1890, published a detailed description of Viscount Enomoto Takeaki's *Kaigai ijū shōrei* and on October 24, 1890, explained the *Nihon shokuminron* written by Tsuneya Seifuku, a member of the Ajia Kyōkai (Asiatic Society) in detail.[48] In the anti-Asian newspapers in San Francisco, including the *Call*, the *Examiner*, and the *Bulletin*, these articles were often conveniently distorted and even fabricated to fit the writers' own sensational commentaries. Chinda mentioned these local newspapers' malicious fake articles in his report to the minister of foreign affairs:

> Local politicians boldly consider issues of Japanese people as oddities and reported them on newspapers impudently. It is despicable for them to cater to their lower-working class community in order to gain their favor. Here, local newspapers do not generally seem to be responsible for their words. I always have to persistently confirm the accuracy of the articles they published on the paper. . . . Furthermore, even though I demand accuracy, not only was I not effective, but I also may have afforded them the opportunity to spread disinformation.

He revealed severe resentment about his consistent annoyance (with this editorial problem).[49]

For example, on May 18, 1892, the year following the incident denying Japanese immigrants entry, the *Call* issued a front-page story headlined "A New Emigration Association Formed in Tokyo." Chinda wrote a long protest citing a passage of false articles published by the newspaper, and stated, "The Japanese government has never given countenance to, much less encouraged, the emigration of common laborers to California." As proof, he cited the short but entire article titled "Japan Emigrants' Association" published by the *Japan Weekly Mail*, on April 23, 1892:

> An association has been formed in Tokio for the purpose of encouraging and facilitating emigration; its method of procedure is to collect candidates for emigration to all parts of the world, subjecting them to due inspection; and, further, to acquire uncultivated land in foreign countries with the object of dispatching emigrants thither, furnishing them with capital on the part of the Association. It will be seen from our advertisement columns that the Association can already lay hand on over three thousand able-bodied and trustworthy candidates for emigration, who are ready for immediate service.[50]

In addition, the *Call* cited a translated article published by the *Japan Weekly Mail* on March 26, 1892. This long article was first published in the *Mainichi shinbun*, written by Andō Tarō, the head of the *iminka* (emigrant section) in the Ministry of Foreign Affairs, who described a private view on emigration. The *Call*, however, cited only the part that was convenient to its editorial and reported it in such a way that readers could misinterpret the view that the Japanese government recognized emigration as a policy for relief of the poor, and that private *imin kaisha* (emigration companies) also supported this kind of government policy to encourage emigration.

The same paper recently printed the following extract from a report of the Director of Emigration of Japan: "The amount of wages received by our emigrants from the first until now is $1,000,000 and the sum at present being paid is $100,000 per month, out of which over $60,000 is either deposited in Government banks or remitted to the families of the emigrants at home."[51]

Thus, arguably, the editorial policy of the "yellow press" in San Francisco was to exploit whatever material was available, in particular, on the issue of Japanese immigration. On the other hand, the articles in the English-language newspapers issued in Yokohama covered the opinions and the activities of advocates for Japanese *shokumin* and *imin*. These were undeniably easily misunderstood on the West Coast, where public opinion had become biased with the desire to stop or limit Japanese migrant laborers' immigration to America. For example, in 1885, the year that *kan'yaku imin* (Japanese government contract laborers) began working in Hawai'i, Andō Tarō issued a statement. Andō served as the Japanese consul general in Hawai'i at the request of Inoue Kaoru, then the minister of foreign affairs. Later, at the request of Enomoto Takeaki, the minister of foreign affairs, he became the first head of the emigration section in the Ministry of Foreign Affairs, also established by Enomoto, with whom he fought at the Battle of Goryōkaku.[52]

Increase of the population amounts to 300,000 yearly, and it is not necessary to dwell upon the insufficiency of the area available within the country to provide for them. No doubt there are many methods by which this insufficiency might be met, but none so effectual as emigration to foreign countries. . . . As experience proves that emigration is much more advantageous to the country [than the opening up of Hokkaido], people generally do not show much eagerness in adopting the alternative scheme. Emigration does not rest upon a dislike to cultivating this country and a desire to go abroad; its advantage is that it makes use of the wealth of foreign lands to increase that of our own. . . . Whether emigration is or is not an advantage to this country may be seen by the experiments tried in the Sandwich Islands [cited in the *Call*].

Thus the total amount imported into the country every year is over seven hundred thousand dollars. If this sum were employed in cultivating the land at home, would not the wealth of the country be at once increased by the introduction of so much foreign capital? The above statement only gives the profit derived from the emigration alone. There are, however, many indirect advantages reaped by the country. Consider, for instance, the original status of these emigrants. They are principally farmers from out-of-the-way places, and they do not even know the use of matches. Therefore their food—rice, dried fish, soy, salted vegetables, and so on—as well as cotton, paper, and other necessaries of life, must be exported from Japan; so that their emigration increases the export trade; and as these articles are sold in the streets of Hawaii, the Hawaiians themselves are beginning to purchase and to appreciate them. If no emigration to that country had been started, no Japanese product would ever have found a market in so very remote an island.[53]

If Japanese people had read this, they would have understood that Andō just repeated the *kaigai hattenron* that was introduced by expansionists including Taguchi Ukichi, Tsuneya Seifuku, Wakayama Norikazu, and Shiga Shigetaka in newspapers and magazines at this time. On the West Coast, however, people perceived this differently. Many (white) residents proudly believed that Caucasians were superior to all the other races in the world, based on an academic theory published in the late nineteenth century. They listened to persistent warnings by "yellow peril" alarmists that proclaimed, "Massive numbers of poor people and contract laborers from Japan are rushing into America, the republic of whites, to try to take jobs away from white workers."

To those residents, articles about Japan's promotion of migrant laborers in the yellow press probably appeared eerie. This was one of the reasons why it was hard for the Japanese government to devise an effective solution to the issue of Japanese emigration around 1887–1890. As Consul General Chinda lamented, arguing against the anti-Japanese view in America would only invite their counterattack.[54] As long as many Japanese shared the opinions of *shokuminron* and *ijūron* about Japanese overseas expansion, and dreamed of a new Japan's future, it was in vain to loudly press Americans on the idea that Japanese had no intention of flooding to America. Americans would have considered this nothing but an unpersuasive excuse.

Japan's Emigration Issue and the Treaty Revision Negotiations

Another significant reason why the Japanese government hesitated to take drastic action to halt the migration of Japanese laborers to America to prevent worsening the anti-Japanese situation in 1891 was the negotiation for the new Japan-US Commerce and Navigation Treaty. The revision of the unequal treaty was a long-cherished desire for Japanese since the founding of Meiji government in 1868. Successive foreign ministers and secretaries made attempts to conclude the treaty but failed. Finally, the negotiation was at its final stages, appearing more promising this time.[55] The Treaty of Amity and Commerce between the United States and Japan concluded by the shogunate in 1858 lacked the principle of reciprocity and was thus considered unequal. Various studies have already demonstrated in detail that the application of the most-favored-nation clause in the Ansei Treaty of Amity and Commerce, in particular, placed the Empire of Japan and its people in an absolutely unfair position compared with that of the United States. Therefore, I don't need to repeat it here.[56]

The Treaty of Amity and Commerce between the United States and Japan did not clearly stipulate details governing Japanese people's entry, residence, and travel in America. However, when few Japanese lived in America, it did not call for a deliberation on whether Japanese people would be guaranteed most-favored-nation treatment under the treaty and would obtain similar rights as citizens of other nations that were guaranteed most-favored-nation treatment. However, around 1891, when the incident of the Japanese immigrants' entry denial occurred, the number of Japanese residents in and near San Francisco was estimated to be approximately four thousand, and the number of Japanese migrant laborers arriving there exceeded more than one thousand per year.[57] Furthermore, the conclusion of a new treaty of commerce based on the principle of reciprocity no longer seemed unrealistic. Therefore, the negotiating parties were going to discuss Japanese migration to a treaty nation in light of the fundamental rights guaranteed by the treaty of commerce. However, the United States had already forcibly pressed the Qing Court to conclude a treaty regarding immigration, with which the former banned the immigration of Chinese migrant laborers for ten years.[58] Naturally, the US government strongly demanded that the new treaty would warrant the right to regulate the immigration of Japanese laborers by domestic legislation.

In August 1892, Mutsu Munemitsu assumed the position of minister of foreign affairs for the Itō Hirobumi cabinet, replacing Enomoto Takeaki, who resigned due to the collapse of the Matsukata cabinet. Mutsu accepted the suggestion by Aoki Shūzō, the former foreign minister, regarding the treaty revision negotiation and decided to discuss it with England, the United States, and Germany one by one. Mutsu also assigned the additional post of minister-counselor in Britain to Aoki Shūzō, who was already the minister-counselor in Germany. While Aoki was negotiating with the British government in London, Mutsu avoided any discussion with the US government.[59] On July 16, 1894, the Anglo-Japanese Treaty of Commerce and Navigation was signed in London. On July 11, 1894, five days before the treaty was signed, Mutsu sent a telegram to Tateno Gōzō, ambassador to the United States. In this message he instructed Tateno to start negotiating with Walter Q. Gresham, the secretary of state, on the new Japan-US Commerce and Navigation Treaty.[60]

The Japanese government had already sent the minutes to Edwin Dunn, the US ambassador to Japan, on February 20, 1894, in which Mutsu emphasized, "The new treaties are to be reciprocal in all their provisions. Consequently, unilateral clauses and engagements hitherto admitted are to be suppressed."[61] However, on July 16, immediately after the negotiation started, the US government expressed its intention through Ambassador Dunn to establish a special clause for the immigration of migrant laborers and to have domestic legislation limit migration if the need arose in the future.[62] The Japanese government, in response, sent back an unofficial message that if the US government agreed to the new treaty, Japan would compromise on the issue of laborer migration, which the US government considered a most challenging issue. A *kunreisho*, an instruction document that signaled the start of negotiation for the new treaty by Foreign Minister Mutsu, was sent to Ambassador Tateno, clearly stating that the Japanese government would not express any objection regarding this matter:

> The US government proposed they might want to add revisions to our provisional treaty proposal. They marked and added revisions to every article and instantly sent them to us. Their letters, privately shown by the United States Ambassador to Japan to the Japanese minister, was that the US government was most concerned about adding the clause limiting the immigration of migrant laborers. On this matter, the suggested revision was that the freedom of residence in the first article of the treaty should be left as is, and that a separate special article about limiting immigrants should be added. Please send them two special provisional proposals as addenda (on a separate paper). Please let them decide which proposal they prefer. As long as they don't lose their spirit, it would not cause any problems even if they revised words. Also, regarding most-favored-nation treatment, the US government traditionally agrees with unconditional treatment. Therefore, if they ask for a revision, . . . it would not be a problem.[63]

The two proposals from the Japanese government for the special provisions regarding limits on immigration are displayed herein as two addenda.[64]

Special provision proposal 1

Separate Article: It being the intention of the High Contracting Parties to severally reserve to themselves full and entire liberty of action in all that concerns the regulation and control of labor and the immigration of laborers, it is declared, with a view to the prevention of any possible misunderstanding on the subject in the future, that each Contracting Party possess, as it did before the conclusion of the present Treaty, the absolute right, by domestic legislation, at its own pleasure and independently of the other, to regulate and control all Questions of labor and to limit, restrict, or prohibit the immigration of laborers into its own territories, without in any way calling in question the provisions of the present Treaty.

The present separate Article shall have the same force and value, as if it were inserted, word for word, in the Treaty signed this day and shall be ratified at the same time.

Special provision proposal 2

Separate Article: It is understood by the High Contracting Parties that the stipulations of the present Treaty do not, in any wise or to any extent, limit and qualify the right enjoyed by each of the Contracting Parties prior to the conclusion of the present Treaty, of regulating all questions; relating to labor and labor immigration; accordingly each Contracting Party is at full and perfect liberty, by domestic legislation, at its own pleasure and independently of the other, to regulate and control all questions of labor to limit, restrict or prohibit the immigration of laborers into its own territories without in any way calling in question the provisions of the present Treaty.

The present separate Article shall have the same force and value as if it were inserted word for word in the Treaty signed this day and shall be ratified at the same time.

The US government, however, counter to the Japanese government's expectations, did not show a willingness to accept the new treaty easily due to the difference in opinion on the limitations on the migration of Japanese laborers, as explained before. The Japanese government thought the reason negotiations were not progressing was that the US government officials did not trust Ambassador Tateno. Therefore, the Japanese government decided to recall the ambassador and assigned Kurino Shin'ichirō, the director of government affairs of the Ministry of Foreign Affairs, as the incoming ambassador.[65] Kurino arrived in

Washington, DC, on August 18, 1894, and started negotiating with the United States on September 21.[66] Kurino urged Walter Q. Gresham, the US secretary of state, to conclude the new treaty promptly:

> Now the discussion with each treaty power has begun and is showing gradual progress. We have already completed and signed the ratification of the treaty with Great Britain ... therefore, if the United States promptly accepts the requests of the Imperial Japanese Government, and completes the ratification of the treaty, the Imperial Japanese Government would appreciate the United States' trust. Also, the existing friendship between both countries would become increasingly cordial, which would bring mutual benefit to the future Japan-US trade relationship.

However, the secretary of state insisted, "the subjects or citizens of each of the two High Contracting Parties shall: have full liberty to enter, travel or reside in any part of the territories of the other Contracting Party." He insisted that it was necessary to add the special clause regarding the right to limit immigration by domestic law and demanded further discussion.[67]

After both countries continued negotiations on this matter, finally, on November 22, 1894, they signed the treaty.[68] They agreed to add the following terms at the end of Article II of the Treaty of Amity and Commerce between Japan and the United States with respect to immigration limits and immigration control:

> It is, however, understood that the stipulations contained in this and the preceding Article do not in any way affect the laws, ordinances and regulations with regard to trade, the immigration of laborers, police and public security which are in force or may hereafter be enacted in either of the two countries.[69]

Inevitably the Japanese government accepted, without resistance, this new Japan-US treaty, including the revised Article II, which would allow the US government to restrict alien immigration by legislating domestic laws, if necessary. The new treaty reflected the intentions of the US government and Congress to align with the establishment of the

Chinese Exclusion Act of 1882. As mentioned before, Congress enacted the Chinese Exclusion Act based on the Treaty Regulating Immigration from China (the Angell Treaty of 1880). The act suspended the immigration of Chinese laborers to the United States for ten years, and subsequently in 1892, this ban was extended for another ten years. By adding this special clause on immigration in the Treaty of Amity and Commerce between the United States and Japan, the Japanese government would not be able to legally object if the US government needed to legislate a similar law limiting Japanese migrant laborers as was done to the subjects of Qing—a country that the Japanese government had always looked down upon. Thus, the Japanese government found itself bound in the new treaty negotiation.

Why did the Japanese government, whose motto was "Never repeat the mistakes of the Qing [dynasty]," make such a compromise? I speculate that the Japanese government considered migrant laborers as despicable lower-class physical workers, different from true "de-Asianized" subjects of the Empire of Japan. The Japanese government tried to persuade itself that limiting the immigration of lower-class Japanese had no bearing on the rights of the subjects of the Empire of Japan.[70] A supporting line of evidence is that the Japanese government voluntarily took action to suspend Japanese migrant laborers' entry to the continental United States in August 1900 due to alarming rise of anti-Japanese sentiment on the West Coast. This was one year after it enacted the new treaty of commerce in July 1899.[71] At that time, the Japanese government probably could not predict that the US government would implement a discriminatory immigration policy based on racial bias after the Russo-Japanese War. What did Japanese unawareness signify? Since, so far, no studies have been conducted to shed light on the relationship between the issue of immigration and the revision of the treaty, much remains unclear. I hope research in this field will be published in the future.

The Japanese Diplomats Stationed in the United States and the Issue of Japanese Migration

So far, I have discussed from various points of view the historical significance and causes of the establishment of the immigration law of

1891 and the incidents of entry denial of many Japanese migrant laborers as a result of immigration inspections based on that law. Now I will
focus on Japanese diplomats stationed in the United States and evaluate
the sequence of incidents.

The Denial of the Poor and Efforts for Mediation
by the San Francisco Consulate

The initial reason for the denial of Japanese migrant laborers was that
they were paupers. Immediately after the establishment of the new
immigration law, the sight of steamships loaded with Japanese migrant
laborers arriving at the port of San Francisco was perceived as "inces-
sant," just as Chinda described in the report.[72] First, at the port of San
Francisco, on March 22, 1891, more than forty migrant laborers from
prefectures including Wakayama, Yamaguchi, and Hiroshima arrived
on the ship *Oceanic*; on April 7, twenty-five from the same prefectures arrived on the ship *Rio de Janeiro*; on April 14, twenty-eight
from the same prefectures plus Kumamoto prefecture arrived on the
ship *Gaelic*; and on April 21, more than fifty migrant laborers from
prefectures including Kumamoto, Nagasaki, and Hiroshima arrived
on the German tramp steamer *Remus*. They all applied for immigration inspection. Chinda observed these people and emphasized in his
report, "Clearly the number of the poor people who would violate the
[new immigration] law was not small." He emphasized that more than
fifty passengers on the *Remus* had a tattered appearance and were low-
class gluttons: "Most of the passengers dressed shabbily. The money
they carried was smaller than twenty yen at most and might be as little
as several tens of sen. They appear to be nothing but the poor." The
racially prejudiced immigration inspectors naturally made a similar
judgment, and among more than 150 Japanese passengers, "except
for a few who brought financial resources, all the others were barred
from landing by the customs officers and detained."[73] This incident
provided a good opportunity for the anti-Asian yellow press in San
Francisco, and it published front-page stories with sensational headlines every day.[74] The articles, Chinda said, were "unbearably exaggerated to appeal to the general public in the area and to try drawing their
attention."[75]

Japanese are swarming here by hundreds. Every steamer from Yokohama brings a full cargo of the pleasant little people from the Mikado's realm. They are picturesque people, as well as pleasant. They are polite, courteous, smiling, and nobody ever has occasion to kick or cuff them, or even to unbraid them. They rarely get into the Police Courts, and there are few if any in San Quentin. But they are taking work away from our boys and girls and away from our men and women. What shall be done about them? Is it not time that some checks were put upon their immigration? They are pleasant people—these Japanese—but the question arises, "Have we not enough of them now?" The answer of all the working girls and boys in California is "Yes, not only enough, but too many. Keep the rest of the crowd out."[76]

As soon as Japanese migrant laborers were denied, Consul General Chinda sent Fujita Yoshirō, a consular officer, to the port and had him investigate the situation. As a result, Chinda decided to appeal the measure taken by the immigration inspector. Simultaneously, he made every effort to write letters of guarantee, obtain documents verifying the identification of people denied entry for being poor, took them in, and helped to find employment for them. He invalidated the immigration inspector's action and succeeded in gaining their entry to the United States, with exceptions of former Amakusa residents who arrived without passports.[77] The former Amakusa residents were clearly in violation of Japanese law. Moreover, they looked so miserable that it was hard to object to the immigration inspector's decision judging them as cashless and poor. However, many sold their property in Japan to pay for the sea fare, and Chinda felt that it was a pitiful hardship to deport them instantly to Japan. Furthermore, he felt that denying them entry could "harm the honor of Japanese people," so he harbored those nine people while searching for guarantors for them. He was able to complete their custom procedures successfully.[78]

Local newspapers sensationally reported that many Japanese migrant laborers faced deportation immediately after the new immigration law was enacted and tried to stir up sentiments that Japanese were undesirable laborers just like the Chinese. Yet in reality, not even one Japanese was denied entry to the United States.[79] However, people such as Collector Phelps, who were fully immersed in anti-Chinese sentiment, would not contain themselves and would strengthen their resolution to deny more people. Chinda was concerned about future consequences.[80]

Thus, on April 24, while the consular officers in San Francisco were busy dealing with the above matters, they received a telegram that the German steamship *Pemptos* had arrived at the port in San Francisco loaded with sixty-seven migrant laborers from Hiroshima and Kumamoto prefectures. They were also informed that customs was already enforcing a very strict immigration inspection and that among the passengers were fifteen likely prostitutes, for whom the consulate would refrain from acting as an intermediary for job placement. Moreover, on April 25, they received a telegram saying that fifty Japanese migrant laborers were arriving on the *China*, followed by two more steamships with tens of Japanese passengers.[81] Consul General Chinda warned that if some of these passengers were denied entry, he might not be able to reverse the ban on all of them as he did before. He stated in a report to the minister of foreign affairs that for immigrants already on the way, it was desirable that he make a tremendous effort to mediate with the customs authority in order to avoid rejection. However, he said, it was naturally not possible "to propose measures that would bypass the laws of the United States for those who are clearly in violation of the new law." Furthermore, he stated that there was no benefit for the consulate to give a guarantee to poor people. Therefore, he said that the consulate would act "to find trustworthy people inside and outside of the country . . . to become a guarantor of these people, and under these conditions, the consulate would request approval for their immigration." He also suggested, however, that the scope of the consulate's action was very limited, and that it was impossible to assist the mass of immigrants. Some Japanese immigrants might have to be deported.[82]

Thus, Chinda requested that the minister of foreign affairs take measures in Japan to ensure that migrant laborers who might be suspected to be "persons likely to become a public charge," or paupers, would not face the hardship of being denied entry and deported at US ports.

If denied entry, the initial desire of those who sold all their property and bought ship tickets would dissolve into bubbles. Their troubles would be unparalleled. Therefore, I would request Your Excellency to notify each prefectural governor of the addendum of the US immigration law. Since people are currently applying for passports, please notify the prefectural governors of open ports to send these applications to the Ministry of Foreign Affairs. With this measure, please send instructions to strictly control people traveling without passports. Those whom local government officials must focus on controlling are prostitutes, contract laborers, the poor, and the unhealthy. I have observed during the immigration inspection of passengers at this port that people who don't carry at least fifteen or sixteen dollars, excluding the cost of the ship ticket, are usually considered poor.[83]

This suggestion by Chinda started a so-called show-money system: before departure from Japan, emigrants obtained money to show so that they would not be suspected of being poor. This practice became widespread. For example, Katayama Sen's *Tobei annai*, issued in 1901, emphasized the need of carrying show money. "To prepare for emigration, even if one is a poor student, he should prepare at least 150 yen. This would be total of 50 yen for the ship travel cost and 60 yen for 'arrival money' (money for show only). The remaining 40 yen can be used for preparing for emigration and as an allowance during travel on the ship."[84] Furthermore, both Chinda and Tateno requested that the Japanese government tighten the control of passport issuance—including inspection of the identification, financial status, and purpose of travel—of people applying for passports for emigration purposes. They also requested that potential emigrants be instructed about the terms and current status of US immigration law so that they would not be denied entry by authorities at a port.[85]

Such requests from diplomats stationed in the United States were sent as official notifications to prefectural governors of open ports, the main offices issuing passports under the Ministry of Foreign Affairs.[86] Thus, the local government branch that served to indirectly control emigrants by assessing those suspected of being poor reinforced emigration control.[87] The yellow press in San Francisco continued to sensationally attack Japanese with headlines such as "A Horde of Indigent Japanese Are Flowing into America." However, according to the consular reports, after 1892, there were few incidents in which the poor were denied entry, and this did not develop into serious incidents.[88]

The Article to Ban Contract Laborers and Its Application for Japanese Migrant Laborers

Before 1891, when immigration inspection was implemented by the new law, the number of alien passengers who were denied entry for being contract laborers, including Japanese migrant laborers, was quite small despite the legal banning of the immigration of contract laborers since 1885.[89] Moreover, the 1891 law made it more difficult for immigrants to appeal for a reversal of the decision made by the immigration inspector in the Treasury Department if they were denied entry for being contract laborers rather than for being poor. The reason was that immigration inspectors judged contract laborers on more concrete evidence such as the possession of a contract or a written or oral guarantee of employment, while judgments of poverty were more subjective.[90] Chinda also pointed out that the denial of contract laborers was a clear application of US law and that its rationale was different from the rationale of denying the poor.[91] Moreover, the clause of the law defined contract laborers' agreements and contracts as those with parol (oral), special (for example, written), expressed, or implied agreements. Therefore, for example, a friend might promise someone in his letter, "If you immigrate here, I will find you a job." If the letter is shown to the inspector at customs, the inspector could consider the letter proof of an implied agreement.

As previously pointed out, in San Francisco, the port of arrival for Japanese, the chief customs collector held anti-Asian views. Influenced by public opinion in the region, he prevented Japanese migrant laborers from entering the country to the best of his ability. As a result, many Japanese passengers were, in fact, denied entry because they had gotten a promise from a friend residing in America that they would have a job after arrival and were thus judged to be contract laborers.[92]

For example, according to the investigation by a consular officer in San Francisco, Katō Unokichi, a Kanagawa prefecture native who arrived on the *Pemptos*, was judged a contract laborer and was denied entry. The report states:

> According to Ukichirō's [Unokichi's] statement, he had a friend in Seattle, Washington, who ran lodgings for mariners. He responded to his friend's letter beforehand, stating that if he immigrated, he would use help in finding a job as a ship crew. When he arrived in America, the customs inspector thought that the boarding master traditionally provided sailors to ships, almost like selling sailors to ships. Therefore, the inspector concluded that the boarding master recruited Unokichi for a business activity; therefore, he would not be allowed entry to the US.[93]

This seems a total distortion or a sophism. The local newspaper's article implied that Phelps, the chief customs collector, distorted Japanese oral statements on purpose to conclude they were contract laborers.

> Collector [of Customs] Phelps [said,] "You ask me how I can tell that the Japanese are violating the immigration law as to contract laborers. I will tell you of one strong, convincing proof of that fact. Before the immigration act of March 3, 1891, was passed by Congress the Japanese who were then coming here were afraid that some restriction would be placed on their immigration. They thought that as many of them were poor and came here without a dollar in their pockets, they would be considered undesirable and would create the fear that they were to become public charges unless they were to show their willingness to show proof of the fact that they came here to work under contract. This was conclusively shown in many cases. As soon as the act of March 3, 1891, went into effect the Japanese coming here found that they could not land if they were to tell of the contracts which they or their subjects had made, and they therefore kept that feature of the business in the background."[94]

As a principle, Phelps judged people who were not guaranteed employment to be poor and, likewise, judged non-poor people with

guaranteed employment to be contract laborers. Therefore, I must say
that it was difficult to prevent denial at customs.

Denial of Japanese Contract Laborers at Customs and the Reaction
of Japanese Diplomats Stationed in the United States

It was troublesome that the denial of Japanese contract laborers
occurred while the consular officers were active in supporting the poor.
The first case of denial at customs occurred when four contract laborers arrived on the *Pemptos* and underwent immigration inspection in
San Francisco on April 29.[95] Chinda considered this a serious incident
and explained this matter to Tateno in a telegram and letter, requesting
countermeasures.[96]

In the report about this matter to Aoki Shūzō, the minister of foreign
affairs, Ambassador Tateno emphasized that the clause related to contract laborers applied to "all people, not only to the Chinese but also
to immigrants from European countries." He cited a case where immigrants from European countries were considered contract laborers,
stating that they arrived "with their passages paid by employers with
the promise of employment in America." Tateno also observed that "as
the number of Japanese passengers to the United States has increased
recently, I heard that some were arriving as so-called contract laborers." He said that, since the implementation of the 1885 Alien Contract
Labor Law, "fortunately, Japanese migrant laborers have never been
denied entry until today." However, due to the new immigration law,
he expressed concerns that this incident might not be an isolated event
and might happen again. "Since customs inspections in San Francisco
have become increasingly strict, many more people might be denied
entry in the future, and the situation will be unpredictable."

Like Consul General Chinda, Ambassador Tateno also recommended a countermeasure of tightening the emigration control in
Japan. "I believe we should issue a notification in Japan or conduct
strict inspection at the departure ports, including Yokohama. It is quite
urgent to prevent damage caused by those who are ignorant of US
immigration laws and fooled by greedy adventurers into traveling to a
faraway country for nothing." Moreover, Tateno referred to the possibility that biased immigration inspectors would make erroneous judgments, and if so, he affirmed that he intended to appeal. "If our people

are denied entry at immigration in San Francisco and have proof of contract laborer status that is deemed insufficient, I will exercise my authority to the fullest." [97]

Tateno noted that "the telegraph message from Consul General Chinda was brief, and the details of this incident are unknown." He reported the concrete circumstances of the incident to the foreign minister, and his instructions with his reasoning to Chinda:

> Aside from the four mentioned previously, several Japanese are expected to arrive on the same ship from the Kingdom of Hawaii. It was evident that these four passengers arrived in America after receiving a promise of employment and wages before their departure in correspondence from their acquaintances residing in America. However, it is still unclear whether their acquaintance is an American or Japanese, or if he is an employer or simply a friend acting as an agent out of friendship. If the acquaintance is an employer, American or Japanese, it would not be possible to deny a claim by a customs inspector in the San Francisco port for being tacit contract laborers. If the acquaintance is a friend and just recommended a job based on friendship, no valid contract exists between them. Therefore, the US had no right to deny their arrival in America. Even though the oral evidence of two among the four migrant laborers contradicted that of their employer or agent, the immigration inspector at San Francisco took their first oral evidence and denied entry without detailed inspection.
>
> This was a very inconvenient one-sided measure, I must say. Therefore, I fundamentally determined to urgently request a clear explanation from the US government. If I recognize that there are enough reasons [for denial], then I have to yield to their deportation on the ship leaving the port of San Francisco today. At two o'clock in the morning ... I sent a telegraph message to Consul General Chinda. I asked him if he could detain the previously mentioned four Japanese in San Francisco in the meantime until I inquired with the authorities and the judgment was issued, with the provision that the Japanese government will compensate the costs for their stay. With this measure, I could try my best to demand consent from the customs collector. If my request is not granted and

Consul General Chinda believes those four Japanese have the right
to immigrate, please appeal publicly to the customs collector and
report in detail to me.[98]

Ambassador Tateno considered this incident important since it was
the first in a series of denying the entry of Japanese by suspicion of contract laborer status, and he expressed his determination saying, "We
expressed our objection to the US government as they were proceed-
ing with deportation and tried every possible means to bring about
Japanese migrant laborer immigration." The steamship, which was set
to send Japanese migrant laborers back, was scheduled to leave San
Francisco that day, and Tateno further explained:

> If we proceed through the Department of State, we would have
> indubitably lost this opportunity. Therefore, this early morning I
> consulted privately with the *zatsumu kyokuchō* [director general
> of miscellaneous duties] at the Department of the Treasury, and
> the following telegraph message was sent to the secretary-general
> of immigration in San Francisco:
>   "Regarding the incident of the four Japanese migrant laborers'
> denial of entry, the Japanese consular officials express objection to
> the decision of your officials. We request a hold on the deportation
> of the four Japanese migrant laborers for a while if you agree.
>   ". . . if, by these procedures, Japanese migrant laborers can stay
> at the port of San Francisco temporarily, we will pay for the cost of
> their stay and the sea fare."

Ambassador Tateno explained the above and requested the home
government's consent.[99] However, he never received a reply or special
instruction from Foreign Minister Aoki.

Since then, the arrival of Japanese migrant laborers was unabated.
The number of Japanese migrant laborers suspected of being contract laborers and denied entry was not as large as in the beginning,
although several cases occurred on every ship. In such cases, Chinda,
following Tateno's instruction, objected to the immigration inspector's
decision and tried to avoid the bitter deportation of Japanese passengers as much as possible. However, some Japanese passengers that were

among those denied entry apparently did carry credible documentation that could be determined as a contract.

> Among the Japanese migrant laborers on the ship *Gaelic* arriving on January 23, 1892, ... two of them ... were judged as violating the law banning contract laborers and were denied entry. ... One man, named Ōgawara, a wood-engraver, was carrying an employment contract with Siegfried & Brandenstein, tea merchants. It delineated the contract between the person and the agent of the company, stating the nature of employment, the amount of payment, and other necessary terms in a standard contract template. It contained additional terms regarding nondisclosure of the contract with others and so on. Since this seemed, at minimum, a true contract, the consul general could not find any grounds for arguing against the contract's validity. If this contract was legally valid, as the US authorities had judged, thus violating this country's law, then it is not within our authority to defend him. If we decided to defend him, our consul general may be judged as harboring a criminal and eluding the law.[100]

Chinda, too, concluded that Ōgawara was a contract laborer. However, he said, "if the US authorities followed the law and punished the contractor Siegfried & Brandenstein or the person, we would naturally infer that the contract should be considered invalid."

He emphasized, "I will try my best to call for removing the ban." Even in this case, he intended to defend a lawbreaker as long as he had a way to do so.[101] Moreover, Chinda insisted that he alone should not make a decision and requested instructions from Ambassador Tateno.[102]

Tateno, replying to Chinda on whether the consul general should always defend and mediate for the immigration of millions of these potential contract laborers, stated that it was desirable not to appeal such cases:

> In the case in which appealing the cases might encourage the US government to establish even stricter laws against Japanese emigrants, it is not recommended to make an objection. If this

happened, when our good people emigrate to America in the future, it would create a major obstacle. Therefore, as an observer of general policy, I think we should not choose a policy that encourages migrant laborer immigration when they might be denied, in order to prevent American complaints. Then we should wait for a good opportunity quietly, and deliberate on future measures before acting. This would be beneficial.

However, he continued, when Japanese migrant laborers travel to foreign countries,

> it is the [San Francisco] consul general's firm occupational duty to protect their benefits, save them from disaster, and strengthen their rights. These duties should not be done lazily. If you exercise your duty as consul general rightfully, it will often cause political conflict. That is one of the difficult parts of your occupational duty, and it is hard to achieve easily and quickly.

Ambassador Tateno emphasized that it was the duty of Chinda, the consul general, to make an effort to reverse the denial of Japanese migrant laborers, including a difficult case like Ōgawara's.[103] Most likely, Chinda was placed in a very difficult position.

Enomoto Takeaki, the minister of foreign affairs, was asked for a response to a question by Ambassador Tateno and responded with *kunrei* (instructions) as follows:

> Japanese traveling to America from Japan suspected of being laborers were subject to deportation decisions by immigration inspectors at the port of San Francisco. I received the consul general's request for my instructions on the future policy encouraging contract laborers to emigrate. . . . San Francisco immigration inspectors judged that those migrant laborers violated immigration law and were denied their entry. In this case, the consul general conducted a detailed investigation and concluded that they, in fact, did not violate the law. His duty is to fully defend them and strive to act as their intermediary for their immigration. If it was our migrant laborers' faults, and they violated the law as the inspector

had judged, then this decision is not within the scope of the consul's intervention. In short, the future duty of the consul general in defending Japanese migrant laborers is to conduct actual investigations. Then you should make an objection stating that there was no evidence for the violation of immigration law. This is my *kaikun* (reply).[104]

The minister's reply seemed to place all the responsibility in the hands of a mere diplomat, a consul general in San Francisco. At this time, the discussion of the new Japan-US Commerce and Navigation Treaty was about to begin. Even Enomoto Takeaki, an advocate of expansionism, may have determined that it was best to avoid creating a Japanese disadvantage in this negotiation.[105] Unfortunately, *gaikō bunsho* (diplomatic documents) do not mention this matter.

Emigration Agents and the Incident of the Contract Laborers' Denial of Entry

It has been pointed out that American immigration inspectors who held biased views against the "yellow race" applied the article banning certain immigrants, contributing to the Japanese migrant laborers' being denied entry. However, the Japanese government too should be blamed for the frequent denials after the implementation of the new immigration law. One reason was that emigration was promoted in Japan. But more importantly, unprincipled emigration agents swindled many indigent migrant laborers who might be denied entry to America. In fact, as Chinda reported, the first time that an unexpectedly large number of Japanese passengers were denied entry was when two German tramp steamers, the *Remus* and the *Pemptos*, arrived simultaneously at the port of San Francisco.[106]

Chinda continued, "Unlike the Japanese who arrived previously, eight or nine out of ten of these laborers were farmers and came to the United States for the purpose of *dekasegi*. Most likely, they have sold their properties to pay for the journey, and once they arrive in the United States, very few of them could support themselves." Many of the passengers on the *Remus* were poorly dressed and denied landing as it was thought they would become a burden on the public welfare. On the other hand, the migrant laborers on the *Pemptos* were "somewhat superior financially, but for the first time, many people were suspected of being contract laborers. As many as fourteen of them suffered the misfortune of deportation." [107]

It was Durham White Stevens, a competent *oyatoi gaijin* (foreign government adviser in Meiji Japan), who indicated that the migration of poor *dekasegi* laborers stemmed from the fraudulent activity of immoral emigration agents. He served as the English secretary to the imperial delegation at Washington, assisting Tateno Gōzō, the ambassador to the United States, in negotiating the new Japan-US Commerce and Navigation Treaty. After the denial of Japanese entry in San Francisco, he submitted a written opinion in which he analyzed the circumstances of this incident as follows:

> The feeling in the United States toward Japanese is very friendly. It is not too much to say, however, that there will, in all probability, be a change in this regard if indigent Japanese continue to arrive in [America]. Already there are indications of such a change in California. Hitherto there has been a widely marked difference in the attitude of the people and press of that State toward the Chinese and their sentiments toward [the] Japanese. But recently, in the controversy regarding the Japanese on the "Remus" and "Pemptos," it was possible to detect in the comments of the San Francisco press that same hostility so often displayed toward Chinese. This feeling may be neither logical nor just, but the fact that it has been manifested for the first time toward Japanese is especially significant in view of the position assumed by the United States Government on the question of Immigration. . . . The fact, therefore, that this question may assume grave political significance, equally with due regard for the welfare of the Japanese who are lured by the false pretenses to leave Japan, render it worthy of the serious attention of the Imperial Government.[108]

In addition, he described the activities of vicious immigration agents:

> There are unquestionably in Japan at present a number of persons engaged in promoting emigration to the United States simply to obtain the passage money of the immigrant. This seemed to be

clear in the case of the steamers "Remus" and "Pemptos." . . .
These people have been promised employment in the United
States by the agent of the steamer, merely to obtain their passage
money, there being no intention to fulfill the promise. The Imperial
Government, I venture to think, should take immediate action in
regard to this matter. Delay will certainly work harm to individuals; it may do injury to important national interests. If there is any
means of punishing the persons who for their own selfish ends
lure Japanese away under false promises, the punishment should
be prompt, and severe. If there is a way to prevent indiscriminate
emigration, it should at once be utilized. Neither the welfare of
Japanese subjects, nor the credit of Japan, will be promoted by the
continuance of the present condition of affairs.

He stated that the top priority was to limit Japanese *dekasegi* laborer
migration and control unscrupulous emigration agents.[109] However, it
took two years for the measure that Stevens proposed to be carried
out. In April 1894, Regulations on the Protection of Emigrants were
implemented to control *imin kaisha* (emigration companies) and emigration agents.[110] Moreover, it was not until 1896 when this imperfect
law was revised, and the more effective Emigrant Protection Act was
implemented.[111] Furthermore, as I state in chapter 5, these laws inadvertently caused problems later.[112]

The Meiji Elite's Biases: "Don't Repeat the Same Mistake as the Chinese"

When analyzing the incident of the denial of Japanese migrant laborers in San Francisco in 1891, we should not ignore the biases that the
Japanese government officials—Meiji elites—held against low-class
Japanese. Chinda was making his best effort to solve this problem by
supporting migrant laborers who were denied entry. However, in reading the details of the consular reports that have survived, it becomes
clear that his actions did not stem primarily from sympathy for the
Japanese migrant laborers' misfortune. It has been pointed out that
most Japanese government officials were of the former samurai rul-
ing class and held a strong bias and contempt toward the working
class. Chinda was the same.[113] In the *jōshinsho* (written statement)
to the minister of foreign affairs, he repeatedly expressed annoyance

and anger over the migrant laborers that he despised as disgracing the Empire of Japan's honor in the United States.[114]

As I discussed in detail in chapter 3, when the entry of Japanese was denied in 1891, anti-Chinese sentiment on the West Coast, and in the San Francisco Bay Area in particular, had not abated.[115] However, except for a few officials, the Japanese did not recognize the impact of anti-Chinese sentiment on the US government's immigration policy, or how it would affect Japanese emigration to the United States. Thus, they did not consider these subjects to be worth serious study. In many cases the Japanese thought that Americans naturally disliked the Chinese, just as the Japanese did. Because Chinda was stationed in San Francisco, he might have been one of the few Japanese government officials focusing on the issue of the Chinese in the United States.[116] However, the entry denial of the Japanese laborers concerned Chinda because of the serious damage it caused to the honor of all Japanese people, not so much because of the misfortune of these Japanese migrant laborers.[117] Not only did he hold a strong bias against low-class Japanese, but he also did not have the awareness that the Japanese were a race similar to the Chinese. His report demonstrated that he was extremely afraid that, as the low-class Japanese congregated together in San Francisco, the center of the anti-Chinese movement, the US government authorities would despise the Japanese, just as Americans did the Chinese.

> Areas such as San Francisco, where Europeans and Asian races mingle, are the most significant place to maintain Japan's reputation. Therefore, it is very important for Japanese people emigrating here to represent the true nature of the Japanese people and maintain Japan's honor. Nowadays prostitutes, the poor, and people in bizarre clothes are constantly coming and going, and it naturally breeds enmity in Americans for our people ... workers and pseudo-politicians would fuel reasons for anti-Japanese sentiment. If Japanese people are publicly attacked like this, it would be a situation we are truly unprepared for. Nowadays we, who are good people, are excluded like the Chinese, who are ostracized by nearly the whole world. The beginnings of this situation are appearing here, and the precaution seems imminent. I, in my humble opinion,

solely hope that you will pay special attention to the Japanese people who would arrive at this port, and make wise decisions.[118]

The warning to not repeat the mistake of the Chinese, who were ostracized "by most of the world," and the goal of maintaining the honor of the Empire of Japan, as stated here, were emphasized as the fundamental issues that the Ministry of Foreign Affairs and the Japanese government should consider when discussing the immigration issue in the United States.[119] Simultaneously, Japanese government authorities and intellectual leaders did not change their disgust and condescending attitude toward migrant laborers.

Many migrant laborers . . . are farmers, all completely illiterate and country bumpkins. In addition, their language and manners are crude, and their clothes are eerie. At a glance, they can be recognized as laborers. When sometimes they gather together and walk the streets of the city, in many occasions, passersby look back and stare at them. The increase in the number of Japanese residents might help Japan, and they could be more or less useful. On the other hand, they lower the American perception of Japanese and attract more contempt. Finally, Americans, acting like politicians pandering to the public, spawned an opportunity to spread anti-Japanese views. This is the problem associated with repeating Qing's mistake. This seems to be an important issue to be studied and discussed today.[120]

An article in the *Kokumin no tomo* also stated,

It is not necessarily an exaggerated criticism that Japanese [migrant laborers in San Francisco] are partly rather inferior to Chinese. In this regard, Ozaki Yukio mentioned the situation as follows:

Since many poor students emigrated to the United States, the sentiment of Americans towards Japanese worsened daily, as the distance between the perception of Chinese and Japanese narrowed. Unless we take action to save the Japanese now, we will be insulted by Americans, concluding with a treaty with articles enabling the immigration bans and disgracing the Empire of Japan. Some newspapers have already increased the use of rude language against Japanese, with their anti-Chinese sentiment expanded to target all yellow races. Moreover, from an objective point of view, Japanese are better-hearted people. Otherwise they are not very different. Regarding business, Chinese use capital to run prosperous businesses including manufacturing. On the other hand, the Japanese are simply cooks or janitors cleaning corridors, bathrooms, and glass windows. They are rather inferior to Chinese and never superior in any way. It is natural for Americans to gradually equate the two races. Asked about American people's attacks on them, the Japanese pedantically argue that they have no faults that deserve to be denied but these arguments are futile, prejudiced, self-righteous opinions. If the Japanese are misled by these people holding such prejudiced opinions, and lazily hold to them over time, it is quite clear that Japan would be insulted by Americans. The society at large would not succumb to such a quibble.

With this momentum, the United States Congress will resolve an anti-Chinese bill sometime in the future. It is worrisome that they will also resolve an anti-Japanese bill. If we don't pay attention to this matter today, I am afraid that we will have serious problems. . . . I must say that the honor of the people of the Empire of Japan will fall to the ground.[121]

Not every elite in the Meiji era may have had this perspective, but this was undeniably a mainstream idea.

Notes

1. The *hōkokusho* and *jōshinsho* (written reports) sent by San Francisco Consul General Chinda Sutemi and US Envoy Tateno Gōzō to the minister of foreign affairs regarding this incident are compiled in "Hokubei ni oite honpō tokō seido oyobi haisetsu 1-ken" dai 1, held at the Gaimushō Gaikō Shiryōkan (Diplomatic Archives of the Ministry of Foreign Affairs of Japan), as well as "Honpōjin no Beikoku imin narabini haisetsu kankei ikken," Gaimushō hen, *Nihon gaikō bunsho dai 24-kan* (jikō 18) and *dai 25-kan* (jikō 18) (Nihon Kokusai Rengō Kyōkai, 1952). The most notable of these are as follows: Kimitsu dai 6-gō, Meiji 24-nen

4-gatsu 25-nichi, Chinda Sutemi yori Gaimu Daijin Aoki Shūzō ate, "Beikoku imin shin kisoku shikō ni tsuki honpōjin tokō torishimari kata ni kanshi jōshin no ken" (*Nihon gaikō bunsho dai 24-kan*, 463–76); dai 45-gō, Meiji 24-nen 4-gatsu 29-nichi, Tateno Gōzō yori Aoki Shūzō ate, "Sōkō ni oite Nihonjin jōriku kinshi sashitome no ken" dai 1 (ibid., 476–77); dai 48-gō, Meiji 24-nen 4-gatsu 30-nichi, Tateno Gōzō yori Aoki Shūzō ate, "Sōkō ni oite Nihonjin 4-mei jōriku kinshi no ken" dai 2 (ibid., 478–87); Kimitsu dai 7-gō, Meiji 24-nen 5-gatsu 7-ka, Chinda Sutemi yori Aoki Shūzō ate, "Honpō tokōsha jōriku kyozetsu no ken" (ibid., 480–87); Kō dai 16-gō, Meiji 25-nen 3-gatsu 4-ka, Tateno Gōzō yori Gaimu Daijin Enomoto Takeaki ate, "Tokōsha torishimari ni kanshi seikun no ken" oyobi fuzokusho 1, dō-nen 2-gatsu 10-ka, Chinda Sutemi yori Tateno Gōzō ate, "Keiyaku rōdōsha torishimari ni tsuki seikun no ken," to fuzokusho 2, dō-nen 2-gatsu 22-nichi, Tateno Gōzō yori Chinda Sutemi ate, "Dōjō ni kanshi kaikun no ken" (*Nihon gaikō bunsho dai 25-kan*, 678–93); Kimitsu dai 14-gō, Meiji 25-nen 5-gatsu 10-ka, Chinda Sutemi yori Enomoto Takeaki ate, "Tokōsha jōriku kyohi ni tsuki zensho saretaki mune jōshin no ken" (ibid., 699–707); Kimitsu dai 15-gō, Meiji 25-nen 5-gatsu 21-nichi, Chinda Sutemi yori Enomoto Takeaki ate, "Honpō rōdōsha ni kansuru shinbun kiji ni tsuki hōkoku no ken" (ibid., 709–13); Meiji 25-nen 7-gatsu 30-nichi, Chinda Sutemi yori Tateno Gōzō ate, "Honpō tokō rōdōsha futō torishimari ni kanshi hōkoku no ken" (ibid., 717–18); and Kōshin dai 86-gō, Meiji 25-nen 8-gatsu 16-nichi, from Chinda Sutemi yori Gaimu Jikan Hayashi Tadasu ate, "Honpō tokō rōdōsha no jōriku torishimari ni kanshi mōshi susume no ken" (ibid., 723–24). Chinda's confidential report included attachments of English telegrams and newspaper clippings; however, these have been omitted from *Nihon gaikō bunsho*. In addition, in 1891 and 1892, the passage of Japanese prostitutes to America's western shores became a problem, but this essay does not touch on the topic. For information on the issue of the passage of Japanese prostitutes, see "Zaibei honpōjin no jōkyō narabini tobeisha torishimari kankei zassan, dai 1-kan: Zai Sōkō ryōjikan no bu," held at the Gaimushō Gaikō Shiryōkan, *Nihon gaikō bunsho dai 24-25-kan*; Yuji Ichioka, "Ameyuki-san: Japanese Prostitutes in Nineteenth Century America," *Amerasia* 4:1 (1977), 1–21; and Donald T. Hata Jr., *"Undesirables": Early Immigrants and the Anti-Japanese Movement in San Francisco, 1892–1893, Prelude to Exclusion* (New York: Arno Press, 1978).

2. Until now, it was considered that the beginning of the Japanese immigration problem started in 1900. For example, "It [was] in 1898 that the United States government, alarmed by the sudden increase in Japanese immigrants, started to become wary of them. . . . With the increasing number and prosperity of immigrants, the anti-Japanese movement was gradually systematized. In 1900 under the proposal of the San Francisco workers' union leader and others, a citizens' rally was opened, and an anti-Japanese stance was adopted where San Francisco mayor Phelan and Stanford University professor and immigration scholar Dr. Ross were present. Following this in 1904 the American Federation of Labor held a rally in San Francisco and passed an anti-Japanese resolution. Anti-Japanese sentiment was high, and in 1905 in San Francisco, the Asiatic Exclusion League (later renamed the Japanese Korean Exclusion League) was formed. They were active not only in California, but also in the Northwest, Oregon, Washington, and Canada, establishing branches and committing to the anti-Japanese movement" (ed. Zaibei Nihonjin Kai, *Zaibei Nihonjin shi* [1940], 1070–71). For English-language research, refer to Thomas A. Bailey, *Theodore Roosevelt and the Japanese American Crises: An*

Account of the International Complications Arising from the Race Problem on the Pacific Coast (Stanford, CA: Stanford University Press, 1934), 1–27; Roger Daniels, *The Politics of Prejudice: The Anti-Japanese Movement in California and the Struggle for Japanese Exclusion* (Berkeley: University of California Press, 1962), 21–24. In addition, the aforementioned Hata, *"Undesirables,"* is given as an example of research directly related to the Meiji 24 (1891) entry denial.

3. Much excellent research has been published about the treaty revision. For the fundamental documents regarding the Japanese side of the conference for the execution of the Japan-US Trade Treaty, see "Jōyaku kaisei ni kansuru ken," ibid., *Nihon gaikō bunsho dai 23-kan* through *dai 28-kan*; and Gaimushō kanshū, "Mutsu gaimu daijin jidai, taibei kōshō," *Jōyaku kaisei kankei Nihon gaikō bunsho dai 4-kan* (Nihon Kokusai Rengō Kyōkai, 1950), 433–46. This insistence by the United States on "the right to regulate and limit immigration by domestic legislation" will be discussed in more detail later in this chapter.

4. Bailey, *Theodore Roosevelt and the Japanese American Crisis*; Raymond A. Esthus, *Theodore Roosevelt and Japan* (Seattle: University of Washington Press, 1966); Akira Iriye, *Pacific Estrangement: Japanese and American Expansion, 1897–1911* (Cambridge, MA: Harvard University Press, 1972). In particular, Iriye's research looks at the early twentieth-century confrontation between Japan and the United States from the perspective of "expansionism" and is of great interest.

5. Refer to endnote 1.

6. Sakata Yasuo, "Shōtotsuten e mukau kidō: Meijiki ni okeru Nihonjin no Amerika dekasegi" (On a Collision Course: The Migration of Japanese *Dekasegi* Laborers to the United States during the Meiji Era) (I), *Kokusai gakuron shū* 3:1 (June 1992), 145–200, and chapter 3 of this volume.

7. Some examples include Japan's *bōchō kiun*, or expansionist spirit; discussions about the new treaty of commerce and "immigration rights"; and growing anti-Asian sentiment in America. These points will be discussed in more detail later in this chapter.

8. For example, see chapter 2 of the aforementioned Iriye, *Pacific Estrangement*: "As the racial connotations in [the remarks made by Theodore Roosevelt and other expansionists] indicate, civilization was becoming a parochial notion, representing the interests of Americans for some writers, Anglo-Saxons for others, and the white race for still others, this was symptomatic of the growing concern with the future of Western supremacy in a rapidly changing world. Herein lie the clues to American imperialism and to Japanese-American estrangement" (27).

9. George F. Kennan, *American Diplomacy*, expanded ed. (Chicago: University of Chicago Press, 1984), 49.

10. The goal of the legislation was considered to be regulating the entry of so-called undesirable foreign immigrants, and unlike the Chinese Exclusion Act, it did not aim to limit the entry of a specific nationality or race. However, in the 1880s, the number of so-called new immigrants, or people from eastern Europe, Russia, southern Europe, and other places that had previously sent few immigrants to the United States, increased dramatically. The Anglo-Saxon citizens, or "old immigrants," who had until then been the mainstream of American society, felt threatened by this, and this is thought to be a major motive for the Immigration Act of 1891. The old immigrants saw eastern and southern Europeans, who made up a

majority of new immigrants, as considerably inferior to Anglo-Saxons, and therefore concluded that they were in general unfit to become part of American society. Maldwyn Allen Jones, *American Immigration*, 2nd ed. (Chicago: University of Chicago Press, 1992), 152–76, 212–38.

11. The common name for this Office of the Superintendent of Immigration was Bureau of Immigration. The position that was established with the 1891 Immigration Act changed its title to commissioner-general of immigration in 1895 (28 Stat. I, 780–81). The Bureau of Immigration was later moved under the control of the Department of Labor, then to the Justice Department; however, its principal duties remained unchanged and it remains today as the Bureau of Immigration and Naturalization. Every year, the Bureau of Immigration compiles an annual report of the commissioner-general of immigration (also known as the Immigration Bureau's annual report).

12. This refers to the Immigration Act of March 3, 1891 (26 Stat. L., 1084), or what is called the 1891 Immigration Act. Under this act, "the . . . classes of aliens [who] shall be excluded from admission into the United States" included "all idiots, insane persons, paupers or persons likely to become a public charge, persons suffering from a loathsome or a dangerous contagious disease, persons who have been convicted of a felony or other infamous crime or misdemeanor involving moral turpitude, polygamists, and also any whose ticket or passage is paid for with the money of another or who is assisted by others to come." Also covered was "the class of contract laborers" excluded by the act of February 26, 1885. The Japanese *dekasegi* workers who were at risk of being banned from entry were mainly paupers or persons likely to become a public charge, and contract laborers. These people were already banned under the 1882 and 1885 immigration acts (contract laborers were banned under the 1885 Alien Contract Labor Law); however, the federal government had not yet established the Office of the Superintendent of Immigration, and on top of this, no immigration inspection was enforced at the ports. Therefore, very few "offenders" of the above clauses were deported. Japanese *dekasegi* workers who were denied entry on the grounds of being contract laborers suddenly increased after the implementation of the 1891 Immigration Act. It is thought that this increase was because so-called assisted immigrants, or persons "whose ticket or passage is paid for with the money of another or who is assisted by others to come" were added to the act. In addition, the Japanese prostitutes mentioned in endnote 1 were banned on the basis of moral turpitude. The full text of the 1891 Immigration Act is compiled in the US Senate, *Immigration Commission Reports*, vol. 39, *Immigration Legislation* (Washington: Government Printing Office, 1911), 98–100.

13. In the American government's immigration statistics before 1904, the Immigration Bureau only recorded the number of people who sailed to the United States as "steerage passengers," who were permitted entry into the country. This was based on the belief that foreigners wishing to enter the United States as "immigrants" had no resources and by no means could afford to sail as "cabin passengers." Sakata Yasuo, "19-seiki kōhan ni Amerika ni tokōshita Nihonjin to 'imin tōkei'—itsuwaru sūji—," *Kirisuto-kyō shakai mondai kenkyū* 38-gō (Dōshisha Daigaku Jinbun Kagaku Kenkyūjo, March 1990), 51–102. Consequently, the legislators of the 1891 Immigration Act may have assumed it would be practically impossible for them to sue the Washington Immigration Bureau for reexamination.

14. Beikoku Sōkō gū Shūyū Sanjin, Ishida Kumajirō henshū, *Kitare Nihonjin—ichimei Sōkō annai—* (Kaishindō, 1886), 4–5; reprinted in *Nikkei imin shiryōshū,* Hokubei hen dai 5-kan (Nihon Tosho Sentā, 1991).

15. Meiji 24-nen 9-gatsu 15-nichi, Gaimu Daijin Enomoto Takeaki yori Kanagawa, Hyōgo, Ōsaka, Nagasaki, Niigata fuken chiji ate, "Beikoku e tokōsuru rōdōsha e taishi dōkoku ijūmin shinjōrei no kitei o ryōkaiseshimuru gi ni tsuki naikun"; Kimitsu dai 16-gō, Meiji 24-nen 8-gatsu 14-ka, Chinda yori Enomoto ate, fuki *(Nihon gaikō bunsho dai 24-kan),* 501–2.

16. Jones, *American Immigration,* 212–16.

17. For example, ibid., 216.

18. Kimitsu dai 16-gō, Meiji 24-nen 8-gatsu 14-ka, Chinda yori Enomoto ate *(Nihon gaikō bunsho dai 24-kan),* 500.

19. In regards to Chief Customs Inspector Phelps, Chinda made an interesting report: "Perhaps because it has not yet been long since the promulgation of the new immigration act, the method by which to implement it does not seem to be settled, and it appears that there is confusion about who is to be the authority. In the beginning, the condition was such that the port's immigration office committee member 'Sorunrē' took over this position. Afterward, the port's chief customs inspector 'Hirupusu' (Phelps) asserted his own authority, and there appeared to be somewhat of a fight over power between the two officials. The main authority figure remained ambiguous; thus for a time there was clearly a misunderstanding about the ban on ship passengers entering the country. In the end, the chief customs inspector finally made a rejection verdict based on the immigration office committee member's reports, but the ban was lifted when the country's Ministry of Finance sent telegraphic instructions to the committee member, who upon receiving this followed the orders of the former and gave permission of entry to each person who was denied entry. As such, rumors claim that the chief customs inspector complained incessantly that the official was abusing his authority. If the implementation of this act causes such a spectacle as mentioned above, interpretation of the new law will bring still more disagreement among the authorities. Between the chief customs inspector and the committee member, it appears as if there was a rift" (Kimitsu dai 7-gō, Meiji 24-nen 5-gatsu 7-ka, Chinda yori Aoki ate [*Nihon gaikō bunsho dai 24-kan*], 482).

20. *San Francisco Morning Call,* May 18, 1892; Kimitsu dai 15-gō, Meiji 25-nen 5-gatsu 21-nichi, Chinda yori Enomoto ate, "Honpō rōdōsha tokō ni kansuru shinbun kiji ni tsuki hōkoku no ken," besshi, "Hokubei gasshūkoku ni oite honpōjin tokō seigen oyobi haiseki ikken" dai 1, held at the Gaimushō Gaikō Shiryōkan. Even though Kimitsu dai 15-gō and a part of Fuzokusho kō-gō are recorded in *Nihon gaikō bunsho dai-25 kan* (709–13), the accompanying English-language newspaper articles were omitted.

21. Kimitsu dai 7-gō, Meiji 24-nen 5-gatsu 7-ka, Chinda yori Aoki ate *(Nihon gaikō bunsho dai 24-kan),* 481.

22. According to US government immigration statistics, the number of people who sailed from Japan to the US continued to increase, from 229 during the 1886–87 fiscal year (from July 1886 through June 1887) to 404 in 1887–88; 640 in 1888–89; and 691 in 1889–90. In 1890–91, the number increased to 1,136, exceeding 1,000 for the first time, and the following year, in 1891–92, the number increased yet again to 1,498. Since then, the number never fell below 1,000.

Sakata, "19-seiki kōhan ni Amerika ni tokōshita Nihonjin to 'imin tōkei'" dai 1-hyō, 68–72.

23. Daniels, *The Politics of Prejudice.*

24. Kuroda Ken'ichi, *Nihon shokumin shisō* (Kōbundō, 1942), dai 2-hen, Meiji shoki ni okeru shokumin shisō, 181–251.

25. Meiji 24-nen 9-gatsu 15-nichi, Enomoto yori Kanagawa, Hyōgo, Ōsaka, Nagasaki, Niigata fuken chiji ate kunrei: Kimitsu dai 16-gō fuki (*Nihon gaikō bunsho dai 24-kan*), 501–2. For more on the Meiji government's emphasis on the "country's honor" regarding the overseas migration of "lower-class Japanese," refer to Sakata Yasuo, "Fubyōdō jōyaku to Amerika dekasegi," ed. Dōshisha Daigaku Jinbun Kagaku Kenkyūjo, *Hokubei Nihonjin Kirisutokyō undō shi* (PMC Shuppan, 1991), 664–80, and pages 102–115 of chapter 2 of this volume.

26. Sō dai 659-gō, Meiji 33-nen 8-gatsu 2-ka, Gaimu Daijin yori kaku fuken chiji ate, "Hokubei gasshūkoku oyobi Kanada imin tokō kinshihō kunrei no ken," "Hokubei gasshūkoku ni oite honpōjin tokō seigen oyobi haiseki ikken" dai 3, held at Gaimushō Gaikō Shiryōkan, 1428–29; and *Nihon gaikō bunsho dai 33-kan*, 461. "Wishing to do what it could to quiet [the campaign against the Japanese], the Japanese government announced in August, 1900, that henceforth no passports would be issued to laborers desiring to go to the mainland of the United States. As a result of this voluntary limitation, which certain writers have called the first Gentlemen's Agreement, the influx of coolies fell off one-half in 1901" (Bailey, *Theodore Roosevelt and the Japanese-American Crises,* 2).

27. Sakata, "19-seiki kōhan ni Amerika ni tokōshita Nihonjin to 'imin tōkei'" dai 1-hyō, 68–72.

28. Kuroda, *Nihon shokumin shisō,* dai 2-hen.

29. For more information on Enomoto Takeaki and the establishment of the *Gaimushō Iminka* (Ministry of Foreign Affairs Emigration Section) and *Shokumin Kyōkai* (transplantation or colonial association), refer to Tsunoyama Yukihiro, *Enomoto Takeaki to Mekishiko shokumin ijū* (Dōbunkan, 1986), 58–79, 167–83. For "Shokumin kyōkai setsuritsu keika," "Setsuritsu shuisho," and "Yakuin, kaiin meibo," refer to *Shokumin kyōkai hōkoku dai 1-gō* (April 16, 1893).

30. For example, Mutō Sanji's *ijūron* (migration theory) is titled *Beikoku ijūron*; however, the discourse itself is on Japanese *dekasegi.* See Mutō Sanji, *Beikoku ijūron* (Maruzen Shōsha Shoten, 1887).

31. Kuroda, *Nihon shokumin shisō,* 211–47.

32. Taguchi Ukichi, "Nan'yō keiryakuron," *Tōkyō keizai zasshi* (1890); referenced in Kuroda, *Nihon shokumin shisō,* 223.

33. Referenced in Kuroda, *Nihon shokumin shisō,* 229–30.

34. Shiga Shigetaka, *Nan'yō jiji* (Maruzen Shōsha Shoten, 1887). See also Tsuneya Seifuku, *Kaigai shokuminron* (Hakubunsha, 1891); reprinted in *Nikkei imin shiryōshū,* Hokubei hen dai 3-kan (Nihon Tosho Sentā, 1991).

35. Shiga, *Nan'yō jiji,* 191.

36. Tsuneya, *Kaigai shokuminron,* 84–85. Tsuneya cites "Mexico, Central America, western South America, Australia, Malaysia, Polynesia" as *shokumin kōhochi* (proposed colonization sites) and discusses these locations.

37. Fukuzawa Yukichi, "Beikoku wa shishi no sumika nari," *Jiji shinpō* (Meiji 7-nen 3-gatsu 25-nichi gō); *Fukuzawa Yukichi zenshū,* dai 9-kan (Iwanami Shoten, 1960), 442–44.

38. Akamine Seichirō, *Beikoku ima fushigi* (Jitsugaku Kai Eigakkō, 1886); reprinted in *Nikkei imin shiryōshū*, Hokubei hen dai 5-kan (Nihon Tosho Sentā, 1991). See also Ishida, *Kitare Nihonjin*; reprinted in *Nikkei imin shiryōshū*, Hokubei hen dai 5-kan (Nihon Tosho Sentā, 1991).

39. For more on *tobei annai*, refer to Yuji Ichioka, Yasuo Sakata, Nobuya Tsuchida, and Eri Yasuhara, comps., *A Buried Past: An Annotated Bibliography of the Japanese American Research Project Collection* (Berkeley: University of California Press, 1974), 42–46.

40. Mutō, *Beikoku ijūron*. For more on Mutō's study abroad in the United States, refer to "Jijoden," *Mutō Sanji zenshū dai 1-kan*, 23–38.

41. Mutō, *Beikoku ijūron*, 277.

42. Ibid., 280.

43. Ibid., 254–58.

44. Ibid., 286.

45. In the 1880s, being a *dekasegi* worker, also termed as a "sojourner" or "bird of passage," was considered the trait of an "undesirable" traveler to those who advocated for the restriction of foreigners migrating to the US. The Chinese workers who were denied entry into the country as immigrants under the 1882 Chinese Exclusion Act were also criticized for sailing to the US as *dekasegi* workers. See Sakata, "Shōtotsuten e mukau kidō (I)," 196–200, and pages 166–68 of chapter 3 of this volume.

46. Iriye's *Pacific Estrangement* is a rare and valuable piece of research.

47. Inagaki Manjirō, *Japan and the Pacific: A Japanese View of the Eastern Question* (London: T. Fisher Unwin, 1890).

48. "The Question of Colonization," *Japan Weekly Mail* 16:5 (August 1, 1891); "Viscount Enomoto and Japanese Emigration," *Japan Weekly Mail* 16:7 (August 15, 1891); "Emigration," *Japan Weekly Mail* 16:17 (October 24, 1891).

49. Kimitsu dai 16-gō, Meiji 25-nen 5-gatsu 21-nichi, Chinda yori Enomoto ate (*Nihon gaikō bunsho dai 25-kan*), 710.

50. *San Francisco Morning Call*, May 18, 1892; Kimitsu dai 15-gō, Meiji 25-nen 5-gatsu 25-nichi, Chinda yori Enomoto ate, besshi, "Hokubei gasshūkoku ni oite honpōjin tokō seigen oyobi haiseki ikken" dai 1, held at the Gaimushō Gaikō Shiryōkan. Even though Kimitsu dai 15-gō is recorded in *Nihon gaikō bunsho dai 25-kan*, the accompanying English-language newspaper articles were omitted. The original text from the article used is "Japan Emigrants' Association," *Japan Weekly Mail* 17:17 (April 23, 1892).

51. "Emigration," *Japan Weekly Mail* 17:13 (March 26, 1892).

52. Andō Tarō followed Enomoto as a *bakushin* (samurai directly serving the shogun) and barricaded himself in *Goryōkaku*. In 1871, he accompanied Iwakura on his mission to the United States (*Nihon rekishi daijiten 1* [Kawade Shobō, 1968], 221). For more on Andō's career as the Hawai'i consul general, refer to Hawai Nihonjin Imin Kankō Iinkai, *Hawai kan'yaku ijū 25-nen kinen, Hawai Nihonjin imin shi* (Hawai Nihonjin Rengō Kyōkai, 1964), 130–133.

53. "Emigration," *Japan Weekly Mail* 17:13.

54. Kimitsu dai 15-gō, Meiji 25-nen 5-gatsu 21-nichi, Chinda yori Enomoto ate (*Nihon gaikō bunsho dai 25-kan*), 710.

55. Kajima Morinosuke, *Nihon gaikō shi 2 Jōyaku kaisei mondai* (Kajima Heiwa Kenkyūjo, 1970), 198–210; "Jōyaku kaisei ni kansuru ken," *Nihon gaikō bunsho dai 23-kan* and *dai 24-kan*; *Jōyaku kaisei kankei Nihon gaikō bunsho dai 4-kan*.

56. For more on the Ansei Treaty of Amity and Commerce (Unequal Treaty) and workers traveling abroad for *dekasegi*, refer to Sakata, "Fubyōdō jōyaku to Amerika dekasegi," chapter two of this volume.

57. Eizō Ōsawa, the organizer of the *Fukuinkai* (Gospel Society) established in San Francisco, wrote in his *jōshinsho* to the San Francisco consul in 1889, "The number of our Japanese compatriots in San Francisco and the surrounding areas has reached 4,000." See Kōshin dai 48-gō, Meiji 22-nen 6-gatsu 11-nichi, Sōkō ryōji Kawashita Toshisuke yori Gaimu Daijin Aoki Shūzō ate, "Fukuinkai kanji Ōsawa Eizō jōshinsho sōfu no ken," fuzokusho, jōshinsho, "Zaibei honpōjin no jōkyō narabini tobeisha torishimari zassan" 1, held at the Gaimushō Gaikō Shiryōkan. On the number of people sailing to the United States, refer to endnote 22.

58. Sakata, "Shōtotsuten e mukau kidō (I)," 179–87, and pages 155–60 of chapter 3 of this volume.

59. Kajima Morinosuke, *Nihon gaikō shi 2 Jōyaku kaisei mondai*, 203–6.

60. No. 315 (A), Meiji 27-nen 7-gatsu 11-nichi, Mutsu Munemitsu Gaimu Daijin yori Chūbei Kōshi Tateno Gōzō ate, "Kōshiki kaidan ni kanshi kunrei no ken," *Jōyaku kaisei kankei Nihon gaikō bunsho dai 4-kan*, 474.

61. Sō dai 4-gō, Meiji 27-nen 2-gatsu 27-nichi, Mutsu yori Tateno ate, "Jōyaku kaisei mondai ni tsuki zaibei honpō Beikoku kōshi ni nakaire no ken," *Jōyaku kaisei kankei Nihon gaikō bunsho dai 4-kan*, 452–54.

62. Sō dai 27-gō, Meiji 27-nen 2-gatsu 27-nichi, Mutsu yori Tateno ate, "Jōyaku kaisei ni kansuru ken" dai 14, *Jōyaku kaisei kankei Nihon gaikō bunsho dai 4-kan*, 474–77.

63. Ibid., 474–75.

64. Ibid., 475–76.

65. Kajima, *Nihon gaikō shi 2 Jōyaku kaisei mondai*, 208. Tateno, too, has implied in his *hōkokusho* to Mutsu that there was a problem. "At the meeting on May 31 . . . the rough seas of our empire's political realm have become increasingly harsh, and on top of this, our government's treaty revision is a massive undertaking and a pressing task with an urgency to reach a satisfactory conclusion. I have repeatedly explained this to the secretary of state and requested that he immediately begin treaty revision negotiations; however, the secretary of state has [in the past] repeatedly expressed his will to speak with me but has stopped at this, showing no indication of answering my request. Due to this, I recognize that to hold a final decision-making meeting by force would place us in an even more unfavorable position, and so I expressed my aim to further reconsider the matter and left" (*Jōyaku kaisei kankei Nihon gaikō bunsho dai 4-kan*, 468).

66. Ibid. Kurino states in his *hōkokusho* to Mutsu, "When I was granted an audience with the president," the president "inquired in detail about the time I spent here previously studying at Harvard Law School, and expressed an unspoken joy that I was offered this respectful duty and returned to this country at this time for treaty negotiations." See dai 32-gō, Meiji 27-nen 8-gatsu 31-nichi, Kurino yori Mutsu ate, "Kōshō kaishihō ni kansuru Beikoku-gawa no taido ni tsuki hōkoku no ken," *Jōyaku kaisei kankei Nihon gaikō bunsho dai 4-kan*, 475–76.

67. Denshin [No.] 14 (A), Meiji 27-nen 9-gatsu 21-nichi, Kurino yori Mutsu ate, "Zenken inin ni kansuru ken," *Jōyaku kaisei kankei Nihon gaikō bunsho dai 4-kan*, 479, and Kajima, *Nihon gaikō shi 2 Joyaku kaisei mondai*, 208.

68. Dai 48-gō, Meiji 27-nen 9-gatsu 27-nichi, Kurino yori Mutsu ate, "Danpan kaishi uchiawase no tame no kokumu chōkan to kaidan no ken," *Jōyaku kaisei kankei Nihon gaikō bunsho dai 4-kan*, 480–83.

69. Denshin [No.] 34 (F), Meiji 27-nen 10-gatsu 26-nichi, Kurino yori Mutsu ate, "Dai 2-jō no shūsei ni tsuki seikun no ken"; Denshin [No.] 984 (35), Meiji 27-nen 10-gatsu 31-nichi, Mutsu yori Kurino ate, "Shūsei shōnin no ken"; *Jōyaku kaisei kankei Nihon gaikō bunsho dai 4-kan*, 488–90. For the full text of the Treaty of Commerce and Navigation and the protocol signed on November 22, 1894, see ibid., *bunsho 308 fuzokusho* (appendix), 500–511.

70. The Meiji "elite" and their prejudice against "low-class Japanese" will be discussed later in the main text. For more on *datsu-a ron* (de-Asianization) and *zai-bei Nihonjin* (Japanese living in the United States), refer to Sakata Yasuo, "Datsu-a no shishi to tozasareta hakusekijin no rakuen—minkenha shosei to Beikoku ni okeru ōshoku jinshu haiseki—," ed. Tamura Norio and Shiramizu Shigehiko, *Beikoku shoki no Nihongo shinbun* (Keisō Shobō, 1986), 47–193.

71. Refer to endnote 27.

72. Kimitsu dai 6-gō, Meiji 24-nen 4-gatsu 25-nichi, Chinda yori Aoki ate (*Nihon gaikō bunsho dai 24-kan*), 464.

73. Ibid. Chinda's assessment of *dekasegi* workers is extremely harsh. "In the past, the Japanese who came to the United States had the purpose to study as students. However, the purpose for coming to the United States has completely changed from studying to *dekasegi*. Likewise, the individuals who come to this country are no longer students, but menial laborers who do not speak English or understand American customs. Furthermore, some cannot even write their names. They come here to seek their fortune with limited travel allowances. As soon as they arrive in San Francisco, they have only meager funds to support themselves. . . . On top of this, recent migrants, unlike traditionally when individuals would sail alone to the United States, come from this prefecture and that district with a group of five or ten people from their hometown, and because of this they are under suspicion of being contract workers."

74. "As the number of our countrymen sailing to the United States continues to increase . . . it is easy to see how much this adds to the strife. This incident is a premonition that calls for prudent preparation, like preparing before stepping on frost. . . . Now, the lower class of our country arriving one after another has at once provoked apprehension in the workers of this land, of course, but there has also been an appearance of those engaged in politics who express curiosity in this matter and attempt to incite the working class. . . . Such is a rumor that often reaches our ears. Consequently, newspapers and the like are also paying plenty of attention to this, and on a daily basis they strive to publish exaggerated articles regarding our people." See Kimitsu dai 6-gō, Meiji 24-nen 4-gatsu 25-nichi, Chinda yori Aoki ate (*Nihon gaikō bunsho dai 24-kan*), 465.

75. Kimitsu dai 14-gō, Meiji 25-nen 5-gatsu 10-ka, Chinda yori Enomoto ate (*Nihon gaikō bunsho dai 25-kan*), 702.

76. *San Francisco Examiner*, April 29, 1892. The article used here is from 1892 and is therefore not immediately after the entry-denial incident; however, these were sent as attachments to San Francisco Consul Chinda's kimitsu dai 14-gō (Meiji 25-nen 5-gatsu 10-ka, Enomoto Gaimu Daijin ate). As previously mentioned, even though the consul's report is recorded in *Nihon gaikō bunsho dai-25 kan*, the accompanying newspaper articles were omitted. These articles can be

found in "Hokubei gasshūkoku ni oite honpōjin tokō seigen oyobi haiseki ikken" dai 1, held at the Gaimushō Gaikō Shiryōkan.

77. Kimitsu dai 6-gō, Meiji 24-nen 4-gatsu 25-nichi, Chinda yori Aoki ate (*Nihon gaikō bunsho dai 24-kan*), 463–66.

78. Ibid., 464.

79. Ibid.

80. Ibid., 465.

81. Ibid. Besides prostitutes, one boy aboard the *Pemptos* also contracted a violent case of syphilis. He was sent back on the grounds that he had little chance of making a full recovery, according to an examination by the resident doctor. See Kimitsu dai 7-gō, Meiji 25-nen 5-gatsu 7-ka, Chinda yori Aoki ate (*Nihon gaikō bunsho dai 24-kan*), 482.

82. Kimitsu dai 6-gō, Meiji 24-nen 4-gatsu 25-nichi, Chinda yori Aoki ate (*Nihon gaikō bunsho dai 24-kan*), 465. In addition, in Kimitsu dai 7-gō, Chinda gives a detailed report of the difficulty they are having in overturning the entry-denial decision. He states, "I had a meeting with the official in charge and firmly requested a more detailed inspection, but he stood his ground to the end. In addition, I also requested a temporary entry approval. To this, he said that we must submit a security of five hundred dollars for each person denied entry; otherwise it will be difficult to give permission to land. Alternatively, a guarantee signed by an American must be submitted. Our consulate will not be a direct guarantor but will still need to provide a sizable amount of security for an American to sign. Ultimately, it will still be in the domain of our consulate's responsibilities." See Kimitsu dai 7-gō, Meiji 25-nen 5-gatsu 7-ka, Chinda yori Aoki ate, 481.

83. Kimitsu dai 6-gō, Meiji 24-nen 4-gatsu 25-nichi, Chinda yori Aoki ate (*Nihon gaikō bunsho dai 24-kan*), 465.

84. Katayama Sen, *Tobei annai* (Rōdōsha Shinbunsha, 1901), 10; reprinted in *Nikkei imin shiryōshū*, Hokubei hen dai 5-kan (Nihon Tosho Sentā, 1991).

85. Dai 45-gō, Meiji 24-nen 4-gatsu 29-nichi, Tateno yori Aoki ate; Kimitsu dai sō dai 16-gō, Meiji 24-nen 8-gatsu 11-nichi, Chinda yori Enomoto ate (*Nihon gaikō bunsho dai 24-kan*), 476–77, 500–502.

86. [No number], Meiji 24-nen 9-gatsu 15-nichi, Kanagawa, Hyōgo, Ōsaka, Nagasaki, Niigata-ken chiji ate, "Beikoku e tokō suru rōdōsha e taishi dōkoku ijūmin shinjōrei no kitei o ryōkaiseshimuru gi ni tsuki naikun no ken"; Kimitsu sō dai 16-gō, Meiji 24-nen 8-gatsu 11-nichi, Chinda yori Enomoto ate, fuki, 501–502.

87. The most effective measure would have been to enforce a "departure examination" at the port from which a ship was departing. The envoy Tateno also wrote to Foreign Minister Aoki proposing such measures. He said, "I believe it is an urgent matter to release an edict in our homeland to enforce detailed inspection at ports such as Yokohama. We must prevent further damage caused by the futile efforts of people who, ignorant of the laws of the US, sail to the faraway country in hopes of making a fortune or adventuring." See dai 45-gō, Meiji 24-nen 4-gatsu 29-nichi, Tateno yori Aoki ate, 477. However, as long as the Ansei Treaty (Unequal Treaty) was not revised, such measures could not be taken at the *kaikōba* (open ports). For more on the reasons why, refer to Sakata, "Fubyōdō jōyaku to Amerika dekasegi," 630–80, and pages 75–115 of chapter 2 of this volume.

88. "Beikoku ni oite honpō imin seigen narabini haiseki ikken," *Nihon gaikō bunsho dai 24-kan, dai 25-kan*, 460–515, 683–733.

89. Contract Labor Law, 1885, 23 Stat. L., 332. Sakata, "Shōtotsuten e mukau kidō (I)," 189–96, and pages 161–66 of chapter 3 of this volume.

90. Ibid.; dai 48-gō, Meiji 24-nen 4-gatsu 30-nichi, Tateno yori Aoki ate, 478–79; Kimitsu dai 7-gō, Meiji 24-nen 5-gatsu 7-ka, Chinda yori Aoki ate, 480–87.

91. Ibid., 481.

92. Sakata, "Shōtotsuten e mukau kidō (I)," 189–96, and pages 161–66 of chapter 3 of this volume; refer also to "Fair Immigration Law Articles and Its Prejudiced Applications" in this chapter.

93. Fuzokusho 20-gō; Kimitsu 7-gō, Meiji 24-nen 5-gatsu 7-ka, Chinda yori Aoki ate, 484.

94. *San Francisco Morning Call*, May 4, 1892.

95. Kimitsu dai 7-gō, Meiji 24-nen 5-gatsu 7-ka, Chinda yori Aoki ate, 480–81.

96. Fuzokusho 1, 2, Chinda yori Tateno ate Eibun denshinsha; dai 45-gō, Meiji 24-nen 4-gatsu 29-nichi, Tateno yori Aoki ate; Fuzokusho 1, 2, Chinda yori Tateno ate denshinsha; dai 48-gō, Meiji 24-nen 4-gatsu 30-nichi, Tateno yori Aoki ate (*Nihon gaikō bunsho dai 24-kan*), 477, 479–80.

97. Dai 45-gō, Meiji 24-nen 4-gatsu 29-nichi, Tateno yori Aoki ate, 476.

98. Dai 48-gō, Meiji 24-nen 4-gatsu 30-nichi, Tateno yori Aoki ate, 478.

99. Ibid.

100. Kōshin dai 27 gō, Meiji 25-nen 3-gatsu 1-nichi, Chinda yori Hayashi Gaimu Daijin ate, "Keiyaku rōdōsha no tokō torishimararetaki mune gushin no ken" (*Nihon gaikō bunsho dai 25-kan*), 685-686. The part that is referenced is fuzokusho 1, Meiji 25-nen 2-gatsu 10-ka, Chinda yori Tateno ate, "Keiyaku rōdōsha torishimari ni tsuki seikun no ken, kō dai 16-gō, Meiji 25-nen 3-gatsu 4-ka, Tateno yori Gaimu Daijin Enomoto ate (*Nihon gaikō bunsho dai 25-kan*), 690.

101. Fuzokusho, Meiji 25-nen 2-gatsu 10-ka, Chinda yori Tateno ate, 690-691.

102. Ibid., 689-691.

103. Fuzokusho 2, Meiji 25-nen 2-gatsu 22-nichi, Tateno yori Chinda ate, "Kaikun no ken"; Kō dai 16-gō, Meiji 25-nen 3-gatsu 4-ka, Tateno yori Enomoto ate, 691-693.

104. Sō dai 55-gō, Meiji 25-nen 5-gatsu 9-ka, Enomoto yori Tateno ate, "Honpō yori tobei no rōdōsha shobun ni kansuru kunrei" (*Nihon gaikō bunsho dai 25-kan*), 698.

105. Refer to "Japan's Emigration Issue and the Treaty Revision Negotiations" in this chapter.

106. Kimitsu dai 7-gō, Meiji 24-nen 5-gatsu 7-ka, Chinda yori Aoki ate, 480. For details, refer to chapter 3.

107. Ibid.

108. Fuzokusho, Washington, October 12, 1891, " 'Suchībunsu' [Stevens] shi hōkokusho"; Kō dai 96-gō, Meiji 24-nen 10-gatsu 4-ka, Tateno yori Enomoto ate, "Gasshūkoku Taiheiyō engan shoshū ni dekasegisuru honpōjin ni kanshi sanjikan 'Suchībunsu' [Stevens] shi no hōkoku sōtatsu no ken" (*Nihon gaikō bunsho dai 24-kan*), 510–13.

109. " 'Suchībunsu' [Stevens] shi hōkokusho," 512–13.

110. "Chokurei dai 42-gō imin hogo kisoku," Meiji 27-nen 4-gatsu 12-nichi kōfu; fuki 1, Kimitsu shinten dai 16-gō, Meiji 27-nen 2-gatsu 12-nichi, Mutsu Munemitsu Gaimu Daijin, Inoue Kaoru Naimu Daijin yori Itō Hirobumi Naikaku Sōri Daijin ate, "Imin hogohō kisoku seitei ni tsuki kakugi yōsei no ken" (*Nihon gaikō bunsho dai 27-kan*), 618–22.

111. "Meiji 29-nen hōritsu dai 70-gō imin hogohō," "Meiji 29-nen 1-gatsu kōfu; Gaimushō rei dai 3-gō, imin hogohō shikō saisoku," Meiji 29-nen 5-gatsu 26-nichi seitei; Fuzokusho, shinten sō dai 1-gō, Meiji 28-nen 12-gatsu (no date), Saionji Gaimu Daijin yori Itō Naikaku Sōri Daijin ate, "Imin hogohō seitei ni tsuki kakugi seikyū no ken" (*Nihon gaikō bunsho dai 29-kan*), 976–85.

112. To examine the true state of the *imin kaisha* (emigration companies), the US Bureau of Immigration dispatched Commissioner of Immigration W. M. Rice to Japan. Commissioner Rice's report submitted to Congress was full of prejudice in the extreme and ended up fiercely stirring up anti-Japanese sentiment. See "Immigration of Japanese," H.R. Doc. No. 686, 56th Cong., 1st Sess. (Washington, DC: Government Printing Office, 1900). For Japan's response, refer to "Hokubei gasshūkoku ni oite honpōjin tokō seigen oyobi haiseki ikken" dai 2, held at the Gaimushō Gaikō Shiryōkan.

113. Sakata, "Datsu-a no shishi to tozasareta hakusekijin no rakuen." On Chinda Sutemi's personal history, refer to Takenori Kikuchi, ed., *Hakushaku Chinda Sutemi den* (Kyōmei Kaku, 1938).

114. Kimitsu dai 6-gō, Meiji 24-nen 4-gatsu 25-nichi, Chinda yori Aoki ate; Kimitsu dai 7-gō, Meiji 24-nen 4-gatsu 7-ka, Chinda yori Aoki ate.

115. Sakata, "Shōtotsuten e mukau kidō (I)," and chapter 3 of this volume.

116. "Tō minato no rōdōsha kaisha ga Shinajin o haisekisuru no kishō ni tomu wa tsuto ni kakka no seichō ni tasshitaru tokoro ni shite . . . ," Kimitsu dai 6-gō, Meiji 24-nen 4-gatsu 25-nichi, Chinda yori Aoki ate, 465.

117. For example, Kimitsu dai 6-gō, Meiji 25-nen 4-gatsu 29-nichi, Chinda yori Aoki ate; Kimitsu dai 7-gō, Meiji 24-nen 5-gatsu 7-ka, Chinda yori Aoki ate.

118. Kimitsu dai 6-gō, Meiji 24-nen 4-gatsu 25-nichi, Chinda yori Aoki ate, 465–66.

119. "Hokubei gasshūkoku ni oite honpōjin tokō seigen oyobi haiseki ikken" dai 1, dai 2, held at the Gaimushō Gaikō Shiryōkan.

120. Kimitsu dai 14-gō, Meiji 25-nen 5-gatsu 10-ka, Chinda yori Enomoto ate (*Nihon gaikō bunsho dai 25-kan*), 702–3.

121. "Nihon to Beikoku," *Kokumin no tomo dai 23-gō* (Meiji 21-nen 6-gatsu 1-nichi), 402–6.

CHAPTER 5

On a Collision Course

The Migration of Japanese *Dekasegi* Laborers to the United States during the Meiji Era (III)

The End of the Sino-Japanese War and the Changing Nature of the Japanese-Labor Exclusion Movement on the West Coast

The Reinvigorated Attacks on Japanese in San Francisco in English-Language Papers in May 1895

As Director Herman Stump reported in the *Annual Report of the Commissioner General of Immigration*, a total of 1,110 Japanese arrived in the United States during the fiscal year ending June 30, 1896, of which 561 entered through San Francisco, 466 through British Columbia to Washington State, and 83 through other ports.[1] The total number of Japanese arrivals declined by 40 people from the previous fiscal year; "the Japanese in this country were decreasing in number, and . . . the apprehension of a large migration from Japan to the United States was without foundation," he wrote.[2] This report suggests that the Bureau of Immigration was not concerned with the arrival of Japanese laborers. Compared with much larger numbers of arrivals—the so-called new immigrants from Italy (66,445), Greece (24,230), and Russia (35,484)—the number of arrivals from Japan was much smaller and apparently did not concern the federal government.[3]

This paper was translated from Sakata Yasuo, "Shōtotsuten e mukau kidō: Meiji ki ni okeru Nihonjin no Amerika dekasegi" (On a Collision Course: The Migration of Japanese *Dekasegi* Laborers to the United States during the Meiji Era) (III), *Ōsaka Gakuin Daigaku Kokusaigaku ronshū 5-kan, 1-gō* (1994). The author intended to refine this article at a later date.

The situation in the San Francisco Bay Area, however, was different, as it was the epicenter of the Chinese-exclusion movement in the 1860s, which continued to develop into strong anti-Japanese sentiment, particularly against laborers, in the early 1890s. The San Francisco–based Consul Kamiya Saburō reported to acting Foreign Minister Saionji Kinmochi on June 12, 1895, suggesting that the situation was no longer negligible:

> The number of Japanese who have arrived in the United States was small during the Sino-Japanese War and did not cause a controversy. The time passed peacefully, until the middle of the month, when a number of Japanese laborers arrived on the ship *Peking* and reinvigorated the anti-Japanese campaign. Only one or two papers initially bitterly attacked Japanese laborers; now it has spread to the most prominent of the three major newspapers, the *Examiner.* The newspaper began attacking Japanese laborers, and I am concerned about the consequences. It takes a different form than the "exclusion argument" that typically resurges at this time of the year. The US immigration officers now tour around the rural area to study the conditions of Japanese laborers and are investigating whether or not they have a labor contract. This situation appears to be serious and I'd like to seek your advice.[4]

He attached newspaper articles from the *Bulletin* issued on May 14 and 15, 1895, and the *Call* issued on June 5 to his report.[5] The *Bulletin* was so inflammatory that it could be described as part of the "yellow press." It directed Americans to be anti-Japanese and ignited sentiment against Japanese laborers.[6] This is the headline of the front-page article:

DEFIED

THE CONTRACT LABOR LAW

Japanese Shipped in Gangs to California

Proof That They Go to Work in the Fields

White Farm-Hands Are Idle by Thousands

Yet Steamer Load after Steamer Load of Contract Laborers

Are Arriving Weekly

The intentions of the anti-Japanese attack were obvious. The article read as follows:

> The United States contract labor laws are being violated every two or three weeks by the Japanese. The country is being flooded with cheap Japanese laber [sic], the little brown men are pouring in upon us in greater numbers than did the Chinese before the Restriction Act was passed by Congress, and the State of California is threatened with an epidemic of cheap labor and hard times in farming and commercial circles. It is time to sound the warning and to expose the ways and means by which certain rural citizens have provided their orchards with fruit-pickers and packers from the ranks of the Japanese unemployed, while white American workingmen stand idely [sic] by and watch the harvest of the Golden State being reaped by the alien hordes of Asia. To all ap[p]earances the United States immigration officers have been neglectful of duty, and, what is worse, alleged American citizens have contracted for cheap Japanese laborers who agree to receive per capita 40 cents and 50 cents per day for twelve or fourteen hours' work.[7]

The article sensationally emphasized that Japanese, the "little brown men," were willing to work many hours for minimum wages that would embarrass American white laborers. Because Japanese laborers were now flocking to California, American workers were losing jobs. The article also criticized the Bureau of Immigration, which did nothing to stop the Japanese from coming, and Americans who hired cheap Japanese laborers. One can infer the intention behind this article was to receive a positive reaction from working-class Americans whose dissatisfaction had grown during the prolonged recession.

These newspaper articles wove erroneous positions and facts to support their arguments. They tried to argue that the state and federal government statistics were incorrect and cited a survey conducted by a publisher to misleadingly state the following: a large number of Japanese arrived in California in violation of the Contract Law of 1885; the new immigration law of 1891 and the Bureau of Immigration generously allowed Japanese to immigrate without any measures; and as a result the number of unemployed white farmers was increasing.

Within the past year about 10,000 Japanese have found employment on farms of San Joaquin Valley, Napa Valley, Livermore Valley, and the fertile valley of the San Gabriel. Especially in the Livermore Valley the busy little followers of the Mikado have wormed their way into every farming industry, until the strange sight of dollarless white laborers, willing to work but unable to secure employment, tramping out of the country, can be seen on the highways that lead from Pleasanton and Livermore.[8]

The article continued:

The law of the United States strictly prohibit[s] the importation of contract laborers, but the statutes are a dead letter. It is almost impossible to prove that a certain laborer has been imported under contract. Circumstantial evidence cannot convict, although in numerous cases it is exceedingly strong. However, the immigration officers could make it very warm for suspects and thus discourage the scheme that is undoubtedly being worked in this port by Japs and whites alike.[9]

The front-page articles in the *Bulletin* on May 15 suggested that Japanese laborers were contract workers and belonged to a "similar category as coolie" workers who were willing to work many long hours for low wages.[10] The lede read:

CHEAP JOHN IS A JAP
You Can Secure Him for 40 Cents
for Which Amount He Will Work Sixteen Hours
Some Interesting Figures Which Show
That a Number of Laborers of Asia Are Due

The article read:

One of the first principles of protection is protecting the American-born and naturalized American laborer. Upon the prosperity of the working classes depends the prosperity of a State; upon the prosperity of the States depends the scope and power of the United States. A crime against one American workingman is just as great in his individual eyes as a crime against a thousand of his comrades. It is an insult to a community for even one poor but honest member of its commonwealth to be asked to stoop lower than the coolie of Asia or the slave of Africa for a paltry 40 cents per day and feed and clothe himself.

The first paragraph of the front-page article is adorned with colorful rhetoric; however, it drew upon the discriminatory law that classified Japanese as aliens ineligible for citizenship and as undesirable immigrants in white American society.[11] The newspaper continued its attack on Japanese just as it did on the previous day:

Certain figures show that the immigration of Japanese into the United States in the past nine months amounts to only 241 souls. These are Customs-House figures and are sadly incorrect. In the past thirty days there have been nearly double that number of Japanese landed on the soil of California.

The influx has commenced again with all its old energy, and the contract labor laws have been broken time and again. The record of only a few weeks shows that 329 Japs have come to San Francisco on steamers and by the Portland route alone, and the contractor at 270 Brannan Street admits that he had shipped over 300 men to orchards and fields in the Sacramento and San Joaquin Valleys alone. He says that he secures 40 cents per day for his men and offered to secure any number of Japanese for a farm for 40 cents a day, the Japs to feed themselves.[12]

These articles are only a few examples. The *Bulletin* and the *Call*, which were leading the exclusion campaign in San Francisco, were full of slanderous remarks against the Japanese. Furthermore, as Consul Kamiya reported, the *Examiner*, which was considered moderate and reasonable, started joining the league, warning against the arrival of many Japanese contract laborers.[13]

Multiple Unfavorable Conditions: More New Immigrants from Europe, a Prolonged Recession, a Worsening Labor Conflict, and Japanese-Exclusion Arguments on the Grounds of Low-Wage Labor

The crash of the silver market in 1892 triggered financial problems in the United States. The country was in a recession. Kamiya reported to Saionji that "641 banks have been closed and 16,000 factories and stores filed bankruptcy, three million laborers or 20 percent of the entire labor force have lost jobs." [14] The recession continued for three years until 1895. As the labor historian Herbert Gutman pointed out, by the 1890s—known as the Gilded Age, when material culture was highly developed and the United States had shifted toward a matured industrial society after the Civil War—violent tensions worsened between a preindustrial social structure and the different systems being modernized amid the development of industrial capitalism. With the rapidly developing industrial labor force, new immigrants began arriving from Eastern Europe and the Mediterranean region, and after the 1880s the number exponentially increased. As a result, the conflicting labor interests in various fields of industry grew in many parts of the United States. The conflict emerged on the grounds of cultural differences, religious backgrounds, and civil consciousness, antagonisms that were increasingly becoming more violent. [15] The Japanese laborers arriving in the United States in the early 1890s constituted new immigrants and found themselves in the middle of the conflict of opposing interests.

However, white racism is an important factor to consider when one compares the situation of Japanese laborers with that of new immigrants from Europe. In the United States in the late nineteenth century, white citizens from different European areas assumed their racial superiority and considered persons of color to be inferior; this white racism became a pillar in the minds of European Americans, as citizens of a developed nation. Against this backdrop, the degree of anti-Japanese sentiment and bullying against the Japanese was much more persistent and aggressive than what the new immigrants from Europe experienced. Moreover, because the "peculiarity" of Asians, including the Japanese, was visibly recognizable, white racism or prejudice led to the perception of Asians as aliens who could not be assimilated into the "white" republic. [16] As a result, this perception was stressed and justified as a national agenda. [17] The late nineteenth century may be characterized by a climate in which very few people questioned this white supremacist view.

The Chinese railroad workers who contributed to the industrial development of the United States between the 1860s and 1880s were excluded as the result of a persistent anti-Chinese exclusion movement driven by racism. The Chinese Exclusion Act of 1882 was an unusual act in the United States because it singled out members of one nationality to be barred from US immigration. Senator Oliver P. Morton of Indiana, chairman of the special committee to investigate the Chinese-exclusion issue, reported:

> If the Chinese in California were white people, being in all other respects what they are, I do not believe that the complaints and warfare made against them would have existed to any considerable extent. Their difference in color, dress, manners, and religion have, in my judgement, more to do with this hostility than their alleged vices or any actual injury to the white people of California.[18]

History has proven that Morton's judgment was not wrong. The arrival of Japanese *dekasegi* laborers on the West Coast inadvertently coincided with the beginning of the recession in the early to mid-1890s. No matter how the Japanese perceived themselves, white Americans viewed Japanese as part of the "yellow race" and cheap laborers, just like the Chinese who were barred from entering the United States. In other words, Japanese laborers were successors to the excluded Chinese laborers. Multiple unfavorable conditions were laid out at the time when the Japanese started arriving in the United States. Japanese arrived in this country bewildered at the unexpectedly hostile environment and were at a loss as to what to do, which gave even more excuse for American exclusionists to exclude the "yellow race" of Asians. Counsel Chinda Sutemi wrote to Foreign Minister Enomoto Takeaki as follows:

> The majority of laborers are from Wakayama, Hiroshima, Yamaguchi and Kumamoto. They are farmers and pure provincial folk whose language and mannerisms are unrefined; they are dressed strangely and they look obviously like laborers. Sometimes

they appear on the street as a group and stare at the passersby on the street. The increase of this type of Japanese would surely result in denigrating the status of Japanese, subjecting them to more contempt. Eventually this country's populist politicians will propagate the argument that the Japanese should be excluded like the Chinese. This matter is an important issue to be well studied.[19]

For the Americans, anything that appeared bizarre was a target for ridicule or insult at the time:

With but few exceptions the [Japanese] immigrants profess to be good Christians and they declare that they are bound for the Japanese Christian missions in this City to learn the English language and learn more of the ways of Christian people and of Christianity. Notwithstanding their professions every Jap has strung around his neck a *kamisama* or praying-bag. These bags contain prayers written on silk or stout paper and are specially addressed to the possessors' household god. The Japs pay their Buddhist and Shinto priests from 1 to 2 cents for these prayers, which service the double purpose of being lucky charms as well as prayers.[20]

Unfortunately, the late nineteenth-century United States was not an ideal destination for overseas *dekasegi* laborers, but the Japanese leaders who encouraged overseas migration, the recruiting agents, and the laborers who wanted to work abroad were not aware of this. These oblivious individuals believed that the United States was the most favorable destination for overseas work and had a strong interest in working abroad, particularly because they would make money doing so. Their attitude gave the Asian exclusionists an excuse to attack the Japanese, whom they regarded in the same way as the Chinese: as outlandish, ignorant, and willing to live miserable lives like coolies.

In the late nineteenth century, Japanese laborers living in a white-dominated society inevitably were perceived to be peculiar and to have a low standard of living because Japanese laborers were unfamiliar with the Western lifestyle. As I explained earlier, the primary purpose for the Japanese to travel to the United States was to work as *dekasegi* laborers: in other words, to make money regardless of the hardships and miserable living conditions. With this determination, some even became so-called *burankketo katsugi* (blanket carriers), or seasonal farmworkers who moved from one farm to another carrying one blanket, forming the bottom tier of the farming population. During the harvest season, some of these blanket carriers who found work in rural areas such as Fresno purportedly slept under trees, in horse stables, or even in the fields.[21] In the summer of 1895, the first group of Japanese who were looking for jobs in Fresno were detained by the police because they were loitering on the street, poorly clothed.

> The number of Japanese arriving in the United States has increased, which naturally saturated the labor market. These newly arrived Japanese looked for jobs not only in California but also in the neighboring states. These kinds of laborers formed a group of about some fifteen or sixteen, wandered in Fresno in Southern California, and were detained by the police officers. Therefore, they reported to the consulate. These laborers stayed in the city for several days looking for jobs but lacked resources to support their living. They were wandering around in the city, which led them to look suspicious to police officers. Such an act not only harmed them but was not in the best interest of the Japanese residing in the region in general. It is a worrisome situation.[22]

Chinda Sutemi, the consul general in San Francisco, made this comment after learning of their situation. He dispatched members of the Dai Nihonjinkai (Great Japanese Association) and an American lawyer to have these laborers acquitted.[23] It is true that many of the Japanese *dekasegi* laborers wandered from place to place looking for jobs and led a life similar to that of homeless people. Those living in the fields were not limited to seasonal workers.

> Circa 1891, a young man found a job as a stable guard in a farm near Fresno during the great harvest season. Many Chinese and Europeans had gathered at this farm for the harvest. One morning this young man picked up a bundle of hay with two hands to transport it to the horses. Suddenly the hay jumped out of his arms

and screamed. In surprise, the young man fell down. A woman's leg came out of the hay. It was a European couple who decided to sleep in the hay overnight. At this time in the countryside, not only Chinese and Japanese but workers in general slept in the fields. In anecdotal stories, some were bit by poisonous snakes while others were stepped on by horses.[24]

The meals of workers were terrible. Their main meals were *dango-jiru* (Japanese dumpling soup).

When [Baba] Kosaburō opened a *ryokan* [inn] in Watsonville in 1895 or 1896, he rented an old house in the corner of Watsonville's Chinatown. The rent for this house was $3.50 a month. He built makeshift bunks and had Japanese working in the region stay there. At that time luxuries such as rice, miso [fermented soybean seasoning], or shōyu [soy sauce] were not available for sale in the rural area. Daily meals of soup with millet balls and flavored with a few slices of bacon were offered to the guests of the *ryokan*. The guests would gather around a pot to help themselves. Nakajima Shūsaburo, who stayed at this *ryokan*, remembered that some twelve to thirteen workers would stay in Mr. Baba's rooms. Every day they would eat millet ball soup, and they became tired of it. Mr. Baba occasionally threw in a few pieces of cabbage and two eggs into the pot. One day eight or nine workers went to the fields to work. Still staying at the *ryokan* were the lazy *shosei* [school-boys]. Mr. Baba would say, "Today I will treat you." People came to the dining table expecting an extraordinary meal but saw the normal soup. When they asked, "Mr. Baba, why did you call this a treat," he replied that the number of eggs per person was greater. When you come to think about it you usually get two eggs per thirteen people and today you have two eggs for five people. The schoolboys laughed at that and said that it was indeed a treat.[25]

Despite their low quality of life, they were able to remit large sums of money to their home country. According to a report from the San Francisco consulate, the *dekasegi* laborers, who numbered five thousand in 1895, managed to send 600,000 to 700,000 yen to Japan. The exclusionists who wanted to expel Japanese laborers used this as a jus-tification; Japanese laborers were not bringing profits to the United States.[26]

Additionally, Japanese laborers unthinkingly behaved in ways that crystalized the impression that they were strong competitors against white workers for jobs. The acting Japanese consul in Vancouver, Kitō Teijirō, reported to the Ministry of Foreign Affairs that "these laborers are not trained in the details of labor market. The Japanese come to North America relying on the correspondence of their friends, increasing pressure on the job market and lowering the wages," sug-gesting that the competition among Japanese laborers was one of the factors in lowering wages.[27] In addition, "it is rightly known that the collapse of the silver currency caused a recession in the United States, leading to shrinking businesses." The ripple effect of the recession was felt throughout the Pacific coastal states. "It spread to British Columbia; the businesses are sluggish now. The state's important industry, the sawmill, was forced to temporarily shut down, and the output decreased. However, if you go southward to the United States, we hear the economy is even worse." The economic situation had become dire. Therefore, about 150 Japanese workers in Vancouver and its vicinity, about 50 in Victoria, and about 300 in Seattle and Tacoma became "jobless or had a difficult time supporting themselves."[28] Despite this situation, "every ship carried fifty to sixty or as many as over a hundred Japanese workers to America." As a result, the Japanese workers competed against one another for jobs, with the managers of farms preferring to hire Japanese who were willing to work for lower wages. Consul Kamiya in San Francisco, who had in 1895 inspected Californian regions where Japanese resided or worked, referred to a case introduced in the *Bulletin*:

> Vacaville is situated about sixty-four miles away from San Francisco. The area is famous for peach production, and today about 450 Japanese workers are engaged in agriculture at orchards or in fruit production. During the harvest season the number increased from 800 to 900. The number of Japanese workers is increasing every year. Vacaville farm owners, based on many years of experience, have, particularly in the last two to three years,

used Japanese workers to gradually replace the white and Chinese workers. The percentage of white and Chinese workers is small now. The white workers are not satisfied with the Japanese and are advocating that the farm owners exclude Japanese. Despite the Sino-Japanese War, which might have alleviated anti-Japanese feeling among the white laborers, those in direct conflict are still advocating for the expulsion and exclusion of the Japanese. One could see the revival of anti-Japanese feeling given the current situation.

In addition to the general economic recession, the working class is increasingly having more difficulty. Some white workers attack our workers, destroy houses, and injure Japanese. Observing the current situation of Japanese workers, it is a matter of concern. Japanese are not accustomed to the local customs, and they are clothed strangely. They are regarded as a disgrace by Americans and do not speak the language. Many cannot even write their names and are subject to Americans' contempt and discrimination.[29]

There had been Japanese-exclusion incidents led by armed workers in various parts of the West Coast. In 1892 a Japanese railroad maintenance worker in Nampa, Idaho, was diagnosed with smallpox; as a result all the Japanese workers were expelled from the region.[30] One year later, in 1893, on the Southern Pacific Railroad at the Doreen Station, a Japanese worker was attacked by a fired white worker.[31] These incidents of Japanese expulsion were reported to the Ministry of Foreign Affairs by the consul.[32]

Undoubtedly, underlying conditions were present for inflammatory newspaper articles to reappear in newspapers like the *Bulletin* in 1895. Except for the consulate officials of the western states who were aware of the difficulty of the situation, Japanese government leaders and intellectuals, who encouraged overseas migration, were not aware of the strong prejudice white Americans had toward the "yellow" race. However, some might criticize this as hindsight. If those leaders did not properly deal with the exclusion activities against Japanese *dekasegi* laborers, they could not identify the potential risks at the time, including the jeopardy posed to future US-Japan diplomatic relations. After the end of the Sino-Japanese War, Japanese leaders were most concerned that the Japanese laborers were validating the exclusionist argument and that consequently, the Japanese would be treated just like the Chinese, damaging Japan's pride as a nation. Supporting this judgment, the leaders held on to a self-righteous sense of reassurance that if they controlled or prohibited the emigration of Japanese laborers who were barely literate and could become an easy target of contempt, anti-Japanese sentiment could be alleviated in the United States.[33] This perception, however, was certainly not shared by Americans.

Anti-Japanese sentiment worsened beyond their control. The Japanese victory in the Sino-Japanese War marked a turning point in the anti-Japanese campaign in the United States. Consul Kamiya, in May 1895, warned that local newspapers were emphasizing that the surge of Japanese migrants was connected to the aftermath of the Sino-Japanese War. Even more unfortunate for the Japanese, the Bureau of Immigration, which was criticized by exclusionist newspapers for its generous inspections of contract laborers, began reinvestigating Japanese laborers who had already been admitted and were working on Vacaville farms but who had caused friction with white laborers. The announced purpose of the investigation was to find evidence that Japanese laborers had entered the country in violation of the Alien Contract Labor Law. Although no such evidence was found, just the fact that investigations were conducted brought the federal government's attention to Japanese laborers. As a result, the Japanese migration issue on the West Coast became linked with the Congress investigation on the impact on US industries by Japanese manufacturers that benefited from post-Sino-Japanese-War low-wage laborers.

A domestic issue relating to a small number of Japanese migrants to the United States became associated with the "yellow peril" slogan that portrayed the Japanese, who represented Oriental civilization, as strong competitors to the white race, who had developed Western culture, society, and industry. The Japanese immigration issue would eventually become one factor threatening Japan-US relations at the turn of the twentieth century. In the next section I will examine how Japanese *dekasegi* in the United States became associated with Japan's victory in the Sino-Japanese War.

The Sino-Japanese War and Reorienting the Exclusionist Argument: The Issue of Competitors and Low Wages

Consul Kamiya provided reference material to Saionji, the acting foreign minister, from an editorial titled "The Wily Japanese" in the *Call* that purported a slanderous link between Japan's victory and the immigration issue, suggesting that all the Japanese laborers who had just arrived on the West Coast after the termination of the Sino-Japanese War were veterans who experienced hardship on war fronts. Indeed, in a *Call* editorial, California State Commissioner of Labor Fitzgerald was quoted as stating, "There are many Japanese laborers in California today who are wearing the military uniform which they wore in the war with China. . . . Since the disbandment of some of the Japanese armies as a result of the treaty of peace, the recent belligerents have been in so great a hurry to come to California that they have hardly taken time to change their clothes." [34] Kamiya interpreted the editorial as suggesting that after the Japanese victory, Japan had emerged as a rising nation in the Orient and that sending low-wage laborers to the United States was an attempt to wage major competition against American laborers. Kamiya also interpreted that this editorial was an inflammatory exaggeration used to create a sense of crisis among many of the readers about the risks of the large influx of Japanese migrant laborers coming into the United States, where white workers were not competitive with such low-wage workers. [35]

As you can see, in May 1895, the Japanese victory reinvigorated the anti-Japanese argument in San Francisco–based newspapers that there was an impending dangerous situation again and ignited the discussion that many Japanese laborers were in violation of the Foran Act. The Japanese victory against China, the "sleeping lion in the East," concerned Americans, particularly those living on the West Coast. As suggested in the *Call* op-ed, the advocates for Japanese exclusion in San Francisco and other West Coast cities feared that Japanese labor migration would be resumed with renewed vigor when the Sino-Japanese War was over. Indeed, as they anticipated, the steamer *Peking* arrived in San Francisco on May 12, 1895, with 120 Japanese passengers in its steerage. [36]

Four years earlier, a sudden surge of Japanese arrivals had also raised anti-Japanese campaigns in the press and among some Americans.

Coincidentally, in April, right after the enactment of the 1891 Immigration Act and the creation of the Office of the Superintendent of Immigration, two tramp steamers, the *Remus* and *Pemptos*, carried an unprecedented large "mass" of 120 Japanese *dekasegi* laborers who were "disreputable in demeanor." These charter ships charged only thirty-five dollars for transpacific travel. Because four of the passengers were contract laborers, they were denied entry; several others were denied entry based on the new immigration law that banned paupers. The *San Francisco Call* and *Bulletin*, which had hitherto championed anti-Oriental causes in the city, also resumed their heated campaign against what they regarded as the illegal importation of "cheap contract laborers from Japan unacceptable to the US society." They argued that Japanese laborers should be banned from the United States just like the Chinese. The San Francisco consul, Chinda Sutemi, called most of these articles outrageous, full of erroneous information.[37]

The anti-Japanese reporting in the press, which began in 1891, continued through the following year but subsided by 1893 for two reasons. First, the Japanese government tightened inspections for passport applications, and *dekasegi* laborers who were likely to be denied entry found it difficult to leave Japan. Second, those who learned about the strict immigration inspection at the San Francisco port changed their port of entry to Vancouver in British Columbia and Tacoma in Washington State.[38]

With such precedents, the anti-Japanese campaign was expected to subside if the number of Japanese arrivals was reduced. Consul Kamiya, however, sent a special alert to the minister of foreign affairs reporting that the Japanese exclusionist argument had taken a different form and the situation should be treated seriously.[39] Kamiya's assessment was based on the fact that an immigration officer and state labor commissioner had started reinspecting Japanese laborers who were already on farms and orchards in the country.

Arousing criticism from the press, the "mass" arrival of the Japanese migrants on the *Peking*, contrary to the exclusionists' expectations, resulted in all 120 Japanese being admitted into the United States despite suspicion of their being contract laborers and a strict inspection by the immigration officers. Needless to say, the Japanese migrants welcomed the outcome. The criticizing articles, however, could no longer sensationally exaggerate "facts" as they did when a few Japanese were denied landing; instead they had to come up with other reasons to instigate anti-Japanese sentiment. The newspapers argued that the "cunning" Japanese found loopholes in the contract labor and immigration laws in order to come to the United States. Supporting this argument, an authoritative US immigration officer was quoted as promising that he would "do all he can to prevent the scheme that the Japs are preparing to spring on our industries."[40]

For the Japanese government, all Japanese emigrants getting permission to enter the United States was something expected and easily justifiable. The Japanese *dekasegi* workers who arrived in the United States were more conversant with the new immigration law and the procedures of the inspection than the *dekasegi* workers of four years earlier, when the new laws were introduced. They were well informed of the procedure when they applied for emigration permission in Japan. The officials of regional government offices that issued passports and the administrative agents instructed migrants to carry thirty dollars to show in order to avoid being considered poor. Thus, the situation four years earlier that called for immediate rejection upon landing no longer occurred.[41] Four years earlier, Japanese migrants with the purpose of *dekasegi* labor had to dispose of their properties to pay for their fare to the United States, meaning that very few of them could support themselves. This situation, however, no longer existed. They were also prepared not to give the immigration officer an excuse to deny them landing based on labor contracts.[42] Therefore, the number of Japanese denied entry to the United States was expected to decrease unless immigration officers purposefully targeted the Japanese.

Unfortunately, this development further increased the suspicions of the exclusionists, who had preconceived notions of the Japanese as cunning, making them determined to bar the Japanese from immigrating. Newspapers redirected their attack toward loopholes in the immigration law and the generosity of immigration officers. Consul Kamiya reported that the *Bulletin* and *Call* repeatedly criticized the "shortcomings of the immigration laws and the immigration officials for allowing the Japanese who were essentially contract laborers and, thus, criminals into the United States." [43]

These newspaper articles led to the reinspection of Japanese laborers who had already been admitted to the United States, creating a situation that the Japanese government could not ignore. US immigration officer Walter P. Stradley and California State Director of Labor Fitzgerald, unable to ignore the severe criticism from newspapers, decided to go to Pleasanton and Vacaville to reexamine the labor contracts of Japanese workers. Although they were not able to find proof, these visits gave the *Call* and *Examiner* a prime opportunity to call for the exclusion of Japanese, just like the Chinese. Consul Kamiya was concerned about this development and stated that the *Call* featured editorials filled with erroneous facts to instigate an anti-Japanese movement.[44]

The sensational articles insisted that the Japanese tolerated deplorable meals and living conditions that white laborers would not tolerate and were cheap laborers like coolies.[45] Supporting these arguments were the relatively high wages, on the basis of just pure dollars, in the United States compared with Japan, and the significant gap between American and Japanese living standards. Furthermore, the prolonged recession in the United States affected the labor force. Coincidentally, Congress began studying the negative impact on US industry from rapidly expanding Japanese exports, sustained by cheap labor, further fueling the "coolie labor" argument.

The following is a headline of an article that appeared in the *Call* on June 11, 1895:

IMPORTED JAP LABORERS
PROOF THAT THE COOLY CONTRACT SYSTEM
IS IN OPERATION HERE
CHEAP HELP FOR FRESNO [46]

Another article appeared on June 14 in the *Call* with the following title: JAPAN'S COOLY LABORER: MANY INTERESTING FACTS LEARNED FROM THE *PERU*'S PASSENGERS. The idea that the Japanese were coolie laborers was presented as fact.[47]

Furthermore, the *Call* on June 11, 1895, provided twisted facts to support the "coolie-like low-waged labor" argument:

The investigation of Japanese cooly labor matters was resumed yesterday by Labor Commissioner E. L. Fitzgerald and Deputy Cleve L. Dam. While the inquiry was confined principally to one witness, many interesting points were brought out, in spite of the witness' desire not to tell what he knows about the contract system which is now filling the agricultural and horticultural districts of the State with cheap cooly labor. One interesting feature was this witness' statement concerning wages in Japan. The farmer, he stated, earns on an average 40 sen or 20 cents a day. Below the farmer are other workers, who earn about 25 sen or about 12 and 13 cents a day and pay for their own board and lodging. It is the latter class that is being imported to this State, where they are only too glad to work for any wages offered. This accounts for the low rate of wages—60 to 75 cents per day—that the Japs are paid in the California orchards and hopyards.[48]

The article went on to reveal a "surprising fact":

The contracts [in Fresno] call for about 2,000 Japanese and Chinese coolies. These cheap laborers are to receive from 50 cents to 70 cents a day and board and lodge themselves. Arrangements have been made with the Southern Pacific Railroad so that the coolies will be shipped from this city to Fresno in boxcars, the same as cattle and hogs. This will materially lessen the cost of transportation. The idea in making these contracts so early is that, as all the coolies in the State are engaged for the season, to wait much longer would make it impossible for the Fresno patrons of cheap labor to secure the required help.[49]

In addition, the *Call*'s article explained that the Japanese were trained to deal with US immigration inspections before their departure.

New features are being brought to light every day by the investigation into the Japanese cooly labor question. The investigation yesterday was held on board the steamer *Peru* that arrived on Wednesday from the Orient. Among the steerage passengers were ten or dozen Japs, who were held on board until Immigration

Commissioner Stradley and Deputy Gaffeney could determine whether they were entitled to land. From the answers and manner of answering questions the Japs show beyond a doubt that they have been coached as to what they should say in response to the Commissioner's questions. When led away from the routine line of inquiry the immigrants become nervous or sullen and rarely anything can be obtained from them beyond "I am telling the truth."[50]

This article ignored the fact that Japanese were not contract laborers and gave readers the impression that the Japanese public and private sectors were "maliciously" plotting together.

The Investigation of Japanese Industry and Low-Wage Labor in Japan by the US House of Representatives

The Committee on Ways and Means at the 54th US Congress's first session in 1896 started an investigation on the rapidly modernizing Japanese industry and its impact on US industries' laborers, in light of low living standards and low-wage labor in Asia.[51] The members passed a resolution in the House "respecting the alleged invasion of the markets of the United States, and the menace offered to American manufacturing industries by the products of cheap Oriental labor, and to determine what is the cause of this menace, and what legislative remedy, if any, should be adopted to avert the threatened injury to American producers." The Committee on Ways and Means was to report to the main session. This resolution did not specify the source of "cheap Oriental labor"; however, Representative Dingley, a member of the committee, admitted in his first report to the main session that the target of the investigation was Japan, saying: "The Oriental country whose actual or prospective industrial competition has suggested this inquiry is Japan."[52]

The first meeting of the American Manufacturing Association (AMA), held in Chicago during January 22–23, 1896, passed a resolution concerning competition from the Japanese manufacturing industry.

Recently Oriental countries, especially Japan, have developed a manufacturing industry at a remarkable rate, and their products were extremely cheap and sold in the US market. Newspaper articles regarding this matter prompted us to investigate whether their competition harms US industry and, if so, what measures should be taken. For this purpose, three committee members were appointed.[53]

The selected three members of the committee concluded that the Japanese competition significantly damaged US industry. Wages in Japan were 10–15 cents a day, about one-tenth the US equivalent. However, they failed to propose any measures against this competition. The AMA's main assembly proposed that this matter should be closely investigated and that it should help the general public become aware of this development. As a result, the main assembly passed a resolution to submit the following report to the US Congress:

> Resolved, by the National Association of American Manufacturers in Chicago, Jan. 22, 1896, That the Congress of the United States is hereby respectfully requested to appoint a commission, or to direct one of its own committees, to inquire respecting the alleged invasion of our market and the menace offered to American manufacturing industry by the products of cheap oriental labor and to determine what is the cause of this menace and what means should be adopted to avert the threatened injury to domestic producers.

This report, which the AMA submitted to Congress, apparently led to the passage of the House resolution to request an investigation.

The first report, dated June 6 and submitted to the main session by Representative Dingley, emphasized that the "Eastern empire," Japan, in the previous thirty years, and particularly the most recent five years, had experienced significant political and economic development brought about by "a rapid Westernizing of her methods of industry."[54] Dingley paid respect to Japanese people's enthusiasm and effort for their country's modernization. He, however, repeated the same rhetoric of criticism as had been seen from the end of the Edo period. He stated that the "Japanese do not have the inventive genius of Americans, or even of Europeans, yet their imitative faculties are wonderful, and their progressiveness exceptional among Orientals. . . . A little rice, costing but a few cents per day, suffices for the food of the masses. The standard of living is so low that the workingmen of the United States would justly regard it as practical starvation. Inasmuch as wages always move with the standard of living of the masses, the pay of the Japanese laborers, who work industriously and patiently twelve hours each day, is as scanty as his clothing and fare."

The investigation report stressed that the rapidly developing manufacturing industry in Japan, backed by low-wage labor, and their cheap products in the market posed an extreme threat to US manufacturers. The conclusion was supported by the following reasoning:

> The Japanese labor [is] likely to soon become as effective with machinery as European labor is. This result will be counteracted, indeed has already been counteracted, somewhat by the inevitable tendency of contact with civilization to improve the standard of living, and consequently the wages of the Japanese workingmen. But notwithstanding the Japanese are more progressive than any other Oriental people, yet it will take time for the masses of Japan to reach even the European standard of living and wages, not to mention the much higher standard of the United States.

In sum, the report submitted by the Committee on Ways and Means stated that Japanese industry was expected to continue to develop rapidly through modernization, but that Japanese living standards would not rise at the same rate; therefore, at end of the nineteenth century, Japanese wages were not expected to rise rapidly. This would allow Japanese industry to compete favorably with European and American industries. As a result, modern Japanese industries would be able to rely on low-wage labor and remain a strong competitor with US industry in the future.

Until then, American anti-Japanese exclusionists' criticism targeted *dekasegi* laborers. Aimed at the Japanese entering the United States was criticism that Japanese laborers, like coolies, tolerated deplorable living conditions and were willing to work long hours at low wages that white laborers would not tolerate. However, if one emphasizes Dingley's argument that, like "cheap products" entering the US market and threatening American manufacturers, Japanese low-wage laborers were entering the United States in massive numbers through immigration companies, then issues associated with the Japanese *dekasegi* system may no longer be dismissed as a US domestic matter. Unfortunately, by the end of the 1890s, the exclusionists' argument appeared to encompass a target beyond Japanese immigrants. The US immigration supervisors played a nonnegligible role in this shift.

> The Japanese were never wealthy as a people. There are no rich men in Japan. . . . The country produces no inventors, no original ideas, except along the line of its peculiar art in curios, silk, embroideries, and pottery, and practically has no literature. Only the Samurai, or soldier class, or nobility have enjoyed the comforts of culture or wealth until recent years, and until this time 50 per cent of the population live in the most squalid poverty, and the remainder of the common people, to put it mildly, are poor. It is not surprising that such is the case.
>
> It is historical that the population of Japan had outgrown the capacity of the soil to furnish food thirty years ago, and they have been enabled to live only by the practice of the strictest economy with food products. Infanticide was popular. Famines were frequent, and loathsome and immoral diseases were everywhere prevalent, which have left their imprint upon the people to the present day. The people were habitual gamblers. In most of the municipalities, forming a city by itself, was a large colony of women for immoral purposes—a system recognized by usage and law and which prevails to this day. In fact, the decencies of life were unknown except among a very few.
>
> It is not possible that a generation and a half could regenerate such a people. There is, it is true, a brighter side to new Japan, a regenerated section of the population, who have taken on European ideas, who are struggling for better things, but the future is still veiled in uncertainty.
>
> It is . . . with [the] class of her people who emigrate [that I have to deal here today]. First, there are a few merchants and businessmen; second, a few students and young men, the sons of Japanese of the better professional and commercial class; third, the great mass of emigrants, say 95 per cent of the whole, who are coolie laborers and small farmers, who class as coolies.[55]

The above report was made by Commissioner of Immigration W. M. Rice, a high-level federal bureaucrat who was ordered in December 1898 to investigate the immigration issue of Japanese laborers in the United States and was then dispatched to Japan. Even considering that this report was written at the end of the nineteenth century, it is hard to imagine this was an official report written by a man with common sense. This quote is from a report that was submitted by Rice to the Committee on Foreign Affairs in the fifty-sixth Congressional Session in 1900.

Rice's long report repeats the exclusionists' criticism and insults from the early 1890s that Japanese were low-wage laborers who tolerated deplorable living conditions like coolies. This was applied to the Japanese population as a whole in many aspects. Rice was dispatched to Japan to confirm that Japanese "coolies" were migrating to the United States en masse. Rice attempted to support his argument by providing a line of evidence that 50 percent of the Japanese in Japan led miserable lives and 95 percent of the Japanese migrants in the United States belonged to this class. This report gave an impetus for universalizing the exclusionists' arguments, which were understood as targeting only certain Japanese immigrating to the United States, justifying its generalization to describe the Japanese as a whole. Through this process, the Japanese border-entry issue developed from a mere domestic issue in the United States at the end of the nineteenth century to a "Japanese immigration problem" at the turn of the twentieth century, later turning into a factor in the deteriorating US-Japan diplomatic relations.

Notes

1. US Bureau of Immigration, *Annual Report of the Commissioner-General of Immigration to the Secretary of the Treasury for the Fiscal Year Ended June 30, 1896* (Washington, DC: Government Printing Office, 1896). Hereafter, I will indicate this publication as *Annual Report 1895–96*. Pursuant to the Immigration Act of 1891 enacted on March 3, 1891, the Bureau of Immigration was established in the Treasury Department and issued annual reports. The first issue covered the 1891–92 fiscal year starting July 1, 1891, and ending June 30 the following year. It is customary for the annual report to adopt the fiscal year unless otherwise stated. In this paper, I use the term *Gasshūkoku* for the United States of America, and the term *America* for North America including British Columbia (Canada).

2. *Annual Report 1895–96*, 14. In this fiscal year, 466, nearly half of the
Japanese who were allowed entry to North America, arrived at the port of Victoria,
British Columbia, and then entered the United States through Washington after
crossing the border. The reasons are as follows. Pursuant to the Immigration Act
of 1891, immigration inspection by the federal government began. Since the immigration inspection was strict in San Francisco, the center of the yellow peril movement, many Japanese were denied entry for violations of the immigration law.
Starting in 1892, many of the Japanese who learned about this before traveling
avoided the problem by arriving at Victoria and crossing the border to enter the
United States through Washington, where immigration inspection was not yet as
strict as in San Francisco. Although the *Annual Report 1891–92* reports no immigrants avoiding San Francisco by arriving in Victoria, the *Annual Report 1892–93*
and *1893–94* show drastic increases: 805 and 772, respectively. (Refer to *Annual
Report 1892–93; 1893–94;* and *1894–95*). This pattern of entry to North America
stopped when the immigration inspection at the Canada-US border became stricter
in 1895–96. For example, refer to Kōkō dai 114-gō, Meiji 26-nen 6-gatsu 6-ka,
Beikoku Chūsatsu Kōshi Tateno Gōzō yori Gaimu Daijin Mutsu Munemitsu ate,
"Gaikokujin no ijū ni kansuru hōritsu kisoku ni ihaishi tōkoku ni raikō o kuwa-
datsuru mono ronshi no ken"; Fuzokusho, Otsukō dai 35-gō, Meiji 26-nen 5-gatsu
30-nichi, Beikoku Chūsatsu Kōshi Tateno Gōzō yori Zai Bankūbā Ryōji Dairi Kitō
Teijirō ate; Dai 76-gō, Meiji 26-nen 6-gatsu 10-ka, Kitō Ryōji Dairi yori Tateno
Kōshi ate, "Beikoku tenjūsha setsuyu kata ni tsuki hōkoku no ken"; Fuzokusho,
sha, Meiji 26-nen 6-gatsu 10-ka, Kitō yori Tateno ate, "Tō chihō yori Hokubei
Gasshūkoku ni tenjyū o kuwadateru mono zōkashi nyūkoku kyohisaretaru koto
ni tsuki hōkoku no ken"; and Sō dai 64-gō, Gaimu Daijin Mutsu Munemitsu yori
Tōkyō fuchiji ate, "Bankūbā keiyu Beikoku ijūsha ronkoku kata tsūchi no ken" in
Nihon gaikō bunsho dai 26-kan, ed. Gaimushō (Nihon Kokusai Rengō Kyōkai,
1952), 731–34 and 740–41. Hereafter I will indicate *Nihon gaikō bunsho*, ed.
Gaimushō as *Gaikō bunsho*.

3. For the total annual number of immigrants, refer to "Table VI Actual and
Total Immigration of the Fiscal Year 1895–96" in *Annual Report 1895–96*, 29.
For new immigrants, refer to Maldwyn Allen Jones, *American Immigration*, 2nd
ed. (Chicago: University of Chicago Press, 1992) 152–238; and Akashi Norio, Iino
Masako, and Tanaka Masako, *Esunikku Amerika: Taminzoku kokka ni okeru
dōka no genjitsu* (Yūhikaku, 1984), 82–125.

4. Kimitsu dai 1-gō, Meiji 28-nen 6-gatsu 12-nichi, Sanfuranshisuko Ryōji
Kamiya Saburō yori Gaimu Daijin Rinji Dairi Saionji Kinmochi ate, "Sōkō sho
shinbun Nihon dekaseginin ni kansuru kiji o keisaishite sendōteki kōgekiron o
shōdōshi hīte Gasshūkoku imin kensakan tō chihō ni shucchō shi honpō rōdōsha
ni tsuki rōdō keiyaku no zonhi o torishirahetaru ken ni tsuki gushin" in "Hokubei
Gasshūkoku ni okeru honpōjin tokō seigen oyobi haiseki kankei ichiran dai 1,"
held at the Gaimushō Gaikō Shiryōkan (Diplomatic Archives of the Ministry of
Foreign Affairs of Japan), 382–400; and *Gaikō bunsho 28, bunsho 1317*, 680–83.
I will indicate "Hokubei Gasshūkoku ni okeru honpōjin tokō seigen oyobi haiseki
kankei ichiran" as "Honpōjin tokō seigen oyobi haiseki ichiran."

5. The text of Kimitsu dai 1-gō, as mentioned in endnote 4, is recorded as *bunsho 1317* in *Gaikō bunsho 28*. However, some excerpts from San Francisco newspapers including the *Bulletin*, May 14, 1895, ibid., May 15, 1895, and *Call*, June 5,
1895, that are attached as Besshi dai 1, dai 2, and dai 3 have been omitted.

6. *San Francisco Bulletin,* May 14, 1895, Kimitsu dai 1-gō, Meiji 28-nen 6-gatsu 12-nichi, Kamiya yori Saionji ate, Besshi dai 1-gō, "Honpōjin tokō seigen oyobi haiseki ichiran, 1."

7. The daily wage of forty to fifty cents for Japanese migrant laborers indicated here was clearly fabricated by newspapers. On April 20, 1895, right before this article appeared, the consul general in San Francisco sent an on-site survey to the Ministry of Foreign Affairs. It stated "Fresno, 207 miles away from San Francisco, is one of the most important areas for Japanese migrant laborers, after Sacramento. The wage of Japanese migrant laborers working in fruit farms in Fresno was eighty cents per day. Many of them were employed via contractors (commonly called 'boss'). When they directly entered into contracts with landowners to work exclusively on their land, however, their wages were reportedly about one dollar twenty cents. The prevailing daily wage of Japanese migrant laborers in Sacramento was still seventy-five cents, the lowest in California. Many migrant laborers, however, chose to work here since they could access San Francisco in winter when farms were closed" ("Beikoku junkai kaku chihō shōkyō narabini zairyū honpōjin no jōtai" [the consular report of San Francisco dated April 20, 1895] in *Tsūshō isan dai 17-gō,* ed. Gaimushō Tsūshōkyoku [May 15, 1895], 3–13). Washizu "Shakuma" Bunzō, who helped migrant laborers find jobs on farms, stated in his memoir that the daily wage of Japanese migrant laborers was seventy-five cents during winter and one dollar and ten cents during summer. Furthermore, he stated that in September 1895, grocery prices were seventy-five cents for fifty pounds of flour, fifteen cents for a dozen eggs, ten cents for a piece of beef, fourteen cents for a piece of bacon, ten cents for one *seki* of rice (six dollars for a hundred *seki*). See Washizu "Shakuma" Bunzō, "Rekishi enmetsu no tan 23—Nijūnendai inaka no seikatsu, Musen ryokōsha no kotodomo—" in the Sōkō *Nichi-Bei shinbun* issued on April 29, 1922. Bunzō, a highly valued writer in Nikkei communities, left valuable documents for researchers, including "Rekishi enmetsu no tan," 1–97, in the Sōkō *Nichi-Bei shinbun* issued between April 5 and July 14, 1922; "Wagahai no Beikoku seikatsu," 1–132, in the Sōkō *Nichi-Bei shinbun* issued between July 10, 1924, and January 23, 1925; and *Zaibei Nihonjin shikan: fu Zaibei zaifu Nihonjin rekishi no minamoto* (Rafu Shinpōsha, 1930). For the business activities of Japanese contractors of migrant laborers and their actual labor conditions at orchards and agricultural fields, refer to Yuji Ichioka, *The Issei: The World of the First Generation Japanese Immigrants, 1885–1924* (New York: Free Press, 1988), 197–281. For the Japanese-language edition, refer to Ichioka Yuji, *Issei: reimeiki Amerika imin no monogatari,* trans. Tomita Torao, Kumei Teruko, and Shinoda Satae (Tōsui Shobō, 1992), 65–100.

8. *San Francisco Call,* May 5, 1895. In the on-site survey conducted by the consul general in San Francisco mentioned in endnote 7, consular officers were dispatched to more than ten regions in three states, including seven regions in Southern California, two in Northern California, one in Oregon, and two in Washington. The breakdown of the number of Japanese residing in each region was as follows. (The numbers are only approximate.)

Southern California
    Pacific Grove   100
    Fresno   220
    Bakersfield   3

Southern California (*cont.*)
Santa Barbara	10
Los Angeles	230
Riverside	30
San Diego	33

Northern California
Sacramento	1,650
Vacaville	450

Oregon
Portland	400

Washington
Tacoma	70
Seattle	450

The report shows that the total number of Japanese residing in these cities was approximately 3,600. It also indicates that the number of Japanese residing in San Francisco and neighboring cities was about 2,400, with 500 migrant laborers working in Idaho. Furthermore, it estimates that the total number of Japanese residing in the territories overseen by the consulate general of Japan in San Francisco, including those residing in other parts of California, is approximately 7,000. See "Beikoku junkai kaku chihō shōkyō narabini zairyū honpōjin no jōtai" (the consular report of San Francisco dated April 20, 1895) in dai 17-gō, May 15, 1895, 19–21. Therefore, the citation of "approximately 10,000 Japanese found employment on farms in the San Joaquin Valley, Napa Valley, Livermore Valley and the fertile valley of San Gabriel" was probably intentionally fabricated. According to the United States census, the Japanese residing in America in 1890 numbered 2,039, with 1,532 residing on the West Coast (Washington, Oregon, and California). The census in 1900, ten years later, showed that the number of Japanese residing in America had increased to 24,326 with 18,269 (75 percent) in the same three states on the West Coast. See Yamato Ichihashi, *Japanese in the United States: A Critical Study of the Problems of the Japanese Immigrants and Their Children* (Stanford, CA: Stanford University Press, 1932), 94. Furthermore, the *Annual Report* of the United States indicates that 8,860 Japanese entered the United States between 1894–95 and 1898–99 (*Annual Report 1894–95, 1895–96, 1896–97, 1897–98, 1898–99*). Therefore, if Japanese working in orchards and fields in those areas numbered 10,000, as the article suggested, this would mean all the Japanese residing in the three West Coast states were working in those areas.

9. Ibid. The 1885 Alien Contract Labor Law was enacted because Congress accepted the argument that some company management, including labor unions, imported unskilled alien laborers at lower wages. American industry, however, had achieved remarkable technological innovations in the late nineteenth century and needed skilled European laborers. Recent research demonstrates that the labor contract guaranteed favorable working conditions for European laborers and that it was used to recruit European laborers to the United States, not unskilled laborers (Jones, *American Immigration*, 161–62). Since the purpose of this law was to prevent the immigration of unskilled migrant laborers, the federal immigration officers interpreted "contractor agreements" more strictly. In San Francisco, in particular, immigration inspectors held strong anti-Asian prejudice and were swayed by local sentiment. Some Japanese were denied entry if they indicated a

letter or verbal promise from a friend residing in the United States that promised help to find a job after their arrival. In some cases, inspectors considered these as contractor agreements and denied entry. Refer to Sakata Yasuo, "Shōtotsuten e mukau kidō: Meijiki ni okeru Nihonjin no Amerika dekasegi" (On a Collision Course: The Migration of Japanese *Dekasegi* Laborers to the United States during the Meiji Era) (II), in *Ōsaka Gakuin Daigaku Kokusaigaku ronshū dai 3-kan, dai 2-gō* (December 1992), 75–88, and pages 204–13 of chapter 4 of this volume.

10. *San Francisco Bulletin*, May 15, 1895, Kimitsu dai 1-gō, Meiji 28-nen 6-gatsu 12-nichi, Kamiya yori Saionji ate, Besshi dai 2-gō, "Honpōjin tokō seigen oyobi haiseki ichiran, 1."

11. For legal interpretations and the historical background of the effects of Japanese ineligibility to attain citizenship, refer to Ichioka, *The Issei*, 154–76, and its Japanese-language edition, *Issei: Reimeiki Amerika imin no monogatari*, 197–281.

12. These numbers were also skillfully manipulated. First, by insisting that the numbers reported by Customs were not accurate, these newspapers attempted to raise public suspicion about the immigration inspection. (Because immigration inspectors, under the supervision of the Treasury Department, were located in each port, the statistics they reported were those of the officials of the Bureau of Immigration.) According to the *Annual Report* for the 1894–95 fiscal year (July 1, 1894–June 30, 1895), Japanese who entered the United States numbered 1,931, with 462 entering through San Francisco (*Annual Report 1894–95*, 8–9; and *1895–96*, 8). Therefore, "In the past thirty days there were nearly double that number of the Japanese who landed on the soil of California" was a groundless claim. To bolster credibility, the newspaper focused on the number of Japanese working at orchards and agricultural fields in Sacramento and San Joaquin Valley (these are close to the actual numbers). By doing so, it attempted to give the impression that the numbers reflected recent Japanese arrivals in the United States, but that figure included the Japanese migrant laborers who had already arrived there. Japanese who came to California from cities in the Northwest, including Portland and Seattle, were domestic travelers and had nothing to do with new entries into the United States as the newspaper insisted.

13. Kimitsu dai 1-gō, Meiji 28-nen 6-gatsu 12-nichi, Kamiya yori Saionji ate, *Gaikō bunsho 28*, 681.

14. Howard Zinn, *A People's History of the United States* (New York: Harper & Row, 1980), 271–72.

15. Herbert G. Gutman, *Work, Culture, and Society in Industrializing America: Essays in American Working-Class and Social History* (New York: Alfred A. Knopf, 1976). This citation is in the Japanese-language edition, Herbert G. Gutman, *Kinpika jidai no Amerika*, trans. Ōshimo Shōichi, Nomura Tatsurō, Nagata Toyoomi, and Takeda Yū (Heibonsha, 1986), 28–29.

16. Alexander Saxton, *The Rise and Fall of the White Republic: Class Politics and Mass Culture in Nineteenth Century America* (London: Verso, 1990).

17. For the anti-Qing movement, refer to Elmer Clarence Sandmeyer, *The Anti-Chinese Movement in California* (Urbana: University of Illinois Press, 1973).

18. Ibid., 88.

19. Kimitsu dai 14-gō, Meiji 25-nen 5-gatsu 10-ka, Zai Sanfuranshisuko Ryōji Chinda Sutemi yori Gaimu Daijin Enomoto Takeaki ate, "Honpō tokōsha jōriku kyozetsu no ken," in *Gaikō bunsho 25*, 702–3.

20. *San Francisco Call*, June 14, 1895; Kimitsu dai 3-gō, Meiji 28-nen 6-gatsu 27-nichi, Zai Sanfuranshisuko Kamiya Saburō yori Gaimu Jikan Hara Takashi ate, "Gasshūkoku imin kensakan honpō rōdōsha torishirabe no kekka ni kansuru ken," besshi dai 2-gō, "Honpōjin tokō seigen oyobi haiseki ichiran, 1," 424–40. Even though the text of Kimitsu dai 3-gō is recorded in *Gaikō bunsho* 28, 683–84, the excerpts from *Call*, June 11, 1895; June 14, 1895; and June 15, 1895 are omitted from the attachment. There were good reasons for newly arrived Japanese in San Francisco to head to Japanese Christian missions at the time. The lodges that served travelers without much cash belonged to Fukuinkai (the Gospel Society), Young Men's Christian Association, United Church of Christ in Japan, etc. So-called English-language classes were also held by these Christian organizations. See Fukuinkai enkaku shiryō, JARP Collection held at the University of California–Los Angeles library.

21. Washizu, "Rekishi enmetsu no tan 23," in the Sōkō (San Francisco) *Nichi-Bei shinbun* issued on April 22, 1922. Later these migrant laborers lived in tents.

22. Kōshin dai 80-gō, Meiji 25-nen 8-gatsu 4-ka, Zai Sanfuranshisuko Ryōji Chinda Sutemi yori Gaimu Jikan Hayashi Tadasu ate, "Kashū Furesuno ni oite Nihonjin kōin saretaru ken ni tsuki hōkoku no ken" utsushi (hasshin bangō kaku), Meiji 25-nen 7-gatsu 30-nichi, Chinda Ryōji yori Beikoku Chūsatsu Kōshi Tateno Gōzō ate, "Honpō tokō rōdōsha futō torishimari ni kanshi hōkoku no ken"; "Zaibei honpōjin no jōkyō narabini tobeisha torishimari kankei zassan dai 1," held at Gaimushō Gaikō Shiryōkan; and *Gaikō bunsho* 26, 717–18. In *Gaikō bunsho* 26, Kōshin dai 80-gō and the fuzokusho of Chinda's report to Tateno, "Dai Nihonjinkai haken'in hōkoku," are omitted. Hence I will indicate "Zaibei honpōjin no jōkyō narabini tobeisha torishimari kankei zassan" as "Tobeisha torishimari kankei zassan."

23. "Dai Nihonjinkai haken'in hōkoku" in Kōshin dai 80-gō, Meiji 25-nen 8-gatsu 4-ka, Chinda yori Hayashi ate, "Kashū Furesuno ni oite Nihonjin kōin saretaru ken ni tsuki hōkoku no ken," besshi, "Tobeisha torishimari kankei zassan, 1." Dai Nihonjinkai, mentioned here, was the former organization of Nihonjin Kyōgikai established in 1900 to manage the so-called Kokushibyō (Pest) incident, Zaibei Nihonjin Rengō Kyōgikai in 1905 and Zaibei Nihonjinkai in 1908. Dai Nihonjinkai was founded in June 1891 to combine Fukuinkai (the Gospel Society), Aikoku Dōmeikai (the Patriotic League), Enseisha, Dōshūkai, and Seinenkai founded by *shosei*. Chinda Sutemi, the consul in San Francisco, served as chairman (Washizu, "Rekishi enmetsu no tan 13, Nihonjinkai no hajime" in the Sōkō *Nichi-Bei shinbun* on April 18, 1922).

24. Ibid.

25. Washizu "Shakuma" Bunzō, "Wagahai no Beikoku seikatsu 108, Shosei jidai yori rōdōsha jidai e ōnami no gotoki paionia seikatsu" in the Sōkō *Nichi-Bei shinbun* on December 12, 1924. Washizu discussed *dangojiru* (Japanese dumpling soup) that he consumed as a migrant laborer as follows: "Tokusaburō Saitō and I participated in fruit harvesting near San Jose in August 1895. . . . After the fifth day of our stay, we were employed to pick plums. I remember that the wage was one dollar and fifty cents for one ton. Both of us entered a small farm with Fujikawa, a native of Yamaguchi prefecture, and started picking plums. However, we could not finish the work compared to what Fujikawa did. After working all day, we could only pick one ton, which meant we only earned seventy-five cents a day per person, for picking plums only near the entrance. The meals at the farm

were mostly *dangojiru*, with tiny pieces of floating bacon. Even though we were pretty lousy workers, we were gourmets. We could not stand eating *dangojiru* every day at all. So we started buying eggs, eating beef, adding rice and soy sauce, and so on. When we became thirsty, we even bought a watermelon. In this manner, our daily earnings of seventy-five cents were consumed for groceries and takeaway food. When we returned to San Jose after ten days' labor, our clothes were ragged. It was a total waste of energy." See Washizu, "Wagahai no Beikoku seikatsu 66, den'en seikatsu" in the Sōkō *Nichi-Bei shinbun*, July 10, 1924.

26. Refer to "Beikoku junkai kaku chihō shōkyō narabini zairyū honpōjin jōtai" (the consular report of San Francisco dated April 20, 1895) in *Tsūshō isan 17-gō* (May 15, 1895), 19–21 and 25–26. Some criticized not only Japanese but also other "new immigrants," including Italians and Greeks, for staying temporarily in the United States in order to remit money to their homeland, without any intention of becoming naturalized citizens. For example, refer to Jeremiah W. Jenks and W. Jett Lauck, *The Immigration Problem*, 4th ed. (New York: Funk & Wagnalls, 1917).

27. Kōshin dai 91-gō, Meiji 25-nen 7-gatsu 30-nichi, Zai Bankūbā Ryōji Dairi Kitō Teijirō yori Gaimu Jikan Hayashi Tadasu ate, "Honpōjin tokō torishimari hōhō ni kanshi iken gushin no ken" in "Zaibei honpōjin no jōkyō narabini tobeisha torishimari kankei zakken dai 2 Bankūbā Ryōjikan no bu" held at the Gaimushō Gaikō Shiryōkan; and Sō dai 59-gō, Meiji 26-nen 8-gatsu 19-nichi, Gaimu Jikan Hayashi Tadasu yori Zai Bankūbā Ryōji Dairi Kitō Teijirō ate, "Kaigai dekasegi rōdōsha torishimari yōken gushin ni taishi kaitō no ken," Fuki, Meiji 25-nen 7-gatsu 30-nichi zuke "Zai Bankūbā Ryōji Dairi Kitō Teijirō rinji hōkoku oyobi kaigai tokōsha ni kansuru torishimari hōhō no taiyō utsushi, in *Gaikō bunsho 26*, 700–703. Estimating the dates of these documents, it took almost a year for the minister of foreign affairs to respond to Kitō Ryōji Dairi's *gushinsho* cited here. The reason is unknown.

28. Dai 123-gō, Meiji 26-nen 10-gatsu 12-nichi, Zai Bankūbā Ryōjikan Jimu Dairi Shokisei Shimizu Seizaburō yori Gaimu Jikan Hayashi Tadasu ate, "Taiheiyō engan hokubu ni okeru rōdōsha shitsugyō ni kanshi hōkoku no ken" besshi, Rinji hōkoku "Taiheiyō engan no hokubu ni oite rōdōsha shitsugyō no ippan," in *Gaikō bunsho 26*, 703–4.

29. "Beikoku junkai kaku chihō shōkyō narabini zairyū honpōjin jōtai" (the consular report of San Francisco on April 20, 1895) in *Tsūshō isan 17-gō* (May 15, 1895), 9–11.

30. Refer to "Beikoku Aidaho-shū Yunion Pashifikku Tetsudō kōji ni jūjiseru honpōjin rōdōsha hōchiku jiken no tame Chinda Ryōji shucchō no ken" (Meiji 25-nen 7-9-gatsu) held at the Gaimushō Gaikō Shiryōkan. Among these documents, Kimitsu dai 18-gō, Meiji 25-nen 8-gatsu 4-ka Zai Sanfuranshisuko Ryōji Chinda Sutemi yori Gaimu Daijin Enomoto Takeaki ate, "Tōkoku Aidaho-shū ni oite tasū no Nihonjin hōchiku seraretaru ken guhin"; Densō dai 102-gō, Meiji 25-nen 8-gatsu 22-nichi Gaimu Daijin Mutsu Munemitsu yori Sanfuranshisuko Ryōji Chinda Sutemi ate, "Aidaho-shū Namupa hoka nikasho e shucchō kata denshin kunrei"; and Kimitsu dai 21-gō, Meiji 25-nen 9-gatsu 17-nichi, Chinda Ryōji yori Mutsu Gaimu Daijin ate, "Aidaho-shū shucchō hōkoku no ken," are recorded in *Gaikō bunsho 25*, 718–21, 724, and 726–27. However, the important documents, the Tanaka Chūshichi (labor contractor) *gushinsho*, were omitted.

31. Kōshin dai 15-gō, Meiji 26-nen 4-gatsu 6-ka, Zai Sanfuranshisuko Ryōji Chinda Sutemi yori Gaimu Daijin Hayashi Tadasu ate, "Zaibei honpōjin tetsudō

kōfu hakugai ni kanshi jōhō sōfu no ken"; (Fuzokusho 1) kaku Kō dai 11-gō utsu-shi, Meiji 26-nen 4-gatsu 6-ka, Chinda Ryōji yori Tokumei Zenken Kōshi Tateno Gōzō ate, "Dōjō no ken ni tsuki hōkoku"; (Fuzokusho 4), Meiji 26-nen 3-gatsu 31-nichi, Tetsudō kōfu ukeoinin Ban Shinzaburō gushinsho, "Minami Taiheiyō Tetsudō shūgyō Nihon kōfu sōnan no ken"; and newspaper excerpts in *Gaikō bunsho 26*, 710–19.

32. Refer to "Honpōjin tokō seigen oyobi haiseki ichiran, 1."

33. For example, Kimitsu dai 1-gō, Meiji 28-nen 6-gatsu 12-nichi, Kamiya yori Saionji ate, *Gaikō bunsho 28*, 683. Also refer to Sakata, "Shōtotsuten e mukau kidō (I) (II)," in *Ōsaka Gakuin Daigaku Kokusaigaku ronshū 3-kan, 1-gō* (June 1992), 145–200 and *3-kan, 2-gō* (December 1992), 35–90, and chapters 3 and 4 of this volume.

34. *San Francisco Call*, June 5, 1895, Kimitsu dai 1-gō, Meiji 28-nen 6-gatsu 12-nichi, Kamiya yori Saionji ate, besshi dai 3-gō, in "Honpōjin tokō seigen oyobi haiseki ichiran, 1."

35. Kimitsu dai 1-gō, Meiji 28-nen 6-gatsu 12-nichi, Kamiya yori Saionji ate, *Gaikō bunsho 28*, 681.

36. "This time, without good reason, the *Call* severely attacked Japanese migrant laborers. They exaggerated ordinary matters to fuel controversy. With the arrival of the *Peking* in the port of San Francisco, the blatant feelings of anti-Japanese might intensify again," in ibid., 682.

37. Kimitsu dai 6-gō, Meiji 24-nen 4-gatsu 25-nichi, Zai Sanfuranshisuko Ryōji Chinda Sutemi yori Gaimu Daijin Aoki Shūzō ate, "Beikoku imin shin kisoku shikō ni tsuki honpōjin tokōsha torishimari kata ni kanshi jōshin no ken"; dai 45-gō, Meiji 24-nen 4-gatsu 29-nichi, Beikoku Chūsatsu Kōshi Tateno Gōzō yori Gaimu Daijin Aoki Shūzō ate, "Sanfuranshisuko ni oite Nihonjin jōriku sashidome no ken"; and Kimitsu dai 7-gō, Meiji 24-nen 5-gatsu 7-ka, Chinda yori Aoki ate, "Honpō tokōsha jōriku kyozetsu no ken," "Honpōjin tokō seigen oyobi haiseki kankei ichiran, 1," 12–23 and 38–71. Even though these *jōshinsho* are recorded in *Gaikō bunsho 24* as *bunsho 222* (463–76), *bunsho 223* (476–77), and *bunsho 225* (480–87), the attached English-language letters and newspaper excerpts are omitted as in endnote 4. For the details or background of the incident denying Japanese passengers' entry in 1891–92, refer to Sakata, "Shōtotsuten e mukau kidō (II)," in *Ōsaka Gakuin Daigaku Kokusaigaku ronshū 3-kan, 2-gō* (December 1992), 35–91, and chapter 4 of this volume.

38. Refer to endnote 2 and the text of this paper.

39. Kimitsu dai 1-gō, Meiji 28-nen 6-gatsu 12-nichi, Kamiya yori Saionji ate, *Gaikō bunsho 28*, 680–81.

40. *San Francisco Bulletin*, May 14, 1895, Kimitsu dai 1-gō, Meiji 28-nen 6-gatsu 12-nichi, Kamiya yori Saionji ate, besshi dai 1-gō, "Honpōjin tokō seigen oyobi haiseki ichiran, 1."

41. Kimitsu dai 7-gō, Meiji 24-nen 5-gatsu 7-ka, Zai Sanfuranshisuko Ryōji Chinda Sutemi yori Gaimu Daijin Aoki Shūzō ate, "Honpō tokōsha jōriku kyohi no ken," in *Gaikō bunsho 24*, 480.

42. For example, a private instruction from the minister of foreign affairs to the prefectural governor dated September 15, 1891, that explained details of customs procedures, stated that "Japanese migrant laborers heading to the United States of America were unaware of the strict US immigration law. Customs inspectors might question their reasons for immigration and the possession of employment

agreements. There were many Japanese migrant laborers who thought they needed to fabricate their contract laborer status. They assumed that they needed to demonstrate secure employment and tried hard to provide proof of contractual status. Such inappropriate answers made contract laborers suspect and caused entry problems," and the minister further ordered prefectural governments to instruct Japanese immigrants of proper means for entry in advance. Naikun, Meiji 24-nen 9-gatsu 15-nichi, Gaimu Daijin yori Kanagawa, Hyōgo, Ōsaka, Nagasaki, Nīgata, fuken chiji ate, "Beikoku e tobei suru rōdōsha e taishi dōkoku ijūmin shinjōrei no kitei o ryōkai seshimuru gi ni tsuki naikun," in *Gaikō bunsho* 24, 501–2. Tateno Gōzō, Chūbei Kōshi (resident envoy to the United States) also stated, "Recently, the Japanese arriving in the port of San Francisco often disobeyed US immigration law and were denied entry. Every time this happens, we and the consul in San Francisco alert the Japanese government. Furthermore, since our government sent many directives to each prefecture and made repeated announcements in their districts, I assume that all Japanese travelers to the United States would be informed of this instruction." Otsukō dai 35-gō, Meiji 26-nen 5-gatsu 30-nichi, Beikoku Chūsatsu Kōshi Tateno Gōzō yori Zai Bankūbā Ryōji Dairi Kitō Teijirō ate, "Ijū hōki ihan tokōsha torishimari kata rinshin no ken," in *Gaikō bunsho* 26, 732. For *misegane* (show money), refer to Sakata, "Shōtotsuten e mukau kidō (II)," 73–74, and pages 202–3 of chapter 4 of this volume.

43. Kimitsu dai 1-gō, Meiji 28-nen 6-gatsu 12-nichi, Kamiya yori Saionji ate, *Gaikō bunsho* 28, 681.

44. Ibid., and Kimitsu dai 3-gō, Meiji 28-nen 6-gatsu 27-nichi, Zai Sanfuranshisuko Ryōji Kamiya Saburō yori Gaimu Jikan Hara Takashi ate, "Gasshūkoku imin kensakan honpō rōdōsha torishirabe no kekka ni kansuru ken," *Gaikō bunsho* 28, 680–84. In Kimitsu dai 3-gō, consul Kamiya repeatedly criticized both the *Call* and the *Examiner* and stated, "Some newspapers in San Francisco, the *Call* and the *Examiner* in particular, wrote inflammatory and exaggerated articles about Japanese migrant laborers' arrival. They bitterly attacked Japanese residing here and reported distorted cases that had nothing to do with violating immigration law, distorted them, and made false accusations on them. They intended to defame our people and nation."

45. For the image of "coolies" held by Americans, refer to Stuart C. Miller, *The Unwelcome Immigrant: The American Image of the Chinese, 1785–1882* (Berkeley: University of California Press, 1969); Gunther Barth, *Bitter Strength: A History of the Chinese in the United States, 1850–1870* (Cambridge, MA: Harvard University Press, 1964).

46. *San Francisco Call*, June 11, 1895, in Kimitsu dai 3-gō, Meiji 28-nen 6-gatsu 27-nichi, Kamiya yori Hara ate, "Gasshūkoku imin kensakan honpō rōdōsha torishirabe no kekka ni kansuru ken," besshi dai 1-gō, "Honpōjin tokō seigen oyobi haiseki ichiran, 1," 424–30.

47. Ibid., June 14, 1895, besshi dai 2-gō, "Honpōjin tokō seigen oyobi haiseki ichiran, 1," 431–40.

48. Ibid., June 11, 1895.

49. Ibid.

50. Ibid., June 14, 1895.

51. "Japanese Competition," reports submitted by the Committee on Ways and Means to the House of Representatives, June 6, 1896, and June 11, 1896: US Congress, H.R. Rep. No. 2279 (Part 1) and No. 2279 (Part 2); 54th Cong., 1st

Sess. (H. R. Rep. Vol. 9, No. 3465) (Washington, DC: Government Printing Office, 1896). Hence, I will indicate the House report as "Japanese Competition," Part 1 (June 6, 1896) or Part 2 (June 11, 1896).

52. "Beikoku Seizōgyō Kyōkai to Nihon seizōgyō no kyōsō ni kanshite ketsugi no ken," Meiji 29-nen 2-gatsu 19-nichi, the consular report by the consul general in New York, in *Tsūshō isan 38-gō* (Meiji 29-nen 4-gatsu 1-nichi), 6–9.

53. "Japanese Competition," Part 1 (June 6, 1896). Translated into the Japanese by the author, then translated into English for this volume.

54. "Immigration of Japanese," a report submitted by the commissioner-general of immigration, May 15, 1900: US Congress, H.R. Doc. No. 686; 56th Cong., 1st Sess. (Washington, DC: Government Printing Office, 1900). William Marsh Rice, the commissioner-general of immigration, arrived at the Yokohama port via the SS *Coptic* on December 18, 1899, and stayed in Japan for three months until he departed from Yokohama via the SS *City of Rio de Janeiro* on March 25, 1899. During his stay he conducted investigations in "Yokohama, Tokyo, Nagoya, Kyoto, Osaka, Wakayama, Kobe, Okayama, Hiroshima, and Yamaguchi." According to the documents in the Diplomatic Archives of the Ministry of Foreign Affairs of Japan, the Japanese government was extremely nervous about the investigation of Commissioner Rice, who was dispatched by the US federal immigration office. The Japanese government gave detailed instructions to local governments to ensure he would not leave with a bad impression and to cooperate with his investigation as much as possible ("Honpōjin tokō seigen oyobi haiseki ichiran, 2," 771–916). Rice's inspection report, however, did not report on the Japanese consideration. Rather, I cannot help think that he deliberately collected facts that would support his view against Japanese laborers. I can detect his malicious intention throughout his report. His main job was to serve as an immigration inspector stationed in Victoria, British Columbia, controlling immigrants entering the United States through the border towns. He returned to his original job after finishing the investigation in Japan. Shimizu Seizaburō, the consul general in Vancouver, described Rice's personality in his report as follows. "Please keep it to yourself but Mr. Rice's personality is crude and he often behaves badly. His words and actions seem unconventional. After fifty-seven Japanese immigrants were sent back home, we sent Ukida, a clerk to the consul general, to his office and had a petty official write a polite letter requesting a rationale for the denied entry. Mr. Rice, with his hat on the back of his head, his feet on the desk, and chewing oranges, said, 'It is not worth replying to the consul on this matter. The Japanese consul general always tries to interfere with our duty. If he is not satisfied with our decision, he has no recourse but to appeal to the proper authority.' Mr. Rice lost his temper and yelled at our official. He left yesterday (May 21, 1899) to assume an appointment as special agent for the Treasury Department stationed in London, England"; and Kimitsu dai 16-gō, Meiji 32-nen 5-gatsu 22-nichi, Zai Bankūbā Ryoji Shimizu Seizaburō yori Gaimu Daijin Aoki Shūzō ate, "Imin Jimukan Raisu-shi shōsoku no ken," in *Gaikō bunsho 32*, 657–60.

55. "Immigration of Japanese," a report submitted by the commissioner-general of immigration, May 15, 1900, H.R. Doc. No. 686, 56th Cong., 1st Sess.

About the Contributors

Yasuo Sakata is a leading scholar of Japanese immigration and emigration studies, having led the field in both the United States and Japan for decades. He received a BA in history (1962) and a PhD in East Asian history (1969) from UCLA. He was instrumental in compiling the Japanese American Research Project and published two related volumes: *A Buried Past: An Annotated Bibliography of the Japanese American Research Project Collection* (1974), with Yuji Ichioka, Nobuya Tsuchida, and Eri Yasuhara; and *Fading Footsteps of the Issei: An Annotated Check List of the Manuscript Holdings of the Japanese American Research Project Collection* (1992). After returning to Japan in 1990, he taught at the Faculty of International Studies, Osaka Gakuin University. He also served as president of the Japanese Association for Migration Studies. His notable publications include *Tairitsu to dakyō: 1930-nendai no Nichi-Bei tsūshō kankei* 対立と妥協: 1930年代の日米通商関係 (Conflict and compromise: US-Japan trade relationships in the 1930s) (1994), co-edited with Kazuo Ueyama; and *Meiji Nichi-Bei bōeki kotohajime: Chokuyu no shishi Arai Ryōichirō to sono jidai* 明治日米貿易事始：直輸の志士・新井領一郎とその時代 (The beginning of the Japan-US trade in Meiji: The era of Arai Ryoichiro, a pioneer of direct trade) (1996).

Kaoru "Kay" Ueda is the curator of the Japanese Diaspora Collection at the Hoover Institution Library & Archives. She manages the Japanese Diaspora Initiative, endowed through an anonymous gift to promote the study of overseas Japanese history during the Empire of Japan period. In addition to performing curatorial work related to traditional archival and rare books, she manages and develops the Hoji Shinbun Digital Collection, the world's largest online full-image open-access digital collection of pre–World War II overseas Japanese newspapers. The digital collection has made a significant impact in the field. After earning a master's degree in anthropology at Harvard Extension School and an MBA at the University of Chicago, she received her PhD in archaeology at Boston University, specializing in the historical archaeology of the Dutch diaspora in Asia. Ueda is also professionally trained as an interpreter and has translated Japanese and English documents throughout her professional career.

Masako Iino is a former president, professor emeritus, and trustee of Tsuda University, Tokyo, and chair of the academic advisory committee, Japanese Overseas Migration Museum. After earning her BA at Tsuda College, Iino received an MA in American history as a Fulbright scholar at Syracuse University. She taught for many years in American history and migration studies at Tsuda University, McGill University, and Acadia University and was a visiting professor at the University of California–Berkeley and Bryn Mawr College. She has also served on numerous committees and boards, including the Japan Society for the Promotion of Science and the Government Committee on the Development of Research Universities. Iino is the author or editor of many books published in Japan, including *A History of Japanese Canadians* (1997), given the Prime Minister's Award for Publication; *Another History of US-Japan Relations: Japanese Americans Swayed by the Cooperation and the Disputes between the Two Nations* (2000); *Searching Ethnic America: Multiple Approaches to "E Pluribus Unum"* (2015); and *Ethnic America* (rev. ed. 2017).

Index